THE INDIVIDUAL
AND HIS SOCIETY

THE INDIVIDUAL AND HIS SOCIETY

*The Psychodynamics of Primitive
Social Organization*

By ABRAM KARDINER M.D.

WITH A FOREWORD AND
TWO ETHNOLOGICAL REPORTS
By RALPH LINTON

GREENWOOD PRESS, PUBLISHERS
WESTPORT, CONNECTICUT

0777337

Library of Congress Cataloging in Publication Data

Kardiner, Abram, 1891–
    The individual and his society.

    Reprint of the ed. published by Columbia University
Press, New York.
    Includes index.
    1. Ethnopsychology. 2. Society, Primitive.
3. Ethnology—Marquesas Islands. 4. Tanalas.
I. Linton, Ralph, 1893–1953. II. Title.
GN270.K37 1974   301.2   74-12883
ISBN 0-8371-7770-7

Reprinted with the permission of Columbia University Press

Reprinted in 1974 by Greenwood Press,
a division of Williamhouse-Regency Inc.

Library of Congress Catalog Card Number 74-12883

ISBN 0-8371-7770-7

Printed in the United States of America

FOREWORD

By Ralph Linton

ONE of the greatest difficulties connected with coöperation between representatives of different sciences is the lack of a common terminology. This difficulty is especially marked in the case of anthropology and psychoanalysis since both abound in vague terms. For the sake of anthropologists who may wish to use this book, it is worth while to try to equate the concepts used by Dr. Kardiner with those with which they are already familiar. While an exact equation is impossible, a general one may be made. Anthropologists define a culture as the sum total of the attitudes, ideas, and behavior shared and transmitted by the members of a society together with the material results of such behavior, i.e., manufactured articles. This concept is so wide that it must be limited or broken down in various ways before it can be used as an efficient tool. Thus for many purposes it is customary to distinguish between material culture, i.e., manufactured articles, and the nonmaterial aspects of culture. It is further recognized that the nonmaterial aspects of culture are so variable as to defy even complete description. Thus attitudes, ideas, and behavior will be found to vary not only between individuals but even for the same individual at different points in time. However, the range of variation with respect to any element of culture—say a marriage ceremony or a belief in the efficacy of a particular form of magic—will be limited and will show a discernible modal point. In ordinary usage the culture construct will be composed of the modes of the variational ranges with respect to each of the component elements.

The construct of nonmaterial culture which can be devel-

oped by this process still has an exceedingly wide scope and it is
advantageous to break it down in various ways when working
on particular problems. One of the most obvious of these break-
downs is the division of its content into behavior patterns,
readily ascertainable from their overt expressions, and the ideas
and attitudes which motivate these behavior patterns. Such a
division is implicit in the recent work of a number of anthropologists, especially Benedict and Mead. The author of the
present work, approaching the problem from the psychoanalytic
angle with a consequent emphasis on personality, uses a different division. He employs the concepts of *institutions* and of
ego or *basic personality structure*. The former is already in
common usage in the social sciences. It differs from the behavior pattern concept of the anthropologists mainly in group-
ing together constellations of functionally interrelated behavior
patterns and treating them as units. The basic personality
(ego) structure will be less familiar. It is a derivative of the
psychological concept of personality and differs from the latter
in that its delimitation is based upon a study of culture rather
than upon that of the individual. Basic personality structure,
as the term is used here, represents the constellation of personality characteristics which would appear to be congenial with
the total range of institutions comprised within a given culture.
It has been deduced from a study of culture content and organization and is, therefore, an abstraction of the same order as
culture itself. In how far this basic personality structure represents a common denominator of the personalities of the individuals who participate in a culture is a point which can only
be settled by actual study of series of individuals in various
societies, and no satisfactory studies of this sort have been made
so far.

Basing his conclusions on the results of clinical pyschoanal-
yses of individuals reared in our own culture, plus the evidence
afforded by the other cultures studied, the author establishes
a dialectic between basic personality structure and institutions.
This dialectic operates through the medium of the individual.

The institutions with which the individual is in contact during his formative period produce in him a type of conditioning which eventually creates a certain type of personality. Conversely, this personality type, once established, determines the reactions of the individual to other established institutions with which he comes in contact and to innovations. Changes in certain institutions thus result in changes in basic personality structure, while such basic personality changes, in turn, lead to the modification or reinterpretation of existing institutions. Thus in the coexisting social and cultural continuums, the individuals who constitute the society are first shaped by the culture's institutions, then shape or create other institutions in turn. Both continuums are in a constant state of change; the society through the elimination and replacement of its component individuals and the culture through the elimination, replacement, and modification of its component institutions.

In the absence of long series of studies of individuals reared under different cultures, the strongest evidence for the validity of the basic personality structure concept lies in the extraordinary coherence of the basic personality structures posited for each society with the same society's techniques for early care and control of the individual. The importance of early experience in the shaping of the personality has been indicated by clinical studies carried on within the frame of our own society and culture. The heterogeneity of our own culture, and the consequent variety of individual experience, has been sufficient to provide some check on the theories of the psychoanalysts. At the same time, certain features are so deep seated in our culture that they form a part of all individual experience. In the absence of exceptions, the results of such features have frequently been ascribed to *innate or instinctive qualities* of human beings. The studies of other cultures here presented bring several of the current beliefs of this sort into question. They also seem to indicate that the findings of psychoanalysts with respect to the influence òf specific early experience on the personality are valid for whole societies as well as for individuals, when the homogeneity of the cultures involved is such as to provide all members of the society with a wide range of common experience. Thus, in a "primitive" society, practically all individuals will be subjected to the same techniques of infant care and will find the attitudes and behavior of all adults with whom they are brought into contact fairly similar at most points.

I believe that the concept of a group basic personality structure will prove valuable to anthropologists in several connections. It suggests a type of integration, within a culture, based upon the common experiences of a society's members and the personality characteristics which these experiences might be expected to engender. This sort of integration differs sharply from that which the functional anthropologists have made a focal point in their researches and from that posited by Benedict in her well known *Patterns of Culture*. The integration dealt with by the Functionalists is primarily a matter of the mutual adaptation and working interdependence of behavior patterns. As such it lies at a rather superficial level, and the picture of culture which emerges is that of a mass of gears all turning and grinding each other. There is no focal point for all this activity, and even the mutual adaptations of the behavior patterns can be accounted for without an appeal to anything more significant than the processes of trial and error. Viewed from this angle, each culture system appears mechanical and two-dimensional. The concept does not even offer a satisfactory basis for comparative studies, since the patterns which interact are never the same in any two cultures. The investigation of this type of integration becomes meaningful only when it is linked with a delimitation of the human needs which all cultures must satisfy and a knowledge both of the historic factors which have brought new behavior patterns into a particular culture complex and of the form which these patterns had at the time of their introduction.

The integration whose existence has been demonstrated by Dr. Benedict is of a totally different sort. It consists in the domination of a particular culture configuration by a particular attitude or affect about which the bulk of the culture's content is organized. This concept appears to be much more fertile than the functional one just discussed, but even so it has certain limitations. Thus, its application presents difficulties in certain cases. Although some cultures show an integration which is sharply focussed upon a single attitude or value, in others such foci are difficult to determine. Many cultures seem to include a considerable series of attitudes and values all of which are significant and each of which serves as a focal point for the integration of a different sector of the total culture. The real problem here is whether the extreme stressing of a single attitude or value at the expense of the rest is a typical or atypical feature of culture organization. This is a point which cannot be settled until more cultures have been analysed, but even if such stressing proves to be typical, a considerable number of culture configurations will remain to be accounted for.

By employing the concept of a societal personality structure it becomes possible to place the focal point of culture integration in the common denominator of the personalities of the individuals who participate in the culture. Culture, is, in the last analysis, a matter of modes within the distributional ranges of the individual's responses with respect to various repetitive situations. The modes of response with respect to each of such situations are mutually adjusted to the extent required to prevent their interference in practice. Such adjustments are the basis of the functional type of integration. The various modes also reflect the presence of a particular system of attitudes and values common to the normal members of the society to which the culture belongs. If this system is strongly dominated by a particular attitude or value, the result is the type of culture integration described by Benedict. The outstanding contribution which the *basic personality structure* approach makes to integrational studies is that it provides a logical place for cultures which are not dominated by an *idée fixé*. The various personality types which it posits as characteristic of particular societies are constellations of distinct although mutually inter-related elements. When such a personality structure is recognized as the focus for the institutions comprised within a given culture, it can be seen that such institutions need not be mutually consistent, except to the degree required for their actual functioning, as long as they are individually consistent with various aspects of the personality structure involved. Thus, as in the Marquesan case, one series of institutions may be oriented about a basic food anxiety, another about what are to us peculiar attitudes regarding sex, and still another about certain hostilities engendered by what are here common childhood experiences. The phenomenon of culture integration becomes three-dimensional, with its foundations firmly rooted in the complex through similar personalities of the individuals whose desires and responses constitute the ultimate reality in the whole culture construct.

Turning from the static to the dynamic aspects of culture, the basic personality structure concept may provide a key to certain little-understood phenomena of culture change. It has long been realized that the reactions of societies to cultural innovations are highly selective and that the selection cannot be satisfactorily explained on a mechanistic basis. While certain innovations may be rejected because they are in direct opposition to existing behavior patterns, or because they would nullify the results of such patterns, others are rejected for no immediately discernible cause. Conversely, new patterns which entail a good deal of readjustment in the pre-existing behavior patterns may be accepted and retained even at the cost of considerable inconvenience. The explanation for this condition would seem to lie in the compatibility or incompatibility of the new patterns with the already established personality structure of the society. Thus, a new pattern for working malevolent magic would be likely to be accepted eagerly by a group in which the normal individual felt insecure and had numerous personal hostilities, while it would be rejected by a group whose members normally felt secure and had few hostilities. To cite another example, the culturally established attitudes of one society's members toward those of another society would be a part of their ego structure under the present definition. Such attitudes apparently play a large part in connection with the transfer of behavior patterns from one culture to another. A society will borrow such patterns from a group which they admire much more readily than from one which they despise.

Still another phenomenon of culture change is illuminated by the basic personality structure approach. It has been observed that, although borrowed elements of culture always undergo some modifications in form in the course of their integration into a new culture, the most extensive changes are likely to be in meaning. Meaning in this case is used to refer to the whole complex of attitudes and rationalizations attached to any pattern of behavior. Thus, in the diffusion of the Sun Dance among the Plains Indians, the actual ritual and ceremonial paraphernalia have remained much the same in spite of repeated transfers, while the significance of the Sun Dance has come to vary widely. In one group it has become primarily a means of obtaining personal visions, in another it is given as repayment for supernatural aid received in time of emergency, while in still another it has become a technique for testing the validity of the claims of a newly announced medicine man. Such modifications can be seen as attempts to adjust the new, objectively received patterns of behavior to the pre-existing attitudes and value system of the borrowing society. That such wide differences in meaning can be associated with closely similar behavior patterns is a proof of the essential looseness of all culture integration. However, in each case, the meanings will be in a close and constant relationship with the basic personality structure of the group. The integration appears to be closer at this point than at any other.

Closely linked with this reinterpretation of borrowed behavior patterns is the reinterpretation of patterns already present in the culture when their current meanings become inadequate or unsatisfactory to a changing ego structure. Excellent examples of this process are provided by certain features of the Tanala and Betsileo cultures described in this volume. There can be little question that Betsileo culture was once closely similar to the present Tanala one and that both have been derived from a common source. They still have a great many behavior patterns in common, and analysis of the two on a formal trait-list basis would indicate a high degree of similarity. However, changes in the technique of rice culture, with resulting modifications in land tenure, lineage organization, and residence, have produced an ego structure for the Betsileo which differs widely from that for the Tanala. This, in turn, has led to a series of significant reinterpretations and shifts of emphasis with respect to particular behavior patterns. Thus, although both tribes believe in the reality of malevolent magic and employ the same techniques for magical offense and defense, the significance of malevolent magic has come to differ considerably in the two cases. To the Tanala, whose culture provides the individual with a large measure of both economic and emotional security, such magic is of minor importance. The average individual does not know how to practice it, and few Tanala, with whom I discussed the matter, believed that they themselves had been victims of it. Sickness or misfortune is ordinarily ascribed to the anger of ancestral spirits and hence is always justified by the individual's own acts, including the infraction of taboos. As the Betsileo's culture provides little security, malevolent magic is an ever-present threat. Most individuals know at least one technique: there are suspected witches in every village, and sickness or misfortune is largely attributed to the magical activities of enemies. Coupled with this there is an increased emphasis on the benevolent aspects of the ancestral spirits, who help much more frequently than they injure. To cite another example, both tribes believe in spirit possession and many of the outward manifestations of it are the same for both. However, the Tanala spirits use the possessed as a medium for establishing contact with the living. They are not hostile to him and do not injure him. The Betsileo, on the other hand, have an order of spirits who abuse and persecute those they possess. The actual insecurity and hostility of Betsileo existence are reflected in a series of reinterpretations of behavior patterns which make these more congenial to a people with increased anxiety.

It will be evident from the foregoing that the concept of a societal basic personality structure provides the anthropologist with a new tool which has important possibilities. It will enable him to organize data of certain sorts in a new and significant way. It may even provide him with the ability to predict, in very general terms, the reactions of a given society to a given innovation, such prediction being based upon the apparent compatibility or incompatibility of the new pattern with the personality structure revealed by a study of the society's culture as a whole. Nevertheless, it must be kept clearly in mind that a basic personality structure is an abstraction and a derivative of culture. It is a long step from the employment of such a concept in cultural studies to the equation of the basic personality structure of any society with the personal character of the individuals who compose that society. This step cannot be taken until we have a series of studies of individuals made by competent field workers, but, meanwhile, a few speculations as to the relationship which probably exists may not be out of order.

We already know a good deal of the relations of individuals to culture. I have discussed this at some length elsewhere and need only summarize it here.[1] No one individual is ever familiar with the whole of the culture in which he participates; still less does he express all its patterns in his own behavior. Instead, each society divides its total membership into a series of categories and assigns different sectors of the total culture to each category. Thus all societies distinguish between adult men and adult women, and expect different activities, knowledge, and even different forms of emotional response from the members of each group. Furthermore, the training of children,

[1] R. Linton, *The Study of Man* (New York, 1936), Chaps. XVI, XXVI.

insofar as it is conscious, is always directed toward fitting them to occupy certain places in society. The boy is instructed in what a man should know, the girl in what a woman should know. The individual's participation in culture is thus primarily a matter of his position in the social structure, i.e., his status. In the formal organization of any society, each status has associated with it a constellation of culture patterns. These patterns are organized and mutually adjusted in such a way that any individual who occupies the status can utilize the associated constellation as a whole. The constellations which belong with different statuses are similarly adjusted to each other, making it possible for the society to function as a whole. Thus the activities of men and of women will each form a coherent whole, yet these wholes will be mutually interdependent for their successful operation. If the man does not hunt and bring home meat, the woman cannot exercise the pattern of cooking which the culture ascribes to her. Because of this formal differentiation in cultural participation, it is a fundamental error to think of a culture as the common denominator of the activities, ideas and attitudes of a society's component members. Actually, such common denominators can be established only for the individuals who have a particular status in common. The culture as a whole is an intricately organized configuration made up of such status denominators.

Even within the frame of a single society and culture the various statuses make markedly different demands upon their occupants. For example, the same society which expects adult males to be aggressive and competitive may expect adult females to be docile and coöperative. One might even go a step farther and suggest that the personalities which belong with the various statuses are often complementary in much the same way that the activities are. Thus the more dominant and aggressive the males, the more submissive the females, the possible alternative to this being constant domestic fireworks. To cite another case, if a society expects its chief to show exalted pride and keen rivalry toward the chiefs of other groups it must provide him, at the very outset, with unusually docile subjects. One suspects that field work will show that a societal basic personality structure is actually a composite made up of the personality norms for groups of individuals occupying different statuses. However, all these norms will probably prove to have in common a certain value system and an organization of basic attitudes. The woman who cannot be aggressive because of the requirements of her status will still believe that aggression is the proper thing for males, encourage her husband and sons to aggressive behavior, and achieve a vicarious satisfaction from their victories. When we have established such basic systems of personality structure correlated with series of statuses in various cultures, we will have a tool of equal use to anthropologists and psychologists.

My own association with the work which has resulted in the present volume began almost accidentally. At the time I arrived in New York, Dr. Kardiner's seminar had already been going on for some years. During this time a number of cultures had been analysed from literature and one, that of the Zuni, from the verbal accounts of Drs. Benedict and Bunzel, who had worked with the tribe. In an attempt to widen the basis for comparative studies I was asked to act as informant for the seminar, giving an account of certain cultures of which I had had firsthand experience and supplementing this, when possible, with personal impressions, episodes, and other material which would not ordinarily be included in a formal ethnological report. It may be well, at this point, to outline the sources of my information.

The Marquesan material was collected during a stay of nearly a year in the Marquesas, in 1920–21. At that time the B. P. Bishop Museum of Honolulu sent Dr. and Mrs. E. S. Craighill Handy and myself to those islands to make a study of the local archaeology and ethnology. Under the division of activities arranged by the Museum I was assigned the task of studying the local archaeology and material culture, Dr. Handy that of studying the nonmaterial aspects of the native life. My work was, therefore, only partially ethnological, and I collected only incidental information on the elaborate rituals which had characterized the culture before its collapse. In nearly all cases where such rituals are referred to, the material has been drawn from Dr. Handy's well-known book *The Native Culture of the Marquesas*.[2] At the same time, the exigencies of my archaeological work, which necessitated long trips to outlying sections of the various islands, brought me into close contact with many of the natives and gave me an excellent opportunity to observe their current patterns of culture. I was able to form genuine friendships with various natives of both sexes and especially with one young man, Fiu, who adopted me as a brother. I am convinced that many of these native friends were no more reticent with me than they would have been with other natives; all the more intimate details of sexual behavior, etc. given in the accompanying account were checked by statements from at least two persons. The old polyandrous household patterns were almost extinct at the time of my visit, but I frequently stayed as a guest in one of the last establishments of this sort. I believe that my reconstruction, based on this experience and on the reminiscences of many of the older people, is essentially correct. Unfortunately I am not a good linguist and never became able to speak Marquesan fluently. However, I knew enough for ordinary conversational purposes, while many of the older natives spoke French or even English.

The Tanala and Betsileo material was collected under somewhat different circumstances. I was in Madagascar from January, 1926, until the spring of 1928, constituting the Captain Marshall Field Madagascar Expedition of the Field Museum of Natural History of Chicago. The Betsileo were visited in the summer of 1927, the Tanala in the fall and winter of the same year. By the time I reached them I was thoroughly prepared to work with them. There are many basic patterns which are common to all Madagascan cultures, while the tribal tongues are all dialects of a single language differing so little

[2] B. P. Bishop Museum Bulletin No. 9, 1923.

that they are, for the most part, mutually intelligible. In spite of a considerable initial understanding of the cultures in question and a knowledge of the language adequate for ordinary purposes, I never felt the same rapport with members of these tribes that I did with the Marquesans. My closest friends were certain ombiasys (medicine men) with whom I was able to exchange professional secrets, but even these were not too trustworthy. Most of the material here presented on the Tanala has previously been published, although with a different organization, in my report on the tribe.[3] The Betsileo material was selected by Dr. Kardiner from my unpublished notes on that tribe.

I am conscious that there are numerous gaps in these factual accounts and that various questions are left unanswered which, it might seem, could have been answered readily enough. I can only say in extenuation that certain aspects of culture which are considered of great importance for psychoanalytic studies are usually accorded little importance by ethnologists. For example, the incident of a Tanala woman, face distorted with rage, beating an infant less than a year old who had befouled her, of the child cowering under the beating without a cry, while the father stood by indifferent, would scarcely be included in a formal ethnological monograph. Many of the details which I have recorded here were, therefore, observed incidentally and not included in previously published material.

Against this may be set the fact that I believe that my sins have been mainly those of omission. When I was not sure of a point I have left it out, and nothing has been consciously changed or added. Of course no observer can vouch for his own unconscious, and the personality of a field worker inevitably influences his results. He pays the closest attention to those aspects of native life which are in line with his own interests and finds certain native informants more congenial than others. However, my observations certainly were not influenced by any

[3] "The Tanala, a Hill Tribe of Madagascar," Field Museum of Natural History, Vol. XXII, 1933.

expectations of what I would find. At the time the Marquesan field studies were made I had no knowledge of psychoanalytic theory or techniques and no interest in the field of personality study. Between the Marquesan and Madagascan expeditions I had read some of the earlier attempts to interpret cultural phenomena in strict Freudian terms, but I had not been impressed. Concepts of complex human instincts and of racial memories seemed so much at variance with what I already knew about cultural phenomena that I simply dismissed the whole matter. It is quite possible that my memory of certain items not recorded in my field notes or journals was influenced by the patterns which I could see developing as the seminar progressed. However, the items in question were not very numerous and the technique of culture presentation provided a fairly effective check on unconscious invention. The life of each group was described in detail before the analysis was begun. I can honestly say that the psychological coherence of institutions which emerged in the course of these analyses was as much of a surprise to me as to any of the students.

RALPH LINTON

AUTHOR'S PREFACE

THE need for coördinating the knowledge accumulated by the social sciences and psychology has long been felt. To this end many worthy endeavors have been dedicated. The present essay is an attempt to forge a technique for such a synthesis within prescribed limits, and on a special type of material. The attempt is exploratory. The material and the limits of the effort are prescribed by our current techniques in the study of contemporary aboriginal cultures and the present status of psychoanalytic social psychology.

The material for this essay was gathered in a group of seminars held at the New York Psychoanalytic Institute during the past three years. The material therefore is the result of a collaboration of two disciplines, psychology and social anthropology. Both disciplines had important stakes in this collaboration. When this work was begun it was difficult to foresee exactly what each discipline could appropriate for its own independent uses from the projected synthesis. It is, however, safe to claim for each some individual gains; but, still more important for both, this attempt has yielded an added conviction that continued collaboration is imperative for the mutual advantage of both. For psychology this work has proved invaluable in describing the influence of institutions on the formation of the adaptive tools of the human mind; and for social anthropology it has demonstrated the importance of understanding the individual if one is to understand the institutions in society.

Such a synthetic effort as is here attempted is properly the task of one who is equally adept in both techniques. Each discipline is, however, a growing and developing field, and it is quite impossible for one individual to be master of both.

Moreover, efforts on the part of psychologist or anthropologist unskillfully to appropriate techniques from the other's discipline are likely to end in dilettantism. And this in turn has in the past resulted in efforts prejudicial to both disciplines and discouraging to further coöperative attempts.

The work of which this book is the record was undertaken in the hope of creating for both disciplines the opportunities to observe their respective techniques in operation and of exchanging observations on the operational efficacy of the working concepts used by each.

The author is by training a psychiatrist, being engaged mainly in the clinical practice of therapeutic psychoanalysis. He makes no claim to being trained in any way as an anthropologist. For the material and its organization he has relied upon those anthropologists who were kind enough to collaborate with him in this joint enterprise. The only contribution the author can claim in the ethnological presentations was to point to those factors in the individual which indicated the operation of certain institutions, factors which might easily elude attention in an ethnographic account.

The fact that the author is the psychologist and not the anthropologist of this attempt at synthesis is an accident of the circumstance that in our present stage of coöperation the psychologist has most of the explaining to do. If the work continues, this situation is likely to reverse itself within the next few years. Meanwhile, the fact that the author is a psychologist will have left its mark on the relative emphasis given each discipline. If this book is overweighted on the side of psychology, this fact is not entirely due to the author's bent and training. Several unavoidable complications are responsible. The psychological aspects of social psychology are the least well understood, and the author felt it to be an urgent need to describe in detail the method of deriving, from the psychology of the individual, concepts that are subsequently used to describe psycho-social constellations. Furthermore many debatable viewpoints in psychoanalytic theory and technique are here presented at greater length than may be of interest to the sociologist or the anthropologist. This is due to the fact that the author has attempted to eradicate some of the past shortcomings in psychoanalytic social psychology as applied to aboriginal culture. Moreover, the newer points of view are not beyond the range of controversy. A third extravagance may be charged against the author in that he has exploited the opportunity of clarifying many problems in psychology, at the expense of the purely sociological aspects. Whereas this procedure redounds much to the advantage of psychology, it is no less useful to sociology, because the ego or total personality is the point of contact between individual and environment. Personality formation is symptomatic of both individual and social institutions.

Although psychology is relatively overemphasized for the reasons stated, the author must confess to some misgivings with regard to how convincingly it has been presented. It is not easy to evaluate how much psychology the anthropologist should know, or to foresee how much demonstration constitutes an adequate proof to those who do not have direct access to the psychological source material. What is included in the book seems adequate for the elucidation of the problems presented by the specific cultures studied, but can by no means be considered exhaustive for the entire province of sociology.

As far as the psychological technique is concerned, it stands on the groundwork of Freudian principles. There are, however, some modifications stemming from a reorganization of the theoretical structure which today seems imperative. In this modification the author does not stand alone. It originated with the work of Ferenczi many years ago, and has grown in importance in recent years. Others who have contributed to this technique are Anna Freud, Erich Fromm, K. Horney, S. Rado and W. Reich. There are important differences among these authors who are now engaged in refining this new technique. To some degree these differences are discussed in the text. The author acknowledges valuable aid from all of these writers, in spite of many views expressed by them with which he cannot concur. At the present time such debate insures against dogmatization and facilitates the process of testing out the validity of working concepts on clinical material of different types.

It took no little courage to override the objections raised by the fact that we have had to present this work with the methodology tested on only two aboriginal cultures. This seemed the lesser of two evils. To wait until we had accumulated a score of cultures would have been the wiser course. But to do so would mean to sacrifice the opportunity for comparison and criticism so vital to any new effort. The emphasis at the present time must fall on the method and not on the conclusions drawn. These latter must, for the time being, remain secondary and provisional.

The anthropological concepts embodied in this work have been drawn from a wide variety of sources. The concepts of society and of culture are as old as the science and have long since become common property. In developing or utilizing the further concepts which are presented here it has not been felt either necessary or desirable to adhere closely to the formulations of any one of the various schools into which anthropology is now divided. Material has been drawn from all of them, although in varying degree. Least has been taken from the evolutionary school, although this has been the one which has dominated most of the previous psychoanalytic approaches to culture. That cultures have evolved is unquestionable; but our present knowledge makes it equally certain that, in this evolution, they have not adhered to the rigid stages which the evolutionists posited. The techniques and conclusions of the modern historical schools have also been drawn upon very lightly. Although these may sometime prove to be of extreme importance for the testing of some of the conclusions set forth in this book, they are not germane to a first attempt. The sociological-anthropological theories of the school represented by Durkheim, Levy-Bruhl, and Radcliffe-Brown have also made only slight contributions. The concepts regarding primitive mentality upon which the rigid theoretical systems of this school are based have not stood the test of actual field investigations. Much more material has been drawn from the work of the functional school, led by Malinowski, and from that of individual students of personality and culture like Benedict, Mead, Bunzel, Sapir, and Linton. In the formulation of the concepts of status and social structure, Linton has been used as the main source, and the meaning of these terms in the present volume is that which he gives them.[1]

During the past three years eight cultures were studied. These cultures, with one exception, were presented by anthropologists. The exception was Western culture, some aspects of which were used throughout as a control, because it is in aspects of this culture that the reciprocal relations between "individual" and "institutions" are best understood. Of the other seven cultures, three were reported by anthropologists who lived among the people of those cultures. Dr. Linton lived with the Tanala and the Marquesans; Dr. Ruth Benedict and Dr. Ruth Bunzel both lived with the Zuni. The other cultures were studied from published material. Dr. Cora DuBois presented the Trobriand, Kwakiutl, and Chuckchee cultures.

The cultures were studied in the following order: Trobriand, Kwakiutl, Zuni, Chuckchee, Eskimo, Tanala, and Marquesan. The first five of these cultures were used as material for developing some concepts with which to proceed, and for clarifying methodological orientations. In each of these cultures, only those points are stressed which aid in clarifying some methodological points or illustrate the manner in which some of the basic socio-psychological constellations were derived. It was not until the Tanala and Marquesan cultures were studied that we found we could make an attempt to survey cultures as a whole. This was due to two factors: our technique in the form of working concepts had become sufficiently accurate to permit such application, and Dr. Linton's descriptions were sufficiently complete to permit us to see aspects and relationships which in the

[1] Linton, *The Study of Man* (New York, 1936), Chaps. VII, VIII, XV, XVI.

presentation of the previous cultures could only be vaguely conjectured. However, in these two cultures, Tanala and Marquesan, although in each instance we are presenting "analyses" of these cultures, we can hardly pretend to have covered anything more than a few elementary points. Much in each culture defies explanation. The methodology cannot be considered complete in any sense. Much that, in the light of present evidence, is considered valid or operationally effective may have to be discarded in the face of new evidence. Many concepts used in this preliminary report may have to be reduced further in a very short period of time.

However constructive this work has been, some aspects of its incompleteness are very blatant. Psychoanalytic technique is at the present time capable of evaluating personality only from the line of sight established by repression and frustration; it does not yet have reliable criteria for pursuing the joyful and creative aspects of personality. This is a limitation of the method and not, as may appear, a conception of the human personality.

ABRAM KARDINER

ACKNOWLEDGMENTS

THE author is deeply indebted to Dr. Ralph Linton, whose presentations of the Marquesan and Tanala cultures made this essay possible. He was kind enough to permit the author to make records of his presentations and to permit their use for this book; to read the manuscript in its initial and final drafts; and to offer many helpful and illuminating suggestions about the book as a whole. Dr. Linton was frequently consulted on the factual material of both cultures. In these personal contacts many important details about the facts and their theoretical implications were elicited which escaped notice in the original presentations. Moreover, Dr. Linton was kind enough to place at the author's disposal his hitherto unpublished notes on Betsileo. The author expresses his gratitude to Dr. Linton for these many offices, both friendly and scientific, which made the collaboration delightful and stimulating.

To Dr. Cora DuBois, who was the first collaborator in this joint enterprise, the author is likewise indebted as well as to Dr. Ruth Benedict, who participated in these seminars, for her continuous interest and help, and to Dr. Ruth Bunzel for her material on the Zuni culture. I wish also to express appreciation to Dr. John Dollard for two seminars on the psychology of minority groups, where problems in the psychology of interference with status and prestige goals, as illustrated by the American negro, were discussed.

The immediate incentive to write this book I owe to the gentle insistence of Drs. B. W. Aginsky and Ethel Aginsky, who also gave many helpful suggestions. Dr. B. W. Aginsky studied and discussed many portions of the first draft, lending his aid on the score of presentation and clarity, and calling attention to several important references,

The author is indebted to Dr. Willard Waller for reading the text and for many helpful suggestions now incorporated in the book.

Dr. Bela Mittelman and Jeannette Mirsky also studied the text and offered many useful suggestions.

ABRAM KARDINER

CONTENTS

Part I

METHODOLOGICAL

This part deals with the derivation of the working concepts to be used. It describes the method by which they were derived from the study of the individual in our culture, and how the psychic constellations derived from this source are to be used in the application to sociology. It also considers other points of view that have been used in similar attempts.

Chapter I

INTRODUCTION

ANY attempt to join the resources of psychology and those of sociology should begin with a clear idea of the needs which such an effort purports to satisfy. Not all psychologies need sociology, nor do all aspects of sociology need psychology. To both disciplines man's behavior is the object of study; but beyond this one point the objectives and techniques differ. A psychology which elects to study the cognitive and apperceptive functions of man does not make contact at any point with sociology. The only psychology directly linked with sociology is one whose chief interest is the affective or emotional life of man, one which studies the genetic aspects of human adaptive tools and the relation which these have to the external forces encountered. On the other hand, a sociology whose chief concern is to correlate the phenomena resulting from the behavior of human beings in groups does not need psychology. The proposition that bad money drives good money out of circulation can be used as a practical guide without any knowledge of the emotional reactions which lie at the basis of this phenomenon. However, when it becomes important to know why this phenomenon occurs, then, among other things, it becomes necessary to appreciate the effects of the anxiety created by bad money. This is a psychological problem.

The fact that each discipline can lead an independent existence indicates that each has work to do alone. In their separate endeavors, psychology and sociology have developed working tools of their own, conceptual systems and techniques foreign to each other. This circumstance becomes an obstacle when they attempt to collaborate on a problem of common interest. For, by this time, they cannot understand one another. It is clearly indicated, therefore, that a way be found for making the experience of one discipline accessible to the other. They are both complicated technologies; but of the two, psychology is less accessible as regards source material and research techniques. It is therefore clearly up to psychology to make the first concession by bringing its techniques or some of its important conclusions to bear on sociology.

In order to do this it becomes essential first to define the interests common to both disciplines. Psychology studies the changes in mental motion which influence or are associated with behavior; it studies the needs, wishes, drives and impulses of man, it studies the behavior of man necessary to obtain satisfaction from the outer world, his fellows, and himself. Sociology studies organized forms of behavior as fixed in social institutions and the changes in these institutions under varying conditions. The effects of institutions on the individual can be traced; and the origin of institutions can likewise be tracked down to the influence of certain pressures on the individual. The individual cannot be studied without the institutions in which he lives, and institutions[1] cannot be understood except as the creations of man. Whether the starting point is the individual or the institution, one must end by knowing both.

This first essential having been agreed upon, we may move to a second, equally important, and that is the unit for study.

All psychologies use the individual[2] as their source. Sociology and other social disciplines are likewise beginning to do so. Sapir[3] says, "It is difficult to see how cultural anthropology can escape the ultimate necessity of testing out its analysis of patterns called 'social' or 'cultural' in terms of individual realities. . . . What this means is that problems of social science differ

[1] For definition of "institution" see p. 7.

[2] Whenever the word "individual" is used, it is intended to mean the individual in a specific culture. No other kind of individual is known, save as a theoretical abstract.

[3] Edward Sapir, "Why Cultural Anthropology Needs the Psychiatrist," *Psychiatry*, I, No. 1, 9–10.

from the problems of individual behavior in degrees and specificity, not in kind." This agreement by psychologists and sociologists is the result of a long process of development. It is universally accepted that there is no form of social organization, be it family, in-group, clan, village, or state, of which the individual is not the unit. Nor can it any longer be doubted that the forces which create institutions must be identified in the individual.

THE INDIVIDUAL AS THE UNIT OF STUDY—
BIOPSYCHIC CHARACTERISTICS

The study of psychology must begin with the biological characteristics of man. These biological characteristics delimit the field in which psychological processes take place. They have an important bearing on the need for social life, and on the behavior of the individual in the social situation. These biological characteristics are of two kinds: the physiological, which govern the organic internal economy; and those which limit adaptation to the outer world. The physiological characteristics of man are like those of all animal life; man needs to draw sustenance from the outer world and to preserve body temperature. The conditions which satisfy these needs are almost uniform for all animal life.

For sociology the phylogenetically fixed biological limitations which have to do with his accommodation to the outer world constitute a much more important aspect of man. The techniques and reaction types which terminate in some form of *adaptation* may be completed at birth, or they may be present at birth as potentialities which later grow and develop. The relative proportion of reaction types fixed at birth to those which are acquired or developed determines, to a large extent, the character of the adaptation of the animal as a whole. Those fixed at birth are not likely to be subject to subsequent direction and modification. The relation between the fixed and acquired reaction types determines the *tempo* of development of effective techniques of adaptation. In general, we may say that man is distinguished from other animals in having a smaller proportion of phylogenetically fixed adaptations. Thus the development of techniques adequate for independent life is slower in man than in other animals.

This basic condition brings with it certain peculiarly human situations. The relationship of mother and child, for instance, is a bio-social one; it remains the prototype of many later types of social adaptation. In man, this dependent period is an unusually long one, and it is during this protected period that the chief adaptive techniques are acquired—a condition true of all mammals, but in lesser degree of complexity than is the case with man. In place of the fixed behavior types of lower animals,[4] man has a phylogenetically determined plasticity. He has in addition some important phylogenetically determined adjuncts, such as erect posture, speech, a complex hand, and a capacity for creating tools. Other peculiarly human basic biological factors should be noted. In addition to the helplessness of the humn infant and the consequent prolonged necessity for a protector, these are: the absence of regulation of the sexual instinct in accordance with seasonal change or conditions of food supply (absence of rutting season) ; the inordinately great changes in needs and functional capacities associated with human growth and development; and finally, the differences in individual capacity due to age and sex, to constitutional variations in strength, skill, beauty, courage, persistence, and intelligence, all of which play an extraordinarily important role in human life.

But we must observe that these features are not absolutely distinctive of human life. The differences between man and the lower animals are largely quantitative. The helplessness of man at birth must be correlated with his far greater potentialities for eventual adaptations and with the manner in which these are acquired.

[4] In the light of recent animal experiments it appears that these reaction types commonly regarded as phylogenetically fixed (instinctive) depend for their development to no small degree on learned reactions.

GENERAL CHARACTERISTICS OF CULTURE

One might suppose that the immature state in which man commences life, the protracted period of dependency, the necessity of the proximity of male and female, and the tendency to enduring unions, are sufficient to make some form of social life indispensable.[5] It is difficult, however, on these grounds alone to account for those units of society which are larger than the discrete family. These larger aggregates, the enlarged family, in-group, the tribe, the clan, etc., can be accounted for only on the ground of expediency due to alteration or extension of needs, or to some emotional source, or both. But this is a purely historical question. The fact is that there are no human societies without these larger aggregations, and we are safe in assuming that man lives in these larger units because this adjustment is required for survival in accordance with his emotional nature. This does not mean, however, that social life is a phylogenetically fixed characteristic of man.

Wherever we find these organized collections of human beings, we find some habitual regularity and organization of interrelations among the various individuals; we find also organized ways of dealing with the outer world in order to derive from it satisfactions essential to life; furthermore, we find organized ways of dealing with the processes of birth, growth, development, maturity, decline, and death, with due regard for differences in age and sex. Whenever there is a persistence or transmission of these organized methods, we have a *culture*.

When we observe the great variety of cultures, we are compelled to see some confirmation of our conclusions about the biological "nature" of man. Clearly, man is not an animal whose *needs* and behavior are all phylogenetically fixed. Only some of them are so fixed, while others are variable in accordance with a large variety of external conditions. Variations in social structure will change some needs, or create new ones. There is in man obviously much plasticity, or, to use the more

[5] This idea is not presented as a hypothesis about the earliest type of human society.

common term, much *adaptability*. For this reason, though the goals of adaptation may be quite uniform, we cannot expect to find any universal patterns or techniques of adaptation.

If man is thus an animal with certain fixed and certain variable needs, the fixed needs being more closely related to those of lower animals, we may expect to find in the multiplicity of cultures some evidence of both. We can even draft a tentative outline of those features which are common to all cultures. Such an outline should give us a general idea of these fixed needs insofar as they are accentuated or controlled by social life. We will find then that all cultures have the following features:

1. They all have some form of family organization which can be identified by some formal arrangement among parents, children, and members of the extended family. The character of the relations and what constitutes the extended family vary.

2. They all have an in-group formation of some kind. The nature and manner of its composition vary.

3. They all have some larger group like clan or tribe based on family organization, based on real or symbolic consanguinity, or based on common interests.

4. They all have definite techniques for deriving sustenance from the outer world. However, methods of coöperation and of organization for labor and division of produce differ widely.

5. They all have basic disciplines; but what impulses, interests or needs they control differ widely.

6. They all control mutual aggression according to a large variety of standards.

7. They are held together by certain recognizable psychological forces.

8. They all create definite and distinctive life goals which vary widely and even change within the same culture.

The units into which culture can be subdivided are very numerous and include every possible physical activity or mental attitude, such as customs, beliefs, practices, regulations that govern all varieties of human relationships, disciplines, etc. One could make an endless series of this kind. For purposes of brevity, it is expedient to establish a concept which can be used as a general name. The one which fits our purpose best is the word *institution*. This concept is to be used as a general name. When it becomes necessary to be specific, to identify the special institution by another designation, such terms as *mos,* family organization, discipline, tradition, custom, etc. will be used.

An *institution* can therefore be defined as *any fixed mode of thought or behavior held by a group of individuals (i.e., a society) which can be communicated, which enjoys common acceptance, and infringement of, or deviation from which creates some disturbance in the individual or in the group.* When we observe some uniformity of behavior in a group, we can speak of *institutionalized behavior.* Institutions are the means of societal continuity and are the effective tools for social equilibrium.

A culture acquires its conformation and specificity from the uniqueness of its institutions. Thus, the need for support in the human child for a prolonged period is met in almost every culture with some uniformity. The infant is nursed and cared for by the mother; but the duration of such care varies. The child must be carried about, but there is no uniformity about how this is done; some tie the child to a cradleboard; others carry it in a container of some kind on the shoulders. So, too, the technique of rearing children differs very widely. Similarly, the need for proximity of male and female is met by an institution that is universal—marriage—but the regulation as to whom one may not marry differs in different cultures. Still more varied are the institutions pertaining to sexual relations in general.

When we have collected, described, and catalogued all its institutions, we have the description of a culture. At this point we find Linton's differentiation between a society and a culture very useful: a society is a permanent collection of human beings; the institutions by which they live together are their culture.

All institutions have one feature in common: they become known to the individual by means of contact with other individuals. The large variety of pedagogical and disciplinary techniques by which mores are perpetuated will occupy us later. Meanwhile, we must recognize that the individual is the carrier of institutions, and the medium through which they are perpetuated. The products of some institutions consist of permanent material fixtures, such as tools, buildings, etc., which are called material culture; but these are likewise the product of techniques which are communicated through the individual. In other words, if we are to apply psychological methods, we must identify institutions as fixed precipitates of the interactions of humans upon one another, and the interactions between man and the external environment. "Culture, insofar as it is anything more than an abstraction made by the investigator, exists only in the minds of the individuals who compose a society." Linton[6] calls culture aptly "social heredity." The characteristics of man which make culture possible are the supreme objects of study. According to Linton, these are the ability of human beings to learn, to communicate and to transmit learned behavior from generation to generation.

THE RELATIVITY OF CULTURES

When an observer from our own culture brings back an account of the institutions of an aboriginal society, there is a natural limit to our understanding of them. Such accounts are usually arranged in a certain order which coincides with the investigator's conditions for systematic thinking, but not necessarily with the manner in which they are functionally integrated in the native mind. Thus one series of institutions can be arranged under the rubric of religion, another series under family organization, and others under such headings as in-group formation and subsistence economy. When all these have been gathered together, we can raise the following questions: Are these institutions causally related to one another? Has subsist-

[6] R. Linton, *The Study of Man* (New York, 1936), pp. 464, 78.

ence economy any causal relationship to social organization? And do both have any relation to the religion? We can characterize this "causal" relationship temporarily by assuming that if subsistence economy and social organization were altered, then the religion would change as well.

The proof of this hypothesis can be settled only in an experimental way; the opinion of an individual, either in the culture under consideration or that of the observer, is not a reliable guide in this matter. The observer has a limited amount of resources to bring to bear on such attempts at clarification. Every observer who goes to a new culture has a mental and emotional equipment of his own. He has lived in a specific culture, and his mental processes are shaped by its concatenations and synchronizations. His rationality is attuned to it, and the unconscious tendency is very strong to interpret the new culture in terms of the familiar one. In the case of a good many institutions, he cannot go very far wrong; but in the case of others, the relationships existing among our institutions are poor guides for such understanding of a foreign culture. It, therefore, becomes imperative to devise some "impersonal" criteria which can be used to obviate the dangers of explanations based on the rationality derived from one specific culture.

THE METHOD OF PROCEDURE

We are then led to ask whether it is possible to develop a method at once universally applicable and free from the inevitable individual and cultural bias of the observer. This book supports the thesis that this can be done through the understanding of the individual who is simultaneously the creator, the carrier, and the creature of all institutions. It is proposed to arrive at such a method in the following way. Let us study the individual in our culture and standardize his reactions to our own institutional complex. Thus we shall have some general information about the effects of certain institutions on the individual. We shall find that the most useful information is that obtainable from the effects of institutions which govern the satisfaction of those prime biological needs, hunger and sex. A second valuable source is to be found in the reactions to the induction of institutions, some of which require the aid of *disciplines;* i.e., the young individual does not naturally accept them and some system of coercion must be used to make him do so. A third source of information is obtainable from the study of reactions of the individual to needs which are accentuated or created by the culture, needs for prestige, status, etc. Once we have these reaction types, we can pursue their influence in the creation of other (secondary) institutions which are not directly offshoots of the first, but are products of the reactions produced by the first on "human nature." In other words we limit our task to finding out whether certain types of institutions bear a recognizable relationship to the pressures created by other more basic institutions such as family organization, basic disciplines, etc.

In this way culture can be seen molding, directing, and controlling biological and social needs, and at the same time determining the conditions under which they can be satisfied. But institutions have another function, to offer placebos and compensations for feelings, arising from the inability to satisfy these biological needs and needs created or accentuated by the culture.

It would follow therefore that institutions should have a certain consistency, not because they need to satisfy any logical requirement, but because they are bound by the possibilities of human reaction types.[7] Their consistency can be discovered only through the nature of the creature whose ends they serve. If, in a particular culture, the biological need of sexual gratification is systematically interfered with, from infancy on, from our knowledge of human nature we can expect that this will

[7] The quest for consistency ought not to blind us to the important fact that in societies where status and class differentiations are rigid, we must expect to find inconsistencies, because one institution serves and abets one group, and another institution another. No attempt will be made in this essay to discuss the problem of status differentiation, its effects on the individual, the conflicts engendered, and their effects on the total culture, beyond what is warranted by the clinical data of two aboriginal cultures.

give rise to a series of reactions, and that these reactions may eventually become petrified in institutions which offer some expression for the effects created by the frustrations concerned. The only practical way to check the truth of this assertion is to compare such a culture with another in which these systematic restrictions do not exist. Although we cannot at the present time adequately answer the questions why one society has institutions which restrict impulses and another has not, we can show the influence of both alternatives on the resulting culture as a whole.

With regard to the question of why this differentiation of the control of sexual and other impulses in different cultures, a complete answer cannot be made without the aid of history; but it is probable that some plausible conjectures can be made after the first problem is solved. However, no attempt will be made to do so in this book.

Our first task is, therefore, to try to understand the reactions of man to our own institutions; to study his reactions with due reference to his development from infancy to the completion of his psychic resources; and to study his reactions, to both gratifications and frustrations. We can then note the psychic constellations created and see the relationship these constellations have to the creation of new institutions or neuroses. Once this is established we can approach some aboriginal cultures and attempt to describe the interrelations among institutions.

With regard to the method of studying human reaction types, there are many psychologies from which one may choose. The essential psychological problem is to chart the effects of institutions on the individual in such a way that the results can be checked and verified, with the aid of concepts which can be commonly understood. Our task prescribes the conditions which such a psychology must meet. It must take into account why cultures can be communicated and perpetuated; it must be able to account for the different types of human personality which develop under different types of strain imposed upon them; it must be able to account for the continuity of behavior types within the individual during his entire life trajectory; it must have a technique for identifying the reactions to satisfactions and frustrations of basic human needs, and tracking down the effects of both on the adaptive weapons of the individual; and finally it must have an effectual method of dealing with the biological considerations we have outlined.

The psychology best known to the author and best able to satisfy these requirements is that conceived by Freud. We shall describe the specific manner in which this psychology will be put to work on our problem in the pages to follow.

NOTE

For purposes of clarity the following definitions are to be noted.

Sexual object: The object through whom sexual satisfaction is to be achieved. Object taboos therefore refer to tabooed individuals.

Sexual aim: The objective of sexual activity, sexual satisfaction. Aim taboos therefore refer to any sexual activity.

Ego: This is used to characterize the total personality as subjectively perceived, in contrast to "ego," which is used in the sense of the Freudian personality scheme, of which the "ego" is only one part, the others being "id" and "super-ego."

Total personality: This is the same as ego from the behavioral point of view.

Basic personality structure: That group of psychic and behavioral characteristics derived from contact with the same institutions, such as language, specific connotations, etc. (See Chap. IV, p. 126 and Chap. X, p. 467.)

Character: This is the personal variant of the basic personality structure.

"Instinct": The word "instinct" is used in the sense with which Freud uses it in all his works, and is the English equivalent of the word *Trieb.*

Chapter II

BASIC ORIENTATIONS

What Features of Culture Are

Psychologically Relevant?

WHAT features of a given society will best show how psychological forces operate in a culture? That is the question we must answer as we begin our quest. We are tempted to say in answer to this, that everything is relevant; but we are quite certain that to accept this as a working basis will prove unwieldy. For if our objective is to find out what different life goals, objectives, conflicts, and anxieties exist in different societies, not all features of a culture will be of equal weight. The kind of rugs woven and the kind of sex mores prevailing in a primitive society are both facts; but they are not equally indicative of the psychic and social pressures in that society. We must decide which is the better indicator of these pressures. And then there is a further difficulty. Not every institution can be envisaged all at once, for a great many institutions do not immediately meet the eye. For these basic data we must depend on someone's observations. What is observed will be, on the whole, what the observer considers relevant, what he makes the object of investigation. His observation will be qualified by his interpretation of what he sees, and his grasp of the interrelations of the various facts. Hence, the data that we finally get are always edited by the personality of the observer, his cultural bias, and his personal, subjective needs. These needs may not go very deep; to take an obvious instance, the observer may feel the need to prove a theory. Similar difficulties are met if we rely on native informants; no two will see quite the same thing. We see then, that everything in a culture is relevant to our inquiry; some features are more specifically diagnostic than others, and we can agree that the question of relative importance cannot be settled by the observer, who inevitably has both a personal and a cultural bias.

The problem of agreeing on our data is thus not easily solved. One may even take the position that because of these limitations we can never know a culture, and must regard the whole concept of culture as an artifact.

While it will not help us to deny that these limitations exist, we must realize that the reverse is also true; that there are certain features of culture that cannot be distorted by any observer. It is quite true that no individual can take in all of a culture, and the same culture will look different to a child, a woman, a man, a chief, a sorcerer. But each individual sees a facet of the same culture, and all persons see certain things in the same way. These, no reporter can distort. Object incest taboos look the same in our culture to a king and a cobbler. Indeed, the chief difficulty in the data submitted on primitive cultures has been due less to distortions than to omissions caused by the cultural bias of the observer, and to lack of knowledge about where relevant data are to be found.

With regard to the question of what we need to know about a culture in order to attempt some dynamic reconstruction, psychoanalysis has educated our sensibilities through intimate study of the individual subjected to our specific cultural pressures. But this exploration has been far from thorough because of the particular objectives of therapeutic analysis. Psychoanalysis has taught us that institutions can be recovered only from the detailed study of human interactions. It has further taught us that the individual cannot explain institutions, but only describe his reactions to them. Through psychoanalysis, the significance of many of our institutions became apparent. Prior to this experience we had completely overlooked the significance of certain types of institution. When we live in a given set of institutions from birth the effects of these institutions

are so completely a part of the personality that we are frequently unable to identify their effects. Our attention is never
called to them save by contrast with a deviation from them,
which then impresses us as a feeling of strangeness. Indeed, the
individual's conflict with these same institutions often can be
identified only by some internal discomfort perceived by the
individual. The fact that living with particular institutions
creates certain blind spots is well illustrated by the "discovery"
of Freud that children in our society have a spontaneous sexual
life. To us it was a disturbing discovery, violently denied and
contested, whereas to a Trobriand or Marquesan it is a self-
evident fact. To Freud it was indeed a discovery, for it had to
be unearthed and deduced from a great deal of evidence that
did not meet the eye.

It may be well, therefore, to begin with some features of our
own culture, with the purpose of presenting the institutional
complex and the range of effects which it creates.[1] We can use
this procedure also to illustrate how deep the psychic ramifications of an institution can go in the mental apparatus of the
individual.

We shall, in the pages that follow, attempt to describe a few
features of our culture in such a way as to show the interactions
between individual and institution. In describing institutions,
various conceptual systems can be used; the information yielded
will depend largely on the limits defined by these conceptual
systems. In this essay our method will be to describe the
institution in accordance with the effects it produces on the
individual. These effects we shall trace by the influence they

[1] Freud is not of the opinion that a specific cultural complex is entirely responsible for the reaction types of the child. He states ". . . a child catches hold
of this phylogenetic experience where his own experience fails him. He fills in
the gaps in individual truth with prehistoric truth; he replaces occurrences in
his own life by occurrences in the life of his ancestors." S. Freud, *Collected
Papers*, Vol. III: *The History of an Infantile Neurosis* (London, 1924), pp. 577–
578. The numerous types of family organization found in aboriginal cultures,
and the various types of discipline extant cast some doubt on the uniformity
of this cultural heritage on which the child is supposed to draw for his unconscious memories. Freud is himself of the opinion that the experience of the
child must be explored before calling on phylogenetic explanations.

have on the final instruments of adaptation, that is, on the ego or total personality.

The relation between individual and culture has been described in psychoanalytic social psychology from two points of view which are in a large measure irreconcilable. Both use the same data; but on the issue of what an institution purports to be, they diverge.

One viewpoint takes the position that man is phylogenetically endowed with certain drives or "instincts" which press for satisfaction through objects in the outer world; that these "instincts," in the course of their ontogenesis, go through certain phylogenetically predetermined and regularly repeated phases of development, at each of which an arrest of development may take place; and that, in some way as yet unknown, institutional systems are derived from these "instincts" and their derivatives according to the extent of their development. The practical result of this line of reasoning is that a culture is described in terms of a subjectively felt drive such as "phallic," "anal sadistic," etc., in accordance with the phases of development established in the individual. The individual is then viewed as driven back upon one of the earlier phases of adaptation because of the Oedipus complex. And this situation is viewed not as an encounter with institutions, but as an unconscious hereditary constellation which acts as the prime mover of the regressive adaptation. The institutions of a culture, from this point of view, are adventitious excrescences consequent upon certain drives seeking for expression, and hence quite meaningless as influences on human nature. The most noteworthy formulation which proceeds from this point of view is that culture is a product of "instinct"-repression. The process which is responsible for this transformation is presumably sublimation. This view should lead to the clinical fact that the greater the repression the "higher" the culture, for more sublimatable energy is at its disposal. But this formulation does not stand the test of clinical verification. This view would account for the *origin* of institutions on a biological basis and limit their function essentially to biological ends.

The other viewpoint, the validity of which we shall attempt to establish, is that the individual stands midway between institutions which mold and direct his adaptation to the outer world, and his biological needs, which press for gratification. This viewpoint places a heavy emphasis on institutions and stresses the significant role they play in creating the adaptive systems of the individual. The institutions in this view can be identified and their effects on the individual traced. But the coördinates against which all these effects are charted are the basic biologically determined needs of man.

Since each of these viewpoints creates its own conceptual systems, we cannot shift between the two; that is, we cannot state on the one hand that a given institution prevents the exercise of sexuality in childhood, and then proceed to describe its effects on the individual in terms of a phylogenetic scheme of biological phases of development and finally proceed to forget the institution which created the necessity for repression. Incongruity arises not only from the fact that different conceptual systems are used to describe the institution, but from the fact that each point of view presupposes a different function for the institution. In the one view, the institution is seen as a by-product of a biological force exclusively; in the other, as an external force—whatever its origin—on the individual. In the first instance the transformation of sexual energy into cultural traits is accounted for on the basis of a hypothetical dynamism called *sublimation,* which stands in the same relation to instinct energy as did the old "conversion" theory of anxiety to repressed *libido.* But the dynamics of sublimation have never been described; the validity of the concept still depends on a succession of phenomena between which a causal connection is assumed—with some justification—to exist. This concept of sublimation thus becomes one of the necessary adjuncts of an "instinct" psychology in which all the phenomena observed must be accounted for as qualitative changes and quantitative distributions of a unitary *"instinct" energy.* The term *sublimation* satisfies a theoretical requirement, but is not necessarily the name of a psychic process. This does not mean that the original observations which record the succession of "instinct" repressions and their sequelae as sublimations are invalid; it merely means that the concept of sublimation does not adequately account for the change, unless one grants the unproved assumptions about "instinct." There is, however, an excellent possibility that common ground between the two viewpoints can be found after the conceptual systems of each are translated one into the other. The possibility that this ontogenetic scheme of development is not phylogenetically determined, but is a product of certain identifiable environmental pressures on the individual, must be seriously considered. But this is a question which cannot be answered until we know more precisely just what are the effects of discipline on the individual in various phases of his growth and development.

Meanwhile, a way must be found to utilize the important knowledge which Freud has described concerning dynamics, and at the same time to pay the closest attention to the institutions which modify the adaptive tools of the individual. Comparative anthropology gives us ample opportunity to do this. In order to achieve it we must shift our attention away from "instinctive" drives as the most effective approach to the study of mental activity, and focus on the relation between institutions and that part of the adaptive apparatus of the individual which is in direct contact with the institutions, that is, the ego. For the concept "instinct" contains too many processes all condensed into one. In biology the determination of an "instinct" was made behavioristically; in psychoanalysis, from subjective conation of impulse. Practically, the concept includes: (1) the cause of an activity; (2) the goal of an activity; (3) the behavior necessary to consummate the activity. These three units cannot be treated as a single entity.

A definition of the *ego* is difficult because neither structural nor functional concepts do it justice. Of the two, the latter are more useful, for we know the ego from its activity. A crude definition would be *the sum total of all its adaptive processes subjectively perceived.* The ego is "located" at the boundary between outer and inner worlds and is molded by influences coming from both; it has perceptive, coördinative, and executive functions; rudimentary at birth, it grows and develops; its functions are modified coincidentally with the size, strength, and potentialities of the individual; it is integrative in its development, which means that all adaptive processes are based on those which have proved expedient in the past. It is the "organ" of continuity and of the organization of experience.

An ego psychology is based on a two-fold assumption: that the adaptive tools of the individual are in part molded by the environment; and that institutions are the result of efforts to control or stimulate behavior. Such a view gives us a conceptual system that is applicable equally to the individual and to the institutions in which he lives.

We can now see the usefulness of our conclusions in the previous chapter. The characteristics of the human ego, its slow growth and integrative character, make the functional role of institutions with which the ego is in contact very great. Those creatures whose adaptations are more fixed at birth than man's do not accumulate new integrations to the same degree, nor are they as susceptible to the influence of the immediate environment as man. Thus, in man, only the drive toward certain goals of adaptation is phylogenetic; but the specific techniques are strongly influenced, if not entirely molded, by cultural influences.

How much influence the culture has varies with each particular activity we examine. Not all impulses are equally susceptible of control. For example, the impulses generally denoted as sexual and aggressive are much more subject to control than the eating impulses. Sexual drive and behavior cannot be influenced to an unlimited degree. The sexual impulse has an organic substratum, and the ideas and activities necessary to bring about satisfaction are subject to development, growth, and integration; hence behavior in connection with sexual aims can be influenced throughout the entire life of the individual. The most enduring influences are the earliest ones, because the resulting executive equipment of the ego to carry out the satisfaction of the drive is to a large measure *integrative*. However, even erotisms can be culturally determined; witness the fact that in some societies nose rubbing is erotically stimulating, and kissing is not. The reverse is true in other cultures. Neurosis is the best general indicator of the various end-results of specific integrative types of activity. Neurosis, however, indicates only variations within a cultural pattern. But the cultural pattern influences the general mold of the adaptation pattern. On this point there is general agreement.[2]

It is then our intention to describe institutions in terms of the premises outlined, and in terms of the effective tools of adaptation, i.e., in terms of the ego. We must now ask, Which individuals shall we choose to illustrate the effects of cultural patterns? Since there are innumerable individual variations, neurosis and character variations, we can follow only one course: to study the range of variations. For evaluating the types of individual variations, and for seeing what all these variations have in common, we have the tools of psychoanalysis.

We shall attempt to describe the interaction between ego and institution in accordance with the following goal: What effect has the institution on the adaptive weapons of the individual? What effect have the needs of the individual on the institution? Practically, we can use the following scheme:

1. To describe the institution, which, for example, interferes with an impulse.
2. To describe the effects of this interference on the individual with respect to the:

   a) changes in the perception of the impulse;

[2] See K. Horney, *The Neurotic Personality of Our Time* (New York, 1937), Chap. I.

b) modification this makes on the executive functions;

c) feelings to those who impose it;

d) unconscious constellations formed by this series of conditions;

e) relation of these unconscious constellations to the actual behavior of the individual;

f) relation between those constellations to *new* institutions (or neurosis).

We shall limit our discussion in this chapter to the reciprocal relations between the individual and our culture in connection with the following: (1) The organization of the family and character of the in-group formation, and the psychological constellations in the individual formed by them. (2) The basic disciplines, sexual and anal, and the consequences, vicissitudes, and basic constellations in the individual derived from them. (3) The psycho-biological factors responsible for the establishment of discipline and its perpetuation; the psychology of dependency and discipline. (4) The various forms of mastery ontogenetically considered and the reasons for studying them; infantile types, and training for adult pursuits generally called "economic." (5) The conflicts derived from the social conditions of work, subsistence conflicts, prestige conflicts, rivalry, and competition. (6) Aggression, its forms, and the effects of social control. (7) Forces that hold society together, external sanctions and their internalization and "super-ego formation." (8) Life goals and ideals in our culture.

THE ORGANIZATION OF THE FAMILY AND THE FAMILY-IN-GROUP

In our culture the organization of the family is on a patriarchal pattern with legal monogamy. Father, mother, and children are the basic unit. Divorce is possible in some cases, but it is not freely encouraged. Collateral branches are held together by ties of sentiment without binding political or economic significance. The larger units of town, cities, states, are extremely mobile, common interests in them being based on utilitarian, and not on blood or in-group loyalties. The town, for example, does not have the character of a clan or tribe, though many of the common interests of its constituents are based on locality.

The limits of the in-group are hard to define, for the traditional family is an economic unit, and relations to collateral branches are not fixed by any convention. For most purposes, in-group and family are one, although transient and labile in-group formations are set up on a large variety of bases of limited character.

The status of the members of the family is pretty well conventionalized; the father is legal head of the household, bread-winner, and executive; he has powers within limits, and he has prestige. Each family lives in a separate abode, and is thus surrounded by strangers upon whom no economic or emotional claim can be made. Within the family or larger in-group created by marriage, the *individual* can make certain claims. The position of women was long subordinate to that of man, but more recently has shifted toward parity.

BASIC DISCIPLINES—INHIBITED AND UNINHIBITED ACTIVITY

Among the conventions in our culture worthy of note are the wearing of clothes and the special disposition of excreta in privacy. These conventions are very far-reaching in their effect on the creation of special psychic constellations with regard to nudity and excretory functions, both of which become related to sex.

Nursing of children is the rule; weaning is instituted between six months to one year (in America). Sphincter control is begun generally within the first year, and generally completed at about two years. Sphincter control is associated with clothing and with a host of subsidiary disciplines pertaining to cleanliness and order. These are all institutions. The variations in the enforcement of these disciplines are infinite, as are also the reactions of the individual to them.

Sexual disciplines are inculcated by a system of prohibitions, direct or implied, and by a conventionalized system of approvals, disapprovals, and withholding of approval. In urban centers the absence of animals, the wearing of clothes, and the convention of living in several rooms with a private parental bedchamber, offers the child few opportunities to observe sexual relations. The usual incest taboos exist pertaining to mother-son, father-daughter, siblings, and other members of the extended family. The taboo refers both to sexual relations and marriage. The isolation of each individual family renders the individuals in the household the immediate objects of sexual curiosity. But it is as much a convention to deny the existence of the sexual impulse in the child as to conceal the activities of the parents. Not only are certain incestuous objects taboo, but as far as the conventions indicate, all other objects are taboo as well. In other words, *the taboo covers both sexual objects and sexual aim.* The sexual organs are recognized only as excretory organs, and as such are identified by name, and these functions are associated with a permissive parental attitude. The sexual organ as a pleasure organ is not recognized; this function is not given a name; and the genital as a pleasure zone is usually an accidental discovery by the child, for which no approval can be obtained. It is one of the oldest beliefs in our culture that masturbation, the chief sexual activity of childhood, is harmful, an idea which is backed by a whole library of supporting legends. The discovery of the child's masturbation by the parent, as a rule, results in a forbidding or punitive attitude by the parent. This behavior on the part of the parent is institutionalized; the behavior of the child, natural. The parent, as a rule, does not know why he interdicts the sexual activity of the child, except that he believes that it causes some harm. This is an opinion which has been backed by authorities who have never subjected this very ancient belief to some empirical verification. The discipline is intended to make the child conform to the institutions. In other words, the discovery of sexual pleasure by the child leaves it without any tools to deal with, no words, and no concepts, and hence this sexual activity has no approved, accepted place in the child's world. It is learned from other children or perverts. The parental attitude of condemnation, neglect, prohibitions expressed and explicit and backed by punishments and threats of harm or withdrawal of support and love, all conspire to leave a certain portion of the child's personality undeveloped. This situation imposes on the child necessities for channeling out new compensations or gratifications in lieu of those denied. The element of pain, in one form or another, has thus been introduced into what is naturally pleasant. The effects of these institutions vary with each individual. The most likely uniform reaction is that it may place additional burdens on other gratifications which carry with them the affect of permissibility, and to place a higher value on the rewards of the renunciation.

The effects of this systematic suppression on the individual must be evaluated in relation to other biological needs, in relation to institutionalized social conditions for securing protection, approval, and love. In other words, we can expect definite things to happen to the developing personality if the child must invent new attitudes to the sexual urge, to the activity in response to this urge, to the parent, and to himself. One result is that his self-esteem suffers. The parent is needed and feared, and must therefore be obeyed; but the hatred to the frustrating parent, though suppressed, must be present somewhere. Furthermore, an element of frustration and pain has been introduced, which must lead to a new method of handling the whole situation, since the influence of culture is continuous as is the sexual urge. Each individual meets this situation in an individual manner. It is necessary for us to trace a few of the consequences.

From the point of view of common sense, one custom or mos is like another. One group of people do one thing, and another group do another. These differences may merely represent different idiosyncrasies or predilections. This view maintains for certain practices but not for others. How a man wears his hair or eats his food may not materially affect the structure of the ego. In the study of sociology, what is important is not the difference in individuality expressed in mores, but whether or not they affect the essential nature of the individual and how they do this. Where a biological drive or an urgent need is interfered with by a mos, consequences follow which have important effects. These effects, however, vary with the time in the life cycle in which they are initiated. If the effect registers on the individual in the early formative years of his life, it will affect the entire growth and development of the ego, at least insofar as the particular function is concerned. If an injunction is instituted against a function that has already been completed, the influence will be entirely different from that in the first case. For our purpose, the kind of interference with the sexual function in the early formative years, and the one which compels a very specific adjustment, is the best suited for study. We can choose the most extreme types of adaptation for purposes of contrast.

All these reactions recorded in the next paragraphs are clinical; they were observed on individuals suffering from severe inhibitions in their sex life. They were partly deduced from reactions to the analyst, and partly from recollections of crucial events in childhood. Psychoanalytic literature abounds in data which support these conclusions. The observations about the course of an uninhibited impulse is a reconstruction by contrast. If the inhibited individual encounters difficulties in certain portions of a completed action, it would follow that the "normal" individual would encounter no such difficulties. Some of these aspects can be observed, others inferred. In the case of the inhibited person, all can be observed, beginning with the complaint of the patient that he is impotent, and that this impotence cannot be explained by the patient in any way, because he has sexual desires just like the "normal" person. For purposes of clarifying the effects of institutions, we can contrast inhibited with uninhibited activity.

When no obstacles are placed between a given drive, for

example, the urge for masturbation in a child, and the behavior necessary to consummate it, the activity leads to gratification. This concept "gratification" is a psychobiological idea; it involves "release," freedom from "tension," and "pleasure." When the impulse arises again, there is an anticipation of the gratification, and there is a mobilization of executive functions necessary to induce the activity or behavior functions which are both psychic and motor. The successful consummation of the activity leads to a feeling of satisfaction, a feeling of ego enhancement, contentment, relaxation, etc. In addition, there is an important consequence in the form of a picture or image of oneself as successfully consummating the activity. This is the basis of the ego feeling which in the vernacular is called "self-confidence." It is expressed in the formula "I can do that."

In the case of infantile masturbation, this attitude acquires a very important significance. The activity between the ages of one and four years takes place at a time when dependency attitudes to the parent are strongest. It is also the time when the social demand for independence, learning the character of the outer world, and how to deal with it, is most persistent, perhaps never equalled again in the entire life history of the individual. The autoerotic activities of the child have an extremely important function in aiding growth and completing the weaning from the mother. Up to this time the mother is the chief support to dependency longings, and also the chief source of gratifications. The discovery of sexual pleasure is an important adjunct in the whole process of weaning.[3] The child also learns to appreciate similar gratifications in connection with activities associated with other portions of the body, such as walking, etc. Uninhibited masturbation adds to the child's mental life an extremely important idea, namely, "I can get pleasure from

[3] The transition from breast to finger sucking and thence to masturbation has been repeatedly noted by pediatricians and analysts. Rank has made this transition and some of the psychic reactions to it the basis of an elaborate system, in which the transformations of "oral aggression" are responsible for all subsequent changes in the individual's psychic organization. See O. Rank, *Grundzüge einer Genetische Psychologie* (Leipzig, 1927), pp. 69–89.

myself," an idea which helps to break the dependency tie on the mother. It is, therefore, an adjunct to growth and not a retarding influence. This is proved by severe cases of frigidity and impotence where this basic idea, "I can get pleasure from myself," is entirely absent in childhood masturbation, and hence never later becomes a part of the individual's sexual equipment in relations to the opposite sex. The destruction of this "confidence" expressed in the idea "I can do that" is likewise demonstrable in functions other than sexual; in the traumatic neurosis this "confidence" is destroyed in those functions pertaining to orientation to the outer world. The whole concept of "will" eventually rests on the ability to form such an image of oneself. *Will* cannot be exercised over functions in the development of which essential details have been omitted. There is no fulcrum on which the lever of action can rest. The result is that the individual strives vainly toward a goal without any instruments to do so with any effectiveness or precision.[4]

The successful and uninterrupted consummation of such sexual activity leads to a confident, eager, and friendly attitude to the impulse when it arises again, and to pleasant anticipations. This is represented by word, idea, and motility constellations that are easily accessible, plastic, and psychically mobile.

Now, when the element of pain is introduced into this activity in the form of threats of punishment and loss of love and support, especially at a time when the child fears punishment and needs protection and approval most, conditions are created which favor the abandonment of the pleasurable activity as an escape from the conflict. The anticipation of punishment backed by sufficient force, direct or implied, does eventually lead to an

[4] The relation between ego psychology and "depth" psychology is well illustrated in the relation between self-confidence and the underlying processes of which it is the end result. The feeling of self-confidence is only an indicator that, as far as the executive aspects of the ego are concerned, no internal obstacle exists that can hinder the execution of an impulse, and that successes in the past have placed, at the disposal of the ego, images concerned with motor activity. These form a striking contrast with the images in dreams or fantasies of individuals who are inhibited. The representations of the ego are those of continuous failure.

abandonment of the activity necessary to satisfy the drive. Instead of a friendly attitude to the impulse, there is an anxiety which is an anticipation of danger. Instead of the self-confidence and the idea "I can get pleasure by and from myself," there appears an exaggerated idea of the cruelty of the forbidding parent. Instead of the attitude of self-confidence, the opposite develops—a lack of it, together with an inordinate increase in dependency and timidity. If the executive activity is completely suppressed, there is established the psychic constellation known as inhibition. Such an inhibition modifies the entire executive apparatus of the child. The perceptions of oneself and of the activity become modified so that the impulse is represented, not in pleasant anticipations, but in their opposite, cruel and hurtful images. In dreams the individual is represented as failing, and gratifications thus thwarted are represented by their negatives. The latter is called a *masochistic version* of the original activity. In many instances the painful element thus introduced clings to the individual's fantasies and anticipations of sexual pleasure for the remainder of his life. He has not only become tolerant of pain; it has become a condition and essential feature of some part of the original pleasure. This whole syndrome is called "masochism."

Now if we use the study of such an inhibition as a demonstration of the force of a group of institutions, we leave ourselves open to a serious objection. One might argue that the case is not proved at all. It may correctly be observed that most people who live under the institutions described do not become impotent or frigid, and therefore, the institutions cannot possibly have anything to do with the inhibition. It thus becomes a purely *individual* problem. That is true enough. There is indeed an individual problem. But it is the institution which creates the conditions against which the individual is pitted, and all individual variations in reaction must be evaluated and standardized against the institutions.[5] We must first investigate

[5] See also discussion on this point in K. Horney, *The Neurotic Personality of our Time* (New York, 1927), Chap. I.

whether all people who live under a certain group of mores have certain features in common, and whether the effect on this very inhibited individual represents the most extreme consequence of what all the others have to some measure. This is what really turns out to be the case in the actual study of a series of individuals from the same culture whether they are "normal" or have similar neurotic disorders. We must expect a range of individual variations in these reaction types.

This problem came up very early in the history of psychoanalytic theory. At first only those very neurotic individuals with severe symptoms were supposed to have an "Oedipus complex." Further experience demonstrated beyond cavil that this complex was not pathognomonic, and was alike present in all individuals, neurotic, psychotic, and normal. What all of these had in common was, therefore, the derivative of a special set of institutions. But how each individual handled those cultural influences is another story. We have reached the point now where we can definitely identify the reactions to these institutions which terminate in severe neuroses, and those reaction types which terminate in a normal adaptation. Whether these basic reaction types are due to underlying constitutional factors or not is a problem that cannot yet be answered. But they can be psychologically identified, and modified, and for the moment that is enough for our purposes.

Food Disciplines

From this discussion of the influence of certain institutionalized mores on the individual, it is hard to avoid the impression that not all mores are of equal importance and influence. It becomes, therefore, a problem to select the mores of the greatest influence. In the previous section we have been dealing with a group of mores on a special need of the individual, the sexual. The sexual "instinct" in man has well-defined characteristics which make such disciplines possible. These characteristics are: (1) that the satisfaction of the sexual craving can be deferred; (2) that it can be vicariously gratified; and (3) that its energy, according to Freud, can be deflected into channels other than sexual (sublimation).

In studying the influence of various types of sexual mores in different societies it becomes a question whether what we have learned about the influence of prohibitions in our culture will serve us in other cultures. Evidence from primitive cultures indicates that reaction types to this "instinctual" frustration are basically the same everywhere though each society dresses the reaction types in its own particular form.

It is quite evident that if we consider the craving for food an "instinct," it cannot be dealt with in the manner of the sexual need. The need for food cannot be satisfied by substitutes; its satisfaction cannot be long deferred; it is not capable of "sublimation." In short, the need for food cannot be dealt with by any *mos* in such a way that the objective can be seriously interfered with. Short of death, however, a great many mores can be elaborated about eating; they can influence what kind of food is eaten, when it shall be eaten, and how. In other words, the subsistence value of food can never be interfered with; the prestige or ritual value of food can be manipulated in various ways. Such mores, if they do not jeopardize life itself, can be tolerated by the individual without creating serious disturbances in internal psychic economy.

There are several important features about the craving for food. The drive to eat is physiologically determined; but the somatic sources of this drive take in the entire organism, not a special set of organs. The mouth and gastro-intestinal tract are the executive organs for this drive, but not the source of the need. The behavior necessary to satisfy the drive insofar as it pertains to sucking, mastication, and swallowing, is reflex, and the infant already has an executive technique at birth. The only modification that takes place is the change from sucking to mastication in the transition from fluid to solid diet. The only anatomical change is the acquisition of teeth. The great changes in the satisfaction of the eating drive do not, therefore, depend on a complicated development of eating techniques.

The technique of procuring food however, is subject to great changes. Sucking is the technique associated with nursing, mastication the technique after weaning. However, for a long time after weaning, the child is dependent on the parent for procuring food. The child is likewise dependent on the parent for protection. Though the functions of orientation and locomotion develop quite automatically, the finer techniques of adaptation, including that for procuring food, must all be taught.

In our culture the reactions to food anxiety must all be highly individualized, because the technique for procuring food is a part of those social pursuits of the individual which we call "economic." Moreover, in our culture there is no generalized food anxiety, since the means of production and exchange are under quite complete control. The anxieties about food are not created by ignorance of effective techniques of production, but from other complications arising from social organization which deal with distribution.

In aboriginal societies, however, where the techniques for exploiting the environment for subsistence vary a good deal because of vicissitudes of climate and the imperfections of techniques, we must be on the lookout for the generalized effects of food anxiety and the institutions consequent upon them.

DEPENDENCY AND REACTIONS TO DISCIPLINE

If we note the protracted period of dependency of the child upon the parent for food, shelter and protection, there are a good many aspects of culture that become clear. We can understand how cultures are perpetuated, the great inertia to change, and most important of all, the means that society has of enforcing its disciplines. The understanding of this characteristic of dependency can moreover show us the origin of certain types of institutions. It follows that if certain institutions, which we shall designate for the moment as primary, create pressures on the individual, the effects due to the pressures may be registered on certain secondary reactions by the individual which also become institutionalized.

We must defer treating several aspects of the child's helplessness and dependency, and for the moment consider only those aspects that have to do with how society enforces its disciplines. From the behaviorist point of view, we could simply say, the parent has the authority to enforce discipline. This is something of an oversimplification. Not all disciplines need to be enforced, and authority often has nothing to do with their adoption. Language, for example, and techniques for mastering the outer world, do not need to be enforced. Authority of parents is, therefore, necessary only in certain types of discipline. We have already seen one typical instance in which the child is compelled to yield to social pressure in connection with the sexual instinct. There are others as well.

What is dependency? It is a basic ego attitude necessary for survival, in response to an anxiety resulting from a feeling of helplessness, or to a feeling of limited resources, strength, or ability. The attitude is one of soliciting support, help, or protection. In extreme instances, it is an actual wish that another person take over all responsibility for the subject's welfare. The subject will, on such occasions, delegate to the object of dependency great powers, will attribute to him abilities to do things which the subject cannot do for himself. The attitude of dependency motivates the desire to be near the object, to do for the object anything that may be demanded in return for protection and help, even if this entails the abandonment of important gratifications. This attitude has an interesting history throughout the life cycle of the individual. It is an attitude resulting from a biological need determined at birth, and remains effective during the formative years. Its persistence after the time when it should normally disappear is an infallible indicator of underlying failure of growth and development of resources. No individual ever loses the attitude of dependency completely, especially in crises that transcend his abilities. But in some neurotic characters it remains throughout life the dominant technique of adaptation.

Dependency in the child is biologically determined; it is

founded on the incomplete and helpless state in which the human infant is born. This seems at first a great handicap and misfortune. On closer inspection it loses this character and turns out to be one of the very biological characteristics that are eventually responsible for the great advantages man enjoys later in life in the form of plasticity and multiplicity of adaptation possibilities over many lower forms of animal life much better equipped at birth.

This biological fact is of the greatest importance for the study of how society is organized and perpetuated. It means essentially that man is a creature with not inborn, but learned, reaction types. But where, one may ask, do the "instincts" come in of which man has at least as many as lower animals? Yes indeed, these supply the drive toward a goal, but they do not furnish the behavior necessary to consummate it. This is a fact of the greatest sociological importance; for it leaves room for the influence of the social environment in molding these behavior types.

This state of affairs depends partly on an anatomical condition. The body of the infant at birth is largely torso and abdomen and head, the extremities being much underdeveloped. The circulation is largely concentrated in the splanchnic area. The central nervous system is incomplete; the tracts which connect the spinal cord with the brain stem do not yet function, which means that directed voluntary motion is as yet impossible. These tracts do not become functionally active until the process of myelination is complete, and this takes place at twenty-four to thirty months. This means that organized tensions, depending on contact with the outer world through the senses and the muscular apparatus, do not yet arise; and that for those tensions that do arise, no executive apparatus as yet exists. The completion of the process of myelination and the completion of sensory-motor executive functions are therefore effected in conjunction with contacts with the outer world. The general direction and character of these contacts are inborn, but the specific technique is learned. This feebleness of the child, therefore, reaps a rich reward later in that the adaptation possibilities are enormously increased. It follows, therefore, that an animal, whose myelination is completed shortly after birth, has fewer adaptation possibilities. Such is the case with the guinea pig, the mouse and the cat. Still fewer possibilities of adaptation exist for creatures whose drives and the behavior necessary to effect them are both completed at birth. Such a creature cannot modify itself, its environment, or its reaction type. If it succeeds, it survives; if it fails, the creature dies.

Thus this initial handicap in infancy gives the human great plasticity and multiplicity of adaptation possibilities. But it also makes necessary a longer social life and a longer period of dependency.

This primary dependency on the female parent is subject to many mishaps. The dependency is a biological need, though no one has given it the name of an instinct. This need may be frustrated or it may be prolonged beyond its normal usefulness. Such vicissitudes, prolongations, and frustrations are in part dependent on the attitude of the parent to the child, but more largely on the attitude of the child to the parent. It may be well, therefore, to examine this attitude from the standpoint of the infant.

To this problem psychoanalysis has made a signal contribution. Freud recovered some of the main ideas about it from the thought processes of compulsion neurotics; Ferenczi took these ideas as the starting point for the investigation of the development of the sense of reality; and Rado has used them to explain some of the basic attitudes of hypnotist and subject, parent and child. Freud noted the "omnipotence of thought" in neuroses, which simply meant that the patient believed his thoughts to have a magic efficacy, and as he had many thoughts hostile to those whom he presumably loved, he had to invent either neutralizing or self-punitive measures. Freud concluded that this must be a dominant idea in infancy. Ferenczi corroborated the Freudian idea, and found it had a much wider application.

In other words, psychoanalysis made the discovery that infants do not perceive their helplessness, but, on the contrary, feel as if they control the world. How does this come about? The helplessness of the child is conceded by the parent, aid is given unsolicited and indications of discomfort are eagerly anticipated or sought out. To be sure the child's needs are as yet limited; he needs only food, maintenance of constant temperature, and care of excreta. The infant has only one effective organ, the mouth, his excretory functions being automatically regulated. The effectiveness of the mouth is due to the fact that the nerves that supply the muscles used in sucking and swallowing are myelinated at birth. The sucking reflex, however effective at birth, must be successful, otherwise it will cease to function and the infant will refuse to nurse. In short, because of the limitations of his needs, and because of the effectiveness of the oral zone for sucking and the fact that the mother can interpret his every discomfort and can do for him what he cannot yet do for himself, the infant can lead a contented existence. But even under these very favorable conditions, the infant's life is not free from tensions. The mother cannot reach every discomfort such as colic or wetness for brief periods.

This period of a child's life is not subject to direct subjection evaluations; that is, the child cannot tell us about his experiences. One can, however, observe that the child shows mimicry of satisfaction from any form of effectiveness. With such crude weapons as he has, he is assertive. And from what can be learned from pathological states, the control over the environment exerted by the infant through the mother's agency is very like the one we subsequently observe in magic practices. Many fairy tales exploit this form of control. The simplest and most complete of these is illustrated by the story of Aladdin's lamp, where the genie obeys Aladdin every time he rubs the lamp, and the boy is, moreover, obligated to the genie in no way whatsoever. A few vocalizations of the child set in motion a series of complicated changes in the outer world which the child does not understand, but which terminate in easing his tension. It is highly improbable that the child has any appreciation of this state of affairs; and it is highly probable that any ideas about it are reconstructions of a later period. During this period of magic control through the mother, we cannot speak of the child's attitude of dependency. For such an attitude to exist, it is necessary to have a wish tension, a knowledge of the inadequacy of resources to satisfy it by oneself, and an attitude of demanding this satisfaction from someone else.

In clinical experience there is another very important idea associated with this period of magic control which has been observed during the analysis of several paranoid characters. These characters, when they establish a relationship with some individual, do not regard the other person as a separate entity, but as an appendage of themselves.[6] As one patient described it, "I have no feeling of separateness from the other person." This has long been described as "loss of ego boundaries," and was generally regarded as a manifestation of "narcissism." Paranoid individuals perpetuate the relationship of infant to mother on the basis of magic control; every other relationship is based on the expectation that the other person will merely be a satellite, to be used to obey and execute their magic wishes, to enhance their self-esteem. This is one of the basic frustrations which make the perpetrator of these imagined frustrations into a persecutor, and hence an object of hatred.

The period of magic omnipotence in the infant does not go on for very long; for the child is propelled by the process of growth, which simultaneously changes both the needs and the resources of the child. However, the resources never catch up with the needs, and the child must now develop new techniques for satisfying them. The technique of magic control begins to fail. At this point we begin to see the operation of a cluster of forces whose varying combinations lead to different results. The environment and the process of growth stimulate new types of adaptation, which later are either accepted or rejected. In the first case, new types of gratification are found, and a feeling of

---

[6] This process is not "identification," but is one which identification later intends to reinstate after the ego is established as a separate entity.

confidence in them established; or, in the second case, the child is timid in accepting them, and clings to the technique of retreat and expectation that the guardian will continue the magic services. Whenever a situation develops which the child cannot meet, and which is accompanied by a recognition of the limitation of his resources and an expectation of outside help, we have an attitude of dependency. One of the most important influences which tend to perpetuate this attitude of timidity and dependency is failure in the newer types of adaptation; dependency really signals the continuation of the inhibitory effects of failure. The attitude of dependency can be said in every case to be due to a failure of resources; but this failure may be due to the social prohibition of the exercise of certain impulses, to constitutionally determined inadequacies or to accidental interferences. It has been found that in the development of new techniques, which are in a constant state of change, failures are frequent. At these junctures, the expectation of magic help is likely to be revived. Occasional invocations of this kind would not be especially injurious; but experience has shown that when the balance between failure and inhibitory influence is resolved by the habitual wish for magic aid and becomes a permanent reaction type, the growth of the ego is seriously retarded, or resources already developed are not available for ready use.

When the ego attitude of dependency is established, the wish for the continuation of the effortless magic control is revived, but as Rado has pointed out,[7] this wish has undergone an important modification. In infancy we assume the child has endowed himself with a feeling of omnipotence. But in the attitude of dependency, he endows the parent with these magical attributes. One may say this is no new attitude, that it is the same as it was in infancy, but the child's sense of reality has grown, and he really appreciates his former delusion of grandeur. Rado characterizes this state of affairs as follows: "This projecting of almightiness on the parent is effected to the end

[7] Unpublished lecture on hypnosis, N. Y. Psychoanalytic Institute, March, 1937.

that the parent will use his power exclusively for the child's benefit. Thus the character of the security at this time is established on the basis that the executive agent is not within itself, but elsewhere. The dependent person submits to this extremely degrading and masochistic relation to God, King, or father in the blind hope that the power thus delegated will be used for the exclusive benefit of the subject." Thus dependency really becomes a technique for perpetuating or regaining the infantile omnipotence. However, it has disastrous results on the effectiveness and independence of the individual.

The persistence of this attitude has countless variations, and we must track down its consequences on the formation of character. It has the most important bearing on the appreciation of how discipline is imposed.

It follows that if the child continues to have dependent attitudes toward the parent, as he must for a long time, he must do certain things with regard to the parent, whose magical aid he wants to enlist. He must make himself loved by the parent, and from earliest childhood he learns that this love can be earned by obedience or acquiescence to many disciplines.

Let us attempt to define two types of discipline, directional and restrictive. The first operates by the imposition of a type of behavior upon another individual by directing the manner in which something should be done; the second by prohibiting an activity or the manner in which it is done. The procedure may be backed by explicit or implied punishment or rewards. Under this general heading of discipline, these subdivisions are necessary. Learning may be considered under discipline; it may carry with it rewards and punishments. But the learning of language by the child, seemingly the least painful of all disciplines, can also be considered a discipline, in that it carries with it rewards and punishment. Perhaps we need one more qualification, namely, that a restrictive discipline must interfere with a person's behavior type, or with a natural proclivity. In each instance, discipline means, therefore, an interference with an existing adaptation, biological or sociological, and limits the opportunity for choice of action.

In the case of many disciplines, children cannot appreciate the goals toward which they are directed. But there is no time in which the child cannot appreciate that if he does not obey he will be punished or not loved. Parents are too explicit on this point. Hence the acceptance of discipline by the child, even though the discipline interferes either with a natural proclivity or a preëxisting adaptation, is imperative in order to conserve the interest of being approved or protected, or for the other real or fancied boon of enlisting the magic powers of the parent. If the child thus abandons, at parental command, an established pleasure, it can do so only in the hope that the parent will protect it against its fears and anxieties. This is as close as we can get to identifying the balance of forces which terminate in the maintenance of those mores which interfere with basic gratifications. There are other mechanisms as well, but we need not examine them now.

We must now follow the consequences of such acquiescence on the part of the child. Out of many reported cases we can take again an extreme instance from a severe compulsion neurosis, which demonstrates the force of dependency in a very dramatic way. The case of a sexual prohibition imposed by the parent upon a very dependent child will serve us. The parent imposes this discipline either by threat of punishment or loss of approval. Very few children believe these threats unless they are convinced of the parent's earnestness. One such patient of mine continued, despite parental injunctions to masturbate in secret; but his mother would find his penis irritated and would accuse him of transgressing. Then one day his mother forbade his eating snow, and as he came into the house she accused him of having eaten snow, which he had. This convinced the patient that mother knew everything, and that there was not much use trying to fool her. Then he abandoned manual masturbation and substituted fantasies of being beaten which terminated in great humiliation.[8] Eventually every time he had a sexual impulse, he represented it either in masochistic fantasies in which he was victimized, or sadistic fantasies in which violence was perpetuated upon others. It then became his task to prevent the sexual impulse from arising in his mind, which proved to be a very difficult one. He had to distract his mind with compulsive rituals of all kinds, the purpose of which was to prevent him from doing some cruel or antisocial act, the form in which the sexual wish now presented itself in consciousness. He did all this to guarantee for himself parental protection. But he also ceased to exercise any control or responsibility over his sexual impulses. This province of his life was now governed by his mother, or was carried over onto anyone to whom he designated this same protective function.

It is clear, therefore, from this case and many others, that when we speak of discipline we cannot speak of parental authority without appreciating that this authority is not exclusively enforced, but is partly delegated by the child. The lever of parental authority rests on the dependency of the child. Authority can thus be defined as a behavioristic concept describing a relationship between subject and object in which the subject takes an acquiescent attitude to behavior prescribed by the object on the basis of power either possessed by or delegated to the object. However, this authority is not always effective with the child if the needs of dependency are not satisfied. Some children will not delegate such authority, out of the conviction, based on experience, that love and protection will be denied even if the renunciation imposed is maintained.[9]

There are several other consequences of the imposition of disciplines which entail abandonment or curtailment of the activity necessary to consummate a drive, although the drive itself cannot be obliterated: (1) The growth of the ego becomes blocked. (2) The activity in question becomes stunted. (3)

---

[8] For fuller presentation of this case see Chap. X, p. 441.

[9] This situation is notably prominent in criminal and paranoid types, and this reaction type lies at the root of most rebellious attitudes.

This combination leads to a definite fall in self-esteem of the child. (4) It in turn retards the development of other activities, because once a repression is instituted it tends to be used again, and the individual knows that the gratification in question is lost to him. (5) Repression creates a basis for hating the parent, a hatred which must be repressed, and which only serves to accentuate the fear of the parent. (6) It makes necessary forms of expressing this hatred, or (7) demands constant creation of new rewards for renunciation. Most of these affect the personal destiny of the individual, but the unconscious hatred of the parent is common to all who live under these institutions. For this repressed hatred, we can expect to see some institutionalized expression.

This series of reactions may be true of the disciplines to which the sexual "instinct" is subjected as far as its infantile manifestations are concerned; but it is certainly not typical of all disciplines. Let us consider the consequences of anal training. As in the case of sexual disciplines in childhood, this is a type of discipline the purpose of which the child can form no idea about at the time that it is imposed. The anal zone is primarily an evacuating organ. At birth it is not under voluntary control, and sensations of fullness of the rectum are not a signal for withholding or expelling. The demand for sphincter control comes at a time when the child is busy learning more things about himself and his relations to the outer world than he does at any later time in life. Numerous difficulties may be encountered in this process of accommodation to the outer world. Anal training is largely a matter of identifying sensations of fullness, learning what they mean, and what to do about them. Since the sphincter is previously uncontrolled and the bowel is evacuated at any time, anywhere, the new training demands a vigilance, a sense of responsibility, and a technique. At first this latter is simple; it is to notify the parent of the need. For purposes of brevity we shall delete considering urethral control as a special case. Anal control is largely a matter of **withholding.**

As far as the pleasure-giving properties of the anal zone are concerned, there is not much doubt about their existence. However, the genesis of these pleasure qualities is very obscure. If we consider that the sensations from the child's own body must be for a time its chief preoccupation, on which the increasing demand of the outer world for attention makes serious inroads, we can venture a hypothesis, subject to later verification, that the persistence of interest in the bodily sensations at anus and urethra are evidence of failure to derive adequate pleasure from other contacts with the outer world.[10] Discipline introduced under these conditions is bound to interfere with these primitive pleasures. True enough, but just how? The sphincter training does not interfere with pleasures of feces passing the rectum. It only interferes with the irresponsibility, and possibly with the desire for freedom, and most important of all, it interferes with the previous omnipotence.

Still another view of the pleasure qualities associated with the anal zone is possible. In paranoid individuals and in extremely dependent characters one can observe another use made of the anal zone. In order to appreciate this phenomenon one must again use a reconstruction of the experiences of the impressions of the child before anal control is instituted. At this period the anal activities cannot fail to be associated with tender maternal care. These activities can therefore acquire the meaning of attracting or soliciting maternal love. Discipline conveys an entirely different set of values to the child. Failure of sphincter control brings not love but criticism, scolding or punishment; the early effect of attracting tender attention now becomes associated with repellent attributes. Many delusions of paranoiacs to the effect that they repel people by the horrible odors emanating from them are frustrate attempts to recapture the early means of soliciting love. Because of the varied and complex associations with the anal zone, a unitary anal erotism is not an effective working concept.

[10] See Chap. X, pp. 424–435.

If the hypothesis about the child's magic control is true, then we can see that the introduction of discipline of any kind reverses the whole previous adaptation. The child now ceases to control the mother, and it must submit to a situation in which very candidly the mother controls the child. Therefore it seems highly probable that such a reversal will register most disastrously on a child who has difficulties in deriving new gratifications from its encounters with the outer world. It is at this point that the real discrepancy between parent and self becomes manifest to the child, when the desire for new experience, which adult activity constantly holds before his eyes, is constantly held in check by his own inadequacies. From this, the element of pain and frustration probably derives; it is subsequently reflected in the sado-masochistic imagery in which these frustrations are described. Rado[11] has expressed himself along similar lines.

The reaction to anal discipline must, therefore, depend on a host of factors which have hitherto escaped our notice. However, if we observe only "instinctual drives" and segregate them from the context of the entire experience of the child's life, we can see in this phase of difficulty in adjusting to new experience, the breaking up of the old illusion of omnipotence, an "anal sadistic" phase of development. However this may be, the fact is that the pleasure function of the anal zone can become overemphasized.[12]

The most important thing to note is that the social demand for cleanliness and orderliness can be met in two ways. The child either accepts it, and because of the wish to ingratiate itself with the parent, becomes clean and orderly, or he revolts against discipline by refusing. But this refusal has a special character; it takes the form of obstinacy. This characteristic

[11] Unpublished lecture. N. Y. Psychoanalytic Institute. November, 1937.

[12] It has been pointed out by Wilhelm Reich (*Characteranalyse*) that the sadism originally considered to be characteristic of anal erotism is to be found associated with every erotism. To this we can add that the study of traumatic neuroses shows that sadism is the currency in which every activity is expressed when its organized forms are inhibited or frustrated.

need not derive from anal training exclusively, but from other disciplines as well. In short, cleanliness and orderliness are forms of acquiescence to cultural demands, and are therefore forms of obedience.[13]

Thus anal training is another instance of how a cultural demand is imposed on the child before he is able to appreciate its significance or to profit from its usefulness. At this time acquiescence is a method of ingratiation. To accept and obey is to establish conditions for being loved and protected. This is the child's first experience with being "socially accepted."

TYPES OF MASTERY, INFANTILE AND "ECONOMIC"

It might be well at this point to review the ground we have covered so far. We started with the idea of finding out what features of a culture are psychologically relevant. We took some of the features of our own culture and attempted, with the aid of what we know of the individual in our current society, to establish the interactions between institutions and individual. But we did this from the developmental point of view. We stressed the effects of two kinds of discipline, those that pertain to sexual and to anal activity, and decided that the most important factor was the dependency of the child on the parent. In addition we traced some of the consequences on the individual, and indicated those that were most likely to have secondary consequences on the culture as a whole. Therefore, we are safe in assuming, as will be demonstrated in comparative cultures, that sexual and anal disciplines are important landmarks of psychologically relevant institutions. We have also indicated that the need for dependency, though we viewed it entirely from the point of view of the child, is a social factor of prime importance. The manner in which a society satisfies these dependency cravings in both the child and the adult is likely to be an important indicator of the general direction which institutions of a culture will take.

[13] Freud, *Civilization and Its Discontents* (Tr. by Joan Riviere; London, 1930), p. 62.

But these disciplines are hardly representative; there are many others which do not have the character of interfering with basic needs. On the contrary, many disciplines encourage and foster curiosity, enterprise, and activity which the individual accepts and follows eagerly. Learning to do as the parent does is not always painful to the child, when he is permitted to do so, and when parental aid is freely given. This type of discipline should be called by another name, preferably "training." Let us, therefore, consider "training" for effectiveness in deriving gratifications from the outer world. These activities generally refer to exploiting the environment in order to subsist economically. The number of activities and skills necessary are innumerable.

During the normal dependent period the child has no direct contact with the technique for subsistence pursued by the culture as a whole. We have already indicated that the biological makeup of man does not permit a very early participation in these activities. This delay is, however, put to great advantage in increasing the potentialities for skill.

The training for "economic" activity in Western civilization is an extremely complicated process, and one which we shall have to subdivide in order to treat its various aspects. We shall consider it under the captions of infantile techniques of mastery, their persistence and influence; the vicissitudes of the technique of mastery; division of function and its relation to coöperation and competition; subsistence and prestige values in economic pursuits; derivatives of prestige and rivalry conflicts; coöperative activities in our culture.

The earliest form of mastery identified in the human infant before myelination is complete is associated with the mouth. Children,[14] before the use of the limbs is very effective, take objects into their mouths. The prototype of this is undoubtedly the nursing experience.

Oral mastery is a phase of every human, irrespective of the

[14] See S. Bernfeld, *The Psychology of the Infant* (New York, 1929), pp. 72–83; 178–186.

culture in which he lives. The study of the traumatic neurosis has shown conclusively that when all subsequent types of mastery become inhibited, this one remains the most unshakable. Many of the pathological manifestations of this neurosis owe their origin to this form of mastery. It is also true that many of the phenomena in aboriginal cultures correspond to types of oral mastery, but not because they "regress" to this stage of development. Oral phenomena may indicate inhibitions of later types of development or failures of resources to cope with certain eventualities. This is notably the case with food anxieties and some of their derivatives. This does not mean that there is any parallel between ontogenesis and phylogenesis. It merely indicates that when all other resources fail with primitive and contemporary man, both draw on the same common ontogenetic experience. It means in addition that where other techniques have not been learned this immediate and universal experience remains the most immediate substitute.

What is there about this stage that is essentially characteristic, and what accounts for its tenacity? The mouth is the first zone of effectiveness, and remains throughout life an important adjunct to life, but its function later becomes specialized. In childhood it is often used as an offensive or defensive weapon, as in biting. But it is the exclusive zone of effectiveness in infancy in relation to the outer world. It is associated with complete helplessness as regards other effective tools; the limbs are useless and sense organs are inaccurate. Moreover, needs are simple, and the actual work necessary to ease tensions is usually done by the mother or someone else. In other words, the mouth is the sole effective organ of mastery during the most dependent state. This type of mastery can be called oral mastery, a term not to be confused with the oral pregenital phase of the libido. As a matter of fact, this type of mastery was described under this libidinous heading; but no distinction was drawn between the utility function of the organ and its pleasure function, and forms of mastery in psychoanalytic literature were considered only as phases of *libido* development. One can say, therefore, that "oral gratification" may stand for the total success of this early adaptation.

There are several types of thinking characteristic of this stage of oral mastery which have often enough been described in pathological states. The child regards the nursing act (or so reconstructs it at a later date) as an act of eating the mother, a naïve form of cannibalism.[15] It contains the idea or constellation "by eating you, I enlarge myself, or absorb you into myself."

We may picture another type of constellation that arises from the act of crying as a magical agency; for it is frequently followed by relief of a tension which the child itself has done nothing to bring about.

We may therefore summarize the stage of oral mastery as one in which the following constellations[16] are created:

1. You (mother) and I are one.
2. By eating you, I control everything; I become you. I can do as you do for me.
3. To separate from you is to lose control over you and over the world.
4. By crying (oral exclamation) I can invoke magic aid.

These constellations are frequently observed in pathological states, not only in the positive form of eating wishes expressed in dreams, but also in their negative form as a fear of being eaten up, which we will take up later in the study of reaction types to frustration. Meanwhile, there are a few important clues to follow. If the oral mastery stage is one that is associated with effortless control, then the return of oral phenomena, associated with inhibition of later developed functions, indicates a return of oral mastery and the attitudes associated with it. This is adequately proved by the traumatic neuroses, where phenom-

[15] This is referred to in the literature as the oral incorporative stage.

[16] The word "constellation" is much better here than the word "inference." The child at this stage doesn't infer anything, but he is able to experience clusters of things in one ensemble, especially if they terminate in a gratification.

ena of oral mastery are often observed in conjunction with an increase in dependency attitudes.

For the study of primitive culture, these constellations based on oral mastery are extremely important in attempting to reconstruct the technique of thinking.

For our purpose it is not essential to trace the growth and effectiveness of those ego functions which have to do with orientation, locomotion, perspective, and the endless skills the human hand is capable of developing. It is necessary to remember but one point—that in association with this development there is a long series of successes, all associated with psychic pictures or images, both of oneself and of oneself in relation to an activity and the satisfactions derived from it. Whereas in infancy walking may be an achievement associated with a feeling of triumph, subsequently the gratification is fastened upon the objective; it is no longer in the act of walking, but in the objective for which the act is instituted. It is a well established fact that traumatic experiences can inhibit these functions of orientation and locomotion.[17] The vicissitudes to which these completed ego functions can be subjected are: (1) The outer world may withdraw its hospitality as it does in flood, earthquake, famine, etc. (2) Some of the functions may become crippled through injury of the executive organs themselves, as in blindness, loss of a limb, and the like. (3) The opportunity to engage them for purposes of subsistence may disappear, as in unemployment. Each of these vicissitudes has definite influences on the personality as a whole.

SUBSISTENCE AND PRESTIGE CONFLICTS, RIVALRY AND COMPETITION

In every society the "growth" of the individual is socially interpreted as an approximation to the state of adult effectiveness. Division of labor in our society makes special problems for the individual. Techniques are so numerous that the indi-

[17] See Kardiner, "Bioanalysis of the Epileptic Reaction," *Psychoanalytic Quarterly*, I, No. 3, 394.

vidual must choose according to aptitude, opportunity, or chance. Thus a great many people work together toward a common aim, and out of their common efforts each derives subsistence. There is, however, a difference, psychologically speaking, between division of function and coöperation. In the former, the abilities and the task are divided so that each does a specialized portion, which cannot be done by anyone else on the particular "team." The special social problem created in our culture by this situation is that the various functions of planning and executing a given task, and the various subdivisions of the latter carry with them relative prestige values which are tangibly reduced to varying access to economic power and the use of the finished product of common endeavor.

Thus the technique of mastery in our culture eventuates in a claim on subsistence means, the limits of which are physiologically determined, and on prestige values of infinite variety and degree. The entire façade of our culture is made up of those institutions which have grown out of our subsistence and prestige techniques, and most of our current "economic" and sociological thought deals with the problems created by these institutions. It is often difficult, when considering current "economic" conflicts, to differentiate between subsistence and prestige values attached to them. It is important to make this distinction because the two problems are entirely distinct psychologically.[18]

The importance of studying the psychological conflicts arising from pursuits that go under the general name of "economic" comes from the fact that economic pursuits are in our

[18] The conclusions about the nature of the psychological fabric of social conflicts must of course depend on the group of individuals from whom they are derived. The conclusions stated herein come largely from the study of bourgeois of the educated type, which may be entirely misleading as regards the same conflicts in the proletarian groups. I am of the opinion that proletarian conflicts differ considerably from those of the bourgeois. They arise ostensibly from subsistence values. But this does not take into account the fact that the psychological situation is entirely different in both. The differences between the two are very difficult to establish because prestige conflicts are, in the culture of democracies, inseparable from subsistence problems.

own culture an essential part of the security system of the individual, and are the direct means of achieving the relative security that each individual enjoys in the group. To appreciate the nature of these conflicts we may contrast the state of affairs in our culture with those in other societies, in which labor is communal and undifferentiated, i.e., everyone can do what everyone else can, and everyone works for a common end, the advantages of which are then prorated. Under these conditions the individual is protected against the consequences of his inadequacies and inefficiencies. His security is not impaired. In a society in which labor is highly differential according to relative skill or importance of the function, the psychological problems for the individual are bound to differ from those in a society wherein skill plays no role. A society in which there is security as regards subsistence does not necessarily confer a similar security as regards prestige. Some societies confer relative security in both; and some in neither.

From the point of view of the individual we must attempt some reconstruction of the meaning of "work" and the emotional ends toward which it is directed. There is, first, the intrinsic gratification in work as a form of mastery. This must be credited with being a basic satisfaction, without conferring on it the epithet of an "instinct." The satisfactions derived from it are common to all forms of mastery. They give the individual a feeling of effectiveness and control. The more completely the individual masters his work, the more complete his intrinsic satisfactions. This factor becomes an important point when we try to reconstruct the satisfactions that come from highly differentiated labor. Without taking into account the psychological problem created by monotony of work, the intrinsic satisfactions can only be partial.

The subsistence gratifications are physiologically based, but carry with them emotional qualities. A full stomach, warmth, health, etc., are satisfactions appreciated in a positive sense, and the need for them is deeply felt when they are absent.

The most difficult satisfactions to appreciate are those that are associated with prestige.[19] We must defer a discussion of the deeper significance of these until we have the opportunity to study the structure of the personality. Meanwhile, we can only touch on some of the social consequences of this conflict. The quest for prestige is the response to a need accentuated by society; society does not, however, create the reaction type, which is only a special version of effectiveness or mastery. The need for prestige, i.e., for a particular kind of effectiveness established by comparison with others, can be emphasized or made unnecessary by the social organization. We must look at it from the point of view of the psychological factors involved, and the particular values in which prestige is vested.

In terms of the libido theory, prestige belongs to a group of narcissistic needs. It depends for its existence on one of the most valuable human traits, the ability to orient oneself in relation to one's fellows. The quest for prestige shows this characteristic of man in a bad light, because it is responsible for many of the conflicts of man with man. However, this characteristic functions on the positive side as well. On this side we are well acquainted with it from psychoanalytic investigations, where it is spoken of as the mechanism of identification. This term merely describes a certain kind of relationship between subject and object.

We can see a bit more of the psychological fabric by examin-

[19] The psychology of Alfred Adler (*The Neurotic Constitution*, New York, 1917), attempted to account for all neurotic disturbances on the basis of the quest for prestige as the "guiding fiction." The neurotic counterpart of this quest was the notorious "feeling of inferiority." As a basis for a system of psychology Adler's ideas failed because the feeling of inferiority was considered a reaction to a guiding fiction and as the motor of neurosis. This was Adler's substitute for "instinct." Further interesting discussion on this topic of prestige can be found in K. Horney, *The Neurotic Personality of our Time* (Norton, 1937). The subject of prestige is almost inexhaustible, owing to the large number of values to which it may be attached, and the fact that these values vary in each society. The subject is discussed on pp. 234 and 337, but the emphasis falls on the psychological aspects and not on the innumerable problems associated with the attainment of prestige. See A. Kardiner, "The Role of Economic Security in the Adaptation of the Individual," *The Family*, October, 1936; and also, "Security, Cultural Restraints, Intrasocial Dependencies and Hostilities," *The Family*, October, 1937.

ing the values to which prestige is attached. Some of these are wealth, class, race, achievement, etc., all of which are instruments of establishing relative grades of prestige. Class lines are moderately permeable in a democratic society and mobility of status is considerable. Property and wealth are fairly mobile, especially through the economic value of special skills.

The prestige value of class and caste is attached essentially to the accident of birth, backed by property and wealth. In democracies the prestige value of wealth is much the same as that of birth in aristocracies. The individual who commands prestige is always in a position to demand awe, love, regard, admiration. Prestige, in other words, is power. It puts its possessor in the position of authority, and those who bestow it in a position of subservience. The desire to acquire it is therefore a response to an anxiety about shame, degradation, self-depreciation. The achievement leads to increase in self-esteem, and an assurance that this self-esteem is mirrored in the esteem of others.

In the social constellation of wealth we see the uses to which "economic" power is put. Wealth has a utility value as a means of exchange with which to command subsistence goods. But in addition it has a magical power to command prestige. Wealth enhances the size of the ego; the more you have, the bigger the ego. The property becomes a part of yourself. This is proved by the content of impoverishment phobias; when you lose money, you lose a part of yourself. Through money you can command love and allegiance. The magical properties of wealth are contagious. People who do not have wealth wish to associate with those who have, as if by so doing they acquire a fictitious or temporary augmentation of the ego. This contagious quality of prestige is an important factor in social solidarity. It tends to diminish the conflicts about prestige by a vicarious satisfaction of the need for it.

The quest for prestige (wealth, esteem, renown, etc.) leads to a special attitude—viz., rivalry—toward others who pursue the same goal. When the goal is to offer one's goods or abilities to a common user, the attitude is called competition. The usual effect of the attitude of rivalry is to engender hostility, the wish to destroy, to diminish the effectiveness of, to intimidate, awe, or humiliate the rival; but in the case of the competitor, the effect is to secure advantage at the other's expense.

The psychological forces that operate in rivalry are best illustrated in sibling rivalry. Here again we must call on neuroses to clarify what goes on. In our discussion of dependency we saw the factors that make for the origin and persistence of this attitude. It is natural to suppose, therefore, that when a sibling is born during the time of the child's greatest need for dependency, the child cannot fail to recognize this event as a call to surrender a portion of his claim on the parent. The greater the need for the parent, the greater the anxiety of helplessness created in the child. There are three reactions possible, (1) hatred of the new child, and a wish to put a stop to its claims, (2) renunciation of the claim on the parent, (3) hatred of the parent. The first cannot be expressed, and the second is very difficult to accomplish. The hatred of the rival and parent leads to innumerable consequences. Let us examine two clinical outcomes of this infantile rivalry situation.

A young man comes with the complaint of kleptomania. The things he feels compelled to steal are in themselves quite valueless, but he cannot resist the temptation when he knows "he can get away with it." The symptom is a very old one, and began in childhood. The child of poor parents, he was the third of five children. His hatred of siblings, both older and younger, was very sharp, but at the present time he shows very little hostility to rivals, and at the same time very little enterprise. His kleptomania proved to be the result of an irrepressible conflict, represented in his dreams always by food. The thing he was thus reclaiming by his stealing was the breast of his mother, which was "stolen" from him. However, this symptom coexisted with another complicated system of compulsive justice, at the basis of which was the formula, "If I get my share, I will see to it that everyone else gets his share," evidently a very happy solution of his rivalry situation with his siblings. However, the compulsive character of his "social justice" indicated that all was not well underneath. It was a façade concealing many deep-seated inhibitions, anxieties about success, fear of letting other people know of his success, together with stealthy efforts at getting his pound of flesh. On the other hand, he always had to protect himself against the hostility of others, which his assertiveness or success would unleash; hence, he always chose the least ostentatious behavior and was completely unaware of his work inhibitions and the role they played in his compulsive "fairness." In short, the price he paid for a system of equalizing sibling rivalries was to submit to a mutual pact of guaranteeing equality, and at the same time venting his pent-up aggression in the form of a kleptomanic symptom. The scheme of preventing the other siblings from getting more than himself led to a plan in which his own activities were tied to the same tether. This is, however, a rather complicated solution of the problem, in which both patient and siblings become subject to the same restrictions. There are others more naïve.

The other instance worth mentioning is the disturbance created toward the object of dependency by a rival. A boy of 15 is brought in for treatment of tics involving mouth and eyes. His current symptoms are obviously related to a severe conflict about the practice of masturbation. However, his symptoms have a long history of which the infantile situation is most important. His mother gave birth to a little girl when he was four years old. The series of changes that took place in his life was momentous. He was moved from his room to another. He remembers being angry when he heard of the newcomer. He seized his teddy-bear that night and threw it out of his bed. His bear was obviously his substitute for going to bed with his mother. The rage against the mother was most prominent in his reaction. Shortly afterward he had a dream which was recurrent many times to date. In this recurrent dream he always finds himself in bed; a large round object approaches his face, and as it is about to strike him he wakes up in terror. This object, according to his associations, has something to do with eating. According to a principle often recovered from psychopathology, our patient is repeating a once pleasant experience, now no longer accessible to him, and with the effect reversed. It is not pleasant, but horrible. This is what the birth of the sibling has done. But at four he was no longer nursing, so evidently it is not the nursing that is interrupted so rudely. But his access to mother and the expectation of his dependency upon her has been broken. He now fears, is distrustful of, and hates his mother and sibling both. Later developments were kleptomania of food objects and a large variety of tics.[20]

In other words, the sibling rivalry terminates in (1) a hatred and hostility toward the interfering object, (2) an attitude of distrust and hatred of the object of dependency, (3) inhibitions.

How does this situation differ in adult conflicts about rivalry? Not much, except in the form that it takes and the terms in which the values are expressed.

We see, therefore, that there are several stereotyped forms in which conflicts about rivalry and prestige eventually assert themselves: (1) some form of aggression, (2) anxiety, (3) inhibition. It would greatly facilitate our study of those symptoms in comparative sociology if we could allocate the social sources of these conflicts. The goal of rivalry is to satisfy or put to rest an anxiety of helplessness. The intensity of this need is obviously a function of the social organization. It depends on how easily the need is satisfied. It follows that in societies where the individual is unprotected, where access to the love and support of others is made conditional upon many impositions on the ego, such as excellence, beauty, worth, etc., anxiety will the more readily assert itself. On the other hand, if the social organization is such that dependencies are freely recognized and easily taken care of, the less will be the anxiety, the less the mutual hostility and the scramble for the secure position.

There is a unit of society which seems to be the determinant of the security which the individual enjoys—the size character

[20] The pathology of this case is further discussed in Chap. X, p. 433.

of the relationships, the lines of dependency and loyalty or of obligation, which are operative in the in-group. In our culture, family and in-group are basic. Many in-groups exist on a basis of partial interests, but in the formative years the in-group is exclusively the family. In it there are only one mother and only one father to take care of all the claims of the siblings. This situation is further complicated by the sexual situation we have already described.

The coöperation of members of our culture is a chapter in itself, one which at the moment we cannot stop to examine. The methods and institutions through which coöperation is effected are too numerous to describe. One individual can participate in coöperative efforts of a large number of institutions. Participation in coöperative efforts is usually motivated by defense of some interest consciously perceived or by a cause which will advance some unconscious interest. Such participation may be a way of identifying oneself with the underdog or with the exploiter, in neither of which the individual has any direct conscious stake.

Aggression—Its Forms and Social Control

In the institutions of our culture and the reactions to them that we have studied so far, there was one reaction type that we encountered with great frequency—aggression. Freud himself was responsible for the attitude that all phenomena about aggression be considered under one category, that of "instinct." The use of this concept to characterize aggression made difficulties, not so much because the observations on which the conclusions were based could not be verified, but because it compelled us to think of aggressive "instincts" as we do of the sexual "instinct," as a drive originating in somatic tensions which demanded periodic discharge. If we apply to the concept of aggression, the distinction between the cause of a drive, the goal of a drive, and the behavior necessary to consummate it, we find that behavior types necessary to consummate aggression are never taught and need not be. The individual always has some technique for its expression, but the expression is controlled or checked by society or its representative, the parent. As regards the drive itself, its somatic sources cannot be identified nor can one definitely classify the satisfactions derived from its exercise. And these questions are evaded by calling aggression an "instinct." Some effort was made to differentiate between the objective and the activity, the objective being "mastery," the activity being aggression. Aggression can be the executive of any drive; mastery and control are simply organized forms of aggression.

Since the activities designated as aggressive are so numerous, and are, in our culture, a definite object of social control, we must attempt to find out which manifestations society attempts to deal with and what measures it uses to that end, as well as the effects of this suppression on the individual.

We might profit by examining what a noted biologist considers the process of adaptation. Uexküll defines adaptation as a process of removal; he states, "It is the removal of all objects in the outer world from the effective environment."[21] Lower forms of life do this by (1) appropriation, eating, or surrounding like an amoeba, (2) extermination, (3) flight. The sense organs, the organs of preliminary exploration, establish contacts with objects in the outer world, and they also preserve the isolation of the individual. All forms of contact with an object can therefore be considered aggressive. But as a rule one does not consider the function of sense organs as aggressive. The types of contact that humans establish take in much more than just appropriation, extermination, or flight. But no matter what their clinical form, all human relationships contain an element of aggression, if by that term we mean energy directed in an active way toward another object in order to establish over it some form of mastery or control; to subject it to ends of utility or pleasure. Utility in this sense becomes the intermediary use for an ultimate gratification.

Uexküll's definition of adaptation applies to the activity that

[21] Jacob von Uexküll, *Umwelt und Innenwelt der Tiere* (Berlin, 1909).

is created by the disturbing properties of objects encountered in the outer world. Quite in line with Uexküll's definition is that of Bernfeld,[22] who groups all mastery impulses and activities as those which attempt to reinstate a state of rest, which aim to arrest the disturbing properties of the object. The act of attention thus becomes a response to a disturbance caused by an intrusion of properties of another object or situation. Uexküll's is an extremely valuable definition for us to bear in mind, especially since aggression has such a specialized connotation, meaning to hurt, destroy, or in some way by force to diminish the effectiveness of some disturbing object or force.

In those forms of mastery used effectively by the individual, the "aggression" is well organized, and anything in the outer world which acts as a disturbing influence is thus "mastered" in an orderly manner which has become habitual. Some of these forms of mastery are (1) to subject objects or individuals to one's utility ends, and (2) to subject them for pleasure ends. But let us suppose that this orderly form of mastery is interfered with so that it cannot be used. Then some crude form of aggression takes its place. The clinical types of "aggression" can be arranged as follows:

The simplest manifestation of aggression occurs when a wish, a desire, or an impulse is not satisfied or is interfered with, e.g., a nursing child has the breast torn away before satisfaction is completed or is refused the breast when hungry. The aggression under these conditions is disorganized. Any bit of self-assertion thus contains an element of aggression; interference with any bit of self-assertion creates more aggression against the obstacle. Socially the most important type of aggression is this form which deals with the interference with self-assertion in adults.

A second manifestation of aggression occurs when there is an obvious failure on the part of the ego to develop techniques of mastery or to derive the necessary satisfactions from them. In these cases we see a persistence of "destructiveness" long after the period when destruction is normally replaced by more

[22] S. Bernfeld, *The Psychology of the Infant* (New York, 1929), pp. 182–191.

constructive types of mastery. Such a case I described in a child who developed epilepsy at the age of twelve.[23] Her failure in effective mastery was noted by her mother, who observed that she was constantly falling down and hurting herself during the learning-to-walk stage. This characteristic persisted long after walking was established. She was always destroying the objects she played with, found the greatest pleasure in boring holes in the walls, etc. These are the kind of cases that are often quoted to illustrate an inborn instinct of destructiveness or an arrest at the sadistic level of development. This observation is phenomenologically correct; but when we speak of it as a stage of development and a fixation at that point, we lose sight of the purpose of the activity and the gratifications to be derived from it. Thus it is made to appear that pleasure in cruelty is an end in itself; really, it is only the same pleasure that is derived from more highly integrated forms of mastery. This is my understanding of the Freudian formulation of the "fusion of erotic and destructive components." This little girl showed these very traits, wanton destructiveness of animals, cruelty to cats and dogs, flies, etc. At the same time she had a mortal dread of being hurt, indicating that inadequate techniques of mastery leave the individual unprotected for purposes of defense, as well as for deriving gratification from objects in the outer world. It was this phobia of being hurt which led quite directly to the outbreak of her epilepsy. In this case the inadequacy was psychobiologically or even perhaps organically determined.

In this particular case the persistence of the pleasure in inflicting pain and destroying objects was a failure of the normal techniques of mastery. Not enough investigation has been done as yet from this point of view to establish this hypothesis firmly. But there is an idirect confirmation of it to be found in the phenomena of the traumatic neurosis. Here the mastery technique is well developed, but becomes suddenly inhibited by virtue of the traumatic experience. In these cases the sado-

[23] See Kardiner, "Bioanalysis of the Epileptic Reaction," *Psychoanalytic Quarterly*, I, No. 3, 426–432.

masochistic destructive character returns. In some instances crude forms of oral mastery are revived.

This type of aggressive or destructive behavior, in lieu of more refined types of mastery, is due, therefore, to failure of development or to inhibition of already developed techniques: in either case the techniques are not available to the ego.

The symptom complex of sexual sadism probably belongs to this category, in which Freud has noted the improper fusion of destructive (mastery) and erotic components.[24]

Aggression is the ego attitude and activity directed toward an object that inflicts pain on the subject or prevents gratification of some essential impulse or need. Aggression toward the object seeks to destroy the effectiveness of the obstructing force. This is the commonest manifestation of aggression, and the one against which most external social sanctions are enforced by police power of some kind. This is really the same situation as the preceding, but relatively it is different. An interfering object takes the place of diminishing resources in the first case, but the resources are relatively inadequate because of the interfering or disturbing object.

Such aggressive attitudes and activities cannot always be consummated. Society can block the activity though it cannot affect the ego attitude. One can hate, though one cannot obliterate the obstructing influence by force. This society can control by institutional sanctions and systematic punishments. The attitude of obedience to these sanctions may become habitual and automatic. This automatic functioning was designated by Freud as due to the activity of the super-ego. It must however be noted that super-ego activity depends on the wish to preserve certain interests with parents or society, whether one speaks of it as an internalized function (super-ego) or regards it as a modality of the ego (conditioning). The effects of repressing the activity associated with aggression are important to note. They are: (a) changes in attitude to and ideational repre-

---

[24] This subject would take too long to pursue and is irrelevant to our main theme.

sentation of the object; (b) changes in representation of the ego; (c) changes in representation of the activity. Take for example hatred of the interfering object, e.g., hatred of the parent who interferes with masturbation. This hatred of the parent, which cannot be expressed, results in inflation of importance of the parent as cruel and bountiful, both aspects being exaggerated. Diminution of self-esteem of the child and inhibition of growth of essential components of the forbidden activity also result. The desire to consummate activity is now represented in cruel or antisocial images. This is the representation of the sexual act which we find in impotent men. Instead of a fantasy of sexual relationship, we find a fantasy of murder.[25]

In other cases the inhibited impulse may be represented as a piece of aggression against the subject. For example, a man has a date with his mistress; she comes late for the rendezvous and leaves him unsatisfied. He does not express his rage, but dreams of a cat (which he immediately identifies as his mistress) that bites him, and he is in a great anxiety lest the cat has given him hydrophobia.

The aggression may increase the conflict about the object toward whom it is directed and end in further inhibitions on the part of the subject. A man with severe rivalry conflicts notes a superior piece of work by a rival. He is deeply chagrined at this, and in his fantasy he destroys the value of this work. But shortly afterward the patient complains of his own incapacities. His abilities become curtailed as the result of wanting to undo the other fellow's work. The same man is subsequently praised for

[25] This fantasy is commonly explained on the basis that the individual is dominated by the "sadistic conception" of intercourse. This in turn is said to be due to the persistent influence of witnessing parental intercourse in infancy or childhood, at which time the child thought the father was doing something cruel to the mother. Careful investigation on this point has shown that this "sadistic conception" is a later reconstruction, after inhibitions become established, but that the original scene made no impression of horror. The inhibition is explained as due to the curbing of an antisocial act. This states the case rather equivocally because it doesn't make clear where its antisocial character lies, whether in the act itself, or in the fact that performing the act breaks an established taboo.

his exceptional ability. This he wishes to use to annihilate his rivals; but he cannot because the ability has the unconscious connotation of a destructive act.

One can explain all these consequences on the basis of the activity of the super-ego. But there is an additional problem of energy charge. We defer discussion on this point. We must stress one point that we raised earlier, namely, that it does not matter much what instincts operate in the creation of a given experience; the form of the experience directly perceived is the effective unit we can follow; we cannot follow instincts because we assume that they are present, and once we make that assumption, we tend to blame the behavior on the instinct. Behavior can be observed; instinct cannot. One can draw conclusions about behavior; about instinct one can only philosophize.

These manifestations of aggression and the consequences of repression have an important bearing on the formation of institutions. It is unimportant to note in our culture where these repressive influences begin in the basic disciplines of the family organization. The existence of social rivalries in our culture, where self-preservation or assertion depends on excelling the other fellow, naturally sharpens the conflicts about consummating the goals of these rivalries.

It must therefore become a differential criterion of comparative sociology to study the basic disciplines in conjunction with the actual life situations which engender rivalry conflicts, in order to see what sanctions are applied to the manifestations, and to see whether the society makes these conflicts unnecessary. We have good reason to believe that the character of the in-group and the dependencies therein permitted have much to do with the opportunities for mutual aggression and for the behavior of the individual, once they exist.

In our culture, sanctions exist against only certain forms of aggression: the destruction of life and property of another person or interference with basic rights. Within the domain of rivalry and competition no sanctions exist, but only certain rules which are perhaps not legally specified. Prestige only goes to him who lives up to the established rules or conventions governing rivalry.

FORCES THAT HOLD SOCIETY TOGETHER

The individual is not the exclusive source—and perhaps not the best source—from which we can form some idea of the forces that hold society together. However, some indispensable details can be recovered from the individual alone. In general it can be stated that a society is held together by the mutual needs of its constituents. These needs may be utilitarian or emotional in character. A culture always prescribes the manner in which the needs of an individual can be satisfied without injuring anyone else or without creating disrupting influences in the society as a whole.

This statement does not, however, take into account the complicated dynamics of the relation of individuals to each other. There are at least two distinct forces operating between individuals which can be identified: these can be designated as centripetal and centrifugal forces. The first binds individuals together, the other tears them apart. Freud called the binding forces the ability of one individual either to identify himself with or to love another. The centrifugal forces, hatred, the wish to abuse or exploit others for one's own ends, and other tendencies, are more complicated.

We may begin with some study of these centrifugal forces. When we hear individuals describe the manner in which they are bound to their society they usually refer to two main factors. The first is the fear of the consequences of certain assertive tendencies on the object toward whom they are directed—if it happens to be an individual, they fear being hated by the object or fear retaliatory measures; if the act is against an individual in a form in which society as a whole has a stake, the anxiety is expressed in the form of fear of certain institutionalized and common protective agencies such as the police. A second fear is not consciously expressed as such; its operation can only be

seen in the resultant activity, that is to say, either the attitude
of assertion or hostility toward another object is inhibited
and no trace of the original impulse can be found, or it is
expressed in such a way that the original aggression is turned
on the subject himself. This is explained as due to the activity
of the super-ego, one function of which is conscience—an internalization of those social forces which were originally prohibitions and were foisted on the individual through the agency
of the parent. The activity of the super-ego is based on an
identification with what was originally an external authority,[26]
i.e., the child introjects the father's teachings and prohibitions.
Then in place of a fear of external authority there is an inner
anxiety. This identification with the father places the child
in some respects in the father's place, acts as a release of anxiety,
places him in an active role, although he does not enjoy all of
the father's prerogatives. This super-ego is likewise influenced
by nurses, teachers, and figures held up as ideals.

Fromm calls attention to the contradictions and the obscurities in the Freudian formulations; he points out that, at
one place, reality testing is attributed to the super-ego, and at
another, to the ego; that self-observation (*Selbstbeobachtung*)
should be a function of the faculty which includes ideals originating in reaction formations against forbidden instinctual
tendencies, and also ideals of conscience. But most important
of all, Fromm points out the loose usage of the concept of
identification, indicating at least three modalities which the
term may describe: an enriching type (Rado calls it annexa-
tional) —"I take the other person into myself and strengthen
myself thereby"; an impoverishing type—"I become a part
of the other person"; and a third modality, founded on the
interchangeability of one person with another, on the basis not
of common characteristics, but of common interests.

Fromm agrees that Freud has, notwithstanding the defects

[20] This entire subject is fully discussed by Erich Fromm in "Sozialpsychologischer Teil," *Autorität und Familie* (Paris, 1936), pp. 80–110. The following
is an abstract of this portion of this paper.

in the formulation, made a substantial contribution to the understanding of why the use of force is so effective in society. It is effective not solely because those who are awed by it fear physical force—if this were so, society would never enjoy any stability—but also because the external force is transformed so as to operate from within, thus becoming a fear of a psychic faculty (*Instanz*) which the individual has erected within himself.

The social force which in the family is exercised as parental authority, particularly that of the father, becomes, through internalization of parental prohibitions and precepts, a faculty with attributes of morality and power in the form of the super-ego. Once this is established, it is easily projected again upon persons of authority, and thus the actual persons in authority are endowed with the characteristics of the subject's super-ego.

The normal super-ego undergoes changes in accordance with the external reality, whereas the neurotic super-ego tends to remain fixed to its infantile conditionings (p. 86). There are individuals in whom the strength of the super-ego is so great as to render them independent of real objects in the real world for maintaining the tonicity of the super-ego. "There are factors whose force is at least not weaker than the fear of the super-ego (by the ego); and they are fear of real objects to whom great power is attributed; the hope of material advantages; the wish to be loved and praised by them; and the satisfactions which the realization of this wish would entail, even the possibility of sexual, especially homosexual, even if unconscious, relations to these authorities."

"The super-ego, inasmuch as it is established through fear of the father and the simultaneous wish to be loved by him, proves the family to be a great help in establishing a later proclivity of adults to believe in and subordinate themselves to authority." But Freud (Fromm continues) overlooked the fact that the most important function of the family is that it becomes the instrument for forging the socially acceptable character. "This is the defect of the super-ego theory." According to Fromm the characterization of the super-ego as the "heritage of the Oedipus complex" is too thin a characterization of the interrelation between the family and the structure of society as a whole. The authority of the father in the family is subsequently supplemented by socially ordained authorities, which are a part of the authoritarian structure of society, and the father is not the prototype (*Vorbild*) of social authority but its replica (*Abbild*).

Fromm points out that social determinants of the Oedipus complex are not universally present, and that the functions of sexual rivalry and all-powerful authority are not universally present in the father in all cultures, but that these functions are divided in some between maternal uncle and father.

Fromm continues to discuss the attitude of fathers to sons, and describes how in peasant families of the last century the son was exploited by the father, whereas in well-off bourgeois families the child was treated as a source of pleasure. These two situations color the rivalries between father and son. In all instances, however, the super-ego owes its existence to the relationship to the father, which is thus filled with anxiety and love, and has many more emotional connections with the social environment than are encompassed within the confines of the Oedipus complex. He maintains that ego and super-ego are not natural phenomena but depend for their existence and character on the life practices (*Lebensweise*). These practices, in the last analysis, include the system of production and the social structures arising from it.

Fromm then investigates the general social conditions giving rise to the necessity for super-ego and authority, and the relation of ego and super-ego to defense against instinctual tendencies (*Triebabwehr*). He states that "super-ego" is a necessary concept for understanding the relationship between internalized defense and authority, and distinguishes between fear of punishment and the wish to be loved by the "authority" and the wish to be loved by one's super-ego. This fear of being unloved by one's super-ego is an irrational anxiety. Fromm finally ascribes the same relationship to the individual and authority- that Ferenczi describes between hypnotist and subject. The expectations, however, are the infantile ones. The function of authority is the suppression and repression of impulses, but it also has an additional function, to be a prototype and ideal to those who are subordinated. This also becomes a part of the super-ego. Thus authority has a double face, repression and ideal formation.

Fromm's treatment of the forces that hold society together is based on the Freudian super-ego theory plus some very impor- tant amendments with which we can readily concur. We can accept his modifications of the Freudian use of "identification"; and his extension of the sources of super-ego formation from the conflict with the Oedipus complex to the larger source of the life practices, the means of production, and the social structure consequent upon them.

In summary we can say that, in his essay on "Group Psy- chology," Freud attempted to answer, on the basis of the libido theory, the question of what held society together. There Freud introduced two concepts: identification and the libidinous ties between individuals, the latter being reduced to forms of sexual love. The "libidinous" aspects of the union of members of society to each other, Fromm supplements by another and much more useful concept—that of authority—with the aid of which many relationships are made clear. It is not the magic eye of the leader who holds the group in place by virtue of their passive sexual love to him, but rather by virtue of his authority. This is Fromm's modification.

If all societies were organized like our own we might get along quite well with concepts such as authority and super-ego. In neither case can one say that these concepts are in error. The only criticism to which they are subject is that they are not sufficiently precise. Questions about their usefulness in other societies arise on two scores. The concept of authority is difficult to apply to certain types of social organization; and the concept of super-ego conceals some very important details which must be brought to light.

Authority is a behavioristic concept; it describes a relationship existing between two individuals or between an individual and a group. It must therefore be examined with regard to the psychological factors which establish it in the subject and object, and with regard to the functions which can be attributed to its action. It must, moreover, be restated in terms of direct experience. The position taken in this book is that direct experience is not to be confused with behavioristic concepts describing the combined effects of different direct experiences, because the behavioristic concept merely gives a name to a phenomenon which may be the result of different types of direct experience.

From the point of view of the subject, authority can be either enforced or delegated. In either case the psychic processes can be understood only from the psychology of dependency. This latter in turn becomes a question of the resources of the ego. When authority is enforced, the psychic resources of the subject are not necessarily impaired and the acceptance of authority may be purely situational. The subject may be obliged to acquiesce to conditions imposed by another in order to conserve certain other more basic interests. An illustration of this is slavery. Delegated authority depends on aquiescence due to defective internal resources of the ego, and is maintained by the expectations of the subject from the object, expectations which in the neurotic individual become magnified to magical proportions. This we found to be the chief weapon that society uses to impose disciplines; and the renunciation of gratifications at parental command is accepted by the child in order to preserve itself or to guarantee the magic services of the parent (Ferenczi and Rado).[27]

[27] This is not true in every case. In many instances the child treats discipline as enforced and reacts with great resistance against it. The gratification interfered with is that of exercising irresponsible autonomy over itself and megalomanic tyranny over parents. The tantrum is the usual outcome of this reaction.

There is a second vital point concerning the functions which can be attributed to the action of authority. Here a distinction must be drawn between the following three functions of authority: the ability to impose restrictive disciplines; ability to frustrate important needs; ability to exploit another individual.

These three functions must be separated, at least when dealing with societies other than our own. No form of social organization is possible without restrictive discipline; but authority either enforced or delegated is not necessary for the ability to frustrate needs. Earlier in this study we called attention to implied prohibitions in connection with sexual discipline, prohibitions which consisted of a nonrecognition, a withholding of words and concepts with which to deal with the pleasure element of sexual activity, although the excretory functions are given names and have a recognized place in the activities of child and adult. The ability to impose discipline exists in every society irrespective of who the executive may be or whether any individual can exploit anyone else.

The Zuni society is an apt illustration. This is a society in which the opportunity to exploit another individual does not exist. No one can subject another to his own ends. And yet the disciplines, though they fall in places unknown in our society, are extremely severe. The most powerful sanction is the provocation of the sense of shame, which is the result of a forceful and universal nonrecognition. The individual is cut off from response (loss of love), but nothing else. In Zuni society this is a serious threat. Because of the peculiar structure of the in-group and the high degree of mutual dependency, this sanction of the sense of shame is extremely powerful and effective.

This ability to impose important frustrations may be held by an individual who has the ability neither to impose discipline nor to exploit anyone by virtue of economic power. An illustration is found in the Marquesan woman, who has no economic power unless she happens to be an oldest child. She does not take the role of disciplinarian; but she can frustrate the dependency longings of the child and the sexual wishes of the adult. Her position in the society is that she is held in awe and disdain, is envied, hated, and in folktales occupies a position very like that of the father in our society.

The third point, the ability to subject an individual to the will of another, can exist by virtue of size, strength, economic power or prestige. The situations are each entirely different in character, and we need not examine each of them now.

Of these three factors, the ability to impose discipline is the most important and the most universal. In some societies, authority in the sense of ability to exploit or to impose frustrations is considered antisocial; this injunction is maintained by rigid disciplines, the power of which depends essentially on the withholding of approval. One cannot attribute the withholding of approval to any exercise of authority.

The reaction to discipline in turn must be evaluated in terms of what the discipline does to other previous adaptations. The reaction types to discipline are crucial in the formation of what is termed the "super-ego." It must be recalled that the concept super-ego was derived from the study of the neurotic super-ego and is hence a derivative of the consequences of repression exclusively. In order to appreciate some of the questions about the super-ego we must survey the various ways in which inhibitions are established.

There are three ways in which an inhibition can be established: the resources to consummate an impulse may be absent; the resources may be present, be exercised for a time and then fail; the resources may be present and effective, but their exercise may be forbidden on pain of jeopardizing other interests. Illustrations of the first type are difficult to find except in constitutionally defective individuals or in certain severe cases of impotence and frigidity where the sexual development did not advance beyond its organization at the time of childhood. The chief symptom here is the ability to take on new adaptations, to find new types of gratification, and the persistence of masochistic techniques. The second type is found in the traumatic neurosis, where inhibitions of effective ego functions are established on the basis of overwhelming failure. Thus, the case of a young man of twenty-five showed that, for two months after a trauma caused by concussion, vision, hearing, skin sensation, taste, and smell all disappeared. The third variety is most commonly seen in the neuroses, where inhibitions are established by external force contained in disciplines. In these cases the function is developed but held in check by anxiety.

The remarkable feature about all inhibitions is the similarity of some of their characteristics and manifestations, irrespective of origin, whereas in other respects the origin of the inhibition decides its manifestations. In most cases it is not difficult to decide which is which, because disciplines make a highly selective series of inhibitions, whereas those of traumatic origin are much more diffuse. The feature all inhibitions have in common is that the executive activity concerned is not accessible. In all cases, if the need for a given activity persists while the executive capacity is inhibited, certain identifiable phenomena take place. This situation is certain to create psychic disturbances. These have already been reviewed (see p. 27). It is important to remember that as a result of these disturbances changes take place in (1) the individual's conception of himself; (2) in the ideational representation of the activity; and (3) eventually, in the gratification anticipated. In (1) the ego can be represented as failing or being overwhelmed; in (2) the activity is represented as destructive; and in (3) the goal may ostensibly become changed to pain instead of pleasure. The entire syndrome goes under the general name of masochism.

Inhibitions and masochistic phenomena can be produced by failure of resources and are not necessarily due to the imposition of force from without. More specifically pertinent to our theme is the fact that masochistic phenomena can be produced without the possibility of the activity of super-ego, conscience, guilt, or ego ideal. The existence of masochistic phenomena is therefore not absolute evidence of super-ego activity.

The super-ego can, however, produce these phenomena, and as we have heard, the super-ego is formed by discipline, or as Freud states it, by an identification with the original executors of the discipline, father or mother, etc. This formulation certainly covers the clinical facts. This concept of the super-ego, however, creates the impression of its being a compartment of the mind, a specialized portion of the ego; and at times it is anthropomorphically treated as a separate individual (Alexander). This is the aspect of the super-ego which creates the greatest confusion.

We can get some aid concerning this by contrasting the "normal" with the neurotic super-ego. This comparison reveals the interesting fact that the difference is not purely quantitative. That is, the neurotic super-ego which is otherwise characterized as "severe," concerns itself with the condemnation of activities which the "normal" individual permits himself. But in addition the comparison shows that the conception of effective reality is strikingly different in both.

In the case of the neurotic super-ego we see the following associated phenomena. There is a feeling of smallness and insignificance, and that the wishes of another person are binding. An activity under condemnation of the super-ego is feared, and its manifestations are crushed in order to escape condemnation or punishment, or in order to guarantee the good will and magic services of the parent who originally imposed the injunction, or of anyone who occupies a corresponding position. The main point about this neurotic super-ego is that it is backed by certain permanent modifications in the perception of the outer world and of oneself, and a combination of the infantile expectations and goals of dependency. If one sees the super-ego as a compartment of the mind, these perceptions of the individual concerning himself and the outer world remain untouched, his goals are not elucidated. For purposes of therapy this representation has great pedagogic advantages.

From the point of view of sociology there is an additional important implication. The super-ego is derived from the impact of the individual with institutions and retains this contact throughout life. It is not a compartment of the mind, but a function of the ego in its adaptive maneuvers. The neurotic super-ego shows the persistence of infantile modes of perception and of establishing relations with others, which, however, remain unconscious.[28]

The case of the neurotic super-ego is a special case. There the severity of the super-ego persists, without regard to realities. The infantile rewards which maintain the neurotic super-ego are not realizable in actual life. But this is not the case with the normal super-ego. The tonicity of the normal super-ego is always dependent on the realities in the outer world, and on the clarity with which these realities are perceived.

The neurotic super-ego in our culture shows an extraordinary attachment to the infantile values associated with the establishment of discipline. We might raise the question what kind of super-ego exists in societies where disciplines are not severe. In Trobriand society for example, love and protection are not conditioned by renunciation of pleasures. Here, a knowledge of the individual is indispensable. In its absence a few guesses are in order. Disciplines exist in every culture, and if the hypothesis about the origin of the super-ego is correct, all disciplines contribute to its formation.

We can consider at least one other method of imposing discipline that does not depend on threats of withdrawal of support or protection, namely, nonapproval. Let us assume that sexual activity is in no way criticized; that anal training is inducted without the ideas associated with dirt and without disapproval. Consider furthermore a society in which all ac-

[28] The biological and phylogenetic orientation of Freud has recently been reiterated by a singular statement of Anna Freud in *The Ego and the Mechanisms of Defence* (London, 1937), p. 171. She decides that there is in man a phylogenetically determined antagonism to his instincts. This is another illustration of how the phylogenetic orientation shifted attention away from sociological disciplinary influences in its efforts to explain certain persistent clinical facts.

tivities are more or less open and can be observed by the child. Under these conditions a super-ego is formed in which punishment plays no part and in which mos has a larger role. The motive power of the super-ego in this case need not be fear, but shame.

In our culture the sense of shame can be stimulated by the breach of a mos. We do not, however, recognize shame as a factor in super-ego formation, largely because of the preponderance of repressive components in our super-ego formation. Nobody can fail to concede the strong relation of the sense of shame to external conditions. The fact that the super-ego in our culture is based on repressions ought not to obscure the fact that it retains a constant contact with the outside world as perceived by the subject.

We remarked a while ago that the tonicity of the normal super-ego depends on the realities of the rewards of being approved and protected, whereas the neurotic super-ego depends on uncollectible rewards which are no compensations for the abandoned gratifications.[29] This idea helps us to understand the functioning of the super-ego in societies where the obedience-love, disobedience-punishment relationship does not obtain. In Zuni and Trobriand societies the loss of recognition is the effective sanction—not guilt or conscience—and is indicated by the high sense of shame. Chuckchee society, however, exhibits a combination of rigid disciplines and an absence of mutual support or dependency; here crime is socially recog-

[29] The concepts of fear of "being abandoned by one's super-ego" or "being loved by one's super-ego" seem to introduce a confusing ambiguity and anthropomorphism. However, these formulations describe an important condition for establishing and maintaining self-esteem. No individual can tolerate behavior or attitudes in himself incompatible with his ideal, which is derived from the social ideal and which eventually represents the condensed effects of discipline. The formulation "being loved by one's super-ego" destroys the relationship which the super-ego constantly maintains with the outer world. This can be easily proved in individuals who presumably have no sense of guilt about certain activities until they are obliged to talk about them to someone else. Under the conditions of secrecy, guilt or discrepancy between ego and super-ego is tolerated without much conflict. As soon as the outer world is included, the guilt breaks out afresh.

nized and taboos are abrogated with comparative ease. Non-aggression in Zuni society can be maintained because of the unusual degree of mutual dependency created by the strong in-group formation.

The relation of repression to guilt and conscience raises an extremely important problem concerning affects (emotions). Whether affect registers differences in energy stasis or discharge in connection with activities which lead to satisfactions, is a problem we defer to a subsequent chapter.

We can summarize our discussion of the forces that hold society together. These forces are basically the ones which make mother and child the first social unit, but their character and manifestations change as the resources of the individual grow.

The concept super-ego can be used, if translated into terms of direct experience, because in studying sociology in a comparative way one cannot look for super-egos. One can look only for that combination of interaction between man and institutions which creates the super-ego. For this purpose we use as our prototype not the neurotic super-ego, but the normal. One can study the disciplines imposed in each society and the relation these have to the establishment of the security system of the individual. This is bound to be reflected in the religion, because religion forms a part of the security system of the group. The technique used to solicit aid from the deity must in every way conform to the character of the disciplines imposed on the child by its disciplinarians. This we shall have to verify in a comparative way. Beyond this no satisfactory answer to the question of the super-ego can be made until the operation of those forces which hold individuals together is studied in societies which exhibit little discipline, no punishment, and no opportunity for exploiting anyone else.

Life Goals and Ideals

What life goals, objectives, ideals does our society create? This is a question which we can answer only with reference to contemporary life in America. Goals, objectives, and ideals have changed materially within the past generation, and the changes within the past two thousand years would make a long history. These goals and ideals have much to do with the particular position in which the individual is born, and the amount of social motility that exists for him. Conclusions about this point may not be valid for more than a few years, because conditions and ideals are constantly changing.

Whereas it is quite dangerous to draw conclusions about life goals and ideals in the past of our own culture, one cannot avoid being struck with some gross changes. "Salvation," by which we mean boons or bliss of some vague kind to be enjoyed after death, seems to have disappeared as a life goal from the life of the modern bourgeoisie. The usefulness of such faith in immortality as a powerful weapon for preserving social equilibrium cannot be overestimated, for men have an extraordinary ability to postpone certain gratifications. The belief in immortality, as Freud has pointed out in *The Future of an Illusion*, was an illusion created by the helplessness of man. To this one may add that it was an expectation of being loved by the parent as in childhood without responsibility. Basically, this idea derives from the disciplines of childhood; hence, suffering is tolerated in the world as a means of being reinstated into the good graces of God. But as Fromm and Reich have pointed out, this illusion was fostered and exploited because it was such an effective tool for social balance.

No such ideal exists in the bourgeoisie of our society. Instead there is the goal of success, and with it the assurance of sufficient self-esteem as reflected in the esteem of others. There are innumerable forms to which the idea of success can be attached. The "narcissistic" goals of prestige are identified in values of power to influence or exploit others, in the great fear of being the underdog, and in the powerful drive to be superior. Since, in democracies, subsistence values and prestige values are intimately bound together, the current goals are for the greater part directed into economic channels for the average man.

The interference with prestige goals in our culture is therefore a potent source of intrasocial hostility, because the ideas by which these goals are connoted, the emotions that accompany them, and the drives necessary to achieve them are not easily subject to repression. In fact, the reverse is true. They are not only not subject to repression, but, for a time at least, were commonly encouraged. In the absence of illusions which make it possible for some individuals to defer gratification of these goals, the social conflict about their achievement becomes all the sharper.

One could go on from this point to discuss the consequences of this conflict, but it lies outside of our immediate objectives.[30]

[30] For further discussion on this point see Erich Fromm, "Sozialpsychologischer Teil," *Autorität und Familie* (Paris, 1936).

Chapter III

PRELIMINARY STUDIES

IN THE previous chapter we have sketched the reactions of the individual in our culture to several institutions. This inventory is far from complete, but is an adequate sampling. The transition from this interrelationship of individual and institution in our culture to the same situation in aboriginal cultures must be made without benefit of knowledge of the individual or of the history of the society. In lieu of an intimate psychological study of the individual, which could serve us as an excellent check, we are obliged to use evidence of another kind. We utilize the sum of all institutions, practices, and beliefs, and chart this against the coördinates established by known reactions of man as studied in our culture. Our license to do this comes from the universality of certain experiences of all humans, no matter what culture they come from, and from the known variations in reaction types to these experiences. All men are born, they are all dependent for a time, they are all subject to disciplines of one kind or another, they all have sexual appetites, they all experience rage when important needs are frustrated, etc. Our scheme of reaction types is drawn from the variations to these universal experiences. And the individuality of a culture depends on how these universal needs are met, curbed, controlled, or frustrated.

The translation of the principles established into a technique requires a further investigation into the debatable questions pertaining to method and procedure. For this purpose we may take some of the features of Trobriand society as described by Malinowski,[1] and use this material to thrash out these prob-

[1] B. Malinowski, *The Argonauts of the Western Pacific* (London and New York, 1922), and *The Sexual Life of Savages* (New York, 1929).

lems, rather than attempt a detailed analysis, which for several reasons we cannot do. The abbreviated description given below is not sufficient to describe the functional interoperation of the various institutions.

TROBRIAND ISLANDS

The society of the Trobriand Islands[2] consists of four clans, each of which is exogamic, with descent reckoned exclusively on the maternal side. The subsistence economy of these people consists in the cultivation of gardens, which, notwithstanding the absence of the plow or draft animals, yield them a plentiful food supply. Yams and sugar cane are their chief sources of vegetable food, pigs and chickens their chief meat sources, though fish are also obtainable. Their food supply is abundant and there is no practical need for anxiety on that score.

The organization of labor for purposes of gardening is contingent upon their social organization. Since the society is matrilineal and all blood relations and personal loyalties are reckoned on the blood ties, the brother of a woman is her official guardian, and her sons work for the maternal relatives, i.e., sisters, under the supervision of their maternal uncle.

The family organization shows striking contrasts to our own. The formal arrangement is the customary one of father, mother, and children living in the village of the father (patri-local) and in the same abode. But striking differences begin to appear when we examine the relations of the individuals comprising the family to each other.

The mother is the sociological center of the family. She creates the child as if by herself, the father having no acknowl-edged role in paternity. This basic idea conditions the rules of descent, inheritance, succession in rank, chieftainship, heredi-tary office, magic,[3] in fact every rule of transmission according to kinship. The father has no ability to impose disciplines on children, this being exercised by the maternal uncle. The term

[2] The inhabitants of the Trobriand Islands are a Melanesian people of negroid type. The particular group studied was a community of about 1,500 people living on the island of Boyoa, lying to the northeast of New Guinea.

[3] Malinowski, *The Father in Primitive Society* (London, 1927), p. 10.

father means to the native "husband of my mother, and a close companion." He takes an active part in the tender cares lavished on infants, invariably feels and shows a deep affection for them, and later shares in giving them instruction. The father means a man who loved and cared for you in childhood.

As the child grows older, Malinowski tells us, the situation changes: the child then learns that the father belongs to a different clan, but that the child's own totemic allegiances belong with the mother. Duties, restrictions, and matter of pride unite him with the mother.

The child's "own" village is where his maternal uncle lives, and there he has his natural allies and rights. In his real domicile the boy is a stranger. In his own (i.e., his uncle's) village, the authority of the uncle increases. The latter has the right to discipline, to give or withhold consent, while that of the father becomes less important.

The disciplines of early childhood are not severe. Anal discipline is slow and gently instituted. Sexual disciplines are remarkable in that their objective is not to prevent the child from any exercise of sexual activity, but to limit the objects with whom it is permissible. Children are permitted any sexual activity within the limits of the object taboos. No sexual activity is permitted the boy with his sisters or his mother or with his mother's female relatives. But these restrictions do not apply to cross cousins, and unions between these are considered the marriages of choice. There are no puberty rites or defloration ceremonies.

The courtship of the young is encouraged and special facilities are created for that purpose. The young pairs meet in bachelor houses where sexual experimentation takes place until a couple decides to marry. Sexual objects must be chosen from the outsiders (Tomakava). This means for the boy that most of the girls of the village apart from his sisters are available sexual objects.

With marriage, however, the period of sexual freedom comes to an end. Fidelity to the mate of choice is then expected and

punishments are instituted for any breach. Marriage is monogamous for everyone except the chief, who has polygamous
privileges. The marriage is consummated with parental consent on both sides, and an elaborate mutual gift exchange. The
marriage itself is signified by the couple's partaking of a common meal. In the marriage, food is supplied by the wife's
family and valuables by the husband's.

The Trobriander is not greatly dependent on supernatural
beings: he has a god whose anger is indicated by severe catas-
trophes such as earthquakes: he has no fear of the dead and
little of death, because after death the individual continues
to lead pretty much the kind of existence he did during life.
Old age and loss of power do not denote death.

The islanders believe the normal status is health; they explain death as being caused by accident. Illness is due to
sorcery, practiced by wizards who are much dreaded; rapid
and sudden disease and death may be brought about by flying
witches of supernatural origin. Epidemics are brought about
by malignant spirits, *tauvau,* who have a permanent abode in
the south. They are invisible and walk at night through the
villages. Occasionally they are transformed into reptiles, when
they become visible.

The belief that sorcery is practiced in the islands is justified;
it is practiced chiefly by men. The child is held to be relatively
immune from sorcery, while the youth or man in his prime is
most susceptible. Commonly, when sorcery is suspected, a relative of the maternal line is blamed.

Life after death is much the same as earthly existence. Communication with the nether world is effected through individuals who go into trances and act as go-betweens, carrying
messages to and from the dead. The invisible dead return to the
living on a special day, on which a special series of taboos are
observed to prevent injury to the dead.

The use of magic is widespread. Magic is employed in making
yam and taro gardens, but not in the cultivation of the cocoa,

banana, mango, and breadfruit. Malinowski[4] observes that magic is used in any enterprise where there is any uncertainty or danger. War, love, disease, wind, and weather are all governed by magic, so in fact is any activity "not yet completely mastered by man."

The technique of magic consists of words spoken by a special agent in connection with rituals. The utterance of the spell is the most important part of the process.

The government of the group is mainly in the hands of the chief, whose power lies largely in the fact that he can preëmpt the services of the magician and has a call on the labor of many men through his practice of polygamy. There is gradation by rank, the divisions being those of commoner and noble, to which prerogatives and privileges are attached. The most obvious sanction found to operate in this society is the sense of shame. Suicide is extremely common, and is most often provoked by a sense of shame.

There is some exchange in the form of barter between individuals. The custom known as Kula is a ceremonial exchange of articles of no definite ownership, which pass from one individual to another until reaching the original holder. It is considered a virtue to pass a Kula article around rapidly to its next holder.

Some of the customs are worthy of note. The Trobrianders do not eat facing each other, but back to back. Food has a high display value and is a frequent vehicle for ostentation. The reverse is also true; having no food is a disgrace, opulence a privilege, and he who has too much or eats too much incurs wrath. The pride that centers in food is shown also by the prominence given in the village to the food house.

There is also an institution which is quite important as an indicator of tension between the sexes. The women have a secret organization to which no man is admitted; a man who approaches the precincts of this organization is liable to harm.

To this brief description we may add one or two myths and

[4] B. Malinowski, *Myth in Primitive Psychology* (London, 1928), p. 80.

legends. Two young people lived in a village with their mother; by an accident the girl inhaled a strong love decoction, prepared by her brother for someone else. Mad with passion, she pursued her brother along a lonely beach, and seduced him. Overcome by shame and remorse, the brother and sister forsook food and drink, and died in a grotto. An aromatic herb grew up through their interlaced skeletons, and this herb forms the most powerful ingredient in the substances compounded for use in love magic. An origin myth tells of a first couple who came out of a hole, a sister as head of the family and a brother as her guardian and provider. They came and took possession of the lands. Usually such stories concern a specific hole and a specific lineage. One of the holes, that of Labaï, has an atypical origin story in which four representatives of the main clans emerged. Another origin myth tells of a primal mother who came out of a hole and gave birth to a boy and a girl. The boy was her guardian, and she had children.

FOCAL IDEAS AND THE TECHNIQUES FOR USING THEM

In the previous chapter we used the procedure of sifting out of the narrative of the daily experiences of the individual in our culture some interactions between institutions and the subject. In such a narrative we get a dynamic picture of the individual in action against a large variety of institutions simultaneously. From this complex account we selected and isolated certain reaction types for purpose of study. We can get nothing from one individual but his direct experiences. Many of the things we call "institutions" do not strike the individual as such. He only knows about them as customs—demands that are made on him—restrictions. He is not even aware of "permitted" activities; he simply carries them on without being aware that he can do so by virtue of the absence of restrictions. With such a story we must deduce the institutions from practice.

In the abridged description of Trobriand culture, we have an entirely different type of data to deal with. Our observer who reports the culture has already done a bit of editing and classification of the data, taking them out of the living context of complex interrelated activities and reducing them to certain definite categories of experience. We have a series of practices, beliefs, customs, etc. Some of the evidence the observer gives us is direct, i.e., how the individuals act and feel. But he has also given us a good deal of indirect evidence, petrified in folklore and myth.

If we are to make some sense out of this galaxy of recorded experience we are in need of some focal ideas about which to organize the material, for the description of the institutions does not supply them. Before we decide which to use, we may survey briefly a few of those which have already been used for this purpose.

Cultures have been described by analogies with the variations found in human character, drawn either from psychopathology, from literary or from mythological sources. Thus cultures have been described as "paranoid," "introverted," or "extroverted"; cultures have been named after literary figures like "Faust," or after Greek deities like "Apollo" or "Dionysus." The effort in all these cases is to convey some general impression of the predominant direction of life goals, of moral values, or of a psychological technique.

Such designations as these cannot claim any great accuracy. No culture is exclusively extroverted or introverted. No culture is predominantly "paranoid." These epithets rely on very vague connotations. The term "paranoid" may refer to megalomania, to persecution, or merely to anxiety, and the reader's selection of one of these depends on his conception of "paranoid." The term "extrovert" likewise can mean any number of things: uninhibited, interested in activity, interested in the outer world; "introverted" may mean inhibited, introspective, interested in fantasy, etc. The designation "Faustian" or "Dionysian" is different in kind from the preceding ones. Here a culture is described in accordance with a characterological type in which the characteristic dominant objectives or values or ideologies are taken as guides to the adaptation of a group.

All these focal ideas are open to the same objection, because they destroy the boundaries between individual and institution. The basic fallacy involved is that, according to any contemporary psychology, variations in human character are created by habitual methods of reacting to external conditions. The character trait may be a reaction formation, a compensation or flight, the nature of which can be decided only from the disciplines or reality situations in the culture. From this point of view, if a group is paranoid, one ought to be able to track down those institutional forces with which all constituents make contact and which terminate in this common trait. However, to regard character as an irreducible racial or cultural idiosyncrasy is at once to use a psychological designation and at the same time to deny the validity of psychological derivation of character.

Perhaps the chief objection to these designations is that they afford no basis for the comparison of the effects of various institutional systems on human nature. This is true of every focal idea derived from the psychological constellations in the individual. The result is no different if, instead of using a character trait, we designate cultures through a formula which expresses "instinct" repression. This latter system of notations has been used by psychoanalysis, which described cultures as oral, anal, or phallic.[5] Nor is the designation of a culture as "secure" or "insecure" any more successful. In this latter case the affect is detached from the circumstances which bring it about. The affect or emotion is not a cause; it is merely an indicator of deeper-lying changes in the individual.

To lose track of the sharp differentiation between individual and group, and of the fact that society is not an individual, is to abandon the chance for any precision in studying reciprocal relations empirically. Character, affect, security, are attributes

[5] For further discussion of this point see p. 391.

of the individual only. A culture is the collection of institutions by which a group of individuals live. These institutions create effects on the individual which may end in security for him, or in paranoid traits, etc.

But this brings up another very important issue. Is there any uniformity in the effects that institutions have on individuals in the same culture? There cannot possibly be any uniformity because there are always the differentiations of sex, age, and status, as well as constitutional differences in strength, beauty, and intelligence. This, however, does not contradict the fact that in any culture all individuals are subject to certain disciplines, as is true of religion, and of prescribed attitudes to members of the family. In other words, a culture creates an orbit within which move all the individuals comprising the culture. This orbit is made up of institutions to which all individuals in a society are subject. Within this orbit sharp differentiations appear for the sexes, primogeniture, and status. It is as untrue to say that all women or all oldest sons in a given culture have the same "character," as to suppose that all chiefs from different cultures have the same character. The distinctions between individual character formations depend on the different habitual attitudes, perceptions, and action formulas to the same external stimuli which each individual creates for himself. So that we can expect to find almost the same differences in character in aboriginal societies as we find in our own, even though the variations in the life destiny of the individual are likely to be smaller in aboriginal society. Gradations in status do not create differences in character. They create differences in opportunity for exploitation of others, for prestige and immunity from some institutional restrictions; but for the greater part these do not influence the character, unless they are accompanied by immunity from the influence of disciplines and restrictions in the formative years. Giving a man a new function in a society does not necessarily alter his character; if it does, the change has a definite relation to his previous character. The underdog who suddenly acquires power will use it differently from the man who is to the manner born. The oldest son in a society where primogeniture confers important immunities is not necessarily the most effective and resourceful individual among the children of his family.

We can summarize this discussion of focal ideas based on analogies with the individual as follows: Comparisons between societies on a dynamic basis cannot be made by general terms describing predominant traits according to affects, pathological syndromes, character traits or characterological types as they are found in the individual. Such comparisons can be safely established only by comparing institutions and then comparing the end results in the individual.

Incest taboos, basic disciplines, techniques of magic and methods of invoking aid from a god are the same for all individuals in a society. It is these institutions which make the cultural orbit. Within this orbit character differences can be individually developed. A group cannot have a character any more than it can have a soul. This anthropomorphism is misleading. What creates the impression of a group character is the operation of general sanctions, which when universally followed may lead to the apparent absence of certain character traits. One may thus observe that the Todas are not jealous. Phenomenologically this observation may be correct; but methodologically, it makes a great deal of difference whether the absence of jealousy is regarded as a racial idiosyncrasy, "a culture pattern," or as maintained by virtue of sanctions. No culture can interdict an emotion; it can only create conditions which render the emotion unnecessary; it can make the suppression of the emotion acceptable; or it may interdict its manifestations. The rest is a problem for the individual. How he handles this problem depends on his character, and that has nothing to do with his status; unless, for example, it is unbecoming to a chief to be jealous of a commoner—and this latter is a *mos*.

If we cannot use these descriptive criteria, then it becomes important to find others that are free of the objections we raised. We can observe the effects of institutions on the individual. We have several to choose from. There are affects, which we can use not as causes, but as indicators of stress. The most universal of these is anxiety. Moreover, the effects of anxiety in the form of organized defenses can be readily identified. Another important guide is in the effects of the frustration of basic needs. A third criterion we can use is to study those conditions which terminate in giving the individual a sense of security and those which fail to do so. Failure in security can be detected by the anxieties it creates and by the compensatory measures made necessary by this failure.

To use these criteria effectively, some knowledge of both normal and abnormal psychology is necessary. We can illustrate this with a practical example. From what we know about our culture we would expect that severe sexual restrictions in childhood, taboos against objects and the sexual aim as well, will in a considerable number of cases produce disturbances of potency in the male. We may confirm this by direct observation, i.e., by finding out whether males in their period of sexual functioning have any impotence. If we consider a society where no such restrictions exist we will expect to find no disturbances in potency. Suppose we then verify this fact, and find no evidence of the aberration. But this apparent absence may be due to oversight. There is a sure way to check on it. Potency disturbances are likely to produce anxiety in any society. In primitive society it is most likely to be rationalized as due to the malevolent magic of someone. If we find in this society the idea that malevolent magic cannot cause impotence, then we can be quite sure that there are no potency disturbances, and the original thesis that sexual restrictions in childhood cause sexual disturbance in adults is highly probable.

Anxiety, however, is not the only affect we need to watch. Others supply us with valuable clues. Jealousy can be used as a valuable indicator. Not alone is its presence important, but likewise its absence in situations where we might naturally expect to find it. Such absence is an invitation to look either for sanctions against its manifestations or for compensations in some tangible form for its suppression.

. As a corollary to this use of affects and of reactions to frustration, plus the effects of these on the total personality, we may use another concept as a focal idea, namely the constellation "security system," which we shall presently explain.

The defenses against anxiety are extremely varied and are excellent indicators of the resources which the indivdual commands, and these in turn depend on the resources available to the culture as a whole. An important problem arises in connection with the practical application of this knowledge. These affects and defenses should be described in the form in which they occur in the conscious ego, and not in the form in which the unconscious constellation derived from them is expressed. For example, if we find a constellation that may be characterized as a "fear of being eaten up," we could do what has been done in the past—describe this in terms of the libido theory as "a regression to the oral-sadistic phase of development." In this form the statement gives us neither information about the institutional source of difficulty, nor a very accurate picture of the effects of the institution on the individual. On the other hand, if we state it in terms of the total personality, it sounds somewhat different. We then state that there is a manifest anxiety, that the form which it takes—the fear of being eaten up— is an unconscious representation of an actual frustration in life. We must make the statement in terms of the total personality because it is this which comes into direct contact with reality. In this manner the external reality or the institution creating the pressure can be identified and studied. The frustrating situation may refer to such things as dependency, sex, prestige, or food. Which of these it is must be decided from the total picture of the culture. We can characterize the two points of view by saying that the first theory uses the oral fantasy of being eaten up as evidence of a substitutive gratification, the other as a diagnostic indicator of a frustration coming from somewhere in the effective reality of the individual.

The dynamics to be used are essentially those described by Freud. The point of departure is that the focal ideas are expressed in the language of experience in which they consciously occur. The unconscious constellation is used as evidence of an institutionally created pressure, and the latter is identified. Thus, when we use a concept such as security or security system, meaning organized institutionalized attempts to relieve anxiety, we are speaking of organized defense provoked by a specific anxiety, which must be identified. Then the anxiety is described in terms of the basic wishes or needs as these are consciously perceived to arise out of food, dependency, and so on.

If we take a focal idea such as security, we may arrange the data so as to study the types of organization which yield a sense of security to the individual and those which do not. However, once we elect such a focal idea, we must remain true to its conditions. We must identify the anxiety and its source, and identify also the institutionalized defense. For example, much has been written about the strivings of man for immortality. This can be regarded in two ways: either it represents a striving for endless life, i.e., a positive wish, or it represents a denial of a painful and anxiety-provoking fact, that of death. Each approach leads to entirely different conceptions of the particular society we are dealing with. The underlying ideology about immortality is a product of many rationalizations; however, these ideas are used as evidence of a wished-for state of affairs. Furthermore, when man uses the phenomenon of dreaming to serve as evidence that the personality is divisible into an actual body and a double which he calls the "soul," he is philosophizing toward a conclusion which satisfies an emotional need—to relieve an anxiety about death. He thus undoes, and at the same time negates, a painful reality. From the point of view of these philosophical systems, one may draw the conclusion that there is a strong drive toward immortality. On the other hand, if it is regarded as a part of a systematic defense against an anxiety, we must look for facts in an entirely different direction. We must seek evidence to indicate why this universal anxiety is so much more exaggerated in one culture than in another; and why the beliefs about it are so much more elaborate in one society than in another. We must examine the conditions in the group's struggles with the environment, seek the factors arising from the social organization which stimulate this fear, and then supply the basic ideas by means of which immortality is described. The Christian idea of immortality thus contains ideas which are wanting in other cultures, such as the Zuni. The former is derived from rigid obedience to discipline and punishment, while the Zuni religion is entirely free from these ideas. In short, although all cultures have anxiety which manifests itself in a drive toward immortality, the factors which emphasize this underlying fear of death must become the object of study. This rational fear may become the carrier of anxieties arising from other hidden sources. This is the phase which must be understood, rather than the final syndrome of the search for immortality.

In other words, we can work from the idea of *security* as defense against anxiety as a pivotal point. If we do not use anxiety as an underlying focal idea, we shall be identifying an endless series of positive wishes, like that for immortality, without first identifying the factors accentuating it. By following this procedure we can avoid being lost in an endless series of rationalizations.

With these considerations in view, we may look at the Trobriand beliefs in immortality. It is not, however, enough merely to identify the presence of this wish which the Trobrianders have in common with all other aboriginal peoples, but we must compare it with the special conditions under which immortality can be lost or gained, and the emphasis that is placed upon it. Immortality among the Trobrianders seems a condition taken for granted for every individual. The relations with the dead are not characterized by great fear. Neither are the ideas about immortality characterized by great expectations, for there are no great dangers to be avoided. The post-mortem world does not serve them as the situation in which all dissatisfactions in the present world will be remedied.

We may safely conclude that the Trobriand ideas about immortality indicate the absence of such an anxiety as is expressed, for example, by the Christian ideas. This anxiety, expressed by complicated conditions for securing immortality, must apparently be of a very specific kind, for it cannot be said of the Trobrianders that they are free of anxiety. It now becomes necessary to identify the sources of their anxieties on the one hand, and to account for the absence of it in places where one would expect to find it. We might correlate the absence of anxiety about death and immortality with the absence of severe disciplines in childhood and the effect this has on the formation of basic ideas and attitudes with respect to parents. However, we have as yet no proof of such an assumption.

The problem of diagnosing anxieties and defenses becomes an extremely important, though difficult, one.

If it were possible to study sociology under the conditions of a controlled experiment, we could quite readily solve the problem of the localization of anxiety. We could take several groups and subject each to a series of conditions which can be represented thus:

1		2	
CONSTANT	VARIABLE	CONSTANT	VARIABLE
A	— X	B	— X
A	— Y	B	— Y
A	— Z	B	— Z

Thus we would have one constant condition and several variables in one experiment; in the other, we would maintain the same variables, and alter the constants. If in the first experiment A were to stand for easy and complete satisfaction of subsistence needs, then X, Y, and Z would represent variations in regulations governing sexual gratifications, X standing for complete absence of control of any kind, Y for aim and object taboos, Z for object taboos only. Then one could alter the constant B by introducing great hardships in subsistence gratifications. If such a controlled experiment were continued for several hundred years we should probably be able to establish definitely the effects of specific pressures acting on humans in relation to certain constants, and we should be able to observe the effects of these pressures on the secondary institutions produced by them and the kind of individual each would create.

Such a controlled experiment is of course impossible, partly because the time requirement for its completion is too great, and partly because it would be impossible to impose controlled conditions on any group. Such a series of experiments are, however, actually recorded in the various cultures extant, but here we are at a loss in reconstructing all the conditions, though some of them are clearly visible. Then there are accidental factors like diffusion, which complicate the picture, and there is the still more troublesome factor of different reaction types to the same anxiety, and finally the fact that the various social pressures have an influence on one another. Food anxiety, for example, may eventually influence prestige mores. The same social conditions do not produce individuals of uniform character. Neither do the same social conditions influence groups in a uniform way. The limits of similarity and variation can, however, be explored with regard to specific difficulties, such as food, sexual, and prestige anxieties.

When we speak of pressures on a group of individuals we mean that certain institutions create great difficulties in the way of satisfying certain basic needs. The most evident of these needs is that of procuring food. It is an important issue to decide how far one can go in tracking down such a difficulty in a culture. Food anxiety will materially influence the behavior of individuals to one another in any society. But this problem is further complicated by the fact that such pressures are never found singly, and that there is no guarantee that the same pressure will produce similar effects in different cultures; the likelihood is still smaller that clear-cut results can be noted when these pressures coexist with others. The same end result can be achieved from different beginnings. This complicated series of interactions thus becomes more difficult to disentangle. The best one can do in these conditions is to deal with those anxieties with which we are best acquainted through our knowledge of man in our society, and then, by studying the interrelations between anxieties and reactions to them, to isolate the various specific cultural conditions which create them. The differences in reaction types of different groups to the same anxiety will of course vary with the resources available to a particular group in overcoming this anxiety. In the case of food, the reaction type depends on the reliability of the technique for procuring and insuring the food supply. It is also important to identify the manner in which such a food anxiety is represented ideationally, for the manner in which a given need is represented is a direct indicator of the resources of the ego to satisfy the need on the basis of a cultural configuration.

In other words, a reaction to a food anxiety must have at least two elements: the ideational representation of the anxiety; and the resources of the personality to overcome it. Ideational representation in the case of food may be expressed by the following ideas: making rational efforts to get food; taking food from some other person; wishing for someone to give it (i.e., another person, or a supernatural being) ; hallucinatory gratification of hunger by fantasy or dream. On the basis of the food anxiety, several other anxieties may appear, the fear of death and disintegration, and the fear of being eaten up. If a rational method, completely under control, is found to suffice, then the other types of representation need not be invoked. Whether rational methods suffice or not depends on the available technical resources. The types of ideational representation depend on and are therefore indicators of the available resources. But these resources are all functions of the total personality. These resources are part of the "cultural" equipment of the group, but they are taken in or mastered by the individual in varying degrees.

Hence, when we speak of ideational representations of a specific anxiety we mean also to imply that the specific form of representation has a definite relationship to the resources available to handle it. In our culture, if someone gets appendicitis, we do not pray or send for a sorcerer to find out who perpetrated the magic, but we remove the inflamed appendix. The technique for diagnosing and removing it is a cultural trait, though not each individual in our culture knows how to do it. Not every individual in a primitive society knows the technique of magic; but the concept of etiology of disease, magic, and what to do about it (consult a sorcerer) is common knowledge.

Let us attempt, with the aid of these guides, to see whether we can discover any sources of anxiety in Trobriand culture.

Several features, here, are very similar to those in our own culture. There is status differentiation of noble and commoner, with gradations of prestige associated with relative status. The four clans are not of equal standing. Distinctions of rank are associated with differences in privilege, food taboos, etc. We do not yet know whether status differentiation in itself can create discomfort, nor do we know the specific conditions under which it may do so. It seems a self-evident fact, from what is ostensibly the case in our culture, that differentiation of status should automatically create anxiety, because of the envy, jealousy, and aggression which it is able to mobilize in the individual. This is not necessarily the case. The anxiety due to status is inversely proportionate to the status mobility of the individual. We can, moreover, expect that if the expression of envy and aggression is prevented by a sanction of some kind, the anxiety is likely to be all the greater. In Trobriand culture the sanctions against mutual aggression are severe. The highly developed and easily stimulated sense of shame, and the frequency of suicide out of motives which one would expect to give rise to aggression against another—these factors point to anxieties arising from status differentiation.

Such an explanation does not, however, seem very satisfactory. There is another factor which must be considered before we can agree that status differentiation with differences in privilege and opportunities for certain types of gratification can create anxiety. This additional factor is whether or not compensations are given the underprivileged for their renunciations. These need not necessarily be of a concrete, real nature; the compensation may be fantastic or illusory. How this factor operates in Trobriand culture cannot be answered from the data we have considered.

We might now look for food anxiety in Trobriand culture. Here the evidence is conflicting. The actual economy seems quite capable of satisfying subsistence needs without much difficulty. On the other hand, food is accorded a high display value, the yam houses are conspicuously placed, and there is evident pride in having enough of a commodity of which there is no scarcity. There is even the denial that food has any value as an essential for life. The natives eat with their backs to each other. But we see no evidence of fear of post-mortem disintegration, and no cannibalism. In short, there is little evidence of actual food anxiety in this society, but considerable evidence that there is some concern about food. The evidence is not conclusive. It may be that food, of which there is plenty, is used as an asset in order to underplay a deficiency in another quarter, or it may be that food is used as a symbolic representation; we cannot tell.

There is one situation, however, in Trobriand culture which merits the closest attention—the family organization and the character of the early disciplines.

In its form the family is quite similar to our own; but the duties, obligations, and loyalties are differently distributed. The in-group is a matrilineal one, backed by the conception that the mother is the sole procreator and that the father has no role in biological parenthood. Hence individuals of one blood, maternal relatives, form the in-group. The economic support, food, and discipline, all come from the maternal line. From the paternal side come all sexual satisfactions, and a kind and friendly attitude from the father. Sexual disciplines do not exist and sphincter control is mildly instituted. Punishments and threats are not used in discipline. Really important discipline does not begin until the individual's resources are quite well developed, when it is the maternal uncle who takes over the role of disciplinarian, and the influence of the father dwindles.

We can easily see from this what kind of an image of the father (i.e., of the mother's husband) is formed; it must of necessity be a kind and friendly picture, because at no time in life, in childhood or thereafter, does the child have the opportunity to associate prevention or restriction with the father, and hence has no occasion for repressed hatred of him. There is no need to submit to disciplines in order to win approval or security. Everything friendly and permissive is associated with the father, all restrictions, sexual and disciplinary, arise from the maternal side. Small wonder, therefore, that such hatreds and hostilities should be directed toward the maternal relatives. The Trobrianders believe that illness is due to sorcery, which is most commonly attributed to the malefaction of a maternal relative. And most significant in this regard is their belief that the child is relatively immune from the influence of magic, which begins to affect them only after puberty. This is testimony to the fact that the child lives in a permissive environment and that he does not begin to have real cause for hostility to anyone until after puberty; and then this hostility must be repressed, because the uncle has a position quite like that of the father in our culture, that of food provider and disciplinarian.

We would, therefore, expect to find in Trobriand society an individual who is strong, self-confident, free from envy, resourceful, and enjoying a high self-esteem. But, while this may be the case before puberty, the evidence indicates that it is not so after that period. There is plenty of envy, and the great sexual freedom of childhood is replaced by a strict monogamous ideal and by a rigid subjection to a large group of sanctions.

The sexual restrictions of childhood concern only the objects (chiefly the sisters), but not the aim. How much hardship this creates is difficult to estimate, because the individual has no restrictions with regard to non-taboo objects. If we take the folklore as an indicator of this pressure, we see that this restriction is felt. The story of the origin of love magic from a plant which grows from the intertwined skeletons of sibling lovers who died in shame, stands in lieu of the usual Oedipus story. The story describes the power of the sanctions against brother-sister incest, and in the place of the paternal rival there is merely the whole weight of a generally held prohibition. This taboo represents the only really serious piece of discipline to which the child is subjected.

If we seek to find hidden sources of anxiety and hatred due to severe disciplines and impositions on the liberty of the child, we see that these are absent in childhood, when the basic adaptations are formed. The ego develops freely, and restrictions do not begin to appear until puberty and marriage.

Nevertheless, there is evidence of a great deal of anxiety, expressed in the form of a fear of sorcery and of flying witches. The existence of women's secret societies from which men are excluded indicates considerable tension between the sexes,[6] and, furthermore, great envy and mutual hostility are evidenced.

Trobriand culture presents an interesting contrast with our own. It raises the question whether basic constellations formed in childhood so completely determine the resources of the ego that the individual is able to handle subsequent problems in accordance with his erstwhile freedom. Let us suppose that in Trobriand culture the child grows up free of the restrictions to which the child in Western culture is subjected. Then, after his personality is completely developed, the Trobriand child encounters serious restrictions on liberties formerly freely enjoyed, and on the opportunities to use those resources which, during development, were free from social obstructions. Can we expect that under these conditions the individual will accept his restricted opportunities without protest? Decidedly not.

[6] Malinowski has never been able to confirm the actual existence of these feminist organizations which subject men to degradations and mutilations. Their existence as a feminine fantasy is nevertheless significant.

Such an individual is under a more serious handicap than one whose activity is restricted from infancy and who has accustomed himself to masochistic adaptations which are socially compatible. But there is this difference between the two: the reactions to the two types of restriction will be different and the cultural precipitates of both will differ radically.

The individual whose expression of biological needs is strangled by social pressures develops a definite attitude to the executives of these disciplines. He acquiesces to their demands in order to conserve other interests, which are to a measure really satisfied. He learns, for example, that if he obeys he is approved and protected. On the other hand, the individual who need not meet these conditions by way of the restriction of essential needs does not form similar basic attitudes of adaptation.

In short, restrictions in Trobriand culture confront the individual after the personality is allowed unrestricted development within the cultural limits. This situation tends to sharpen the conflicts between individuals with regard to advantages they all want later on. The margin between defeat and success thus becomes an extremely narrow one, and there are no reactions midway between the two that are accessible or acceptable. Perhaps it is this which accounts for the efficacy of the sense of shame, and the readiness with which the Trobrianders commit suicide as a result of failure or degradation. It gives the individual a low frustration threshold.

THE ROLE OF FOLKLORE AND MYTH

We come now to a consideration of the role we should assign to folklore in the system of diagnostic criteria. There are two uses to which folklore has been put: as a kind of historical record; and as the expression of the pressure of certain social conditions currently prevailing, on the products of fantasy.

The difference between these two uses is best illustrated by a familiar example, the stories which have the pattern of the Greek tale of Oedipus. Freud holds that this is a combination of a historical event and a biological tendency of man. We can indicate a third possibility, that the Oedipus tale and the complex found in contemporary individuals have nothing to do with the remote past, except insofar as the same type of institutions which created the complex in the remote past still exists in some form today. Nor is it a process of the racial unconscious; but both are produced by the same institutions which are a specific type of patriarchal family organization, operating on a given biological make-up of man. Alter the social organization, and with it the specific disciplines attached, and we create a different ego structure; and hence, theoretically speaking, either no Oedipus tale at all, or a version of the story which bears the imprint of the specific conditions prevailing in a culture.

This does not mean that myths in primitive culture or in our own culture may be interpreted as containing a record of the past, and may therefore be used to reconstruct some theory about social origins. It is an open question whether survivals as such can persist in a culture where they no longer serve any functional purpose. When social organization changes, the basic disciplines to which the individual is subject change with it, and new interests arise in the culture, which these stories must serve. In our contemporary culture such revisions and carefully edited "histories" are constantly in process. It would be safe to credit the possibility that the same process occurs in primitive society. Purely historical and unrevised tales can theoretically exist in a society which has undergone no change, or in a society where written and uncensored historical records exist. Egypt has such written records, but they have not escaped editorial revision. Very often one finds synoptic tales where the layers of change are definitely in evidence.

For a comparison of these two orientations, the historical and that of functional integration, we may review an interesting experiment made by Wilhelm Reich[7] on the basis of material of Trobriand culture and then examine whether or not the folklore of a culture yields material for both points of view.

[7] *Der Einbruch der Sexualmoral* (Berlin, 1932).

or whether these are mutually exclusive. On the basis of current mythology, one cannot reconstruct with any degree of certainty the institutions in a culture that existed in the past. One can trace migrations, diffusion and combinations of certain elements, and can reconstruct historical contacts. This has been done effectively. But the myths in each locality have the stamp of that particular locale.

Reich observes that the brother in Trobriand society acts toward his sister in every way as the husband in our culture, except that he does not have sexual intercourse with her. Sex mores, as we have observed, are sharply divided into a premarital and a postmarital phase, the former being characterized by complete freedom associated with parental approval, whereas after marriage, continence and fidelity are expected and deviation from them is punished. In addition, Reich makes much of the question of dowry, and points out that cross-cousin marriage tends to keep property in the male line.

Reich answers these questions by an ingenious theory of the origin of the mores, especially the one dealing with brother-sister incest. He takes his clue from several origin myths, which he uses unquestioningly as historical evidence. The myth which he singles out is that of the original mother who came out of a hole and gave birth to a boy and a girl who lived together in incestuous union.[8] The girl gave birth to children, and the boy took care of his sister and her children. There was thus originally one clan, one village, one garden, one magic for gardening or fishing, one rank, and one origin. Reich's interpretation is: Originally there were two communal societies organized on a matriarchal communal basis with brother-sister marriage. These two communities were brought into conflict with each other due to the necessity of hunting—apparently in the territory of the other group—or of exchanging goods. Since the women do not come along on the hunt, the men away from their women

[8] The author has been able to verify only the myth that the mother came out of the hole and that the boy and girl were born, but not that they lived in incestuous union. This story accentuates the actual practice that the man is his sister's guardian and her children's disciplinarian.

must be abstinent, and they therefore take the women of the other clan from their original husbands. This is a theory of external imposition of incest taboo. But the marauders compensate the original men with goods. The dispossessed brothers then seek revenge, with the result of mutual murder and great mutual anxiety. Efforts at reconciliation are made, and some regulation of the disturbing situation is effected through exogamy, but with the effort to retain former economic advantages. This is the prototype of the marriage in Trobriand society; exogamic marriage, with the brother working for his sister and her children. The victorious clan retains its victory by enjoying higher rank, and a chief chosen it enjoys polygamous rights. This is the origin of exogamy and patriarchy.

The argument has some plausibility; but it is hard to see what advantage is gained by the new arrangement. The groups now hunt on each other's territory and have relations with the women of their rivals, but owe economic obligations at their original home. It is hard to see who gets the "economic" advantage, the men or the women, and which group. Reich evidently discards any idea of intrasocial rivalry among the members of each clan for the women. According to this system, the man who surrenders his sister must be compensated, and the woman becomes an economic pawn. The fact is that in Trobriand society the woman is indirectly the instrument of economic power, which is notably visible in the polygamous chief, who thus has a call on the economic resources of many men.

It is interesting to note here that similar origin myths appear in other cultures. The Egyptian origin myth is one in point. Thus Khepera, the beetle god, who pushes the sun across the heavens, is the progenitor of all the gods. By an act of masturbation, he creates the twin gods Shu and Tefnut, who live in marriage and procreate Geb and Nut, who do the same, and procreate the gods Osiris, Isis, Set, and Nephthys. The story of Osiris is unquestionably a composite,[9] all characters in the story

[9] See A. E. W. Budge, *Osiris and the Egyptian Resurrection* (New York, 1911), I, 1–98.

having led independent careers before being merged into the Osiris myth. But the interesting point is that a male god procreates parthenogenetically. One can with some justice claim that this creation myth was based on an earlier myth in which the woman was the sole progenitor, and that the myth of Khepera was a "patriarchal" edition of the older story. That may be true; but the meaning of "patriarchal" is very obscure. The increasing importance and prestige of the male must be the result of a complicated series of changes in personal and social values. One cannot, therefore, take myths at their face value. The illustration from Egypt indicates that myths have a functional relationship to the social organization, and when their usefulness is exhausted, they are changed. Without a historical orientation on the relation of myth to social change, inferences about the past are pure guesswork. Anthropologists have demonstrated that myths are constantly undergoing revision.[10]

Reich sees in Trobriand social organization evidence of the mixture of matriarchal and patriarchal patterns. This mixture is nothing unique; it is found in many cultures. The premarital sexual freedom he regards as a survival of early matriarchy, and postmarital stringency as due to the despotic influence of patriarchy. The institution which marks the transition is the dowry by which the man compensates the erstwhile possessor of the woman for taking her away for sexual purposes. Dowry is the original form of goods and capitalism; and the sexual persecution of the child, who is an economic pawn, becomes the privilege of the father. The argument is not very clear. How does the premarital chastity of the woman increase her economic value in a society where the connection between impregnation and intercourse is denied? It is still harder to answer how it increases the value of the male who is subjected to the same persecution. He thus becomes more easily subject to the father's domination. As a matter of fact, this is the practical effect which sexual prohibitions in childhood have, but we question whether the subjection of the child was the original motive; for if it be

[10] F. Boas, in his Introduction to J. A. Teit, *Traditions of the Thompson River Indians* (New York, 1912).

so, the group must have known in advance the effects of this sexual restriction. This is very unlikely.

The trouble with the theory seems to be that matriarchy and patriarchy are accepted as basic power or political orientations in which the essential conflict concerns the relative prestige of each sex. If we accept matriarchy and patriarchy as basic motive influences, we may agree with Reich. If these patterns are end results and not causes in themselves, then we must look for the underlying causes for the change.

Roheim[11] suggests some of the changes of value in the transition. He suggests that property, in the transition from matriarchy to patriarchy, is changed in value from a formal or ceremonial relationship to a practical and erotic meaning. "Erotic significance" of property is an incomprehensible formula. However, if we state that the property has a utility value, that it is to be used directly or indirectly for remote pleasure gains or for enhancing the size and importance of the individual, we can understand this better, and put it to some use. This significance of property would be coincident with certain other social changes, necessitating an alteration in the orientation of the ego to an increasing sense of individuality, a sharper sense of the value of one's attributes in comparison with others. All of this might explain the increase in the sense of the value of property in relation to individuality or in comparison with others, and this in turn has a relation to division of labor, skill, and capacity for work. But it would not explain the necessity for making durable property transmission through the male lineage—which Reich regards as essentially connected with patriarchy—and the introduction of sexual restrictions.

Reich's theory about social origins, as well as others based upon mythological material, cannot be proved unless the accompanying social changes are known. Myths cannot be used to clarify social origins. These tales and folklore are commentaries on current social organizations, and demonstrate attending conflicts with certain qualifications which we shall discuss

---

[11] Quoted by Reich, *Der Einbruch der Sexualmoral* (Berlin, 1932), p. 65.

in connection with Marquesan culture and folklore. It is impossible to determine how much lag there is in folklore, and to what extent old patterns that have actually disappeared in practice are continued in stories. Therefore, the use of mythology as a source from which exact historical reconstruction of the continuity and change of cultural institutions can be made, is, to say the least, hazardous.

In his most recent book, Géza Roheim[12] attempts by a compromise to bridge the gap between ontogenetic and phylogenetic conceptions of society. He maintains with great emphasis the fantasy of social origins as originally proposed by Atkinson and later adapted by Freud, and buttresses this hypothesis with "proof" by analogy. The social organization of higher apes is discussed at great length, and this description strongly supports the thesis that higher apes live in hordes with strong emphasis on the dominance of the more powerful males. The result is that these stronger males preëmpt all sexual prerogatives, to the great discomfort of the weaker males, who are thus condemned to a kind of enforced bachelorhood. These observations can stand on their own merits: however, when they are used to support the theory that human society began in this way, the difficulties begin.

The theory of human social origins is not what creates the difficulty in Roheim's theory: this lies in the insistence that the facts pertaining to these origins are remembered (unconsciously) or perpetuated through myths, and that the guilt of the primal parricide is likewise perpetuated in some mysterious way; and that the evidence for this can be recovered from myths of aboriginal man and the dreams of contemporary individuals.

It is quite new in Dr. Roheim's work to find the following statement: "What is the unconscious material from which the demons are formed? From Uran-Tukutus dreams we already know that they are projections of the members of the family, and we can unmask father, mother, and child in the guise of these supernatural beings. They evidently represent the un-

[12] *The Riddle of the Sphinx* (London, 1934).

sublimated part of the emotional and libidinal relation between members of the family circle" (p. 29) . However, in attempting to evaluate what these tensions between child and parent are he concludes: "We can hardly err in seeking in the primal scene[13] the source of all belief in demons" (p. 31) . In other words, according to Roheim, the effects of these early impressions endure irrespective of any sexual restrictions subsequently imposed on the child, or of the absence of such restrictions. This conclusion is not borne out by clinical experience. Such impressions of parental intercourse are reconstructions at a much later date by inhibited individuals in societies where sexual restraints are severe. If this is the case, how can the dreams or fantasies be used as indicators of social origins?

This Roheim does in the following way: "If we attempt to derive the specific traits of individual cultures from the infantile experience of the individuals who live in these cultures, we must admit the possibility of describing the origin of culture in general in ontogenetic terms, that is, of deriving it from a specifically human form of childhood, from a permanent, universal and at the same time historic, cause" (p. 173) . "There remain however certain elements that cannot easily be derived from the Oedipus Complex as it is played out in the individual family . . . . I refer to myths. The peculiarity of these tales is not that they can be analytically interpreted as more or less distorted representations of the Oedipus situation. They describe the conflict as between *the one and the many,* between the superman and humanity. Moreover they are often concerned with some event in the primeval history of man, with some decisive change, such as the origin of civilization or of a particular culture that is associated with their tragedy" (p. 174) .

In other words, it is the myth interpreted as a record of history which is the link between ontogenesis and phylogenesis. The fact that parents are represented in myths as demons is a representation of a current conflict between child and parent; but the fact that the conflict is represented between a super-man

[13] Primal scene means the observation of parental intercourse by the child.

and humanity—that's history! This is a very arbitrary deduction, not based on any known principle in psychology. One can establish no rule, aside from convenience, about when to use an ontogenetic and when a phylogenetic interpretation.

It is quite evident from the material that Roheim advances that the binding link between present and past is by way of institutions, and not through recollections, unconscious memories, or myths. As the institutions change (i.e., the family organization and disciplines imposed on the child), so do the products of fantasy of those who live under them. There are only a limited number of types of family organization and disciplines in childhood. If this is the source material, then the whole theory of social origins is gratuitous and distracting. It is difficult to work with the belief that characteristics ontogenetically acquired will be transmitted by heredity, when the whole biological organization of man points away from the influence of phylogeny. The thing transmitted is the primary institution; the fantasies resulting from the pressures created by these institutions on the individual do not need to be inherited. Each individual can create them afresh.

It is this latter consideration which makes us pause at the unguarded use of myths and folklore made by Freud and Reich and Roheim. If folklore gives us clues about the current social tensions, we can draw conclusions about "origins" only if we have the complete record of the changes in folklore and myths. Egypt gives us a good opportunity to do this for a segment of its history covering some 2,000 to 3,000 years. But is is another question whether we can use conclusions about Egypt as indicators of what happens in every society. The evolutionists did this, because they assumed the regularity of "evolution." There are psychological considerations which make such regularity highly improbable. If we dismiss folklore as an accurate historical guide, and attribute to it only a functional significance, then we have severed one tie with historical reconstructions. We would even go further than that, and say that folklore may contain elements of history; but that what is historical in it is

of relatively little importance, because the history is distorted
to the use of expressing current conflicts—conflicts of a general
kind created by the existing social organization—but retaining
nothing of the remote past, except perhaps the characters.

The whole question of origins has, through the evolutionary
school, acquired an inflated importance, because the discovery
of origins became an "explanation" of society. By this process
the whole dynamic significance of institutions was overlooked,
and no room was allowed for social change caused by the interaction of individual, institutional, environmental vicissitudes,
and accidents. The particular diagnostic syndromes which the
evolutionists caught are without question important and correct. Matriarchal and patriarchal are two such facets. But these
are only descriptive syndromes and tell us nothing about the
conditions that create them. Hence we cannot attribute to patriarchy as such any motive power. "Patriarchy" is an end-result
arising from a highly complicated series of circumstances. In
other words, taking one of Reich's arguments, patriarchy is not
despotic because of some inherent quality concealed in masculinity, nor are matriarchal societies permissive because mothers
are kind; nor is this likely to be due to the influence of the
concept of "property." There are many other identifiable influences, all dynamically interrelated.

In short, we abandon the quest for origins as an explanation
of society, and substitute for it a study of the dynamic relationship between man and institutions. We can take as a base line
some of these institutions, as specific family organizations and
basic disciplines, and attempt to see what happens as we alter
these conditions. This is as close as we can get to the conditions
of "experiment" in sociology.

Chapter IV

SECURITY SYSTEMS AND BASIC PERSONALITY STRUCTURE

OUR discussion of Trobriand culture did not include enough material to permit much more than to state more precisely the problem of individual and culture. We attempted to use the affect of anxiety as a clinical indicator of the conflict between the individual and the effective external reality insofar as it consisted in the institutions with which he makes contact. Even the most cursory comparative survey of different cultures would show us that this effective external reality is entirely relative.

In regard to impulse control, we found in Trobriand culture a specific problem. What happens when the sexual impulse is unrestricted in its development, but encounters strong obstacles later? We might contrast this with the question, What kind of personality develops when the development is restricted and complete liberty is conferred afterward? The results are certain to be different in the two cases.

In order to make such comparisons, we must establish the coördinates with respect to which the variables can be charted. The variables are institutions composing the effective external reality, and the constant, the biological needs of man.[1] The items to watch in the individual are the internal adjustments required by this effective external reality, the anxieties and frustrations it creates in the individual, the defenses mobilized, the internal psychic elaborations of these, and the types of fantasy life that emerge.

[1] These needs are not so constant either; for the sexual need can be manipulated in a great many ways, whereas other biological needs are much less plastic.

The important thing to note about different types of effective reality supplied by different institutional systems is that each demands different types of adaptation to guarantee the individual security within his own environment. Another consequence is that each type of effective reality creates its own conceptual systems. The concept "father" is very different to a Trobriander from the same concept in our culture because of the actual differences of experiences genetically conditioned and cumulatively integrated.

The security system of the individual can be defined as that system of adaptations which insures the individual acceptance, approval, support when necessary, esteem, and maintenance of status. It demands impulse control and development of resources along specific lines.

The security system of the group can be defined as the activities or attitudes expected of each individual which safeguard the group against dangers coming both from without the group and from within. In the first group belong such different activities as warfare and religion. The dangers from within the group are the disrupting influences of individuals or groups within the society. The security systems vary widely, but, generally, sanctions, compensations, and force are the chief methods of dealing with these disrupting influences which come from within.

Sanctions are the most effective, and are the most important if they begin to operate in the childhood of the individual and thus become incorporated into the personality structure as the individual's effective tools of adaptation. Thus the genetic and cumulative character of human adaptations terminates in making the individual an ally in the perpetuation of adaptations the purpose and function of which he may not be in the least aware.

The following sketches can be used as illustrations of different types of security systems of the group, and different security systems of the individual, in the face of different systems of effective social realities created by each culture.

The Zuni

The Zuni live in a stretch along the Zuni River which courses between the Rockies and the Sierras. Zuni Village has a population of about 1,900. Their environment is a very inhospitable one. The summers are hot and the winters cold, rainfall is uncertain, and floods are very damaging. Sandstorms are frequent and devastating. Despite the poor environment the Zuni have lived by agriculture for over 2,000 years. Hunting has ever been an important pursuit; but this has more recently been replaced by sheep owning, a shift in emphasis from skill to wealth. They use no plows and no animals in agriculture. Food, however, is abundant. They live in houses which are built for defense. The family consists of woman and husband, daughters, and their children. Lineage is reckoned through the mother; the Zuni are matrilineal and matrilocal. The father's social role is distinctly subordinated. Property belongs to the entire group, and land is exploited by the common labor of the men for the benefit of the clan. Marriage is monogamous, but easily broken. One marriage at a time is the rule, and there is no occasion for secret affairs. The woman chooses the man. No one has any stakes in a Zuni marriage. Infidelity is common and divorce easy.

There are thirteen clans of varying prestige. All women in a clan are called "mother" and all fathers' brothers are called "father." The biological father has no particular authority, the latter being altogether a vague concept to the Zuni. The strongest family loyalties are toward the maternal relatives. There is a complete governmental structure copied from that of the Spanish invaders; but it is a mere shell, as no one wants political authority, and there are no political sanctions.

The religion is very elaborate. The chief religious issue is rainfall. The gods and the dead are all benevolent spirits whose chief function is to produce rain. There is no fear of the dead; there are no horrors associated with death. The dances, in which the men wear masks, are sacred magic rites with which to influence the *catchinas* or rainmakers. The dances are magic rites through which the Zuni solicit the gods to meet their needs.

The details about their sex mores are lacking, but in general there are few taboos. There is no premium on female chastity. Initiation rites for the male are mild and are preparatory for enterprise, not punitive as they are in many primitive societies. There is no authority vested in the father, and the mother remains the most stable figure in the community. The role of male and female in this culture is different from that in ours, the mother dominating by her interest and influence. Concerning early discipline it is known only that the child is nursed long and treated very tenderly. The Zuni do not know what punishment is, but they concentrate a great deal on building up a sense of shame in the child. Sorcery is the only crime prosecuted by them.

Now let us evaluate this culture according to the criteria already established. The biological conditions of life—the high fecundity, and high death rate—keep the population constant. Hence no pressure is created from this source for change in economy. The environment, though difficult, yields enough food, but uncertainty of rainfall is a constant and insurmountable source of anxiety. The Zuni technique of mastery is simple, a primitive horticulture that has not changed in 2,000 years, though their economy, as has been said, has shifted in some respects from skill to ownership, i.e., sheep raising.

Their social organization is matrilineal and matrilocal, and from all indications the greatest repression falls on the impulse for mutual aggression. There are numerous instances which indicate that emotions and aggression are generally played down. Their institutions tend to make these traits useless. There is little necessity for competitiveness, or for any form of overt aggression within the group. This does not mean that envy and jealousy are absent. It merely means that the social organization diminishes opportunities for their exercise, and in addition powerful sanctions against their exercise exist. Outside the group the Zuni have plenty of aggression; they are warlike, but perhaps not as warlike as their neighbors. They have ritual dances to immunize from guilt the man who has taken an enemy scalp. There is general communal coöperation, and there are no sanctions to enforce it except the feeling of shame. If we are correct in assuming that in religion we ought to see the resultant of anxieties proceeding from the economy and from intrasocial tensions which need to be repressed, we ought to find here a religion which satisfies few needs; and that is exactly what we do find. It is a religion which satisfies the only anxiety these people have, rainfall. There are no other symptoms of strong intrasocial tensions; there is no fear of the dead, and there are no complicated rituals to placate them. There is no strong and exacting deity or graded hierarchy of gods; there is no suicide, a concept which only makes them laugh. There is no place in their organization where tensions are allowed to accumulate so far as first to suffer repression and then to influence the objectives of the growing ego. Sibling rivalry is taken care of immediately by adequate substitution of a number of mothers. And since in childhood these longings are not repressed, no particular tension is created as a result of a wish for authority, for there is no opportunity to exploit anyone. Authority is diffused. Hence, the adult ego has no particular use for these concepts, and the emotions that attend them are stillborn. The ego has little anxiety to drain. The religion of the Zuni derives chiefly from anxieties related to the outer world, and not from intrasocial sources. Religions are very different in those societies where mutual hostility is great, e.g., Egypt and Greece. However, where the Zuni do vent their aggression on an enemy by scalping, they need an antidote to immunize the offender from guilt. This proves that there is plenty of aggression, but powerful sanctions oppose its use within the in-group.

Their phantom government, with its teeth drawn, is note-worthy. As we have noted, the form was copied from the Spaniards, but in actual practice has no resemblance to its prototype. It has no function; and nobody wants political authority. The Zuni seem to know that authority brings hatred.

We must also note the psychological prominence of the women. From the forlorn attitude of the male and the secret societies of the men, we gather that the society is not only polarized toward the woman, but the child-bearing function of the mother seems to be the object of endless admiration and wonder, and that the men have consequently formed a secondary in-group. The dreams of several women reported by Ruth Bunzel again indicate a basic anxiety, the fear of being separated from the mother, and fear of desertion.

Concerning the intrapsychic forces that maintain the stability of this culture, we again encounter the feeling of shame as the most powerful.

Now there are several features of Zuni culture that we must note very carefully. There is a great exaggeration of value attached to dependency on the mother, a fear of aggression within the group, and a limited ability to exploit the environment. The incompatibility between dependency and fear of aggression or self-assertion is a clinical fact verifiable in any case in which inhibitions or limited resources can be noted. I shall return to this point later, in the hope of getting some clue to the incentives for inventing a more effective technique for mastering the world.

We must note in this culture a new principle at work. The Zuni exerts a repressive influence over all aggressive impulses, even though the organization of his society tends to supply few provocatives for this type of response. These aggressive impulses if exercised, would have a very disturbing influence on the culture. But sanctions of this kind cannot be enforced on the basis of authority, nor even on the basis of the sense of shame. These sanctions must be backed by the positive knowledge of mutual advantages; when it is broken the common security is molested and anxiety is released. The Zuni is, therefore, a society in which the individual is protected by mutual guarantees against isolation, a feeling of impoverishment, ego deflation, humiliation, starvation, and exposure. Hence these people need not have recourse to other means of supplementing the prevailing security, as for example, by wealth or prestige. Wealth accordingly has no significance. Property rights are neither clearly defined nor strictly enforced. Envy or covetousness and many other homely vices surely exist, but to a diminished extent; they are treated as antisocial and cannot gather much momentum or reap great rewards. Property is appreciated as far as its utilitarian value is concerned, but it is shorn of its magical properties to command love and respect for its possessor. Hence generosity is the rule, murder and theft are rare. As one thinks of this culture, one is immediately struck by the absence of the tendency to self-aggrandizement which in our culture seems so natural.

We might compare this latter phenomenon for a moment with one found in our culture, the common objective and goal to be "on top," to surpass, to achieve a position of dominance. This is commonly regarded directly as an instinctual character. It is sometimes called a "self-maximating" tendency. What happens to this tendency in Zuni? Obviously inflation of the ego is not an end in itself. What would be the narcissistic (sexual) interpretation of self-maximation? This has nothing to do with the pride in efficiency or effectiveness which can exist without any self-glorification. Can we formulate any definite ideas about this culture concerning the manner in which those anxieties are put to rest, which in our culture express themselves in the wish for power and wealth? I think we can. The weakness of the individual against the outer world is cushioned by a strong in-group formation in which mutual dependency is recognized. Anxiety about one's helplessness does not have opportunity to gain much momentum. There is no chance for the individual to feel small by comparison. The individual is protected against the typical sibling rivalry conflict, "You suffer less or enjoy more than I do," and inflation of the parental imago is prevented by the device of perpetuating the guarantee of maternal care equally for all. This is what seems to be the effect of the enlarged in-group.

The whole point of Zuni culture is therefore the formation of a powerful in-group, with great increase in security for the individual. The sanctions against mutual aggression can be easily enforced because the advantages to the individual are perceptible, and he can cash in on conformity.

THE KWAKIUTL

Among the Kwakiutl we observe a culture in which security of the individual may be seriously impaired, notwithstanding guarantees of subsistence. The conflicts about prestige can so overshadow subsistence as to render the latter a relatively unimportant issue in the individual's life.

The Kwakiutl inhabit the heavily wooded section on the coast of British Columbia on Vancouver Island. They live chiefly by fishing, as vegetable food is very scarce. The population in 1900 was about 2,000. They live in clans, each of which occupies a village on terraces along the beach. Their abodes are of wood, with rooms arranged according to rank. Their social organization is a mixture of patriarchal and matrilineal features. Marriage is typically exogamic, and sex taboos and disciplines are rigid, though details about such taboos outside of exogamy are scant.

Subsistence is guaranteed by communal labor in clan groups with stringent regulations governing hunting and fishing. Poaching is punishable. Clothing, food, and shelter are the same for all ranks. Food and shelter are the concern of the family by groups, and labor is communal. However, all intrasocial tensions are grouped around the prestige economy, which is entirely distinct from subsistence economy; and this extends to every aspect of their lives except food and shelter. Prestige value is attached to anything and everything, names, privileges, rank. Even membership in the clan must be earned by a very complicated system. There is graded rank, i.e., nobles and commoners. The chief receives twenty percent to fifty percent levy on the subsistence activity of groups.

The tangible prestige values are capital, interest, and conspicuous waste. The Kwakiutl use a currency of blankets and coppers. The conspicuous waste is consummated at feasts called *potlatches*, in which property, blankets, boats, slaves, and coppers are either given away or destroyed by burning. The oldest son is most highly favored and is the recipient of the greatest prestige values. Wealth is circulated by a system of obligatory gifts, which are always returned with interest, and wealth is manipulated much as it is in our culture.

The use of wealth or prerogatives is to shame rivals. The emotional tensions of these people oscillate between uninhibited self-glorification and constant anxiety of being outdone and humiliated. The fear of being seen in shame is so violent that they have been known to bribe witnesses not to notice their shame. Death is a disgrace, and to wipe it out you may inflict corresponding shame on someone else. The idea seems to be "I am not in disgrace, but you are"! It needs but a glance at this social situation to see that intrasocial tensions must be kept at a boiling point, remarkably enough without involving subsistence interests.

Let us examine their religious practices, and see whether these afford any drainage for the pent-up affects created by the mutual hostility, and whether it coincides with what we would expect to find, a typical Oedipal situation of some kind. Though their institutions permit ample opportunity for expressing aggression in unsublimated or displaced forms, even unto murder, through which means a man may acquire names, titles, wealth, etc., their religious practices show deeply repressed anxieties, and methods of draining these. We find here typical Oedipus myths and rituals. Note how these are absent in Trobriand and Zuni cultures.

The following is a typical myth:.

The young hero visits the Cannibal; the Cannibal is away, but the youth comes upon a woman from whom a taproot is growing down into the ground. She advises him how to over-come the Cannibal and gives him supernatural means to do so. The Cannibal returns and subjects the hero to a series of com-petitive tests. The hero wins out, and having killed the Can-nibal, tries to take the woman home with him, but cannot because she is rooted to the ground.

This is a typical Oedipus story; judging from the fact that such myths are absent in the Zuni and Trobriand cultures, we surmise that they are not reminiscences of the murder of a primal father, but that their sources are to be found in social organizations where mutual antagonism is high, and sexual restrictions stringent.

The Kwakiutl pantheon is not well organized; there are a vast number of supernatural beings, including a Salmon Chief and many others.

The initiation rites may be considered part of their religious practices. The initiation into the cannibal society consists of sending the youth away for four months, during which time he becomes cannibalistic. At a ritual séance he runs around in an ecstatic state, biting pieces of flesh out of spectators. There are dances and exorcisms; he remains taboo for four months under food restrictions, and then returns. He is finally tamed of his supernatural possession, and resumes normal life.

Why does this community have to create this drastic ritual? In preparation for what life situation? This ritual affords plenty of abreaction for both group and victim. The novitiate is ob-viously tortured for hostile wishes toward rivals, and must suffer many privations for it. The youth is first sent away, then returned after privations and purifications. The mutual fear of the growing youth and father are manifest, and in these rituals repressed hostilities of both are mutually expressed. Ritual and myths resemble closely those in Western culture, and according to our scheme of criteria represent avenues of drainage for repressed affects accumulated from the intrasocial situation with its intense rivalries, and from sexual and other restrictions.

The social situation here is such that it creates the greatest amount of tension, rivalry, hatred, and desire to excel. Most of the anxieties of the Kwakiutl proceed from these sources, and not from their struggles with nature, which is a complete contrast to the Zuni. No wonder that they are constantly oscillating between feelings of humiliation and megalomanic boasting. This anxiety of humiliation seems to have many expressions, for example, fear of being eaten up, fear of magic, fear of the dead, and fear of degradation.

We have yet to say a word about the external and intrapsychic forces for maintaining social stability. Although sense of shame is inordinately sensitive, sense of guilt seems to be lacking. A person who loses a relative by death can wipe out the disgrace by killing a person of corresponding rank, and even the score by saying, "It is not I who am mourning, but you."

It is interesting to contrast the security system of the individual in Zuni and Kwakiutl cultures. In the Zuni the social mobility of the individual is very free. There are few goals that are not within reach of each individual. In the Kwakiutl there is no such mobility. There the individual is born with a status; the rank in family immediately sets a natural limit to the goal. The oldest son gets most, the youngest gets least. To such younger sons there is possible the achievement of some status by a large variety of competitive efforts.

It is unfortunate that in this culture our knowledge of childhood disciplines is defective, so that we cannot draw any trustworthy conclusions about their influence on personality formation. The cannibal story recorded is an indicator of strong rivalries with siblings and father. There are, in other words, severe obstructions to the free development of the individuals toward goals on which the highest social approval is bestowed. The anxiety expressed in the form of fear of being eaten up is also there; but we cannot definitely establish its significance. Our only guide here is the institutional expression of the importance of face-saving, fear of humiliation, and the socially permitted channels through which status can be achieved, namely inheritance, purchase, murder, and becoming a religious person. The anxiety caused by shame of lowered status can be gauged by the fact that the men bribe witnesses by gifts not to notice their humiliation. This extreme reaction to humiliation by suicide or starvation indicates the terrific tensions lying back of the loss of face.

The contrast of Zuni and Kwakiutl culture moreover, is marked as regards the feeling of security for the individual in relation to in-group formation. The in-group formation in Zuni society protects against loss of self-esteem as well as subsistence needs.

Frustration in Kwakiutl culture probably involves cravings for dependency. This may be the significance of the anxiety in regard to being eaten up, and of the outburst of cannibalistic impulses in the possessed youth. However, since our information about early training is lacking, proof of this point must be deferred until another culture is examined in which this information is available.

It is essential for us to have a complete record of the life cycle of the individual in relation to institutions because we need such a record as a guide to basic constellations set up in the individual. These, if they become a part of the ego organization, predicate in part the formation of institutions. Immediately the hen-and-egg question is raised: Which came first, the specific personality organization or the institution which created it? This is a historical question. But one thing can be stated with certainty: given certain basic disciplines, whatever be the source from which they arise, these will create a definite type of personality which will lead to the formation of institutions according to the need and perceptions of the personality. We shall be able to prove this in cultures where we can better study the mutual relationship between personality organization and institutions. We cannot answer this question in reference to Zuni and Kwakiutl culture because here the information about life cycles and institutional disciplines is defective. One additional conclusion forces itself from this contrast which we cannot observe in our culture; we noted that in our culture, subsistence and prestige values were all mixed together under the general head of "economic." Kwakiutl culture teaches us that "economic" as used in our culture is not synonymous with "subsistence."

CHUCKCHEE AND ESKIMO

Another contrast of security systems is to be found in Chuckchee and Eskimo culture. In the societies we have reviewed there were no really serious problems connected with subsistence economy, though the Zuni have·no small amount of trouble with their subsistence needs.

The Chuckchee are a subarctic people living in northern Siberia. The group under consideration are inland or Reindeer Chuckchee. A population of about 12,000, divided into twelve territorial units, live in about 650 camps, each containing about fifteen people. They live by raising reindeer, which they use for food, clothing, shelter, draft animals, and trade. They do not use the deer for milking.

These animals are imperfectly domesticated and consequently are difficult to manage. The people must accommodate their lives to the cycle of reindeer life. After the breeding season the deer move north to pasture land. The vicissitudes of the Chuckchee depend on habits, diseases, enemies (i.e., beasts of prey) of reindeer; on theft and trespassing on the part of their fellows; and on the hazards of weather, extreme cold and ice. The care of reindeer requires doggedness, strength, and persistence to an unusual degree.

Everyone in this society over ten years of age works; there is little leisure. Because of their particular economy the Chuckchee are nomadic; they do not live in permanent abodes, but in temporary shacks or tents consisting of a single room.

Since ownership is individual and the vicissitudes of reindeer life are highly variable, some will be rich, that is, have large herds, and others, poor. These latter can attach themselves to the richer members of the camp as assistants.

With regard to habits or discipline, information is not complete. Sphincter control is expected at the age of three. The Chuckchee eat their food boiled, but they use no vegetable foods. It is a mark of distinction to be a big and fast eater. They are fond of intoxicants. The most prominent traits of their character are persistence, doggedness, obstinacy to the extent of murder if thwarted, quarrelsomeness, and resentfulness to authority.

The family consists of one husband and one or more wives, and children, the sons living to the rear of the father's house. The family is stable, the other social units are not. The organization is patrilineal and patriarchal. Grown children may, however, leave the household. There is no clan feeling, and one's most dependable fellows are one's campmates. Loyalties follow lines of common interest and not blood ties, though blood revenge occurs for violence to family members. Marriage takes place early, the man serving the bride's father for a time.

Sex morality or discipline seems, in general, to be lax, but information on this point is not accurate. The usual incest taboos exist, but are often breached in the case of father-daughter and brother-sister. There is no word for chastity, and women may have illegitimate children. Rape is frequent and does not carry with it serious punishment, but does incur ridicule. Monogamy is the rule, one-third of the group being polygamous. Marriages are easily broken, especially if a man loses his herd. Romantic marriages are not frequent but group marriage is common. Groups of two to ten men from different bands, friends or cousins, but not brothers, agree to share each other's wives. There is no emphasis on paternity and there is no infanticide.

Childhood is largely an imitation of the life of the elders. Childhood is over at ten, and lazy sons or sons-in-law are sent away. Labor is divided between the sexes. The women are treated as inferior beings and do a great deal of hard labor. The aged suffer the same social degradation here as they do in most societies in which strength, and not skill, is the main attribute necessary for survival. The parents are often killed, or beg to be killed by their sons. Outside the family, murder lets loose a feud which can be bought off. Murder is common; life is devaluated. Suicide is common because of loss of spouse or because of anger. Fear of the dead is inordinate. The Chuckchee cut the throats of the dead, and fear being pursued by them.

We have here a people whose opportunity to exploit the environment is limited, because of climatic conditions. Their economic fate depends on chance, doggedness, and on the vicissitudes of an unmanageable animal. Property depends upon a perishable object, subject to weather and disease. Hence there is a great amount of insecurity which touches both on subsistence and on relative status, prestige, wealth, and poverty. To survive, traits of skill, strength, and hardiness are needed. Since the opportunity for dependency on anyone else is lacking, the people are inhospitable, selfish, stingy, aggressive to an inordinate degree, and resentful of authority. These traits are necessary adjuncts to survival and enjoyment of social prestige, and originate in the inability to be dependent. There is little differentiation of labor, the only distinction being master, hireling, and child.

What is of extreme interest for us with regard to the personality resources of the Chuckchee, is how they think about the outer world. It is important to examine their thought processes—which are typically "animistic"—in greater detail. Their world is dominated by spirits, whom they fear. This fear is expressed as an anxiety lest the spirit get inside of them, crawl into the body, cause disease, and eat it up—this last is the basic fear.

Their religion is shamanism—the individual control of spirits, which are mastered by a technique corresponding to mastery by oral means. No definite origin is ascribed to the spirits, but they are probably the dead or living to whom the individual is most ambivalent. The shamanistic séance seems to be induced by a kind of auto-hypnosis in which the shaman dominates the spirit.

One cannot avoid the impression that this type of mastery over spirits has some relation to the absence of opportunities for dependency; by this we mean that the individual is thrown absolutely upon his own resources. The expectation of help cannot be realized. This fact must drive the individual into a desperate fight with reality, and a hatred of those from whom he expects help and cannot get it. The young can claim it for a brief period, but the aged cannot claim it after their strength fails. Nothing remains for them but to seek death. The economy likewise permits no feeling of security, as it depends on factors that never fall within human control.

With regard to the forces that hold this society together, we must note a paucity of external agencies such as police or government. There is a moderate obedience to disciplinary taboos, and the intrapsychic forces, i.e., super-ego formation, conscience, guilt, are all exceedingly weak. We cannot expect anything else, because the tonicity of the intrapsychic forces depends on the security the individual has in being loved and protected if he conforms. There must be a reasonable expectation that these conditions will be fulfilled, if conscience or guilt is to play any role. Analogies are dangerous, yet it is hard to avoid the impression that this society is organized like a criminal gang, where coöperation for common gain obtains, but emotional relationships are weak.

The basic weakness in this society lies in the fact that neither the economy nor the social organization fosters any high degree of trust. Mistrust is the rule, and the inability to trust in anyone must lead to a deep-rooted suspiciousness, eagerness to exploit, fear of being exploited, grandioseness, fear of degradation, brutal methods of insuring security at the expense of others, and a minimal sense of responsibility to anyone else.

In this society again, we encounter the warning that strong intrasocial hostilities do not arise exclusively from the severity of disciplines imposed on the sexual impulse. Here it seems to have a relation to two identifiable factors: (1) A shifting economy, which permits no sense of control, and in which skill and hardiness do not always reap their reward, and in which no one can take pride in records of achievement—there are not even permanent abodes or records of past accomplishments; (2) their social organization, in which mutual responsibility is underplayed, so that there is no expectation of help, but only the necessity of bowing to fate. No wonder they overemphasize property and cling to it as long as possible. No wonder they are inhospitable and exploit those whose fate is worse than their own and resort to theft and murder. Dependency is even held up to ridicule. To characterize someone as "he who has been helped" is an insult. The repudiation of the idea of dependency is surely making a virtue of a necessity.

We can use their religion and folktales as a check. Their gods are cruel and hostile to humans, whom they devour. There are typical Oedipus stories with a particular slant, in that they emphasize chicanery and trickery to achieve the end of escaping the fate of being eaten up. We must note the absence of exaggerating the properties of gods who will be kind to them if they are obedient. The cruel manner in which the Chuckchee treat their dead, slitting their throats to make sure they will not revive, is another symptom of their strong mutual hatred and distrust.

We can check on the correctness of our conclusion by contrasting this culture with the Eskimo. Here, the "economy" as regards subsistence is even more precarious and uncertain than that of the Chuckchee. Starvation is a more realistic threat, and the vicissitudes of the hunt are much more dependent upon skill. Moreover, large quantities of food cannot be stored. The Eskimo, then, do not have nearly the economic security that the Chuckchee have.

Notwithstanding, we have the same emphasis on skill, strength, fear of dependency, and incompetence. The Eskimo kill their children and elders in the face of starvation. They coöperate to hunt, and divide game according to responsibility in the kill. But they are easy, light, kind, and not hostile. There is ease in the family and in the village, and a high degree of individual freedom. The Eskimo gods take cognizance of sin, recognize guilt, and reward expiation. There is no theft among the Eskimo. Paradoxically the stealing of wives, though a common occurrence, cannot be considered in this category. Women are stolen for definite economic reasons, to demonstrate prowess and as a part of institutionalized rivalry games. The individual suffers no exploitation of any kind by anyone else, and even the socially organized games of humiliation break down easily into general good humoured festivities.

In short, the "economics" as far as subsistence ends are concerned cannot be held exclusively responsible for all ideologies and morality.

The influences of social organization, the basic disciplines, love relationships, and opportunities for dependency make themselves felt in the prevailing types of character formation, religion, and folklore.

Conclusion: Basic Personality Structure

From the contrast of security systems we may attempt to abstract some tentative conclusions about the nature of security within the group; the conditions under which sanctions can or cannot be maintained; the effects of discipline; and the sources of intrasocial hostility. For the time being it is more important to appreciate these concepts and to learn how to follow their interconnections than to be too much concerned over the correctness of our conclusions concerning specific cultures, conclusions which depend ultimately on the completeness of the data submitted to us.

In each of these cultures we noted different types of external reality to which the individual had to accommodate himself, while at the same time we assumed that the biological needs of the individual in all of them must be quite similar. The external reality is of two kinds; that which concerns the natural environment and the specific problems of adaptation that each brings with it; and the institutional system, which in each culture makes such different types of demand upon the individual. The adjustment required by different environmental realities and those created by the mores that govern human relationships must in each culture produce different end results in the personality, such as different thought processes and sequences, and different fantasy life. A cursory comparison of the folklore of Trobriand and Kwakiutl culture shows that each is the product of different life goals, different perceptions of institutional realities, different impulses which must be controlled and different methods of controlling them.

Each culture showed us that the problem of adaptation for each individual (leaving out considerations of sex differences, status, and age) is pointed in specific directions. Some problems of adaptation in one culture create few difficulties, while in another they form the main façade. The problem of mutual aggression in Zuni culture is solved by a rock-bound series of guarantees, which make the exercise of aggression less necessary or less rewarding; whereas in Kwakiutl or Chuckchee culture, the security of the individual depends on the cultivation of effective forms of aggression. In order to maintain equilibrium in each society, the psychic task is different. In Kwakiutl society the individual is up against authority and power; in Zuni, no one has authority, no one can exploit or use another, but notwithstanding this, rigid disciplines exist, which demand impulse control in different places from that demanded in Kwakiutl. In Zuni culture mutual dependency free from burdensome conditions is the claim of every individual; in Kwakiutl, mutual dependency is localized to subsistence needs only; in Chuckchee, it is nowhere available. Chuckchee requires the cultivation of submissive attitudes to insure security under some conditions; in Zuni, they are not necessary under any conditions. Such techniques are a part of the weapons of adaptation; hence it is not remarkable that the Zuni when they are in a helpless state and need to implore the gods for help, will merely implore, and will not institute privations and frustrations upon themselves in order to move the gods to aid them. The mere fact that a people will use such a technique in a helpless state is a proof of its expediency in accordance with their own actual experience. And the only experience the individual can use for this purpose is his own experience with disciplines imposed on him, and the actual gains received in consequence of obedience to them.

In short, the effective reality which the individual confronts and to which he must accommodate himself is created alike by the external physical environment which he must master to satisfy needs for food and shelter, and by the institutional realities which demand impulse control or exercise. The sense of reality which the individual has is determined not only by contact with the physical world, but also by the concatenations and expediencies which are deduced from contact with institutions and their human executives. As it is "logical" for an individual who has learned from the beginning of his life to believe that if he submits to certain arbitrary disciplines which deprive him of pleasures he will continue to enjoy protection, so it is logical for him to deprive himself of pleasure in order to please a deity. Once the relation between impulse control and an ulterior gain becomes experientially established, this syndrome becomes a part of his reality sense—a part of his "common sense."

The case of discipline is, to be sure, an extreme one; there are many other influences of milder character. The withholding of appreciation of a given activity will often discourage its continuation. The case of deliberate discipline is, however, our best illustration. It follows that the earlier these disciplinary influences are established, the more likely they are to dominate the individual's sense of reality. The differences in the cultures we have surveyed can be studied in accordance with the character of the disciplines they impose, the impulses they control, the age at which they are instituted, and the degree of persistence of the social demand for their control.

The security system of the individual depends on how effectively he can conform, and the tax on the resources of the individual depend on how difficult it is for him to meet the conditions. Some are easier than others. A sexual taboo system which involves only sisters is easier than one which involves sisters and every other sexual object and aim as well. Only a Zuni can tell us what special difficulties are created by the necessity to control aggressive impulses.

There are two points about impulse control which are of the greatest importance for the individual and for the group. They are at what time of life the discipline is instituted, and what are the gains or rewards for this control—in other words the social conditions which make such control acceptable.

The first problem we saw illustrated in Trobriand culture; free exercise of sexual impulses (barring females of the maternal line), permits the personality unimpeded growth in the formative years. Then comes a reversal of social attitude after marriage. The consequences of this situation we have already discussed.

The second point, the gains or rewards of impulse control, is one of the most important factors contributing to social stability. From the psychodynamic viewpoint, when, in order to safeguard other interests, an individual is trained to curb an impulse (or rather the manifestations of it) he can do so with comparative ease if the other interests are satisfied. If the latter satisfactions are withdrawn, we can only expect an outburst of aggression of some kind. If the society is so organized as to offer no rewards for impulse control, then this aggression must in itself receive some social recognition. It is no accident that there is no crime or suicide in Zuni, for the provocations are fewer and the gains from repression or control of aggression far outweigh the advantages from theft and murder. No such system of rewards or guarantees exist in Chuckchee, hence we find plenty of crime and suicide. In other words the stability of a culture which demands important impulse renunciations does not depend on a compartment of the mind called the super-ego, but upon those forces in the society which keep the super-ego in line. Where the rewards of impulse suppression cannot be realized by the individual, the super-ego loses its tonicity. This is true not only of those societies where impulse control is instituted early in life, but as well of those where it is instituted later. In Tanala society we shall see an illustration of the deterioration of the super-ego consequent upon the inability to collect rewards of impulse control.

If from all this we wish to extract some general formula about the sources of intrasocial hostilities, we must recognize that this situation is very complex. We can use only a few guide lines which have some universal applicability. Hostility is a symptom of frustration actually experienced, anticipated, or assured by existing inhibitions; from what these frustrations arise and in what form they find expression, must be determined for each culture separately. It is quite true that we can depend on certain basic needs of the human subject, when frustrated, to cause anxiety or hostility. But this guide is not accurate enough. There are various forms of hostility; some of them are overt, others encapsulated. These latter in turn depend not only on whether a given need is frustrated, but also on whether the other available satisfactions are sufficient to prevent these shunted hostilities from breaking their bounds. In other words, instead of looking for isolated frustrations as sources of effective hostility, we need to look for a satisfaction-frustration balance which can be maintained under some conditions and upset under others. In general, the balance lies between restraints and rewards, prohibitions and permissions, satisfactions and frustrations. Furthermore, there can be no absolute or universal yardstick about what constitutes a frustration; the frustration threshold of the Trobriander, who is raised on a high level of satisfaction during the formative years, seems very delicate when compared with that of the Eskimo. This frustration threshold was recognized by the first man who commented on the sufferings of the millionaire who was "down to his last yacht."

Thus far we have considered the security system of the individual. But this security system is only one part of a larger unit which is important for us to identify—the basic personality structure of the individual.

Environmental conditions and some aspects of social organization included under the term primary institutions create the basic problems of adaptation for the individual. To these he must develop certain methods of accommodation, because they are fixed and unchangeable conditions. Food scarcity, sexual prohibitions, disciplines of one kind or another are conditions which the individual cannot directly control; he can only take an attitude to them and accommodate himself according to an array of patterns which have some variety. The basic constellations in the individual created by these conditions are his ego structure, subjectively considered, or his basic personality structure, objectively considered.

The ego structure is not, however, an organization with unlimited possibilities. It has a tether. It is tied to the biological nature of man and to his phylogenetically determined characteristics. If the external conditions and basic primary institutions vary in different cultures we may expect that ego structure will vary also. Common sense confirms this conclusion. It is taken for granted that a Zuni is different from an Eskimo. If one were to ask the average man why he thinks so, he will correctly observe that these two people have lived under different conditions. It is the task of social psychology to dissect this practical observation of common sense into its constituent elements. Common sense, however, gives us another practical judgment, not on the difference between Zuni and Eskimo, but on that between two Eskimos. The average man knows this fact from experience with individuals in his own culture; he knows they are all of different character; and to this fact our average man takes a very practical attitude. These observations of common sense are correct, but not accurate enough.

These two concepts of ego or basic personality structure and character are seemingly overlapping concepts; in reality they are not. Character is a special differentiation of ego structure arising within it. Ego structure is a cultural precipitate; character is the special variation of each individual to this cultural norm.

In the survey of the cultures we have presented we cannot study character, because we are not dealing with specific individuals. But we can study basic personality structure. Under this heading we can include:

1. Techniques of thinking, or idea constellations.
2. Security system of the individual.
3. "Super-ego" formation. A "super-ego" based on obedience to discipline will be different from that in a society where the child is not punished. In the latter we may find its only manifestation in a sense of shame, without guilt or conscience.
4. Attitudes to supernatural beings (religion). The techniques used to solicit aid from the deity are indicators of the relations to parents.

Several questions on ego structure immediately occur. What place does status differentiation have in this category? A king and a commoner may be on opposite sides of a certain situation with regard to subsistence or prestige. But the roles of both are merely different facets of the same ego structure. The character of each may eventually be very different because the higher status may confer important immunities from certain training. The king may be in a position to persecute, the commoner to be persecuted. Yet both are reacting from different polarities to the same ego situation. The same holds for sex and age differentiations.

Ego structure or basic personality is important for us to understand if we are to understand secondary institutions; for they are derived from the constellations created in the ego structure by the basic effective realities. We might ask, for example, where did the idea of embalming originate? Where does the idea come from that the way to create a god is to feed him human victims to be cannibalistically incorporated? Is it not from an anxiety created by food scarcity, at least to start with, although the institution may persist with a new meaning after the original anxiety which provoked it has disappeared? One may ask in connection with this hypothesis, what about diffusion or the contagiousness of certain institutions? No incompatibility exists here. In any given culture in contact with another, only those traits are diffused which create no serious incompatibilities or may even be helpful to the existing basic personality. The Zuni adopted their governmental form from the Spaniards. But they adopted only the form, not its spirit or character, because it created too many incompatibilities with the Zuni ego structure. They had no conception of the use of authority as a weapon to exploit anyone. This characteristic was not diffused.

The concept of basic personality structure thus becomes an important tool in our research. It is qualified to act as a mirror of the institutions which helped to create it as well as the adaptive weapons of the individual once it is established. This concept obviates the hopeless task of dealing directly with biological forces within the individual, and confronts us with the finished products of the interaction of biological forces and external realities. Such end results are the only forms in which we ever get to know "instincts" or drives. Thus if we encounter in the folklore of a society a constellation like the Oedipus complex, instead of leaping from this phenomenon directly to some biologically determined drive, we can proceed to examine the conditions in the actual experience of the individual which contribute to the formation of such a constellation. As conditions vary, so will the basic personality structure. This latter concept lends itself, moreover, to empirical and comparative methods. The only alternative is the hypothesis of Freud, which is to be discussed at length in a later chapter and which assumes that such a constellation as the Oedipus complex is a biological datum. The maintenance of this hypothesis is, in turn, contingent upon the untenable assumption of the inheritance of acquired characters.[2]

[2] The origin of Freud's position with respect to this problem dates as far back as 1896–1905. During this time Freud was occupied with the problem of tracking down a specific etiology of neurotic symptoms. His clinical researches led him definitely to the study of the sexual development of man. In considering this development Freud had some definite coördinates: he knew that there was a defensive process which he designated as repression; he also knew that there were repressing forces operating in the individual, though at that time he did not come to grips with their precise nature. It was in his attempt to deal with these repressing forces that Freud made a crucial decision, the influence of which is still present in his latest work. He did not consider that the actual life situations were responsible for mobilizing these repressive forces in the individual. In *Three Contributions to the Theory of Sex* (New York, 1910), p. 38, he states ". . . this development (of loathing, shame and moral and aesthetic ideation masses) is organically determined and can occasionally be produced without the help of education. Indeed education remains properly within its assigned realm only if it strictly follows the path sketched for it by the organic determinant." His later ideas about the super-ego were also dominated by the assumption indicated. He attributed the operation of these repressive forces chiefly to phylogenetic or organic influences. Actual life situations and education were influential only in touching off phylogenetically predetermined patterns. It is partly the task of this book to show that the introduction of the actual institutional realities as a prime factor in mobilizing repressive forces in the individual leads to different interpretation of facts so accurately noted by Freud.

Part II

DESCRIPTIVE

This part deals with the application of the principles arrived at in Part I to two aboriginal cultures described by Dr. Ralph Linton.

Chapter V

MARQUESAN CULTURE

By Ralph Linton

THE Marquesans are a Polynesian people living on a series of islands in the central Pacific about ten degrees south of the equator. Physically they were, and are, an extremely fine group. They resemble South Europeans, although they are somewhat flatter as to nose, fuller as to lips, and darker in color —about the shade a South European becomes after a summer on the bathing beach. The men average from five feet nine to five feet ten inches tall, with splendid muscular development; the women are outstandingly handsome even by European standards. Because of their isolation, however, they have developed little resistance to disease and fall easy victims to the contagions introduced by the whites.

Although the Marquesans have been under French domination since 1842, they were among the last of the Polynesian groups to become Christianized. They drove out missionaries and resisted white influence as long as they could, but at the time of my visit in 1920–22, Marquesan was already a broken culture. It was possible however, to reconstruct the conditions of the old days from the accounts and reminiscences of old men still living in the islands.

When the Marquesans were finally forced to submit to white domination, they adopted the only means of dignified and effective resistance which was open to them; they ceased to breed. This was a perfectly deliberate measure, the people preferring extinction to subjection. I visited many villages populated entirely by persons of early middle age to old age with not a single child in the group. On Tahuata, the island next to the one on which I was living, there were over two hundred deaths for every birth.

Environment and Economy

The Marquesas are a series of high islands, very rugged and mountainous. At the Western end of Hiva Oa, a cliff, straight as the wall of a house, rises from the sea to a height of 2,000 feet. The natives believe this to be the place from which the spirits of the dead leap off to the bottom of the sea, whence they travel eastward to Hawaiki, the mythical land from which all Polynesians came. At the top of this cliff lived a single priest whose duty it was to watch this leap and presumably say farewell to the ghost as he passed on to the next world. The priest kept records of each death and birth by means of a long cord, tying a knot for each birth and untying a knot for each death, thus keeping a sort of informal census for the group.

The islands have no coastal shelf; the coast goes down with no barrier reef, making fishing difficult and dangerous. The interior of the islands is extremely rugged, consisting chiefly of sections of blown-up volcanic craters with peaks four to five thousand feet high. Many of the larger islands have never been traversed even today. The coast is made up of narrow valleys cut off from one another by ridges so high and steep that in many cases one can get from one valley to another only by sea. There is considerable timber in the valleys and also on the slopes at the eastern ends of the islands. The uplands are covered by a growth of low ferns, across which one can see for many miles. There are a few ironwood trees, but most of the high country is open and waterless.

Since the islands are only ten degrees south of the equator, the climate is warm, with little seasonal change. Being north of the trade winds and consequently devoid of seasonal rains, the islands are subjected from time to time to long and destructive droughts, which lead to serious crop failures and even to shortage of drinking water, as the streams go dry. This state of affairs has had considerable effect on the life of the people. In good seasons there was plenty of food; but one of these droughts, which might last as long as three years, used up all the stores of food and caused genuine starvation; sometimes it drove the natives to hunger cannibalism. A severe drought of this sort could cut the population by a third.

Agriculture was practiced under difficulties because of the steep slopes, very little of the land being level enough for irrigation by the crude native methods. The staple crops in other Polynesian countries, the taro and the yam, were of very little importance here. The Marquesans were dependent almost entirely upon the tree crops—breadfruit, cocoanuts, bananas—and on sugarcane. Another important crop was the paper mulberry, a domesticated tree with very long slender stems from which the natives made their clothing. These tree crops required no intensive cultivation. When a child was born, the father planted a breadfruit tree and a cocoanut tree for the new addition to the family. These trees would provide the child with food as long as he lived. All trees and gardens were individually owned and inherited. A certain right of eminent domain was invested in the chief, but he was hesitant to take a garden from even the lowliest native for fear of retaliation through magic.

In good years there were four breadfruit crops, the first of which was gathered communally. When the fruit was ready for gathering, the chief sent out messengers announcing the event; everyone turned out to gather the crop, which was cut up, fermented, and stored in great communal pits hidden outside the village so that they would not be discovered in case of an enemy raid. The pits were enormous; I have seen some as much as twenty feet across and twenty feet deep, cut into rocky soil. The pit was lined with leaves, and the breadfruit paste was wrapped in packages which preserved it so well that it never became too old for consumption. The entire yield of the first crop went into these large pits, which were opened only in time of famine. The second crop was similarly preserved, but was stored in the household pits. There were no rules governing the second harvest; each household put down as much as it wanted. In good years the breadfruit harvest was more than enough for everyone, and in a run of good years the pits would be kept full. Considerable labor was necessary at the time of the harvest, but in the intervals there was little agricultural labor, and the men fished and amused themselves as best they could.

The concept of property was very strongly developed and all objects were individually owned. At the same time there was recognition of the paramount rights of the group, whether family or tribe. When the interest of the group was thus involved, one might not hold out property without committing offense. Land was administered by the chief for the benefit of the tribe, but trees and crops were individually owned. Until the crops were gathered in, each man retained his individual ownership, but as soon as the goods had been brought into the house, they belonged to the family and were prorated by the household head as needed. Although everyone was well aware of the ownership of every object, wealth was concentrated in the hands of family heads and eldest children, who became, theoretically, heads of the household from the moment they were born.

Agricultural property was vested not in land but in trees or gardens, which might be scattered all over the valley, a circumstance which caused considerable confusion when the French tried to take over certain land. The natives were ready to give up the land but claimed the trees. Birds and a few wild pigs furnished the only game on the islands. The wild boars were ferocious beasts, and were hunted in a manner which was a test of sportsman's courage. The boar was driven down a mountain path on which the hunters would wait, knife in hand, to attack the animal as it charged.

Domesticated pigs, although not an important economic asset here, deserve special mention. Since a pig had to be fed on the same sort of food as human beings and in the same amount, keeping a pig was equivalent to adding another member to the family. A pig, therefore, was not simply a pig, but a pig plus the food and labor that his care had involved. His importance was ceremonial rather than practical. These animals were considered essential to all rites of adoption, marriages, funerals, and various other feasts. The place which the head of a household achieved in the next world was directly dependent upon the number of pigs which were sacrificed at the commemorative ceremonies held for him some time after his death.

Chickens were of little economic importance. Eggs were never eaten; the fowl themselves served as food only occasionally, and were never included in the menu at important feasts. Cocks were valued chiefly for their iridescent feathers, which were used for headdresses and much prized.

Fishing was the main source of flesh food and was highly organized on a common basis. Each tribe had its sacred place for fishermen with a shrine and a master fisherman, who was also a priest. His duties included proper care of the fishing gear and images, and the keeping of the taboos which surrounded the fishermen during their time of service. At this period the men lived in a sacred enclosure which women were forbidden to enter, and no man could have contact with women or with anything made by women during this time.

The fishing canoes were individually owned, but the catch was divided on communal lines. The first fish were set aside for the fisherman-priest and the special gods; after that, what remained was prorated among the population. Shell-fishing could be engaged in by anyone at any time, but big fishing was always communal. Single canoes were warned against going out alone, for some fishing banks were ten or twenty miles from land, and a single canoe could easily be cut off by enemies. Most of the fishing was done with giant nets which were let down between the boats. The big fish, rays, shark, etc., were harpooned and were an important article of diet, although the flesh of the rays was so strong that it had to be hung up for days before it could be eaten. Turtles were highly valued and, for sacrificial purposes, were considered equivalent to a human captive. Surplus fish were either sun-dried or salted. The Marquesans, unlike the other Polynesians, attached a tremendous value to salt and combed the rocks around the cliffs for it.

Mention should be made also of kava, a narcotic drink made from a root, which was chewed up, usually by the boys and girls, as they had better teeth than their elders, spat into a bowl, and fermented. Its effects were mild. The drinker became extremely sensitive to sounds or disturbances, and desired to be let alone. Kava parties were not convivial affairs; the participants after two or three cups of kava each, settled back comfortably and talked very little. Since there was very little land on which the kava root could be raised, the drink was a luxury and reserved for the household heads.

The last item in connection with food is cannibalism. In the old days the Marquesans were vigorous cannibals, and from my talks with the old men who had indulged in the practice, I am convinced that, while there was ceremonial cannibalism, there was also eating of human flesh because they found it good. This is one of the few regions where women were permitted to eat human meat. Although there was eating of enemies because of revenge obligations, there was also plain meat-hunting of enemy tribes for food, especially at times of food shortage. Another indication that cannibalism was not merely ceremonial is that these people ate everyone from infants up. The purpose of ceremonial cannibalism is to absorb the good qualities of the individual one is consuming, but the Marquesans had a preference for children too young to have attained admirable qualities. There were also stories of man-eaters, people who developed a pathological fondness for human flesh. Such a man would kidnap children of his own tribe or even kill and eat his own wife or children. There was ordinarily no cannibalism within the tribe, although in times of extreme famine an inspirational priest might designate certain victims who would be killed and eaten. Sacrifices to the gods were not eaten, the idea being that the entire individual was left to be consumed by the gods. Revenge victims, however, were always eaten.

Famine was a constant and entirely unpredictable threat. The fear of famine resulted in a tremendous value being placed on food. Marquesan eating habits and everything associated with food show the effect of this periodic shortage.

At the age of ten every child went through the ceremony of sanctifying the hands; after this, he could prepare food for himself and others. The cooking and eating were done in separate houses set twenty yards or so from the main dwelling. No one ever ate in the dwelling house or near the food-storage house. Food for men and for women was prepared separately and even cooked at different fires and in different utensils. Most foods were eaten by both men and women, although there were some food taboos for women. There were a number of permanent taboos on food; certain foods could not be eaten by persons in certain occupations; taboos were imposed for several months before a feast, largely to insure bountiful provision for the occasion. A family head might taboo the crop from certain trees in preparation for a betrothal or other ceremony. However, taboos on specific foods were not highly developed. This may have been due to the periods of famine, when such taboos would have seriously interfered with survival.

The social value of food is reflected in many ways; first, in the regulation about its use, and again in the tremendous elaboration and decoration of the various objects used in connection with food. For example, the breadfruit pounders, made of rock and weighing from one and a half to three pounds, were usually carved in a design of human faces. The labor of such carving was enormous, as the stone was very hard and the only thing available to cut it with was the teeth of rats. To carve the top of a pounder would take all a man's spare time for six months. Similarly, the utensils from which food was eaten, the cocoanut cups and containers in which spare food was stored, were carved with extreme delicacy and elaboration, for the Marquesans were artists of a high order.

Food was kept in a special storehouse mounted on posts and taboo to women. Food was one of the few things subject to theft; members of the same family would steal food from one another, but nothing else. The high value placed on food was clearly shown in social observances. Every form of social advancement was linked with some ceremony involving a feast. The natives took delight and pride in the amount of food produced at these feasts, sheer bulk being more important than the delicacy of cooking or preparation. Taboos would be placed on perhaps two of the staple foods, so that no one could eat them for months, and there would be a great accumulation by the time the taboo was removed for the feast. The family would starve themselves for weeks in order to fatten the pigs for the event. Even tribal wars were suspended when a feast was imminent. Neighboring tribes would be formally invited to join the festivities. An enemy never attacked if he knew a feast was in preparation. After the feast, however, when all were beginning to suffer from indigestion, fights were very likely to flare up, and the visiting tribe often had to run for home.

The Marquesans had the belief, common to many primitive peoples, that certain types of illness were caused by the absence of the soul. Their method of restoring the lost soul was another testimonial to the importance of food in this culture. The *tuhunga* (medicine man) built a small house, in front of which he placed food saying, "Soul, this is for you." The soul, unable to resist the lure of food, returned to the house and was snatched by the waiting *tuhunga* and returned to its proper place. He usually had many scratches to show for his struggle with the lost soul.

There was plenty of timber and bamboo on the islands, but stone suitable for implements was irregularly distributed. The Marquesans' material culture was extremely rich, perhaps the richest in the Polynesian area, characterized by a tremendous amount of decoration and elaboration of detail. A primitive craftsman, carpenter, or canoe maker would have half a dozen adzes, each for a special use. A tattooer would have in his kit ten or fifteen bone combs of different sizes for making various designs. The people took delight in fine craftsmanship and great pride in perfection. A master worker enjoyed much prestige.

There was sharp sex distinction in the manufacturies, women being of minimum importance. They could make mats, baskets, fans, and bark cloth, but only about fifteen percent of the articles used by the tribe were made by women. A man could use mats or baskets made by a woman, but he could not wear bark cloth that had been made by a woman not related to him by blood. Even a wife was barred by this taboo, so that when a woman did make bark cloth, it was for the use of her brother or nephew, not her husband. This was the only place in Polynesia where the natives had no decoration on their bark cloth; they merely dipped it occasionally in saffron to dye it yellow. All the women's handiwork was similarly crude and simple.

The men's work, in contradistinction, was of tremendous economic importance. All the production of food, with the exception of gathering shellfish, done by both sexes, was men's work. Men built the houses, made the cooking utensils, did their own cooking, and not infrequently cooked for the entire household. In short, men were in complete charge of the economic situation.

MASTER CRAFTSMEN

The institution of master craftsmen was saliently characteristic of Marquesan culture. All men knew how to make everything that they needed, but the degree of skill differed and there was great respect for experts. The master craftsman was a person of importance and had the opportunity to accumulate wealth.

At the upper end of the scale of master craftsmen were the house and canoe makers, who were also organizers and directors, and the artists, who were master carvers. These *tuhungas* worked mostly on order; they joined the employer's household, received food during the time they were working on a job, and were presented with a liberal gift on departure. The *tuhunga* could afford to be temperamental, for because of the peculiar religious sanctions, no other man could carry on a job which one man had started. If the builder quit in the middle of a job, the employer would have to start all over from the beginning with another craftsman. A part of the *tuhunga's* training was the learning of the chants that accompanied the creation of any object. A food bowl made without the proper magic ritual would be just a bowl. It would have no real place in the universe and consequently no value. Thus a man brought in to finish an uncompleted job would be able to tell where the other builder had left off in the actual construction of the house or canoe, but he would not know what magic had been used or how far the ritual had gone, and therefore would be unable to proceed with the task.

The magic chants were in part a formula for the work, so that if a man knew the charm he could not forget the process, but the ritual was also part of an actual creation, beginning with the genealogy of the universe, building step by step, and finally calling upon the essences of the things to make their contribution to the art of creation, which was regarded as a sexual act. By the aid of these spiritual powers, the craftsman built the object into the universe.

The rank of *tuhunga* tended to be hereditary, since a father was likely to teach his craft to his son, but it could be attained by anyone with skill. However, one had to pay for the privilege of studying under a particular master in any one of the crafts, and of being approved and graduated by him.

The prestige attached to skill was present in all occupations and at all social levels. Even the chief would be proud to be classed as a *tuhunga*. The chiefs regularly maintained carvers and other master craftsmen as members of their households, the fact that they were rich enough to do this contributing to their prestige.

DISTRIBUTION

As to technique of distribution, everyone had free access to all materials within the tribal territory. There was no personal ownership of fishing banks or hunting places. However, as certain things occurred only in certain territories, various tribes specialized in particular occupations, such as canoe making or carving. The products were distributed by means of a thoroughly organized trade in the form of social visits with gift exchanges. A tribe specializing in yellow dye would arrive with canoe-loads of the stuff. These expeditions were led by the chief, who was accompanied by perhaps one hundred men. They would start with a formal social gathering, during which sexual hospitality was usually extended to the visitors. Then the cargoes were presented. No mention was made of payment, but just before the visitors left, they would suggest indirectly that there was a shortage of a certain commodity in their tribe. Their hosts would then beg them to accept of their surplus of this commodity. The exchange was carried on with mutual benefit but no attempt to drive a shrewd bargain. Although a few objects might be brought for personal trade, the main load of the tribe's specialty was owned by the chief, and private individuals could not use any of it for trade purposes. Trade was organized by the chief, but at the close of the transaction, the goods would be prorated to all members of the tribe. Individual surpluses were exchanged on a quite similar basis, care being taken to eliminate the profit motive in all cases. These trade visits were still going on while I was in the Marquesas, although they had become of little importance.

Imperishable property, such as weapons, carvings, tools, and ornaments, was constantly changing hands, but the objects retained their names and individuality in the transfer. Gift exchange was as essential to social prestige as the giving of feasts. There is no question that, by primitive standards, the Marquesans were a wealthy group. All the early explorers made mention of the great number of things they had in their houses, rows of weapons, carved bowls, mats, etc. The explanation lies in the fact that they had a great deal of leisure, which they employed in making things. These articles were accumulated and handed down.

The Marquesans had a high standard of comfort. Their beds were the most luxurious to be found in the South Seas. The entire rear half of the houses, which were often fifty or sixty feet long, was given up to the beds. The bed had a foundation of springy brush, cocoanut fronds, ferns, and layers of grass, on top of which were placed woven mats. A polished cocoanut log running the entire length of the house served as a pillow. These beds were softer than many European beds, and the natives loafed on them when they had nothing else to do. They also built sloping back-rests on the stone house platforms so that they could sit there in comfort and watch everything that went on up and down the street. Clothing was unnecessary in this climate, but the Marquesans made elaborate ornaments for festival wear.

An ambitious, skillful man could use the leisure periods between harvests to create a surplus through craftsmanship or pig tending. However, if one was not ambitious, one could spend his leisure time loafing, singing, playing musical instruments or games, and, even to a considerable degree, in sexual play.

ATTITUDE TOWARD OBJECTS

There was an amazing degree of individualization of objects among the Marquesans, everything being personified. Just as each individual was a distinct entity in his tribe, so every axe or food bowl or canoe was also a distinct entity and had a name. The same names were given to objects as to people, the names for weapons being taken from ancestral names of the owner's family. All canoes were given names, and a house not only went through the process of creation, but was hung with a loin cloth so that it would be decently clad when occupied.

It is difficult to say just how much the natives actually believed in this personification of objects. A properly made object achieved greater prestige value with use. A club which had killed three or four men had a tremendous amount of *mana;* the more *mana,* the greater the distinction of the weapon. The people had a sense for heirlooms; old objects which had been handed down had more value than new ones, even though the new one boasted finer carving. Sacred objects, if carried away, had the power to return to the tribe. Objects might be clad but they were never fed; the nearest approach to this being the attitude toward the war canoes. When such a craft was initiated, it was launched over the body of a victim, a rite which was supposed in some way to make the canoe stronger.

The practice of naming was carried to still further lengths. An important person, a chief or an inspirational priest, had distinct names for the different parts of his body, ten or twelve different members being named, the most honorable names being attached to the genitals. This practice held for both sexes.

Name exchange between friends was common. In such exchanges the personality of each participant was fused with that of the other. When together, each addressed the other by his own name. When a native killed a man, he had the right to use the dead man's name, which he frequently did, especially if the victim was more important than the killer. The weapon with which a man was killed might also be given the name of the victim.

Master craftsmen were sought in name-exchange relationship by people from other tribes, and consequently had considerable freedom of movement. A *tuhunga* frequently had several *enoas*, or blood brothers, often in other tribes. When one was *enoa* with a man, one had equal rights to his property and stood in the same relation to his relatives as he did.

SOCIAL ORGANIZATION

The basic social units were the tribe and the household. There was no clan organization within the tribe, which was in theory an extended relationship group, all of whose members traced connection with an original ancestor, either through actual descent or by adoption. Family lines and ties, aside from those between child and mother's brothers or father's sisters, were rather loose. Mother's brothers and father's sisters were the individuals to whom the child looked for sponsorship in all ceremonies, his relationship to them being closer than that with his own parents. On the other hand, his mother's sisters or his father's brothers were outside the picture and had no particular functional relationship.

Within the tribe, great attention was paid, at least in theory, to descent. All the Marquesans prided themselves on long genealogies. It was not unusual to have genealogies traced back for sixty to eighty generations, though these earlier ancestors were usually gods or legendary figures. However, authentic genealogies for twenty-five generations do exist and can be checked with the accounts of other Polynesian groups, in cases where the ancestors have migrated from other islands.

In theory, social rank was determined by primogeniture; that is, by descent through eldest children, irrespective of sex. Failure to realize this fact has made much trouble for some students of social organization in Polynesia, who have attempted to build up a case for patrilineal or matrilineal descent. Marquesan society was primogenital, but in a small group of this sort other factors entered in. There were rarely more than 1,000 members in a tribe, each related to the same remote tribal ancestors through half a dozen different lines. Since the Marquesans traced descent through the parent of highest standing in each generation, there was always some point in the line of descent at which one of the ancestors was higher than a contemporary ancestor of some other individual. Genealogies could thus be used to justify actual social relations. The various households went up and down in social prestige and position, and household heads selected which of the possible relationship terms they would use on the basis of which was superior or inferior. Because of the in-breeding, it was always possible for a person actually on top to find a line of descent that was higher at some point than any other line.

TRIBAL ORGANIZATION

The tribe was a strictly localized group, all of whose members had a common ancestry, at least in theory. Adoption was considered the social equivalent of birth. In spite of the rivalry among various households, the tribe had an elaborate internal organization and presented a united front against outsiders. There was considerable contact with members of other tribes, under conditions of truce at feasts, trading visits, etc. The natives knew all the outstanding individuals from other tribes and had accurate information as to their activities. The Marquesans were cautious in making blood brotherhood with members of other tribes, each man trying to secure an *enoa* whose status was as high as or higher than his own. But in spite of the wide knowledge of one tribe by another, the relations between tribes were always at least covertly hostile, and wars flared up from time to time.

The tribes were sometimes fused by marriages or adoption between families of ruling chiefs, but such unions were uncertain for some generations, at least until a number of similar bonds had been established between the households of lower status on both sides. Other households, particularly those with long-standing blood feuds, would often try to prevent such unions. For example, I heard of a case in which an intertribal marriage had been arranged, but another household of high status in the tribe, who had an unsettled feud with the bride's family, killed one of the men escorting the bride to their village, thereby breaking the marriage contract and keeping the feud going. This household had several revenge victims coming to them before the score was settled, and did not intend to allow things to be settled peacefully.

Each tribe, like each household, had a physical center. This community center was rated as part of the chief's household establishment, and although used by the entire tribe, was considered his property. The central feature of this community center was a huge feasting place and dance ground called the *tohua*. The building of this structure entailed an incredible amount of labor, since many tons of rock had to be moved in. The *tohua* was often three to four hundred feet long by forty or fifty feet wide, and might be built up twenty feet high on the lower side. In the center was a level floor for dances and exhibition of food; all around this was a series of platforms which were assigned to the various classes of the population as grandstands. Attached to the regular *tohua* would be, first, the altar platform, which was the seat of the ancestral gods; then a seat for the chief and his immediate family, and after that the platform for the priests, that for the *tuhunga*, and that of the warriors, a large affair having a permanent house which was taboo for women; lastly, there were a platform for women and children, and a big platform for visiting members of other tribes. A new *tohua* was usually built for the eldest son of the chief, an act which raised the status of the chief's family and the tribe.

The tribe also had one or more sacred places in the hills which were used for human sacrifices and for the final disposal of the dead. There were also the sacred place of the fishermen and the great food pits. All this property belonged to the tribe, the fact of tribal membership entitling anyone to its use.

THE HOUSEHOLD

The Marquesan household was polyandrous, there being usually two or three men to one woman, while in the household of the chief there might be eleven or twelve men to three or four women, one head wife and subsidiary wives. Well-to-do households would usually add one or even two wives to the establishment some years after the initial marriage of the household head. All members of such a group had sexual rights in each other, the arrangement constituting a sort of group marriage. A chief or head of a rich family would sometimes arrange a marriage with a young woman because she had three or four lovers whom he wished to attach. The men would follow the woman; in this way the family head could build up the man power of his household. Only the poorest households at the lower social levels were monogamous, and there was much envy of rich households by poor ones.

Household, rather than family, is the proper term for the basic social unit of Marquesan society. Households were graded in prestige. The basis of the grading rested primarily in man power; the more active adult males the household had, the more it could manufacture, the more work it could do, and the more wealth it could accumulate. There was not much prestige, however, in a mere hoarding of wealth; it was conserved only to be expended at the time of big ceremonials, when the total wealth and the amount of disbursement at feasts were important factors in determining the relative prestige of various households.

There was a consistent attempt to make hereditary the higher prestige status, but the groupings never became rigid and the various households in reality were always going up or down on the social scale. Social rank was concentrated on the eldest child, through whom the whole household attempted to raise its position. Although the eldest child inherited the status of the household, if this was not maintained by feasts and ceremonies, some other household, working hard together for advancement, would raise their position and outdistance the older and better-established group. Since there was a good deal of vertical mobility for the household and also for the individual, social classes were not fixed.

The household had an elaborate physical establishment. There was a large sleeping house with magnificent beds. The house, which was quite perishable in itself, was erected on a stone foundation; the larger the stone used, the greater the prestige of the family. The house platforms of prominent households would contain rocks weighing two or three tons, which were worked into platform walls and often had to be lifted by sheer man power to an elevation of four or five feet above the ground. The size of the stone thus advertised to all the world the number of men that the household could call upon to help in its house-building. In theory, a new house platform was built for the eldest son shortly after he reached puberty, when he was getting ready to take a wife. At that time all the men already in the household and all their relatives would work on the house.

Near this dwelling house, but at ground level, there was a separate house for cooking and eating. Cooked food, being non-taboo, was kept away from the house so that it would not injure the *mana* of the house or its inhabitants. There was also a storehouse for food and for taboo objects. This was usually elaborately decorated, raised on posts, and set at some distance from the main dwelling. The old men past sexual age spent much of their time here, very often sleeping in the storehouse. The storehouse was taboo to women, and young men could enter only after a considerable period of sexual abstinence.

There was also, as part of each household establishment, a sacred place. Sometimes this was a small house on a high platform, sometimes only a curtained end of the sleeping house. The sacred place was used in connection with the treatment of the dead, and for keeping ancestral skulls and sacred objects. The dwelling house and storehouse were elaborately decorated with carvings on the posts and dyed sennit laid on in elaborate patterns on the rafters.

This establishment, representing a considerable outlay of labor, was inherited by the eldest child, unless the household was rich enough to build a new establishment for the heir. Even if the eldest child was a girl, she might inherit the household; there are numerous cases of women who became hereditary family heads, although households frequently adopted a boy for this position. The younger children had none save occupational rights in the household, although they did own the trees which were planted for them at the time of their birth.

The eldest child of either sex, or the child who was adopted to take the position of the eldest, became the official head of the household from the moment of birth or arrival. One is struck by the fact that in the Marquesan myths the story of a man always ends when his first child is born; after this event, he drops out of the picture and the saga continues with the adventures of the child. Of course, in practice, the father administered the household group until the child reached maturity, but socially the child outranked his father from the moment of birth.

The household consisted of the main husband, the wife or wives, and a series of subsidiary husbands. Even with plural wives the men in a household far outnumbered the women. The numerical disparity of the sexes on these islands was puzzling. The Marquesans swore that they did not practice infanticide, yet the ratio of males to females was about two and a half males to one female. It is probable that they did away with the younger girls but kept the practice from cultural notice. The motive for this is hard to ascertain, but it is reasonable to suppose that the group were merely breeding up to their food resources. In good seasons they had more food than population, the surplus being used to fatten pigs; but for bad seasons, when food was scarce, it was necessary to keep the population down by limiting the number of child-bearing women.

The average household consisted then of a household head, a group of other men, and a single wife. The second husband outranked the other subsidiary husbands and took charge of the household in the absence of the head. He also exercised preferential sexual rights with the wife, either with the first husband's permission or during his absence. In the chief's establishment all the husbands would have certain sexual rights with the chief's wife, but when there were a good many husbands, they lived in another house and were called over at the will of either the chief or the wife and rewarded for good service by a night's pleasures. In theory, all members of the household had sexual rights; even servants had access to the head wife if she so wished; actually, the first husband ran things and distributed favors, although it was to his advantage to see that his underlings were sexually satisfied, so that they would work for his house and not wander off with other women.

The household also included the children of the women, either real or adopted, and old people. The Marquesans were perfectly familiar with all the phenomena of physical paternity, but they simply did not count it in their social system. Questioned about his parentage, a native would say, "So-and-so is my real father, but the head of my household was Such-and-such, son of—" and go on back through the genealogy of the head. Even in the polyandrous households a woman always knew who the actual father of her child was, and presumably the head of the household also knew, but was not especially concerned about it.

When a man came into a household, he brought no property except his trees and a few personal possessions, but he shared in the products of the household and worked with the other husbands under the direction of the household head to accumulate wealth to raise the status of the group.

Only younger sons became subsidiary husbands, except in cases where a family was so poor that it could not give its eldest son a good start; he might then attach himself to the household of a chief or a wealthy family. There was no fraternal polyandry, brothers always attaching themselves to different households. A secondary husband could secede if he so wished and join another household. He could even set up a separate establishment of his own if he could accumulate enough wealth for the purpose, but this was difficult since the household head had a claim on his work.

The first-born child was really a symbol through which the status of the household was raised. A series of ceremonies was held in his honor from birth on, the size and expense of these ceremonies determining the prestige of the household. Adoption of a child from another household to take the place of the first-born, if there was no son, was a very expensive proceeding, involving a large exchange of household goods and pigs and the giving of feasts. Adoption of a first-born really fused two households into one, a fact which raised the prestige of the eldest child and, through him, of the group backing him.

The formal betrothal and marriage of the first-born with a mate from another household entailed still more elaborate property exchanges. It is interesting to note in this connection that except where the ceremony was used for purposes of social elevation, there was no formal marriage; the eldest son merely took, without ritual, the woman he wanted as wife for the establishment.

When a line which had been building itself up over several generations had wealth enough to rival the chief and was moving toward chiefly status, the chief often avoided conflict by marrying the daughter of the rising household, if first-born, to his eldest son, or else by adopting the eldest son of the other household to be his heir. The chief, in order to preserve his dynasty, had always to keep a weather eye on these rising families.

When the chief adopted the eldest son of another household, the child naturally moved into the chief's establishment. However, the activities of his original household were still focused on him. No other heir was set up by the latter and in time the household dissolved. The former family establishment was abandoned and might be left standing empty for generations. Occasionally some family would take up residence in an abandoned house, but such persons were considered squatters, for a household which had not built its own house had no social status. As a result of this attitude, the Marquesans spent the greater part of their time building house platforms. There was an amazing collection of stonework scattered about. One was seldom out of sight of abandoned house platforms in the valley, a fact which testified, not to a large or shifting population, but simply to the necessity for building a new house for the eldest son whenever the household group could afford it.

These adoptions and marriage alliances, which marked the rise in the status of the household and fixed new rank, required wealth, as did the proper ceremonies to maintain the child in his new position. Families were constantly trying to raise their status, which could be done only by accumulating and dispensing wealth. Man power was the outstanding requirement; the more adult males there were, the better off was the household. Since there was also a certain amount of feud and blood revenge even within the tribe, a family strong in man power could in such affairs triumph over a weaker household. Consequently the household welcomed a new man. The man's attachment to the household was voluntary, and persuasion was required to win his allegiance. The wife was very definitely held out as a lure to attract men to the household, so that the household head sought to get a woman who was beautiful and sexually desirable. Only the eldest son had rights in the household into which he was born; a younger son had to attach himself to some other household, and naturally went to the one where the woman was most attractive to him. The handsomest and most sexually skillful girls were sought in marriage by eldest sons, for the sexual attraction of the women promoted the prestige and power of the household.

The head of the household had authority as an organizer but as he was socially outranked by his eldest son from birth, he could not prevent secondary husbands from leaving at any time that they considered themselves ill-used. The effective power lay in the hands of the woman, since by the distribution of sexual favors she controlled not only the head husband but all the subsidiary husbands. In the ordinary household, where the head had simply picked a woman without formal ritual or gift exchange, she could leave at any time she wished. The wife made practically no direct economic contribution to the household. Her job was to please the husbands. After a woman had passed active sexual age, she would take up certain simple manufactures. The woman who was herself the eldest child had a most enviable position. She owned the establishment and ruled openly, calling husbands at will and dismissing them if they displeased her. The head husband in such cases was merely the wife's deputy, who ordered the household according to her wish and direction.

Very little authority was exercised over children, and practically none over the eldest who, as has been explained, outranked the parents. These infant family heads could do practically anything they pleased. In the valley of Puamau, I once visited the local chief, who had a boy of eight or nine. When I arrived, the chief and his family were camping in the front yard, and the boy was sitting in the house looking both glum and triumphant. He had had a quarrel with his father a day or two before, and had tabooed the house by naming it after his head. Until he lifted the taboo, no one in the family could enter the house. The family were thus uncomfortably camping in the open until the child could be persuaded to lift the taboo and allow them to enter the house again.

The child's strongest attachments were to fathers' sisters and mothers' brothers, who were not members of the household. These were the people who stood as the child's sponsors in all ceremonies, and received a large proportion of the gifts distributed at the time of the various ceremonies marking the promotion of the child from one age status to another. There were few formal claims on the child for loyalty or assistance. He was under no obligation to the people who looked after him, and even when he grew up, his relatives made little claim upon him beyond expecting him to aid in case of a blood feud. There did not appear to be any very close emotional attachment between the child and the adults of the household. Children were respectful but indifferent toward their mothers; they seemed much more interested in the males of the household.

Social Grading

The tribal organization centered in the chief, who was both administrator and a symbol of the group. There was constant mention of the genital organs of the chief, which were given names indicating their vigor and size. The chief presided at all the great ceremonies, but had no priestly duties and never officiated at sacrifices. He did not go to war because of the extreme danger to the tribe's prestige if he were captured. He had the right to impose taboos in preparation for feasts and also to announce communal activities. For example, he set the time for the fishing parties to go out, and when the first bread-fruit was ripe, he summoned the group to the harvest by having his servant blow a blast on a trumpet. In case of dispute, the chief did not administer justice. All that he could do was to intervene through his messengers, announcing which side he would back. When the chief gave backing to one side, the other usually withdrew and the dispute died down.

The chief's household was of the regular type except that it was larger than the others, usually having extra wives attached to it. Honored visitors would be received into the house and extended the privileges of the head wife. A chief kept craftsmen in his household all the time; some were attached permanently, others were accepted as members of the household while working on an assignment. The household also included messengers, executives, and servants. On rare occasions, as has previously been observed, a woman might be the tribal head.

Next to the chief, and at times ranking above him in the social scale, stood the inspirational priest of the dominant tribal god. When inspired, he outranked everybody else, but, of course, inspiration was sporadic. He was usually a close relative of the chief, generally a younger brother, and was chosen for manifestations of possession. He held office for life. When he died, his successor would be possessed by the god. Occasionally a woman would be possessed; but man or woman, the inspired individual was almost always from the chief's family. There were, however, occasional cases of authentic possession by members of households other than the chief's, which were nevertheless accepted by the group. Beneath this highest inspirational priest were a number of other priests who belonged to lesser gods. These might be either men or women, their importance depending on their inspirers.

The higher inspirational priests were usually heads of households. The authenticity of possession by an important deity in the case of a secondary husband was likely to be questioned. A candidate for the priesthood was taboo while possessed. The higher inspirational priests could seize servants by thrusting a staff between their legs and telling them to follow. This demand was made in the name of the god; if the man refused, he was cursed and might die.

In addition, there were the ceremonial priests, who were always male. They had no claims to supernatural powers but were specialists in dealing with supernatural things. The main ceremonial priest took charge of all ceremonies, saw that rituals were properly performed, and had final disposition of the dead. He had a number of assistants, who were divided into different ranks, the one next in line succeeding the main priest on his death. To become a ceremonial priest required many years of training. The candidate had to learn the rituals, chants, genealogies, creation of the universe, etc. Anyone could become a ceremonial priest, but the post tended to be hereditary. It was a well-paid profession. The ceremonial priests were called in to instruct the eldest child in the ancient lore. At such times younger children could sit in and learn also, but the more esoteric knowledge was given privately. The social rank of these priests was uncertain. Many of them were household heads, and were in demand as household members as they were well paid, and consequently a financial asset to the family.

Below the priests ranked the *toa*, the important warriors. These were high in prestige but did not outrank the *tuhunga*, or skilled craftsmen. A good warrior had to take at least one head, and therefore the *toa* tended to be troublemakers and to stir up wars. The *toa* and the *tuhunga* together formed the council of the chief, though the household heads also sat in. There was no formal calling of the council. Toward evening everyone would drift over to the assembly place; perhaps the young people would start a dance; the older ones would sit and talk; questions would be thrashed out, and at the end of the evening the point would be settled. An agreement would be reached without anyone, even the chief, putting forward a vigorous opinion. The chiefs, in spite of their power, were never oppressive, for there was the constant threat of other strong households, and if the chief became unpopular, allegiance would be shifted to another powerful household head.

All positions except those of ceremonial priest, war leader, and *tuhunga* were open to women, although a woman of high status usually had to be an eldest child. Sex lines were not sharply drawn, and a girl was even sometimes adopted as a first child. This was usually in the case where two families wished to unite their lines. Primogeniture and skill were more important than sex in determining social status. The high status of women, it should be noted, was out of proportion to their economic importance.

Life Cycle of the Individual

The state of pregnancy brought additional prestige to the woman. At this time she exercised control over the head husband as well as the secondary husbands. He became subject to various taboos as she became pregnant. I did not discover whether or not intercourse continued after pregnancy began, but there was no idea that the child was fed by the father through the act of intercourse. The father had to stay near the mother to protect her in the latter months of pregnancy. Both parents had to observe certain food taboos.

Deaths during pregnancy and labor were frequent, which occasioned much anxiety and speculation among the natives. They believed that the deaths were caused by malevolent magic or possession by evil spirits. There was also not infrequent occurrence of feigned pregnancy, which was undoubtedly of neurotic origin and may have been motivated by the desire on the part of the woman to exercise the privilege of control over chief and secondary husbands that went with the state of pregnancy. When the feigned pregnancy failed to materialize it was believed that the child had been carried away by the *vehini-hai* (female ogres) or that a *fanaua* was responsible.

During the latter stages of pregnancy the household head was required to stay near the house to guard against evil influences. When the birth was due, a small house was built for the delivery, sometimes on the house platform, sometimes at a distance. If the birth took place in the regular dwelling house, the house would be considered defiled and would have to be burned. The father assisted at the birth if necessary. There were no midwives, for it was believed that malevolent spirits were present at this time and women were afraid to go near. In extreme cases, the man would massage the abdomen, or get on top of the woman, holding her by the shoulders and pressing down to facilitate the birth. Immediately after delivery the mother severed the umbilical cord, biting it off or working it off with her fingernails. The father then took the afterbirth and buried it in a wet place, for if it were buried in a dry place the child would not thrive. The mother then took the child to a stream and dipped it under the water three or four times. The average stream, it may be remarked, ran down from the mountains icy cold. The mother next bathed herself, and immediately after this, the household head had intercourse with her, the idea being to restore the uterus and other organs to their proper position. (This was also done in cases of prolonged menstrual bleeding and was considered a prophylactic measure undertaken for the sake of the women, though menstrual blood was considered unclean.) The child was then fed with chewed shrimps and cocoanut milk. No swaddling clothes were used. The infant was simply laid on bark-cloth, not on the bed but on the stone floor inside the house. The bark-cloth was changed from time to time as needed.

The child was bathed twice a day up to the age of three or four years, after which bathing was less formal since the children were in and out of the water all the time anyway. Marquesan children often learn to swim in shallow pools before they can walk. The natives are unable to imagine anyone being unable to swim. There have been cases in which whites were allowed to drown simply because it never occurred to the natives that the men couldn't swim and that the fuss the unfortunate whites were making was anything but a joke.

At the time of the birth a feast was given, at which the household head was presented with a pig in recognition of his service in donating the child. He was supposed to eat the entire pig himself. The relatives closest to the child, that is, the father's sisters and the mother's brothers, had their hair cut at this time, the shorn locks being made into a set of ornaments, a shoulder cape or a kilt, decorations for knees, ankles, elbows, and wrists. The fully equipped male in full regalia looked somewhat like a poodle. The hair was handled by professional curlers, being wound on tubes, wrapped in fibre, and baked. The child did not wear these ornaments during infancy. For special state occasions before the age of puberty, the heir would be dressed and decorated, but, ordinarily, children of both sexes went nude.

Adoption was extremely common even in ancient times. That of first-born children, as a method of fusing family lines and avoiding competition, has already been mentioned, but younger children were also adopted into younger child status. Such children were often asked for before they were born and the request could not be refused without causing serious insult and possibly a blood feud. The child was usually transferred to its new household at the age of two to four months and its real parents were expected to make the adoptive parents a substantial gift to cover the expense of rearing it. Such a transfer would terminate the nursing period. Many women are said to have objected strongly to this practice and it is one of the reasons ascribed for the dropping birth rate during the early period of European contact. The natives could control birth through their knowledge of perversions and mechanical abortion and women were often unwilling to go through the trouble of producing children when they knew that these would be taken away from them. Since the rearing of children was largely in the hands of men, the effect of this custom was to emphasize still more strongly the role of women as sexual objects, minimizing the importance of their reproductive functions.

The Marquesans believe that nursing makes a child hard to raise and not properly submissive. There was probably a certain amount of nursing, dependent upon the will of the mother, but in any event the nursing period was very short. Women took great pride in the firmness and beautiful shape of their breasts, which were important in sexual play. They believed that prolonged nursing spoiled the breasts and consequently were reluctant to do it. Feeding times were irregular and dependent on the convenience of the adult rather than the protests of the child.

I saw only one small infant during my entire stay in the Marquesas. It must have been about six months old, but I never saw it nurse. The feeding process was brutal. The child was laid flat on its back on the house platform while the mother stood alongside with a mixture of cocoanut milk and baked breadfruit which had been made into a thin, pasty gruel. She would take a handful of this stuff, and, holding her hand over the infant's face, pour the food on its mouth. The child would gasp and sputter, and gulp down as much as possible. Then the mother would wipe off the child's face with a sweep of her hand and poured on another handful of the mixture.

There was no particular effort at anal control for small children until they were a year or so old. The adult merely changed the bark cloth on which the child lay. Later the child might be picked up, carried a short distance, and held out to perform its functions. With adults the excretory functions were private; they usually sought retirement in the bushes. I have no data on thumb sucking beyond the fact that I never saw any child doing it. Nor did I ever see any of the postural attitudes common to European children who show embarrassment in the presence of elders by sticking their thumbs in their mouths. (The men smoke moderately but there is no chewing of gum or nuts as a form of mastication pleasure. I have, however, observed men sucking the breasts of women when it was evidently not a preliminary form of sexual excitement.)

From birth on, the child was never alone. The small child was under constant threat from the female ogre spirits, *vehini-hai*, who are supposed to steal small children and eat them. As the child grew older and began to wander, there was the additional danger from cannibals. If enemy raiders did catch a roving child, he was certain to be eaten or sacrificed. Children under four years were not tortured but if offered as sacrifices were simply strangled and taken to the sacred place in the hills, where they were hung up with hooks through the mouth and offered to the gods in this way.

The child, then, was under supervision all the time, usually by the secondary husbands. The man would go about his work, keeping an eye on the infant. The child was played with occasionally when the adult was not too busy, but there was no constant attention. The child found early in life that it got nowhere by yelling, for if the adults were busy, they just let it cry. However, if the child became too troublesome, an adult might quiet it by masturbating it. The masturbation of female children began very early; in fact, from the moment of birth there was systematic manipulation of the labia to elongate them, as elongation was considered a mark of beauty.

There was little discipline, and as has been said before, no discipline whatsoever for the eldest child. There was, however, constant danger from taboo infractions, the supposed dangers from ogres, and the real danger of cannibals. The terror which adults felt when a child got out of sight was genuine, and, of course, strongly affected the emotional response of the child. The child was not intimidated or coerced, but it was impressed upon him that if he wandered away, he would be in constant danger, from which only the adult could protect him. The supervision, however, was of a rather diffused sort. The danger stressed was not in being away from any particular person but in being alone. No economic responsibility of any sort was imposed on the child before puberty. The child was not taught any arts or crafts, but led an entirely carefree existence.

When the youngsters were eight or ten they began to form into gangs. Both girls and boys were in such groups; more boys than girls because of the before-mentioned sex ratio. The unit was vaguely defined, and was composed of children born within three or four years of one another, with occasionally younger children active enough to keep up with the gang. The group usually remained together until the members began to marry and settle down. There was a tendency for these gangs to gather about the eldest child of a chief or of one of the more important families. This leader, who might be either a girl or a boy, dominated the group. From the age of ten on, children were largely independent of their households and families. The older gangs were familiar with the taboos and dangers and could look after themselves. They spent most of their time fishing and raiding plantations for food when they were hungry. There was no wanton mischief or deliberate vandalism; they simply amused themselves. A child might be away from home for two or three days on one of these gang expeditions. The children did whatever they wanted to do. When hungry they went to the nearest house and were fed; at night, since every house had a bed at least thirty feet long, they were accommodated wherever they chanced to be when night fell.

Leadership in the gang was based on ability, so that often a particularly strong and active girl would be the leader. There was not much fighting among the children, but when a fight did break out, the girls were quite capable of taking care of themselves. Marquesan children had extraordinary self-confidence and composure. On one occasion I visited a valley where white men rarely penetrated. I paid a call upon a particular household to which I had an introduction through native friends of mine. I called a greeting at the door of the house and was met by a little girl of about five. Although she had probably never seen a white man before, she welcomed me with perfect composure, explained that none of the elders was at home, but invited me into the house, spread out the proper mat, sat down, and entertained me graciously until her elders arrived. This fine feeling for the social graces, which was typical of the Marquesans, was also observable in the life which the children led among themselves away from the adults. They seldom played group games of any sort, but they danced and sang in imitation of the elders and also copied the occupations of the elders for their own amusement. These children were not *kaioi* or members of adolescent bands; they did not become *kaioi* until after puberty, at which time the whole gang passed into the *kaioi* stage together. When the group married, they tended to become members of the same households, as they had formed attachments for one another and had had considerable opportunity to become accustomed to each other.

Sexual play was a regular practice among the children from the earliest period. The adult attitude toward it, if not one of active encouragement, was at least that of mild amusement. Intercourse was frequently witnessed by the children in the dwelling and also at the periods of license which followed the feasts. Regular intercourse began before puberty with patterns of group sexual play, two or three girls in the gang serving a number of boys in rapid succession with the other boys looking on. Occasionally there were individual affairs. Sexual techniques were learned through imitation of the adults. Masturbation in childhood was inducted by the parents; whether it was practiced afterward in the face of opportunity for intercourse, it is impossible to say. Homosexuality was present in the form of mutual masturbation, but I have no data as to its frequency. The gap between adults and children was such that it was impossible for an adult to win the child's confidence. Relations between them were amiable but entirely disassociated.

Clothing was assumed shortly before puberty. The eldest child was clothed for ceremonial purposes from time to time from infancy onward. I heard of one small boy, an eldest son, who left his family in a huff because they wanted him to wear a loin cloth to a ceremony. Later in life the clothing, so far as males were concerned, was mainly decorative. The decent costume for males was to have the foreskin drawn over the glans and fastened beyond it with a thread wrapped around and tied. Thus attired, a gentleman was properly clothed, but if the thread slipped, it was a case of indecent exposure.

Young people between the age of puberty and marriage formed a group known as the *kaioi*. Readers familiar with

Polynesian literature will recognize immediately the resemblance of this to the Tahitian *arioi;* the words are cognates. The Marquesan group, however, was not a formal secret society and was limited to individuals within this age bracket. These young people were the principal entertainers for the tribe, being called upon to sing and dance at all ceremonies and feasts, for which they received liberal rewards. From time to time the *kaioi* would go on tour, performing their dances in the villages of other friendly groups. These trips would be announced as visits to the eldest child of the local chief, but were really planned in order to show other groups what fine dancers the *kaioi* were. The dancers would be feasted and given gifts after the entertainment.

The costume of the *kaioi* was elaborate, particularly that of eldest children, who were resplendent in hair ornaments, ruffs, anklets, etc. Their bodies were dyed a bright red, their barkcloth garments bright yellow. The young people, the girls in particular, spent hours on bleaching processes. The Marquesans had discovered a preparation which removed most of the skin color. The girls would paint themselves all over with this stuff, sit in the shade until it was completely dry, then wash it off in the stream. They emerged from this process with skins as light as those of South Europeans, but exposure to the sun brought the color back in a day or two and they would have to start bleaching all over again.

The *kaioi* dances usually concluded with sexual exhibitions reminiscent of the modern Parisian peep-show. In addition to this, the girls of the *kaioi* group were expected to entertain visiting males sexually, and they took great pride in the number of men they could satisfy in an evening. Except for taboos in the case of siblings and parents, there was complete sexual license among these young people.

Instruction for the child did not begin until late in the *kaioi* period. Of course the children picked up plenty of things informally, but there was no regular instruction in arts or crafts until the child was in his late teens. The eldest children were instructed in chants and genealogies by the ceremonial priests; during the teaching of the more esoteric lore, both teacher and pupil were under rigid taboos. There was also an informal kind of teaching by the ceremonial priests. The young people would come to a priest in the evening and ask him to teach them a chant. He would ask them which one they wanted; the youngsters would name a chant. The priest would pull out his string record, a series of knots tied in a long cord sometimes woven into a basket shape, the knots representing the stanzas of the chant. Girls and boys learned the chants together in this informal fashion. The boy, about the time he was tattooed, began to study to be a *tuhunga,* ceremonial priest, or a member of whatever profession he chose.

A small ceremony was held for girls at the time of their first menstruation. At this time the girls would go to a particular place long associated with the family line, where the ancestral spirits were supposed to come. First menstrual blood had to be buried in a sacred place to prevent loss of vitality in the girl. There was no ceremony for boys at puberty, but at the age of ten or twelve, a superincision was made; that is, the foreskin was split along the top. This was a group operation including all boys who were old enough for it, not necessarily all members of the same gang. In the case of the eldest child of an important family, some slight ceremony attended the operation.

Girls were tattooed at about ten or twelve years of age, before they became *kaioi.* Tattooing was not regarded as a puberty rite for either males or females. The Marquesans explained that they did not tattoo until after puberty because the process of growth would spoil the design of the tattooing. The girls were tattooed individually with no special rites, although a daughter of a chief or a rich household might be taken to a sacred place for the process Women were tattooed from the waist down, and on the arms and hands, with a series of markings above and below the lips, and with a design behind the ear. The breasts, body, and back were left unmarked. A small feast was given after the tattooing of a chief's daughter, at which the girl danced on a raised platform in the *tohua* (tribal assembly place) to exhibit her new decorations.

The boys were tattooed in groups, with an eldest son of a chief or rich household acting as sponsor. The father would collect food in preparation for this event, and at a given signal the *kaioi* group to which the boy belonged would raid the father's house, carrying off all the food and occasionally other things, though as a rule the household carefully put away everything except the food. The father also had a special house built for the tattooing of his eldest son.

The tattooer started on the most important victim, tattooing a square foot at a time; before resuming the operation, four or five days were allowed to elapse for the skin to heal. During these days the tattooers worked on the other boys in the group so that they all were completed at about the same time. The extremely painful operation was done with little combs made of bird or human bone set in a handle. The instrument was tapped into the skin with an ironwood mallet, and then the pigment was rubbed on. There was profuse bleeding. The victim was allowed to yell as much as he liked under this operation, in fact he took pride in the noise he made and in the number of other *kaioi* required to hold him quiet so that the tattooer could work accurately.

A tattoo artist took great pride in his skill. No preliminary marks were made on the body to indicate the design. In learning the craft the novice would use bamboo cylinders as pattern boards to give him experience in throwing his curves properly, or he might induce some individual to let him practice on him. He had to pay a small fee for this, for if the work was poor it would be a social disability to the victim later on. The tattooers sang a chant as they worked; it was principally a repetition of the theme, "How beautiful this is going to look, how well I should be paid for such fine work."

The tattooing of the boys was a labor of some weeks, during which time the entire *kaioi* group was fed by the father of the principal boy. When his stores began to run out, the boys were fed by their own households. All male tattooing was extraordinarily complete, the entire body, even the eyelids, being covered with intricate patterns. The chief had more elaborate hand tattooing than ordinary men and his toes were decorated, too. There were various markings for the face which were probably of tribal significance. I once saw a man who had the crown of his head beneath his hair tattooed. It was not infrequent to have the mouth tattooed right up to the gums and on the tongue—not to mention more sensitive portions of the anatomy.

The first tattooing was done in the *kaioi* period, but when a man was about thirty, particularly if he was a great warrior, he would have himself gone over again, at which time all the blank spaces in the design were filled in. Tattoo designs came out indigo blue in the young and bluish green in older people so that old men were often completely green. Not to be tattooed was to be indecently naked.

When the tattooing was completed a feast was held at which the newly tattooed boys exhibited their decorations. The girls attended this ceremony also, and at the close of the festivities put on their own dance. Instead of dancing naked as usual, they wore for this occasion full pleated skirts, which they lifted during the final song to expose their genitals. However, all sexual play was prohibited at these feasts, the girl's gesture merely indicating that the end of the *kaioi* period had come and that it was now time for the young men to choose mates and settle down.

Girls were instructed in sexual matters from an early age, trained to swing their hips and walk in a provocative way, and to assume postural attitudes which were highly charged with sex. There was extreme development of erotic technique, both sexes taking genuine pride in their erotic skills, which they discussed without reservation. It was taken for granted that almost any chance meeting between young persons of opposite sexes would, unless they happened to be siblings, result in intercourse. The girls began their dances completely attired but finished in complete nudity, with the expected results. At the close of the feasts, particularly when visitors were present, there would be multiple copulation in public, the women taking pride in the number of men they could satisfy before tiring. One nice old woman boasted that she had once taken on the entire crew of a whaleboat and had been able to leave them all happy. Under such circumstances, however, the woman rarely had more than one orgasm.

In addition to these public affairs, there were, of course, many private ones. These involved even more elaborate forms of sexual play, with the woman definitely dominant, and the man playing up to her erotic wishes. His role was to excite the woman by sucking her breasts and cunnilingus until she was excited to a high pitch and gave the signal for intercourse. These erotic preliminaries were quite devoid of tenderness, and often involved scratching and biting on both sides. The sexual play was apparently of greater importance than the actual orgiastic experience.

All Marquesans were sexually potent, but the potency of the woman was dependent upon these elaborate preliminaries, without which it was impossible for her to have an orgasm, a trait not uncommon in primitive societies and due perhaps to early conditioning in prolonged inorgiastic play. I never heard of a case of impotence among males, nor were there any stories of malevolent magic being used to produce loss of potency, although magic was used against men in other connections. The absence of this belief is fairly accurate proof that the phenomenon of impotence was unknown.

The natives never revealed the identity of their partners when discussing their love affairs. A man once told me of an experience he had had with a woman who was so slow in reaching the pitch of excitement necessary for intercourse that he had broken away and refused to continue. The woman thereupon attacked him savagely, biting and clawing; it was to explain his honorable scars that he told me the story. He seemed to consider that the joke was on the woman, but refused to tell her name.

I heard of no cases of female homosexuality, which would

indeed seem unnecessary in Marquesan society. There was some homosexuality among males; pederasty, however, was rare, the usual form being mutual fellatio. There were occasional cases of transvestites who assumed the woman's role and sometimes entered the household as subsidiary wives, though they never became head wives and were held in considerable contempt.

The erotic skill and attractiveness of women had considerable bearing on their social status in mature life, as the most desirable girls would be chosen for head wives in important households. The women had a great deal of social mobility, since a man picked his wife on a basis of sexual attainment rather than rank, and the competition was keen, the women vying with one another in the excellence of their sexual techniques.

The idea of exclusive sexual possession was almost lacking in the Marquesas, and was certainly socially disapproved. There were a few monogamous unions based upon it, but such an arrangement doomed the household to insignificance. Apparently there was a distinction between the gang sexual activities and the private affairs previously mentioned. In the former a girl gave herself to every boy in the gang at one time or another. In the latter there was selection, and rebuff might result in suicide. Such suicides were stereotyped. Men climbed a tall cocoanut tree and dived off head first; women ate a poisonous fruit. Beautiful girls were often exceedingly cruel and fickle in their dealings with their lovers. They would lead them on and then rebuff them publicly. A standard story in the islands, which may not be true but is quite in line with native attitudes, is that of a white man who fell in love with a beautiful girl. She refused to give herself to him unless he would have his face tattooed in native fashion. He submitted to this, then she laughed at him publicly and told him he was now so hideous she would have nothing to do with him. The man lived on in the islands for years, unable to return to his own people, while the girl enjoyed her triumph. Unmarried men frequently committed suicide because of rebuffs; married men rarely if ever. Unmarried women, on the other hand, rarely committed suicide, while married ones might. Thus if a woman's main husband appeared too interested in another woman she would first threaten suicide, and then, in many cases, carry out her threat. Her death would not bring the vengeance of her family on the husband, but it would grieve him, bring public censure, and also break up the household. The secondary husbands would leave and he would have to attach himself to another household in a subsidiary position. How far these practices are to be interpreted as expressions of jealousy is a question. The main factor seems to have been wounded pride.

After marriage there was little if any overt expression of jealousy on the part of the men. It must be remembered that the household was normally made up of a girl and a group of boys from her gang who were particularly attached to her and to each other. Jealousy between plural husbands or even between married men over some woman outside their households was considered very bad manners. Such men never quarreled over women when sober, but when drunk there were numerous fights, some quite serious, when knives were used. The participants were much humiliated when they became sober, and there would be an exchange of apologies the next day. In a well established household there was no quarreling over the wife.

There were various forms of marriages, the most formal being that between the eldest son of the chief of one tribe and the eldest daughter of the chief of another tribe, a union which would unite two lines and promote peace between the two groups. The betrothal in these cases was made in infancy, and during the period of the engagement feasts given by one family or the other. The marriage was an elaborate ceremony with extensive gift exchanges. The group who went to the neighboring village to get the bride carried live pigs lashed to a tremendous timber frame. This delegation would be attacked by the men of the receiving group, who would attempt to drive them off and carry away the pigs. Later there would be a return ceremony with another offering of pigs.

Only a household well up in the social scale could afford a

formal marriage of this sort. The ordinary marriage involved no ceremony or gift exchanges and was merely the selection of a permanent partner by the eldest child as the hereditary household head. Unmarried individuals then attached themselves to these households in subsidiary positions. Because of the shortage of women, almost every girl had an opportunity to become the head wife in a household. Only rich households had subsidiary wives. Monogamous marriages occurred only among the very poor or in rare cases of strong personal attachment.

Old age brought no prestige in the Marquesas, and respect for parents was impossible in a society where a man was outranked by his son at birth and merely acted as regent until the child was old enough to marry. The high point of life for the Marquesan came during his years as active head of the household. The only people who remained important in old age were the inspirational priests. Ceremonial priests, when they became too old to officiate actively, had to give up their positions. The old women carried on most of the woman's work in the house, while the young women entertained the men; old men could always find odd jobs to keep themselves occupied. The old were neglected but were never killed or mistreated for fear that they might take revenge later, when they became ghosts.

There was very little quarreling among the Marquesans, and that only when they were drunk. Theft of food was not infrequent but was not seriously regarded. The owner of the food would be irate and would punish the thief if he could catch him, but the man who got away with the theft successfully would boast about it later when the owner's annoyance had had time to subside. There was practically no theft of anything except food, probably because all household objects were individually made and decorated so that the stolen article would be promptly recognized. There were some killings, almost invariably for only two causes: sexual jealousy during drunkenness, and revenge, usually by sorcery, for previous killings. The Marquesans had no form of legal procedure in handling crime. Each household was supposed to take care of its own interests.

The Marquesans gave the appearance of being friendly and open with whites, but were actually very much on guard. It was impossible to tell what was going on in their minds. They manifested their pleasures openly but seldom gave way to grief, although they flew into occasional fits of rage. They regarded death with the utmost composure. An old woman who lived immediately behind my house died of tuberculosis during my stay in her village. When it became apparent that she was not going to live much longer, her husband and four sons built a magnificent tomb for her. They reported each day on how it was coming along, and she was very proud and interested in the work. As she became worse, they started her coffin, building it on the front porch of the house so that she could watch the construction.

The strongest expression of emotion I ever saw was that of an eighteen-year-old boy to whom I gave a mouth organ. He had never seen one before and listened fascinated while I tooted on it. When I handed it over to him, he blew one note, then leaped into the air about four feet with a loud whoop. He did not thank me—that came later—but started off at a run, playing the instrument for all he was worth.

The average Marquesan had a horror of being laughed at, an aversion which was a powerful factor in maintaining the mores of the society, for the nonconformist was certain to be subjected to ridicule. Since the Marquesans are essentially a polite people, the handling was gentle from our point of view. They seldom ridiculed a man to his face, but he was nevertheless aware of the joking and talking that went on behind his back. If he was present at the informal assemblies of the tribe, there would be slighting allusions made to him and his foibles, the humor of which would be highly appreciated by the rest of the group. It was easier for the native to conform to the standards of the community than to be exposed to this sort of thing. This fear of ridicule was undoubtedly an important factor in the prevalence of suicide because of jilted love, which was previously discussed.

WAR

Wars were constantly being waged between tribes. One of the principal incentives to warfare was the need for captives for human sacrifice. Human sacrifices were demanded by the gods and were also necessary for the deification of dead chiefs and inspirational priests. Another cause for war was blood revenge, for whenever a member of the tribe was captured or killed, his relatives had to avenge him.

The economic motive in war was not of great importance. Since most of the wars were in the nature of rapid raids carried on along the borders, the invaders did not actually get into the territory of the other tribe and therefore neither carried off a substantial amount of goods nor drove the enemies off their land. However, in individual fighting, the victorious warrior was permitted to claim the weapons and ornaments of his victim and also, if possible, to carry off the body of the dead enemy to be eaten. In such an event the head was kept as a trophy and the warrior usually took the name of the man he had killed. These skulls were carefully prepared, and were worn at the belt at dances and on war parade. Hands of victims were also sometimes dried and worn as waist ornaments. If a warrior acquired too many skulls to be worn conveniently in this fashion, he would cut them up and wear only a section of each. If the victim was a woman, the warrior might not keep the skull, but he would cut off the genitals, dry them, and wear them attached to a lock of his hair. The long bones were kept and utilized for ornaments, decorative handles for food vessels, etc.

When engaged in formal war, the men lived in a special house which was taboo to women. They were allowed no relations with women at this time, since abstinence was believed to increase their fighting power. The women were also subject to taboos at this time; they had to sleep in the grandstands of the assembly place; they could not light a fire, bathe, or let down their hair; they could eat with their husbands only on the morning before the men went to battle. The younger women followed the army and cheered from the background, rejoicing over captives. Women could prevent wars if they so desired. They had only to announce, "'This road I name after my genitals," and any man who passed that way was certain to be killed. The inspirational priests took omens before the warriors went into battle to determine whether or not the time was favorable, and the ceremonial priests performed sacrifices.

None of these war expeditions was at any great distance. The war might be with a tribe which lived only a mile away. The fighters would frequently call a halt for meal times, and fighting usually was stopped before dark, as there were unpleasant demons abroad after nightfall. In the valley of Taipee, which is only six miles long and half a mile wide, there were three tribes which had been at war with one another for generations. Since individual head hunting and raiding to take captives for sacrifices went on continuously between formal wars, the people of the valley lived in a constant state of jitters.

Formal wars were declared by the chief, and the forces were mustered under the leadership of the *toa* or skilled warriors. There was no drilling or military instruction. The battles in the field were merely scrimmages directed by the *toa*, or individual combats, the object of which was to get the body of the enemy. There was one old gentleman in the valley in which I lived who had been the proud possessor of a whaling harpoon with a rope attached. He had achieved a great reputation as a warrior with this weapon, for with it he could spear a man and haul him back in record time.

Small raids were carried on at any time. A favorite trick was for a party to go by war canoe to a valley and land two or three men under cover of night. At dawn the raiders would creep into the village and pick off any early risers who came out of their houses. They would rush their captives back to the shore, signal the war canoes, and be off before the rest of the village was awake.

Each valley had its fort, or forts, which were usually built on high spurs in the mountains. Here the chief, protected by a special guard, took refuge along with the old women and children. This was not because he was lacking in courage but because, as the focal point of the social prestige of the tribe, he could not be exposed to capture. The stigma of having one's chief tortured and eaten by one's enemies would be a disgrace that would ruin a tribe socially for generations. Inside the fort was a rock enclosure in which the chief sought refuge in case the fort was taken. A complete victory resulted in a thorough looting of the enemy territory and the carrying off of the images of the gods. These sacred objects were considered to have lost their *mana* after such a defeat and so could be handled with impunity. The triumphant return was celebrated by a great feast, with torture of captives and human sacrifices to the gods. The captives' remains were cooked and eaten, and the feast ended with a period of general sexual license. This is about as close as anything could be to the old missionary idea of a cannibalistic orgy.

In spite of this picture of warfare and its tremendous ceremonial importance, casualties were not very high and the natives actually showed no great courage in battle, although they yelled and capered and made a great noise. Even the greatest of the *toa* rarely had more than four of five killings to their credit. Weapons were large and showy but not well adapted to vigorous hand-to-hand fighting. Some of the Marquesan clubs were eight feet long, made of ironwood, and weighing as much as twenty or twenty-five pounds. A direct blow from such a weapon would kill a man, but if the wielder of the club missed his aim, it would take him thirty seconds or so to get the club back into position.

Revenge was a sacred duty. The male relatives of a man who had been killed shaved one half of their heads until their kinsman had been avenged. As raids were constant and most of the village was related to one another, these half-shaven heads often appeared to be the typical male headdress. Mourning for a relative who had been killed by a member of a hostile tribe was lifted by the eating of a victim from the offending tribe, all participating in this feast except the parent of the original victim. Cannibalism is taboo for women in most primitive groups, but both women and children participated in the cannibal feasts in the Marquesas.

The highest honors went to the warrior who captured his victim and brought him back alive, though he also received credit for an enemy killed in battle. Captives taken alive were tortured and put to death in various ingenious ways, by dismemberment, evisceration, and other methods. Under rare circumstances an extremely handsome man or woman might be adopted, but this broke up the revenge pattern and made complications. Children under three years old did not count as revenge victims, and were consequently not subjected to torture. They were eaten, however, or sometimes strangled and hung up on hooks in the sacred place as a feast for the gods. Victims taken as sacrifices to the gods were not tortured, save in rare cases. They were usually killed quickly and suspended on trees in the sacred grove by means of a hook through the jaw. Occasionally they would be hung up in this fashion while still living. When the bodies decayed they were buried in a special pit. From a social point of view, being eaten was worse than being killed and was a disgrace to the family. For this reason, if a captive had a relative in the valley at the time he was brought in, his kinsman would attempt to have him consecrated to the god immediately so that he would be killed at once and not tortured or eaten.

Certain regulations mitigated these tribal wars. The mother, sister, aunt, or wife of an individual who had been captured and eaten in revenge could go unmolested to the valley of the captors and curse them. She laid a special curse on the man who had been responsible for the capture. The woman painted her body in a particular way in red, white, and black, put on a kilt of leaves, and carried food, which she threw down in the road before the house of the killer. This food would lure the soul of the slain man and also that of the killer on whom she sought revenge. If the soul of the murdered man was in the lead, the woman would rejoice, for that gave her assurance that the killer would be captured and eaten in turn. She would dance before the killer and rain curses upon him. He was expected to treat this exhibition with an attitude of lofty scorn.

RELIGION

In accordance with the rest of the culture, the religion of the Marquesans was highly organized with elaborate development of formal beliefs and rituals. Deities were of two sorts: first group included the great creation deities and the minor deities —personifications of natural forces, the sea, the rain, etc.; and the second, gods of human origin. Unfortunately most ethnological workers in Polynesia have been greatly and too exclusively interested in the great deities. Volumes have been written on the trinity of Polynesian gods, but it is my opinion that in most sections of Polynesia the great gods meant little or nothing to the average person. This was certainly so among the Marquesans. The creation gods and the gods of natural phenomenon were mentioned in chants and also in work rituals which were closely associated with their natural provinces. Thus, if a Marquesan was making a canoe, the god of the sea and of the winds would be invoked, and the spirit of the wood would be called upon to copulate with the master craftsman for the purpose of bringing forth the canoe. However, there were neither temples nor sacrifices to these natural gods, who were regarded as impersonal principles.

The second type of deities were gods of human origin; these were the active and important gods, for the natives felt that only human spirits were really interested in human beings. First of all, there were the tribal gods, who were the spirits of dead chiefs or inspirational priests. Then there were the gods of the trades, who were deified spirits of famous craftsmen. To understand these deities it is necessary to digress at this point to explain the native ideas on death and on the constitution of the individual and the soul.

According to the native belief, each living individual had a double or *uhane,* corresponding to our concept of the astral

body. This double was material, though of an extremely tenuous form of matter, and had the exact appearance of its living
counterpart. During sleep this spirit left the body and wandered
about freely, meeting the spirits of other sleeping individuals
and conversing with them. Any transactions made during these
conversations were considered valid and had to be fulfilled by
the person on waking. These spirits were also seen by persons
in the waking state, particularly by the priests, who frequently
had to deal with straying spirits of the living.

At death the *uhane* left the body permanently. The natives
believed that there was a whole series of upper and lower worlds
to which the spirits of the dead went. Dead chiefs and priests
of the higher order were deified by means of human sacrifices—
ten human sacrifices, one for each of the ten parts of the body,
were the necessary requirement for deification. These sacrifices
had to be performed before the body was finally disposed of,
thus giving the tribe a year or more in which to seize the captives and stage the ceremony. Persons who were sacrificed for
deification ceased to have any existence as distinct individuals,
since the soul of the dead chief or priest absorbed into itself
the souls of the human sacrifices, and was in this way raised to
superhuman power. The newly made god then rose to the sky
world where dwelt the creation gods and the previously deified
priests and chiefs. Such a god returned to the tribe frequently,
not so much to punish his descendants as to demand sacrifices
because he was hungry, or to aid them if they were in difficulty.

This deification of chiefs through human sacrifice had occurred well within the memory of a number of the old men
with whom I talked during my stay in the islands. One man
told me that he remembered the death of his chief about 1865
and the subsequent deification by the proper ritual. During the
lifetime of the chief, his tribe had suffered numerous defeats
at the hands of the tribe from the neighboring valley. After his
spirit had been deified and his body disposed of, the chief's
skull was placed on the prow of a war canoe in which his followers made a raid upon the enemy valley. They returned

victorious with several captives. The power of the deified chief was thus established and he was the god of the valley, speaking to his people through the mouth of his own inspirational priest. An old man from the island of Ua Pou told me of another instance of the power of a deified chief, which he remembered from his youth. When the chief was old and knew that he must soon die, he said to his followers, "Soon I shall become a god; what do you desire that I do for you after I go to the sky world?" The people asked that he take away the *nonos,* a kind of sandfly which infested the island and caused much distress by its vicious bite. He observed that this would be difficult but that he would do his best. Soon after, the chief died but was not properly deified because the tribe was unable to obtain sufficient captives for the ceremony. The chief, however, overlooked this omission and went to work on the sandflies, so that within three months all the *nonos* had disappeared from the island. This chief is still the dominant deity of Ua Pou. I visited his tomb, a white-washed structure of concrete with a cross at one end and a carved stone image on the other.

The gods were almost all males. Theoretically, women could hold the highest rank, but in practice few women were actually household heads, rulers of tribes, or inspirational priests. In rare cases the eldest daughter of a chief would become chief-tainess and rule in her own right, although as a rule the chief adopted a boy if his eldest child was a girl. Such a woman might be deified, but the most powerful deities were invariably male.

Those whose rank did not entitle them to a place in the sky world went to one of the three lower worlds. The lowest of these was the most desirable, while the highest one, the one immediately adjoining the world of living and therefore the easiest to reach, was highly unpleasant, dark and muddy and short of food. The world to which a man went depended on the number of pigs sacrificed at his memorial feast. Those for whom there was only one pig, or none at all, went to the poorest world. The head of the household of the dead person, some time before the memorial feast, went to each house in which

the head husband or head wife was a relative, recited his genealogy, and called upon the household to give him pigs. They
were obligated to give him at least one on such occasions. The
number of pigs a man could collect was an indication of the
extent of his family connections and the wealth of his family
line. He would then bring all the pigs back, and the household
would fatten them for six or eight months, scrimping on their
own food in order to increase the size of the pigs. Several families would do this simultaneously. Finally the great feast would
be held, with the eldest children of the related households as
the official sponsors and donors of the pigs. The pigs were killed,
roasted, and laid out on banana leaves so that all could feast
their eyes and observe how many animals had been offered, the
number of pigs fixing the individual's status. The pigs were
apportioned by the head ceremonial priest or sometimes by
the chief.

There was no particular fear of the dead in the flesh and very
little fear of ghosts. The Marquesans took it for granted that
the members of one's family were lingering about the dwelling
after death but intended no harm. The living spoke of ghosts
with the greatest casualness; they were constantly seeing and
hearing them. Any peculiar or unexplained noise would be
attributed to the ghosts and considered of no importance.

Bodies of the dead were mummified and kept in the dwelling
or in the sacred place until preparations for the memorial feast
were complete, an indeterminate length of time. The outer skin
of the cadavers was rubbed off with rough coral, thimbles of
skin being left on the ends of the fingers, which were pulled
back over the nails—a device also used by the Egyptians. The
body was eviscerated through the anus and through incisions in
the skin, then rubbed with cocoanut oil day after day until it
finally dried up and achieved a fair degree of mummification.
Small children were not mummified but women were accorded
just as careful treatment as men.

In the island of Nuku Hiva, this mummification was carried
on in a separate house built on a high stone platform; but in

the southern islands, the process was carried on right in the house, with the daily life of the family going on around the corpse, which lay upon a bier. The family would carry the body out into the sun and rub it down with oil, then carry it back into the house when the sun went down. When mummification was fairly complete, they dressed the body in its best clothes and seated it in a squatting position with the arms crossed and the chin on the knees. They held it in place with wooden supports and kept it sitting so in the most honored section of the house until after the memorial ceremony. The remains, usually in a fairly disreputable condition by this time, were then taken to the shrine of the tribal gods and turned over to the ceremonial priests for final disposition. No one but the priests knew what really became of these bodies. An old man who had been an assistant to a ceremonial priest told me that he had helped to carry the bodies away but was never permitted to be present at the final disposal. The heads were often removed and saved, and also a few of the long bones would be selected to be worked up into ornaments for relatives of the deceased as pleasant mementos.

The skulls of the chiefs were kept in the temple and brought out from time to time to adorn the prows of the war canoes to give them *mana*, or were exposed in the fishing house to aid in bringing a favorable catch. Skulls of family heads were returned to the household, where they were kept in the family shrine— either a small house outside, associated with the death house, or a curtained-off end of the dwelling with shelves. Sometimes faces of bark cloth were built upon the skulls and painted with the personal tattooing of the individual.

Each tribe had one or more sacred places hidden far back in the hills. These places were taboo to most men and to all but the few highest ranking women of the tribe. The power of this taboo was demonstrated to me by a strange experience. A man of about fifty-two or three had volunteered to take me to one of these sacred places, the central shrine for one of the two big divisions of the tribes on the island of Hiva Oa. The man was apparently uneasy about his promise, and went up to the sacred place alone on the day before he was to take me. He came back looking very ill, said that he had seen a spirit and was going to die. He took to his bed and three days later he was dead, apparently scared to death.

In each of these sacred places there was a sacred grove, a series of platforms with images, etc. Near the house of the inspirational priest was a curious structure shaped like an obelisk, fifteen feet on a side and sixty feet high. At the tribal assembly place there was another sacred place which was open to all and used for small and unimportant sacrifices. Human sacrifices were all carried on in the sacred groves back in the hills. Some one tribal god was always in the ascendancy at any given time, the dominance shifting with the result of the oracles given by his inspirational priest and with the god's power to fulfill the demands of his followers. In other words, the god most worshipped was the one who worked most effectively; he was usually a deity recently dead.

The priesthood was highly organized with two classes, the inspirational and the ceremonial. Each important god had his own inspirational priest, although two or three lesser gods might share a priest among them. The inspirational priests of the highest gods outranked even the tribal chief. These priests were graded in duties and power in accordance with the importance of the god they served. Women could be inspirational priests but were rarely possessed by a god of high rank. The inspirational priest demonstrated his fitness for the office by being possessed by the spirit of the god immediately after the death of the previous priest of this particular god, or immediately after the deification of a new god. In other words, as soon as a vacancy in the priesthood occurred, everyone would be waiting expectantly to see who would become possessed. The individual thus chosen was seized with violent twitchings, made strange sounds, and finally, after emerging from the hysterical seizure, pronounced an oracle.

The inspirational priests of the higher gods were thought to have supernatural powers. They could fast for a month at a time, lie down on the water and go to sleep, see things happening at a distance, and make fatal curses. This latter ability was very useful, for the priest could take property from an individual just by the threat of cursing him if he did not hand over what the priest desired. The priest could also make a man his servant by approaching him and saying that he must serve him or he would die.

The priests demanded human sacrifices for their gods and kept things generally stirred up. At times of great possession, a high priest of a particular tribe would dress up in special costume and make a trip involving a circuit of the hostile tribes. He was protected from injury in enemy territory by the fact of his possession, which was respected by everyone. As he passed from one territory to another he would be possessed in turn by the dominant god of each locality, who would accompany him on his journey, and his *mana* would become stronger and stronger. When the priest returned to his own tribe, he would enter the sacred place and, in a fury of physical possession with appropriately wild gestures, would demand human sacrifices. Since he had been in a position to make a careful survey of enemy villages during his circuit, he could tell the warriors of the tribe just how to go about picking off captives in the tribes he had visited, so that these raids never failed.

The ceremonial priests, who were always male, made no pretense to inspiration but were considered skilled craftsmen in working with the gods. They knew all the rituals, sacred lore, and family genealogies. They presided at ceremonies, were called in to make charms and recite appropriate chants and rituals at the various individual life crises, and also instructed the children in the lore which it was proper for gentlefolk to know. They were the scholars of the community. The position of the ceremonial priest tended to be hereditary, as a father would try to pass on his craft to his son.

Each craft had its deity, a great *tuhunga* of the past. A man who made canoes would call upon the god of canoe makers, and would often make an offering to the god before beginning his task. The *tuhunga* were also priests to the gods of their crafts, though they had little formal ritual and, except in the case of the fishermen, no sacred place.

Below the gods was another series of supernatural beings, the *vehini-hai,* or wild women. The natives were not clear as to whether or not these spirits were of human origin, but they did have human form. They were malevolent toward children, watching them continuously, sometimes merely making them sick and at other times stealing or eating them. They were also dangerous to young men. Appearing as beautiful women, the *vehini-hai* would present themselves to some charming young man in a lonely place and invite him to go along with them. If he complied, they would lead him to their caves, where they would turn back into ogresses and devour him. Occasionally however, the *vehini-hai,* instead of eating her victim, would try to establish him in an affectionate relationship, which was, needless to say, a very uncomfortable and dangerous position for the young man. The men who had encountered these *vehini-hai* said that they usually appeared as beautiful young girls, but that they were always hungry, and if one could steal glances at them when they were off guard, one could see their eyes shoot out and their long hungry tongues pop out and lick the ground. This was warning that one's associate was an ogress and not a lovely lady, and that it was time to get away.

Still another series of supernatural beings were the *fanaua.* They were the spirits of dead men who became the familiars of women, helping them and injuring other women at their bidding. They never operated against men. No woman had more than one *fanaua.* This spirit might be the ghost of a male relative in the ascending generation, i.e., a father, grandfather, or even some important member of the family several genera-tions back. In such cases his relations with the woman were prob-ably not on the basis of sexual attraction, although I could get no exact information on this point. The *fanaua* might also be a nonrelative, a spirit who had fallen in love with the woman. After death her spirit was united with his, as in marriage, a relationship which might or might not be unpleasant to her. *Fanaua* of the second type seemed to be more numerous and more active, and more to be dreaded than those of the first.

The *fanaua* attacked other women at the bidding of his woman and also protected her from attacks of other *fanaua*. The techniques of *fanaua* attack were primarily connected with pregnancy. The *fanaua* might destroy the child in the womb (cases of neurotic symptoms of imaginary pregnancy were, as has been said, a fairly common phenomenon here) or cause the woman to die, during either pregnancy or childbirth. Practically all such deaths were explained on this basis.

The woman knew she had a *fanaua* by the fact that a spirit came to her in dreams, frequently of an erotic nature. Other people knew that she had a *fanaua* by observing what happened to women who antagonized her. Although the woman herself never announced the fact, the knowledge that she was being aided by a spirit spread around the community. The wife of my craft instructor had a *fanaua* of minor power, the spirit of her father, and other women did not fear her much; but the wife of the pastor had one who had been a paramount chief of the island of Tahu Ata some two hundred years before. This spirit was very powerful, and the pastor's wife was feared accordingly. The women were very reticent about the whole *fanaua* belief, probably because it was a source of great anxiety and mutual suspicion.

Offerings were made to living women who were known to have *fanaua* in order to keep the familiar from working harm. A woman who had a *fanaua* was welcomed by the males of the same household because such a familiar offered the most direct method for protection of property. The woman's familiar never operated against her husbands and could even be invoked to help them indirectly by attacking women of other households whose men had wronged them. In one instance, a chief had expropriated a garden which belonged to a household of low rank. The wife sent her familiar to make the chief's wife sick and give her the appearance of pregnancy. When the chief's wife realized that her illness was due to magic, a ritual was performed to discover what *fanaua* was causing her trouble. As soon as she and her husband, the chief, learned the name of the *fanaua,* they knew who had sent it and why. The chief thereupon returned the garden, the spirit was called off, and his wife was well again. In cases where restitution was not made, however, the attack continued until the woman died.

Occasionally women who had *fanaua* were killed by the irate relatives of women whom their spirits had attacked. This was the only case in which men killed women, and even this seems to have been somewhat unusual and to have resulted in a blood feud.

The incidence of *fanaua* was about one to every three women. The *fanaua* themselves were graded in power, a *fanaua* who was a relative being considered more effective for defense than for offense. He protected his women against the attacks of other *fanaua* but would not act as a strong or constant aggressor against her enemies.

The *fanaua* belief had still another form. Not only the spirit of the woman who had the *fanaua* was united to him after death, but also the spirits of all the women whom he might have killed. For the victims, at least, this was a highly unpleasant relationship, and could be escaped only by directing the spirit to kill another woman to take the place of the first victim. A woman who died in childbirth was thus assumed to be united to a *fanaua* after death and eager to kill some other woman in order to escape from him. She might indicate the new victim to him, not out of personal animosity toward this woman but merely as a means of getting herself out of a bad spot. It was therefore dangerous for a woman to approach a place where a *fanaua's* victim was buried, since by doing so she might attract the dead woman's attention. Such victims were buried in places remote from the village, a small stone platform being erected over the grave. Men frequently made offerings at such places to placate the dead woman and prevent her from choosing a victim from their households.

Fear of women who died in childbirth and special burial rites for them were practically universal in Polynesia, but this was usually rationalized by reference to the jealousy and malevolence of the spirits of unborn children. These hated the living because they themselves had been defrauded of the pleasures of living. I believe that among the Marquesans this general Polynesian pattern had been reinterpreted to conform to local ideas. The whole pattern of *fanaua* seemed to be peculiar to the Marquesas. There were familiars and various forms of spirit possession nearly everywhere in Polynesia, but the relationship was usually established on some other basis.

The basic pattern of the *fanaua* beliefs was clear; women controlled male familiar spirits in two ways. One of these was through a kinship bond, which made it possible for a woman to control the ghost of a male relative in the ascending generation, but only if he offered himself voluntarily. The other method was that in which the woman maintained relations with the *fanaua* through her sexual attraction. This was also at the will of the male spirit, who fell in love with her. This relationship was comparable to the individual affairs which existed between adolescent males and females of the *kaioi* group. The woman's death, after which she became the wife of the *fanaua*, corresponded to the change in relationship which came with marriage and the founding of a household. As has been said before, if this permanent relationship proved unpleasant, she would try to persuade the *fanaua* to kill some other woman to take her place.

Magicians, as distinct from possessors of *fanaua*, might be either men or women. The magician also had to have a familiar spirit or spirits, but one became a magician either through election by a spirit or by studying magic, with the subsequent acquisition of a spirit. In the latter case, the magician, after he had completed his training but before he began to practice, had to kill a close relative in the ascending generation by magical means. This relative could be either male or female, but the most effective way for a magician to acquire a powerful familiar was for him to kill his own mother. The magician dominated the spirit of the person he had killed and forced it to serve him. Magical familiars might be of either sex and could work against either sex. Magic might be performed either by sending the spirit directly to make the enemy sick or by using bait. Illnesses of pregnancy and childbirth were always ascribed to *fanaua* and never to malevolent magic. The use of bait followed a familiar magical pattern, the bait consisting of some of the individual's hair, or if this was impossible to obtain, a part of his clothing or some other object which had been in close contact with him. However, I was told by natives that in such practice one was not operating on a part of the personality of the victim, but rather giving the familiar spirit his scent, like putting a dog on the trail. A familiar thus put in touch with an object would then follow up the person to whom it belonged and injure or kill him. The attacking spirit would be called off by the magician if payment was made. It is interesting to note that there seemed to be no rituals in Marquesan magic to preserve work in progress from injury through the magic of rivals or to prevent the success of another person in his work. The presence of hostile magic was shown by sickness or death, not by work failure. If a work project, which usually had certain rituals connected with it, failed, it was because the worker had not done his magic correctly, not because of any fault in the magic itself.

One rather puzzling aspect of Marquesan magic was the complete absence of charms to be worn either for defense or to insure success in any activity. The whole idea of wearing charms appeared to be foreign to them. During the war I had become accustomed to wearing an identification tag around my neck and was still wearing it when I arrived in the islands. The natives were much puzzled by this and were quite unable to understand the charm explanation which was given. Some practitioners had images of their familiars but these were not necessary.

FOLKLORE AND LEGENDS

From Handy's[1] volume we take some of the Marquesan legends. One story deals with the *kaioi*, who play a game of spear throwing. The hero says his spear will pierce Temooniew's ear. He pronounces a spell over the spear, and it does as he wishes. She takes the spear out and goes into the cave. He then goes to look for a mast for his canoe, and lands in Temooniew's cave. There he finds a tall tree which he fells, but Temooniew holds the crest. He climbs up and Temooniew threatens to kill him for piercing her ear and cutting her down. He makes her his wife, though she demurs but gives in finally, after "showing evil ways," i.e., she licks her lips and sticks out her tongue.

She prepares food of rats and lizards. He offers to take her to his country, where the food is good. He goes away after some piece of deception. She follows him, casts a sleeping spell over his folks, steals him while asleep, and carries him back to her cave. He awakens terrified. She scolds him for his deception, and threatens to kill and eat him. He begs her not to eat him, and excuses his lying. Then they make peace, she goes to his country, and becomes good. Then she has children, and the story ends.

Another tale concerns a woman who has three children, whom she raises instead of giving them away for adoption. She sends them for food; they get it and then go to sleep. The mother steals the baskets of food and conceals them in her back. The children miss the food baskets, but the mother denies knowledge of them. She sends them out again, and the same thing happens ten times. The children then suspect that the mother is a cannibal. The children deceive her and bring a

[1] E. S. Craighill Handy, *Marquesan Legends* (Honolulu, 1930).

basket of eels, which the mother puts in her back, and she dies. Before dying she tells the children to plant a seed on her back. Since they fear her ghost, they bury her in the ground, and a fruit tree grows. The girl wants the seed. They eat the fruit and fell the tree, and the mother comes to life again. Then the mother pursues the children, and threatens to kill and eat them. They flee from her to an island which the mother cannot climb. There they have no food, but they plant the seed that came out of the mother. It grows and they eat the fruit. The mother succeeds in getting on the island, and finally wants to climb up on the girl's hair. She does so, and when the brother cuts her hair, the mother falls and dies. The children now feel safe. They take the corpse of the mother and bake it. There is no mention of their eating it. One brother is a glutton, and eats not only food but utensils. He meets his death by eating forbidden cocoanuts belonging to a chief. The girl is wooed by two chiefs, one of whom kills the other.

Another story deals with a handsome married man who is carried away by the *vehini-hai*. The wife sets out in pursuit, but cannot catch up with him, and dies. The three wild women suggest eating the youth. One of them suggests that there is nothing to gain from eating him. The good ogress cautions the bad, and the latter is transformed with beauty. The woman ceases to be a man-eater, and the captured youth stays with them.

Another story deals with father-daughter incest. A man is married to a woman, but when she is three months pregnant, he deserts his wife for a new woman. The first woman has a daughter, who grows up to be very beautiful. The father of the girl hears of her beauty, and among others seeks her favors, not knowing it is his daughter. He comes while the mother and her brothers are away looking for food during a famine. He takes the girl. The mother returns and the girl tells of her adventure. The mother recognizes the man as the girl's father. The woman reproaches first the daughter, and then the father, and then presents them to each other, i.e., father and daughter.

All that seems to happen is that the girl is ashamed, and the mother forbids the girl to have intercourse with any other man. But not for long, for the men soon set out to get the girl a man with a skin as white as cocoanut.[2] They find one, but he deserts her; she dies of grief, but is revived by his longings.

[2] White skin is considered in Marquesas a mark of beauty.

Chapter VI

ANALYSIS OF MARQUESAN CULTURE

ONE could hardly wish for a better text on which to test the validity of the method and conclusions we have submitted than that which is offered in Dr. Linton's description of Marquesan culture. Together with the additional information included in Handy's *Marquesan Legends* we have enough data to permit us a wide view of the structure of personality in this society and to point out the functional interconnections of the various institutions. This does not mean that the data satisfy every requirement. We could have used a good deal more information on specific points; this lack, however, could not be identified until after the significance of the missing information became apparent. Such information could become accessible only through the intimate personal study of a number of individuals of varying function and status, from each sex. Such material would give us a more vivid picture of the society in action, and point up the dynamic interconnections between institutions, connections whose significance is in part destroyed by the necessity of the ethnographer to edit and classify his data. We therefore may expect our analysis to have many gaps and to fall short of the ultimate check on the individual.

For our purposes, this account has an added virtue in that it concerns a society and culture presenting many dramatic contrasts with our own. This is a circumstance which we can put to good advantage. If our conclusions about the interactions between individual and institution in our own culture are correct, we ought to be able to substantiate their validity by contrast. If one set of institutions creates certain psychological constellations in the individual, then we ought not to find the resultant constellations in a culture from which the given institutions are absent.

The evidence that Dr. Linton gave us is of several varieties. Much of it was derived from actual experience, some from the accounts of informants, and lastly, but of extreme importance, some came from personal impressions concerning the feelings and attitudes of the natives. Our ethnographer reported that the children of this culture behaved in an unusually confident manner. He further observed that the women were treated with a certain consistent aloofness and disdain. These impressions are of great value. But there may be some question about the advisability of treating these impressions with the dignity of established facts, and counting on them for important conclusions. These impressions, though they stand apart from the ethnological account, can be neither isolated nor fortuitous phenomena, but must be connected with the institutional ensemble. They are bits of indirect evidence, the end results of a complicated series of interactions. We cannot check the correctness of these impressions; but the fact that the observer noted them is an indication for us to see whether they have a psychological plausibility and consistency.

GENERAL SURVEY

In order to study a culture systematically, we must first establish what may be called a psychological focus. The array of institutions which seemingly have little connection with one another is somewhat bewildering. Moreover, it is difficult to make any subjective evaluations about the relative importance of one feature over another. The safest procedure, therefore, is to deal first with those features whose significance we can identify and on which we can get some psychological orientation. If we were to attempt any explanation of the "race suicide" of this people, we would expose ourselves to a situation too difficult to solve, and one in which all efforts at empathy must fail. Nor can we trust their rationalization that they do not want their children to be slaves of the French. We do not understand this culture well enough to appreciate the psychological incompatibilities created by the contact with French institutions.

But there are certain other features, the significance of which we can immediately identify. It is impossible to escape the conviction that we are dealing with a culture in which food anxiety plays a prominent role. If food anxiety is not felt for long periods—for the food supply is plentiful between famines—then it is at least likely that many of the institutions were originally defenses against this anxiety, though they may serve other purposes at the present time. But the anxiety of unpredictable famine is sufficiently real to keep these institutions alive and endow them with some function of defense against or compensation for this anxiety.

A second focal point which we can immediately identify is the numerical disparity between the sexes and those aspects of social organization contingent upon this basic fact. This is a circumstance which must influence the adaptation of every individual in the society.

A third focal point is the character of the basic disciplines to which every individual is subjected. Here the contrast to our own culture is most striking. It is this feature which arouses the greatest curiosity, and which gives us the best opportunity to see the effects of the absence of prohibitory disciplines in contrast with other cultures where they are present.

These three focal points are enough to begin our investigation. After we trace the ramifications of the constellations created by these factors we may be in a position to attempt the answer to other questions. Some of these are: What kind of personality structure develops under the influence of these institutions? Where is the control of mutual aggression focused? What kind of "super-ego" develops under these conditions? What are the products of fantasy characterizing a creature of these institutions?

THE SHORTAGE OF WOMEN

The fact that there are two and a half men to each woman is a basic social condition. The cause of this disparity is a matter of considerable moment, but one about which we cannot draw any certain conclusions. If it is a natural phenomenon, it has a different meaning from what it would have if it were artificially induced by female infanticide.[1] The natives deny the practice of killing female children, and no observer has ever brought any conclusive evidence one way or another. Whatever its cause, this shortage of women produces a situation which affects every aspect of Marquesan society. It influences the structure of the family; it affects the relation of children to parents and to secondary husbands, and of the men to each other. It likewise produces an unusual rivalry among the women.

Let us consider first the situation as it concerns the men. By all the standards known in our culture—and in others as well— there ought to be considerable jealousy among the men, both in courtship and between chief husband and secondary ones. However "natural" such jealousy may be, we must recognize that the intensity of the wish to possess a woman exclusively or to displace anyone else who has her, must depend on a host of subsidiary conditions, which can greatly intensify this feeling. The significance of paternity, the existence of venereal disease, the economic obligations to the woman associated with marriage, the existence of romantic love, the special value placed on male potency—all these factors may greatly intensify jealousy, but do not create it. When we find three men living together in marriage with one woman without any manifestations of jealousy, we must assume either that it is not felt or

---

[1] There are societies in which the ratio of males to females is the same as in the Marquesas, and for which it could be definitely established that there was no female infanticide—the Samaritans and natives of Easter Island. This numerical disparity in the Marquesas is known to have existed for centuries before the French took over. This fact can in no way be related to the "race suicide" which the natives have put into effect. See H. M. Huxley, *The Jewish Encyclopedia* (New York, 1916), Vol. X, pp. 675–676.

that some adjustment has been made to the situation by the men through a system of suppressions or compensations, and that some advantage can be gained through these devices.

In most instances the chief and secondary husbands get along harmoniously. However, it has been noted that jealousy appears not infrequently when they get drunk, but the offender apologizes when he sobers up. Occasionally a murder out of sexual jealousy occurs. Moreover, Marquesan men are known to kill themselves out of frustrated love or the inability to gain access to a particular woman. This occurs principally among the unmarried men and occasionally in the case of a married woman who falls in love with a man other than her legal husbands. It is also known that sexual jealousy frequently arises among the children during their premarital sexual exercises. The mere fact that jealousy appears is enough to indicate that it is kept in check under ordinary conditions, and that strong tender and sensual attachments may take place.

The factors which militate against overt jealousy are quite numerous. First there is the fact that the child observes one woman caring for the sexual needs of several men in the child's own household. Then there is the fact that the sexual aim is never subjected to any prohibition, and can be exercised freely by the child under conditions very like those of the adults. These factors would tend to an attitude in the man permitting sexual gratification to others with the same object without fall in self-esteem. This situation might also tend to lessen the opportunity for creating the association between tender and sensual relations. In a society where sexual relations are unobstructed in childhood, the significance of tenderness in such relations is likely to be obscured. The fact is that everyone gets plenty of opportunity for sensual gratification, barring of course the limited taboos pertaining to siblings and parents.

We would expect these factors to tend toward diminishing the functional usefulness of jealousy as an expression of injured self-esteem. Its appearance is therefore all the more remarkable, and is conclusive evidence that all these above-mentioned factors do not obviate jealousy. They tend to diminish only the jealousy that is an indicator of fallen self-esteem, but not the jealousy arising out of a strong biological attraction. In the former, the play of emotion arises largely from comparison with another man, who has legally established claims; in the latter, it arises from the strong need for the loved object. We must look for another interplay of forces which make the suppression of jealousy acceptable for the preservation of other major interests—a suppression maintained either by sanctions against its manifestations or by a sure knowledge of the disrupting influence of jealousy on the whole society. Jealousy among men would disrupt the whole production system; jealousy among women would not, and hence among the latter it is overt and violent.

No mention was made of sanctions against jealousy; but there is plenty of evidence that a major interest is preserved by its suppression—the solidarity and coöperation of the men for purposes requiring common coöperation is assured. Upon the men falls the major part of the obligation for food production and manufacture of articles for use, and this fact is ultimately related to their food anxiety. The women are taboo in places where men need to coöperate to procure food, as in fishing grounds. Women are taboo to warriors before battle—one of the commonest taboos, and one usually rationalized on the basis that sexual relations deprive the man of strength. Moreover, a woman can stop a war by naming the road after her genitals. This latter custom lends itself to two possible interpretations: that to fight over a woman's genitals means disaster; or that the woman can exercise great power over men through her ability to deny them sexual favors. These explanations are speculative. They point in the direction of an unconscious feeling of danger consequent on quarreling over the woman. The explanation that this power of the woman to stop a war is due to the castration fear of the men is out of context.

It is inadmissible in a culture where knowledge of the function of the sexual organs in both male and female is learned from earliest infancy, from observation and direct experience.

But there are other more immediate grounds for the suppression of jealousy: beyond doubt, the chief husband and the secondary husbands derive mutual advantages from this suppression. The chief husband, far from being manifestly jealous, uses his wife as a decoy to attract desirable men as secondary husbands. By this process the prestige and power of the chief husband are enhanced. The chief husband has therefore much to gain from keeping the secondary husbands satisfied sexually, for sexual union takes place by the latter only with the chief husband's consent. The secondary husbands, on the other hand, have much in the way of security to gain from loyalty to the chief husband, and if it is an important household, much in the way of prestige.

This playing down of jealousy and the preservation of male solidarity have some very interesting sequelae. There is, first, a decided diminution of the importance of paternity, though the biological fact of paternity is fully appreciated, and the woman always knows who the father of her child is.[2] This understressing of the specificity of fatherhood is all the more remarkable where genealogies are reckoned by primogeniture, i.e., through the oldest child, male or female. A further proof of this laxity is shown in the frequency and ease of adoption and its standing as the social equivalent of the biological tie, and the fact that the oldest child becomes the inheritor of the familial *potestas* irrespective of who the father is, though in most instances he is the chief husband.[3]

There is a second and more important consequence of the unconscious overemphasis of male solidarity; that is the fact that, despite her scarcity, the woman is treated with an aloofness and disdain, and that in folklore the woman is constantly

---

[2] This is due to a special contraceptive technique practiced by the men (Linton).

[3] In a way, primogeniture in this culture has the significance of a matrilineal descent, except where adoption has taken place.

put in an unfavorable light and represented as a voracious cannibalistic beast. If we assume that the folklore is handed down largely by ceremonial priests, who are exclusively males, we may see some evidence of prejudice in this one-sided representation. But this prejudice is a male point of view, and proof positive of the deep-seated hatred and mistrust of woman. We can therefore conclude that one of the consequences of the suppression of jealousy among the men is that the aggression expressed in the affect of jealousy or hatred by one man against another, is displaced on the woman.[4]

This disparaging attitude toward the woman has many determinants in this society, and is something we cannot fully appreciate until we investigate the consequences of the Marquesan basic disciplines and the relation of the children to the mother, father, and secondary husbands.

INTRAFAMILIAL RELATIONSHIPS AND BASIC DISCIPLINES

The preceding discussion covered to a large extent the emotional relationship between chief and secondary husbands, as far as sexual jealousy is concerned. Other aspects of this relationship as regards relative status, prestige, economic power, ability to impose discipline, and ability to exploit must be deferred until we investigate the relation of the child to the household organization, and follow the lines of loyalties, disciplines and obligations consequent upon it.

For this purpose the approach should be: What are the direct experiences of the child in regard to infantile care or neglect; who are the objects with whom care, solicitude, or neglect is experienced; and what are the consequences? What disciplines are instituted with regard to food, sphincter control,

---

[4] Dr. Willard Waller communicated to me an interesting experience he had while teaching in a coeducational college where the ratio of boys to girls was four to one. The girls were distinctly in disrepute, and slighting remarks by any teacher about the "co-eds" made him very popular with the boys. The mutual antagonism between the men would be too great in open competition; disparaging the woman is a way of making her less desirable, and hence makes the renunciation less painful.

and sexual activity, and by whom? What are the obligations and responsibilities of the child? If our study is oriented from a genetic viewpoint, this informaton is important to trace the attitudes of the child toward other individuals and to its own resources—in other words, to the basic personality structure.

The child is not breast-fed, and the feeding procedure as described is rather harsh according to our standards. The infant is exposed to the shock of cold water baths. These facts cannot in themselves be of any great significance as regards permanent effects on the child's development. They are, however, characteristic of the attitude of mother to child. Maternal care is a secondary interest to the woman, the basic one being that of courtesan to the men. The breasts have a high erotic value to the woman as a sexual stimulus, and their use as feeding organs for the child is thus sacrificed to their sexual significance. For this the unconvincing explanation is offered that a breast-fed child becomes troublesome. The absence of breast feeding is the first in a long series of frustrations which the individual suffers from the woman.[5]

Anal training is inducted gradually, and apparently without the aid of punishment. In fact the child is not punished for any of its misdemeanors.

The most important discipline, or rather the absence of it, is in connection with sexual activity. The remarkable fact about this is that the natives recognize the sexual impulse in childhood and accord it the right of free exercise. One may even say that they go further than that; they induct the child into sexuality by masturbating it to keep it quiet. This fact is, however, not unequivocally indicative of a permissive attitude, for apparently no one has any stake in the child's sexuality. It is likewise an indicator of maternal neglect. In the case of the

[5] At this point we can be justly questioned on the license to call this a frustration to the child. The influence of breast feeding on the infant unquestionably extends beyond mere nourishment. Experience with war babies, most of whom were abandoned by their mothers, showed a very high mortality rate, and experienced nurses knew that fondling, caressing, and otherwise stimulating the child had a value in restoring them to health. Ferenczi observed on this point that "unloved children die."

girls, their labia are manipulated as a placebo, but also to encourage the growth of large labia, which to the Marquesans are a mark of beauty. In other words, there is social recognition of all sexual activity in childhood, and there are no restrictions against encouragement to exercise it freely; it is allotted the same place in the child's world that it occupies in the adult's. The taboos refer exclusively to objects, i.e., to siblings and parents. These taboos surely exist in regard to marriage and are probably maintained for sexual intercourse as well. The absence of fraternal polyandry is a fair indicator of the observance of taboos against siblings, as well as the suppression of jealousy between likely rivals. Furthermore, this free sexual situation is maintained with unbroken regularity from childhood on, and the sexual conflicts of the adult are no different from those of the child. Since the numerical ratio is about the same in children as adults, the rivalry situations are the same in both. So that the marital situation really introduces no new conflicts, and hence jealousy can be handled according to patterns learned in childhood.

As far as these disciplines are concerned, we may expect them to have a pronounced effect on the developing resources. We may expect consequences in two directions: in the attitude of the individual to these resources, and in the attitude toward those under whose care these resources develop.

Concerning the first, one can expect that sexual development is unobstructed in any way; that sexual gratification will be used as a placebo for frustrations experienced elsewhere; that potency disturbances will be unknown both in men and women; that the entire sexual training would tend to make for a special type of relationship to the sexual object. The sexual act is used by the Marquesans as an intoxicant during orgies (in conjunction with cannibalism), though we cannot tell from the evidence how much it is used as a reaction against frustrations. In view of their attitude to food, the sexual act is undoubtedly used as flight from anxiety. Potency disturbances are unknown in either sex, the best proof of which, in addition to the direct clinical evidence, is the fact that although malevolent magic is practiced, no one was known to complain that it was used to take his potency away. Nor has magic ever been used so far as is known, to take away a woman's potency, though it is used by one woman against another through the *fanaua*, to destroy the child in the uterus. This is in contrast to what is frequently found to be the case in societies where potency disturbances do occur; black magic is there used as an explanation of the phenomenon.

A corollary of the absence of potency disturbances is the fact that male potency (and fatherhood) is not especially played up and is not especially a means of enhancing one's self-esteem. Prestige is not gauged in terms of potency, but in terms of one's being a good food provider. With regard to the type of object relationship which the absence of sexual restrictions fosters, we woud expect that there would be a tendency to emphasize the sensual rather than the tender aspects. In other words, "romantic love" is the exception; the emphasis falls on the orgiastic aspects of sexual relations exclusively. This leads to the question of the sociological sources of romantic love, one on which a good deal more comparative study is necessary. From this culture, in contrast to our own, romantic love appears as a "hysteroid" phenomenon, the accentuation of which must be related to the overemphasis of the protective aspects of parenthood, and strong sexual aim and object taboos.

The second consequence of the absence of severe disciplines is concerned with the attitude toward those who care for the child. Here the situation is rather complicated because of the division of this care among father, mother, secondary husbands, maternal uncle, and paternal aunt. The influence of these two latter is remote. They have nominally the position of formal disciplinarians; but since there are no rigid disciplines, their functions are reduced to being sponsors to the child in some ceremonies.

The chief influence of the absence of restricting disciplines and the instrument of punishment as a means of coercion is on the constellations created around dependency. Here a sharp cleavage occurs in the resulting attitudes toward the father and secondary husbands, in contrast to that toward the mother.

We have seen from the study of our own culture that discipline has certain definite effects on the personality, and the specific reaction to it determines in part the character of the individual. An extreme instance of the complete compliance with discipline will serve to demonstrate its effects on the adaptive equipment of the individual.

A man of thirty-seven with a severe obsessional neurosis has, among many other symptoms, a particular anxiety of not being able to sleep. This fear he circumvents with a ritual in which the chief element is drinking a pint of gin. This fear of not being able to sleep applies only to nocturnal sleep, whereas when fatigue overcomes him during the day or Sundays, he sleeps quite naturally. Not being able to sleep has a long series of vague horrors associated with it, rationalized in various ways, none of them very convincing. However, the whole ritual is part of a preparation for his analytic hour, which comes in midmorning. So great is his fear that he may come late that he actually arrives half an hour before his appointed time.

His sleep anxiety has a long and complicated history. As a child he showed the usual resentment about going to bed. This resentment was greatly increased by the circumstance that his life as a child was regimented to an inordinate degree, and the most stringent prohibitions on masturbation, games with boys, and other normal pursuits were motivated by the desire of the parents to keep him from harming himself, and to make him into a perfect man. The chief conflict about masturbation was resolved with a complete compliance to the discipline, but with the added problem of how to prevent the impulse from arising in consciousness. Sleeplessness was associated with the desire to cheat on the taboo on masturbation. But sleep itself eventually became, not an enjoyable relaxation, but an acquiescence to discipline and all disciplines. At the age of six he was forced to go to bed for two hours in the afternoon. This was one discipline which he had the courage to cheat. He smuggled paper and crayons into his bed and spent his two hours in the most hectic imaginary activities, performing great exploits.

At the present time this patient spends most of his time getting himself into a frame of mind to be compliant to every demand made on him. Within the framework of his compliant system it is, however, very easy to detect his resistance to this discipline, for he rarely recognizes an autochthonous wish and even such wishes are immediately transformed into commands from someone else. So that instead of showing his defiance by coming late, he comes early. Instead of going to sleep because he is tired, he is insistent on not going to sleep because it is a duty, and because he may do some forbidden thing (masturbate) if he does not. To circumvent this system, he must narcotize his resistance with alcohol. The following dream is one he had after a *natural* sleep. "I am making love to a beautiful girl. The scene shifts. I am in a room where there is a strange figure, like a sculptured bust. This statue begins to talk in an insolent and petulant manner, and I get more and more angry at the figure. Finally I take a tumbler with some fluid in it and smash it against the figure."

The figure he identifies as that of an elderly friend who is impotent, and also as himself. The petulance is his own for being castrated (impotence being one of the patient's symptoms) . This aggression the patient immediately wishes to crush, and does so by narcotizing his aggression with alcohol. Making love to the girl is easily recognized by him as his repressed wish—which is vaguely expressed in the dream, but immediately interrupted by the fantasy of crushing his own aggression, which in turn is due to frustration of the sexual wish.

Since this is a dream of an uninduced sleep, we can see what our patient accomplishes by alcohol. To prevent the sexual impulse or wish from reaching consciousness is an essential part of his security system; but no less important is it for him to prevent his protest against this frustration from asserting itself. The dream dramatizes this situation quite accurately: a sexual fantasy occurs; it is immediately stopped; he is angry at this stoppage, now existing in the form of impotence; his castrated self cries out at this outrage; his other (repressing) self crushes this protest with alcohol, and all is well again, as far as keeping the sexual wish at bay is concerned. But the next day he is prostrated with the conflict.

The entire adaptive system with which this patient is operating is characteristic of the issues and problems of his fourth year of life. It represents one very extreme type of acquiescence to discipline. For our purposes it is important to dissect out the individual components. First, a system of defenses must be made against the forbidden impulse to prevent its emergence. A second defense must be made against the aggression caused by the frustration; the aggression is directed first against the parent who is the actual frustrating agent; but as it cannot be expressed (because the patient needs the parent's protection, care, and perhaps love), this aggression is then directed against himself (by a process the dynamics of which we shall later describe); the merits of the parent must be enhanced in proportion to the inhibition, with the result that the image of the parent becomes inflated in two ways—his power is exaggerated both to do harm and to do good. The harm is largely a reflection of the fear of being abandoned by the parent, and the protection and love which are the reward for repression become inflated in importance. Though this patient is now thirty-seven years old, this protective goal is still a dominant one in his adaptation. What he does not know is that the ability to exercise the forbidden impulse would at once deflate the value and importance of parental protection (or that of anyone else in loco parentis), and would, furthermore, enhance his own powers, and make the aggression provoked by his frustrations unnecessary.

This digression was necessary in order to clarify some of the features of Marquesan personality structure which are obliged to attribute to the absence of any disciplines such as we have described in our own culture. The problem in Marquesas divides itself into two separate parts. The weapon of discipline is not effectual only by virtue of the power of the parent to impose it; but its most important adjunct is the dependency of the child on the parent. In this regard, the dependency of the child in Marquesan culture is unequally satisfied by mother, father, and secondary husbands, and the fate of each constellation must be pursued separately.

One immediate consequence of the relation of children to parents (in this instance chiefly to fathers) is the absence of abnormal inflation of the parental image. The course of growth from a helpless state in infancy to adulthood plants one ineradicable constellation in every human, the expectation of help by some superior being, when the individual is confronted with a situation transcending his powers. It is natural, therefore, to expect that when he calls upon this superior being to aid him, he will utilize the same techniques which he learned from h's experience in winning protection from parents. Thus, in Marquesas, the absence of discipline does not do away with the necessity for a deity; but the technique for soliciting his aid is not by renunciation of gratifications. In Marquesas the loyalty of the group to a deified human is not bound by the mere fact that he was a progenitor, but is entirely contingent on the good deeds which the deity performs. Should the god fail to do these, his failure is not interpreted as an evidence of the god's anger, to offset which a series of punitive frustrations must then be imposed on the group for the purpose of nullifying the effects of pleasure, acting as a token of repentance, and hence as a claim for reinstatement into the good graces of the god. On the contrary, the failure of a god is interpreted merely as a sign of his inefficiency, and the group is free to shift its loyalties to another deity. This is one of the consequences of a child's having several protectors in the secondary husbands; if one fails, another helps. Suffering has no value as an agency for moving the god to use his magic powers in the individual's behalf. The direct testimony about the friendly relations between children and their fathers we have heard; but this evidence as to their attitude toward a god confirms the fact that the basic constellation that obedience and ingratiation confer security is not formed.

The attitude toward the father and secondary husbands is bound to be free of ambivalence; the child does not need to inflate their importance by increasing his dependency through restrictions. This raises an extremely important issue, the role of dependency in the security system of the individual. In Marquesas the individual has in certain basic aspects the opportunity for unrestricted development, and he has a security system based upon effectiveness and less need for dependency. The world of the child is like that of adults without the responsibilities. The dependency of the child is on a rational basis, not neurotically exaggerated—for there are many real dangers in this society from which the child needs protection. There are the dangers of breaking taboos, the dangers of being carried off by cannibals and eaten, and then the special danger of being carried off by the *vehini-hai*. The security against these dangers is derived from the father and secondary husbands. This entire situation prevents the formation of the constellation in the individual, "If I obey you, you will protect and care for me." Or, "If I want to be protected by you I must renounce certain gratifications and suffer." The positive side of this is the formation of the constellation "I can will and act for myself."

The relations of the child to the mother are of a different order. Whereas she is no more disciplinarian in the sense of a restricting influence than is the father, she fails the child as a protective influence. The role of the woman as mother and later as a sexual object is a frustrating one. It seems to be due to the ratio of men to women, and to the fact that the woman must cultivate and concentrate upon sexual techniques, to the disparagement of her tender relations to the child. The only other way one can speak of this fact is to say that the women are relatively devoid of "maternal instinct." One may even say that the encouragement of the child to sexual satisfaction is a way of shunting these dependent attitudes into sensual channels. The mother keeps the child quiet by masturbating him, and not by tenderness and care which he needs during the formative years.

Whether it is due to the absence of maternal interest in early life or to the subsequent frustrations from women due to numerical shortage, there is much indirect evidence that the longings for protection and love are not satisfied. In other words, the insecurity is caused by frustrated dependency longings, and is aggravated by real dangers in the outer world. The evidence in support of this is to be found in the folklore, where the woman is represented as the cannibal, as the seductress, as a siren-like creature, as the thief of children's food, and as the exploiter of children and young men. None of these characterizations is warranted by any of the actual practices of the Marquesans. But if we regard this indirect evidence as a neurotic distortion, it can be explained. We must seek the actual frustrations lying back of this grotesque representation of the woman. The only clues are maternal neglect in childhood and the sexual experiences of the adult, which have the unconscious significance of frustrations. The adoption of a child into another family after it had become attached to its own parents must, from the point of view of the child, be considered a real danger provocative of anxiety.

The question of dependency of the child in this culture is difficult to analyze because of the complicated actual situation. The real protectors of the child are the secondary husbands, and to a lesser degree the father. The mother as a protectress and caretaker suffers by comparison, in addition to the fact that she neglects the child. This lays the basis—together with the absence of restricting disciplines—for a friendly attitude toward the men, which predisposes to the later ease in repressing jealousy and which automatically puts the mother in a bad light by comparison. Do we in addition need to predicate that there are certain needs of the child which the mother alone can satisfy? I believe we do; because the frustrating experiences with women are not confined to childhood. Dependent and sexual attitudes seem to fuse to create this frustrating image. There is no time in the entire life cycle of the individual when the man can learn to trust the woman and think of her as one whose interest and loyalty he can count on. As far as the woman is concerned, as a child she is exposed to the same frustrating experiences, and immediately afterward is thrown into the same sexual role as the mother.

Such a representation of woman in folklore and myth can be approached from several viewpoints: it may represent some situation in the remote past, which was the result of circumstances long since forgotten, but which has been perpetuated and given new meaning in current life; or we may infer that the myths as they stand today are already adaptations of older ones, and hence express current conflicts and frustrations. The first view cannot be substantiated, and whether it is true or not does not much alter the attitude we are obliged to take that they express current strains. This raises the whole question of the function of fantasy. Our premises and methods prevent us from assuming that these fantasies are autochthonous creations unrelated to the realities in the living social situation.

If these myths are responses to current realities, we must first ask what kind of real situation can create such a representation. Among such possible situations are cruel treatment, the imposition of severe disciplines; the failure of the object to satisfy an important craving, thereby creating in the individual the necessity for repressing this craving. But the only factor we can definitely identify in Marquesas is the last of these.

Regarding the content of these myths, the woman is represented as a cannibal, as exploiting young men, as sacrificing the children's interests to her own, and as stealing children's food. Representing the woman as a cannibal is a serious distortion of the reality, where the men are the actual cannibals and child hunters. The frustrations obviously deal chiefly with food and sex. One may say that this is merely a convenient

way of representing the fear of starvation, and the blame
for the absence of adequate protection falls upon the mother.
According to Rank, this fear of being eaten up by the woman
represents a wish to return to the uterus. In this form the
interpretation is quite meaningless. Why should they wish to
return? This is the kind of interpretation commonly used in
psychoanalysis where the "unconscious" content (return to the
womb) is taken to be the motive for the fantasy, without
reference to the particular frustration to which the fantasy is
a reaction. Roheim would regard these fantasies as reflections
of a terror created by the boy witnessing parental intercourse.
This excites the boy, but his masculine pride is injured:
"when she seems to refuse him, he turns her into a cannibalistic
demon."[6] This is an interpretation which is very tenuous, and
incompatible with another interpretation which Roheim
makes: "Every trauma for which the mother is responsible
contains within it the danger of unsolved tasks and disap-
pointed wishes and may help to build the sinister conception
of the mother as a wild cannibal with a dangerous genital
organ."[7] It is to be noted that the conception of the dangerous
female genital is absent in Marquesas. It is this feature which
makes it all the more likely that the trauma in question is not
sexual in character.

The fact that the mother causes frustration is definite
enough. But there is still the problem of exactly what this
frustration is. If we regard it as dependency, need for support,
why is this not satisfied by the secondary husbands and father?
Or is there something specific about maternal tenderness which
the male guardian cannot supply? One may ask the same
question about the frustration of the adult men in the woman.

In this society the male, as child or as adult, shows the inability to trust, or to feel that the woman is devoted to him.
It is a question whether this is a basic human need. We do not
know very much about the role of maternal tenderness in the

formation of the personality; we know only that the original helplessness and protracted development make the maternal tenderness[8] a satisfying response to the dependency of the child. Nor is it at all understood in what relationship this dependency of child on the mother stands to the development of sexual attitudes. Without an understanding of this, no convincing answer can be given concerning the significance of the Oedipus complex. The feeling of frustrated dependency is related to what dangers the child has to face, and though the child is not restricted, the actual dangers nevertheless remain real.

The situation in the Marquesas is strikingly different from our own. In our culture the dependency situation between child and mother is not distorted by absence of care, but by the introduction of restricting disciplines; in Marquesas the normal dependency is frustrated, but no restricting disciplines are imposed. That absence of restrictions is no compensation for the necessary care is amply proved by the derogatory representation of the mother in Marquesan folklore. Restrictions do tend to increase and prolong this dependency, with resulting inflation of the parental image, but they evidently satisfy an important need in the child. Maternal tenderness is apparently an important adjunct to growth and development.

The further consequences of the relations of the child to parents in the Marquesas are: a precocious independence—a fact that Dr. Linton called to our attention—and a self-confidence remarkable in comparison with European age-behavior standards. This is indicated further by the institution of children's gangs, which to all intents are a replica of the adult life without its responsibilities.

The sibling situation in the Marquesas shows no very unusual features. The absence of fraternal polyandry and the fact that a man can wear clothes woven only by one of his female

[8] For a very suggestive treatment of this theme see Margaret Mead, *Sex and Temperament* (New York, 1935). The contrast in maternal tenderness in Arapesh and Mundugomore is very striking.

relatives, who are sexually taboo, indicates the binding character of these taboos. However, sibling rivalry is unquestionably diminished by the existence of equal opportunities for sexual gratification and by the fact that siblings have common friends in the secondary husbands and one common "enemy"—the mother. The importance of the oldest child we shall treat later; but there is no indication that this situation causes undue conflicts.

We would expect that the tenderest relations in the family would exist between father and daughter. The fact is that there are no mother-son incest stories, but those between father and daughter are described.

There are two other problems which are related to the ratio of men to women: the special importance of primogeniture and general importance of children, and the problem of homosexuality.

The investiture of the oldest child (male or female) with the familial *potestas* and the reckoning of genealogies along lines of oldest children are phenomena which we cannot explain. There are too many unknown factors. These phenomena may be related to the relative difficulty in impregnation, the difficulties of labor, etc. There is only one aspect which we can see, and that is in relation to the rivalry situation between the men. Handing over the *potestas* to a young child who cannot use it may have the effect of diminishing hostility between men. It really means that the man enjoys the highest prestige during the time when he is least able to use it to anyone's disadvantage. In the folktales Dr. Linton observes that the parents disappear from the story as soon as the child is born. Moreover, this same child must surrender his prestige probably while he is still a youth. It may thus be regarded as one of the safeguards of male solidarity. But this is not certain. This feature suggests in addition that the culture is centered more about the child than is ours.

This problem of the significance of the child is extremely

difficult to solve from the material at hand. The various facets are contradictory. On the one hand, there is the suspicion of female infanticide; on the other, the heightened significance of the oldest child—male or female. There is evidence of great desire for children, yet judging from the personal and food taboos imposed upon parents, there is probably also unconscious hostility to the child in a society where food anxiety is prominent.

The institution of free adoption both of oldest and younger children has many implications. Fecundity may have been generally low or very uneven. By this custom the adopted child could be used as a pawn in the status ambitions of the foster parents. If an unborn child could be thus freely demanded, and its delivery made certain by threat of a feud, there is every reason why women would resent the bother of child-bearing through fear that their children would be taken away. This may be the actual situation in back of the phenomenon of the *vehini-hai,* the *fanaua,* the feigned pregnancy, and the wish for women to destroy the child in another woman's uterus.

The feelings connected with this custom undoubtedly differed in parents and children. To the adoptor it was likely to bring prestige; to the actual parents chagrin, and to the child anxiety.

The relation of the males to each other has one other important aspect, that of male homosexuality. The fact is that this perversion is common enough. Male transvestitism is also known to exist. This perversion must be accounted for on one of four grounds: biologically determined inversion; strong hatred of the father, with abandonment of sexual goal to insure his love and support; a love tie based on mutual hatred of women; or a love tie based on a scarcity of women, and hence a supplementary sexual gratification. This could only be settled by a study of the individual. However, from the arrangement of institutions, we can safely rule out the element of father hatred. It is not without significance that the perversion of fellatio and not anal intercourse is the form in which it is expressed. This points strongly in favor of its being a supplementary activity, in fact a form of making good a long-felt craving for dependency which cannot be satisfied by the woman in this culture. Representation of the penis as a feeding organ is often found in their folk tales, especially in those written from the point of view of the woman.

Food Anxiety

Subsistence economy is the rational method of dealing with the problem of insuring food supply and shelter. It requires techniques of production, of distribution, and of preparing for eventualities of failure. The ability to guard against food anxiety depends essentially on intellectual and technical resources, means of exploiting and controlling the natural environment and animals. A third element in the control is the social organization for coöperation toward these ends. But there are always elements, such as weather and rainfall, which are beyond control.

The technical equipment of the Marquesans is adequate under ordinary conditions. Under conditions of drought it fails. The social organization for coöperative effort is rigidly maintained, but chiefly by an inner feeling of its importance rather than by punishments for the individual who fails. The social organization in this respect is communal in some respects and individual in others. It is important to note that practically all of production is in the hands of men.

The rational methods for dealing with food anxiety consist of storing food, and increasing the prestige of the experts who perpetuate the techniques (*tuhungas*). The range of social mobility the *tuhunga* enjoys is an indication of the underlying food anxiety (though other craftsmen enjoy the same). His position cuts across class lines and tribal lines. *Tuhungas* are most eagerly sought out for blood brotherhood (*enoa*) and hence enjoy immunities from enmities to which the others are subject. Likewise they are admitted to deification.

The magical forms of insuring food supply are of the customary kind, through the propitiation of a god. The procedure is by entreaty and sacrifice or offering, which is merely another way of feeding the god.

Notwithstanding the adequacy of techniques of and organization for production, there is evidence of an exaggerated anxiety about food. There is first of all an overvaluation of eating itself, the emphasis falling on bulk and not on quality. The taboos surrounding eating and cooking, the consecration of hands, the great care in making food pounders, and many other practices all point to this anxiety. Cannibalism is one more important evidence of food anxiety.

The effects of food anxiety are important for us to track down. But in order to do this we must formulate some general ideas about the significance of food. The satisfaction from eating is the earliest and most constant experience of all animal life. The importance of food for the intactness and effectiveness of the ego cannot escape any living thing. It is, however, more than that; eating is a pleasurable activity in itself, because of its gustatory stimulus and because of the sense of fullness which follows it. Eating may furthermore be used as substitute for other gratifications when they fail, or for relieving anxieties coming from other sources. However, there is no reason why food should be used for that purpose in the Marquesas, for sexual development is unrestricted, and the basic pattern of exchanging food for sex is not formed. There is no unusual amount of chewing pleasure, no undue amount of smoking, though men have been seen sucking women's breasts when this was not a preliminary to sexual activity.

The reactions to food anxiety which we have described can be called normal reactions. For our purposes we must note another group of reactions which may be indicators of quantitative differences or degrees of depth of the underlying anxiety, and hence require more extreme defensive measures. These constellations are derived from the unconscious elaborations of ideas pertaining to the intactness and effectiveness of the ego. The defensive measure cannot be understood unless we understand the stimulus to which it is a response, and the forms which this anxiety takes in dream and fantasy. The institution which purports to assuage this anxiety is derived from a certain unconscious image.[9]

Let us consider the idea of fear of losing the effectiveness of the ego. How can one insure against it? One can enhance its size, power, and prestige; or one can make duplicates of oneself by giving oneself many names. This latter is a noteworthy institution. The ideas pertaining to intactness are much easier to identify, for they are expressed in overt fears of disintegration. Against this fear there is a rational defense to prevent disintegration, which is the institution of embalming. But there is a second more important fear, the fear of being eaten up, and for this there are two defenses, embalming and cannibalism. A third guarantee, universal in distribution, occurs in some form of the idea of immortality.

The relation between ideas about intactness, immortality, power, and eating is to be found in their process of creating a god. He is an individual who was important in life, a *tuhunga*, chief, inspirational priest, whose powers are augmented, perpetuated, and rendered immortal by a process of eating ten human sacrifices, one for each part of the body which receives a separate name. This fantasy is in itself a description of the manner in which the feeling of euphoria and power are induced in this culture by food, and this in turn is an indication of how deep are the anxieties from this source.

One of the legends[10] describes these relationships between many names and eating and rebirth. The story of Tohe-Tika is as follows: He is born after a gestation of two months, and goes to live with the gods. Three months later in a dream of his mother he demands breadfruit and fish from her. She sends two of her brothers, the formal disciplinarians, who get the food, but on their way to the god, they eat it up. The god discovers this, and he cuts off his uncles' heads. The mother then sends

---

[9] These hypochondriacal fears cannot very convincingly be derived from the "castration complex," and much important information would be lost by considering all anxieties as replicas of a universal castration anxiety.

[10] E. S. Craighill Handy, *Marquesan Legends* (Honolulu, 1930), p. 107.

two other brothers, who repeat the same performance. Finally, the parents set out themselves. The god finds them, but the parents flee. The god then goes away to live as a man, and marries. One day he and his father-in-law go fishing, and the net gets caught. While the god is in the water, a shark bites off his head. The shark brings the head to the god's parents. Through the great power of the god, the mother conceives again, and gives birth in one and one half months. The god takes the child, and makes it into his arms and hands. In two months she gives birth again, and he makes the child into his trunk, and so on, until he is restored to his integrity. Then the people fear him because of his great power.

This fantasy contains a persistent demand on the mother for food. This complaint is tied to a fantasy of incompleteness which is remedied by successive births, after which the god eventually emerges omnipotent and fear-inspiring. These re-births reëstablish the integrity and euphoria of the ego. The fear of being eaten up is likewise remedied by rebirths. Food is used to remedy frustrated feelings of dependency and intact-ness. The hostility to those who steal the food and consequent vengeance by cannibalism is striking. At each rebirth the hero regains those parts of the body which are each given separate names. Simultaneously this story indicates the unconscious hatred of the child as one who may eat the food his parents and relatives would rather have themselves.

Whereas no special psychological difficulties are presented by embalming and the other phenomena which we traced to food anxiety, cannibalism is more difficult to elucidate. All phe-nomena of cannibalism cannot be explained on a unitary basis; it undoubtedly has different meanings and may be the expression of different motives. One can differentiate at least the following: hunger cannibalism; necrophagia—eating the corpse; vengeance cannibalism; gustatory perversion. The case of hunger cannibalism needs no explanation. Necrophagia can be the expression of a strong love tie, and the eating of the corpse a last rite of perpetuating the existence of the deceased as well as of absorbing his valued qualities. Cannibalism as a gustatory perversion is mentioned because it is often offered as a rationalization. This can be ruled out as a real motive. The most baffling is the vengeance cannibalism.

"Vengeance cannibalism" is a poor term to describe this complicated phenomenon. Under most conditions it is a sufficient satisfaction when any mastery impulse diminishes or annhilates the effectiveness of the opponent. The most extreme form is to kill the opponent. However, the added feature of eating the enemy raises the question of the origin and meaning of this activity. To call it a derivative of hunger cannibalism, i.e., an institution founded originally on necessity and subsequently put to other uses, still leaves the latter question unanswered.

The only approach to the problem which promises some aid in understanding this complicated behavior is to study it in cultures where there are some records of its significance. Such records we find in Egyptian mortuary literature. The evidence from that source—too lengthy to be presented here—indicates that cannibalism in Egypt began as necrophagia, was practiced in the form of "vengeance cannibalism," and that a reaction formation set in due to factors we cannot trace, which ended in a fear of being eaten up. Necrophagia and hunger cannibalism have very different meanings; the first is motivated by the desire to perpetuate, the other to destroy the object eaten. But from a psychological standpoint both have a common source, the early experience of being fed by the mother, where the constellation "I devour you" or "I take you into myself" becomes a basic prototype of a dependent relationship. The cannibalistic significance of eating has often been recovered in children. In Egyptian literature, Osiris is often represented with grain growing out of his body, and as saying, "I am a grain." Frequently in Marquesan legends, a tree grows out of the mother's body, which the children eat. The change of attitude in necrophagia to the eating of an enemy is thus drawn from the same source and represents basically an anxiety of need for support or a need for food.

The "fear of being eaten up" is a constellation often found in individuals in a helpless state. The derivation of the cannibalistic impulse from frustrated dependency is, however, not a direct one. The phases are as follows. An observation confirmed by everyday experience is that "love can turn to hate." Because of its frequency, this observation does not offend common sense. Of similar character is the observation that an inability to trust another object to satisfy certain emotional cravings leads to the perception of being injured by that object, whereupon active steps in the form of aggression against the object are taken. The form of aggression derives its character from the nature of the impulse in question. The frustrated impulse leads to the perception of the object doing the negative of the wish to depend on the object: the wish to eat the object becomes the fear of being eaten. It is this perception against which an aggressive attitude is taken—"I eat you up." Exactly this same process takes place when love turns to hate. It has been called by Anna Freud "identification with the aggressor," but this does not accurately describe the steps involved, because the term "identification" describes an arbitrary change of ego attitude without describing its antecedents. Nevertheless, Anna Freud's designation does justice to the facts descriptively.

The story of Hansel and Gretel describes this cannibalistic wish as arising very explicitly from frustrated dependency and starvation fear. In this story the cruel mother starves the children and throws them out into the forest. In the forest they dream of a fairy godmother (the protecting mother) who promises to look after them. The next day they come upon the witch who tries to lure the children to the door of the oven, to push them in and make gingerbread out of them. However, they succeed in pushing the old witch into the oven and make gingerbread out of her. It is the kind father who rescues them and brings them food.

The manner in which the cruel mother who starves them is turned into a witch with the intention of eating the children is very explicit. The wish to "eat" the mother is likewise very clear. In contemporary individuals fantasies of being eaten up are likewise provoked by frustrated dependency wishes. A patient whose life was a sheltered one, though filled with anxiety, reacted to the analytic situation after it became clear to him that the analysis would attempt to break up his neurotic security system. He then reacted to me as a disturber of his dependency in the following terms. He dreamed of an enormous spider who approached him with open fangs; he tries to kill it but awakened in terror. His association is the nursery rhyme about "Little Miss Muffet sat on a tuffet eating of curds and whey; along came a spider who sat down beside her and frightened Miss Muffet away." I was naturally the spider with the open fangs, threatening his curds and whey—his infantile, dependent, and feminine position.

We return to our remarks about Egypt, where the connection between the fear of being eaten up and cannibalism and embalming is very aptly illustrated: On the tombs of the great pharaohs, who were buried beneath mountains of granite, and whose bodies were embalmed for eternity, were engraved descriptions of the post-mortem adventures of the departed king. When he comes into heaven, he feeds on the gods. He has a retinue of slaves who hunt the gods like wild beasts, lasso and dismember them; they are then served the king for food—to this same king whose great fear is that he may be devoured.[11]

The gods upon whose bodies Unas fed were snared by Am-Kehuu; they were examined as to their fitness and condition by Tcheser-tep-f. Finally the gods were bound by Her-thertu, and the god Khensu cut their throats and took out their intestines. A being called Shesemu cut them up and cooked pieces thereof in his fiery cauldrons. Thereupon Unas ate them and

---

[11] J. H. Breasted, *The Dawn of Conscience* (New York, 1933), pp. 88–90; A. E. Wallis Budge, *The Gods of the Egyptians* (London, 1904), I, 33–38.

in eating them he also ate their words and power and their spirits. The largest and finest of the gods he ate at daybreak, and the smaller-sized ones for meals at sunset, and the smallest for the meals at night; the old and worn-out gods he rejected entirely and used them up as fuel in his furnace.

No matter from what standpoint cannibalism is considered, one always comes upon this basic idea of absorbing the qualities or substance of the object eaten, based upon the first eating experience at the mother's breast. In the Marquesas this fear of being eaten is expressed in many ways and leads to a good many different kinds of institutions, the purpose of which is to relieve this fear. It is this anxiety which undoubtedly increases the hostility between tribes. The rage engendered by these anxieties can most easily be expressed on those whom one has no reason to love.

We see, therefore, that food scarcity in Marquesas leads to certain constellations of a hypochondriacal character within the personality structure of the individual. It is from these constellations that the secondary institutions are derived. Thus fears of losing intactness and effectiveness lead to configurations of incompleteness, rage, fear of being eaten up, and the wish to eat others up. From these are derived multiple naming, myths of successive rebirths, embalming, cannibalism, and the establishment of being a good feeder as the measure of prestige, much feasting with emphasis on bulk, and a euphoria based on the prototype of a full stomach.

Raiding in order to capture children for cannibalistic purposes is undoubtedly known by every child to be a masculine pursuit. In Marquesan legends, however, it is not the men who are cannibals, but women. The reasons for this distortion we have already discussed. The dynamism pursued in this particular case is characteristic of this culture. The myths further describe a relationship between the fear of being eaten up and the sexual act, where the penis is obviously used as a feeding organ. The manifest content of these myths says that the woman loses her cannibalistic qualities when the man satisfies her sexually. The man is represented distinctly as the exploited victim. This we can understand only if we follow a little farther the relations between the sexes.

RELATION BETWEEN THE SEXES—NEUROSES

From a purely behavioristic viewpoint there is very little evidence of tension between the sexes. The women are treated with disdain and aloofness, yet as oldest child the woman becomes heir to the rights of primogeniture and may hold the office of inspirational priest. This is enough to show that she is not discriminated against socially. She has, moreover, complete mobility in marriage. Her chief weapon is her sexual desirability, which moves her easily through class lines. The tensions do not arise from any rivalry situation between the sexes. We have already concluded that this rivalry situation between the men for the woman is settled in an amicable way. But the rivalries between women are not so peacefully solved. The character of the inner relations between men and women must be derived from the legends and religion, since we have no biographies to draw upon.

As we have seen from the character of the early disciplines, there is very little chance for failure in development of the activity necessary to consummate the sexual act. The taboos which concern objects are not enough to interfere with this development. Any difficulties between the sexes must arise therefore from the external social conditions. There is evidence of sexual conflict on both sides. The feigned pregnancy of the women and the institutions of *fanaua* and familiars testify to the presence of neurotic disturbances in both. This must be examined for each sex separately.

In the first tale about Temooniew, the sexual act from the point of view of the male is regarded as an act of prowess, which makes the woman angry. The hero vanquishes her cannibalistic traits by intercourse. But after this point it is the woman who steals the man away and exploits his sexuality. Her cannibalism reappears at any dissatisfaction with the man.

The actual facts about sexual life are that the woman will on occasions satisfy many men in succession, but her private orgies are largely with individual men. Over these latter encounters the woman evidently exercises the option of consent. The sexual orgy is so arranged that most of the time is consumed by arousing her with cunnilingus and other perversions. At a given signal from her the man completes the act until she has an orgasm. The act is arranged for her special satisfaction. No special premium is placed on male potency, since that is taken for granted. In the sexual act it is the woman who is the initiator and aggressor. Since intercourse is optional with her and requires the consent of the chief husband, the husbands must feel that they can be exploited by the woman. This situation places a high competitive value on the woman's capacity to dispense favors and puts the man in the position where he suffers by comparison with other men and may be cut off from sexual satisfaction should he fail to please. Thus the women, through their scarcity, are in a position to tyrannize over the men. Moreover, the men are given little opportunity to feel that they control the situation, and no opportunity at all for the security that goes with a tender relationship.

In many of the tales the man occupies a position very similar to that of the innocent girl in Western rape stories. He is stolen for his sexual usefulness to the woman, and constantly threatened with being eaten up should he fail. Only the affect of being exploited is comprehensible from the direct evidence supplied by prevailing social conditions. The other anxieties, like the fear of being devoured, seem to come from several sources: first the frustrating mother who cheats the child of tenderness; then the man's inability to possess the woman exclusively and feel that he can trust her; finally his inability to impregnate the woman at will, for contraception is necessary to keep parenthood straight. All in all, the man is much on the defensive in his entire sexual role.

The question of why the sexual act allays the cannibalistic impulses in the woman is more difficult to answer. The penis is given the significance of a feeding organ.[12] This fantasy has a striking resemblance to the one found in our culture, where the fear of being devoured by the woman is represented by the vagina dentata. The customary explanations concerning this as a castration anxiety or a fantasy of returning to the mother's womb are highly cryptic and meaningless unless we identify the anxiety in real life of which this is an elaboration. And on this point, beyond what we have already indicated, our analysis fails us. This can be thoroughly tracked down only in the individual; the institutional framework merely supplies the setting.

We can thus conclude that despite the plentiful opportunity for sexual union, the "sexual impulse" in its broadest sense is not satisfied for the male. In the place of the usual "castration complex" of the male there is the fantasy of being devoured by the woman. This is a remarkable distortion of reality, for in this culture it is the man who is the cannibal and child hunter. But he is in no way associated with restricting sexual gratification. The usual dread of the father is absent and there is no general fear of mutilation. The scarcity of women, the inability to trust them; the inability to impregnate them at will; all of these introduce elements of anxiety which for reasons already discussed make women into hostile and secretly hated objects. To the male it appears as though the woman rules the roost; and the suppression of jealousy between men puts her in an unfavorable light. Though she has no economic or disciplinary power and no ability to exploit anyone, she has an ability to frustrate several important needs.

The best proof of the sexual dissatisfaction of the male and of the ability of the woman to exploit this dissatisfaction for settling the problems of jealousy between women is to be found in the institution of *fanaua*. These are vicious male spirits who "sell" their post-mortem magical powers to the woman of their choice in return for sexual favors. The man is thus used as a

[12] One possible explanation is that the woman has the same frustrating reactions to the mother that the man has. Her sexual activity is likewise an attempt to make up in sensuality what it lacks in tenderness and support.

tool with which one woman can avenge herself on another. But true to the morals which prevail in this society, the *fanaua* will not attack the husband of the woman whose ghostly paramour he is. The familiars are kindred to the *fanaua*. They may be incestuous objects, hence taboo. Both familiars and *fanaua* are testimony to the fact that the man in this society is the underdog sexually, and that the woman is well aware of this power to exploit the male by her ability to satisfy his sexual needs. These spirits make their presence known to the woman through her dreams. To the man this institution is a promise that sexual dissatisfactions can be remedied after death.

But the woman is not free of "sexual" conflicts either. Though her sexuality has a scarcity value, a fact which renders the role of woman socially preferable, she has neurotic disorders coming from other sources. First, she is the victim of the same maternal neglect as the male, and is soon thrown into exactly the same role as her mother. Sexual indulgence is a palliative for the cravings for maternal affection in childhood, and later a placebo for restrictions on pregnancy. There is one difference, however, in that the relations to father and secondary husbands are bound to retain more tenderness and less anxiety than that of the boy to the mother. Perhaps this is why stories of father-daughter incest are present, those of mother-son absent.

The father-daughter incest story reported by Handy is a Marquesan Electra tale. The girl connives at the father's wish for intercourse, not knowing he is her father. The mother is jealous and prohibits any further contact. There is no punishment for the offense beyond a mild scolding.

The jealousy situation between women does not need to be repressed for any reason, and judging from this story, and the social situation as a whole, the jealousy between women runs high. It is distinctly a prestige problem for the woman with a high premium on beauty and skill in the sexual arts. The gain is marriage to the most powerful man, for there are no social barriers to the woman's mobility. This is a situation which would tend to increase rather than diminish sexual jealousy between the women, though no woman fails of opportunities either for sexual gratification or marriage. In the role of wife, the more attractive and skillful she is, the more men she can attract to her household.

The neurotic manifestation of pseudocyesis (feigned pregnancy) is related to the jealousy between women regarding prestige and pregnancy. The motives for this cannot be adequately traced from our ethnological account. We would need to know whether it is related to a general difficulty in becoming pregnant, whether it is the unmarried woman who feigns pregnancy, the childless married woman, or the mother after her first child, etc. It is known that the pregnancy of the woman immediately enhances her power over the chief husband, a right which she does not ordinarily enjoy. He immediately becomes subject to many taboos. Yet it would be difficult to assign this enhancement as the motive for feigned pregnancy.

The whole phenomenon of pregnancy is filled with mystery to the Marquesans. Deaths during pregnancy and labor are frequent. The only clue we have to this feigned pregnancy is the superstition that the woman whose child disappears from the womb has been taken by the *vehini-hai* and devoured, and that a woman who dies in childbirth is the victim of a *fanaua,* which means in a practical way that she was killed by another woman.

We can only venture a few guesses. If the death during childbirth is the victim of a *fanaua* then it is the *work* of a male spirit acting under the direction of another woman. Hence it merely means that the women are very jealous of each other's pregnancy and feel extremely hostile to each other. The source of this fantasy is what one woman feels toward another woman. Most of the victims of sorcery are women. On the other hand, it is the actual deed of a male spirit who is sexually dissatisfied. We can therefore say that the man has a feeling of animosity to the child who steals his sexual object. The fact that the father is given a pig to compensate him for any sacrifices he will make for the child is a reflection of the fact that this hostility to the child is a part of the general food anxiety. This is furthermore borne out by the fact that the dead child is feared, for it has been deprived of the right to eat and live.

There are many other reasons why women feign pregnancy. It signals a high degree of triumph over the resistance of the men and over women rivals. More than this we can get only from personal study of the woman.[13] The wholesale practice of adoption may be the actual institution from which the *fanaua* and *vehini-hai* take their origin. The jealousy among women because of children, together with the fear of having their off-spring taken away places an undue emphasis on the child, and the enhancement of the child's prestige may in part be due to this. As we have seen, the institution of adoption is the meeting place of many conflicting attitudes.

This culture, with its sexual conflicts, demonstrates the re-markable fact that serious disturbances in the sexual sphere, in the larger sense, can arise in a society where the institutions permit unrestricted development of the activity necessary to consummate the sexual act. This merely rules out disturbances of potency in one form or another. Disturbances in the relation-ship between the sexes in this society have their roots not only in food anxiety and in the scarcity of women, but also in the absence of tenderness.[14]

There is one final sexual issue in this culture, the castration complex of the woman. Its customary form in our culture is the wish on the part of the woman to assume male status, or envy of the penis. The classical theory about this "complex" in

[13] This pseudocyesis can be construed as a guilt phenomenon, consequent upon the actual practice of infanticide. There is little, however, to indicate that fe-male children are elect victims of *fanaua*. The pseudocyesis may likewise be a part of the effort on the part of the woman to "identify" herself with her fetus, and this in turn is traceable to the frustrations by the mother.

[14] The only psychotic disorder mentioned by Dr. Linton is that of pathological man-eating, when a man would kill his own wife and children. Cannibalism within the tribe was definitely regarded as aberrant and punished, except when designated by the inspirational priest in famine. We can venture the guess that these are some form of involutional melancholias.

our culture is that it begins with the idea that the female believes that her organ is a deformity, meaning the absence of a penis; and that she has lost it, been deprived of it, and has hopes of growing one in place of the lost member. The literature is too voluminous to review. The main ideas about its origin are that the sight of the male penis is a blow to the self-esteem of the little girl (the narcissistic theory), and another is that it is the social status of the male which incites the real envy, the penis being a symbol of prestige.

Our material supplies little direct evidence on this point. But we can raise some questions about it. The author cannot subscribe to either of the two main views expressed about the origin of the castration complex in the woman. He has seen many cases in which it was conclusively shown that the envy of the penis or ideas of its loss originated after childhood masturbation had been effectively interfered with, or some element of pain introduced into this activity. In other words, it has the same origin in the female as it has in the male. The conviction that the penis has been cut off is a rationalization of an actual fact, that the child's pleasure organ has actually been taken away, or at least its free exercise stopped. Prior to this, the idea of the loss of an organ does not occur to the little girl. And since in our culture, even when masturbation is permitted, it is impossible for the child to get full social approval for the activity, the female castration complex is bound to be practically universal, by virtue of the implied disciplines.

It becomes, therefore, a test case to prove the female castration complex in Marquesan culture where female masturbation in childhood is encouraged; where the significance of the sexual act in adults is permitted full imitation by the child as soon as this is possible; where the woman has a high and assured scarcity value, where, therefore, she has a high social position and enjoys the capacity to exploit men by her sexuality. If the mere sight of the male organ inflicts a narcissistic injury, then it ought to be present in Marquesas or any other culture, irrespective of the opportunities to exercise the vagina as a pleasure organ. In the folklore the woman is not represented with phallic attributes;[15] it is the male who occasionally dons female manner and role. Nor is there any evidence of female homosexuality. The only female hysterical symptom is a feigned pregnancy, a very feminine role. In the Marquesan culture, feminine rivalry is with the other woman for female excellence, for children, and not with the man, for either his sexual organ or social status. It is difficult on any grounds to see why the woman in this society should want to be a man.[16]

We may now summarize parental conflicts centering about the child. He is hated as one who eats the parents' food. To allay this hostility the father is given a pig as compensation; the mother deprives him of the breast; both parents are placed under food taboos during pregnancy and the father is compelled to act as protector. On the other hand the child is much desired; his value is enhanced because of the scarcity of children, and high honors are thrust upon him. He becomes a pawn in the prestige conflicts of the parents; he is a factor in the status of the father, and for the mother a weapon to shame other women (hence, the feigned pregnancy). Since the child may be forcibly adopted, this symptom is a compromise between the wish to have a child and the wish to cheat the one who may steal it away.

Status, Authority, Prestige, and Power

The social organization of the Marquesans presents one very unusual feature, the importance of primogeniture. Its im-

[15] One might claim that this is not complete evidence because the female is there represented as the male sees her, and that ceremonial priests being all males, no female point of view is permitted to intrude.

[16] However, those who insist on any evidence to prove a theory will find in the prolongation of the labia, in the long tongue which the cannibalistic ogress sticks out, phallic symbols, and regard the cannibalistic woman as one who wishes to castrate the man because of penis envy. With these views the author cannot concur, for they are totally inconsistent with all the evidence. One could force the issue on the female castration complex by interpreting the feigned pregnancy as really having the unconscious content of a penis. If so then the incentive for this equation of child and penis must come from some phylogenetic source and not from the actual frustrations experienced in real life.

portance rests on several associated factors: that the family *potestas* is vested in an individual who cannot use it, that this oldest child outranks the father and can put him under severe restraints if he so chooses, and that rank and genealogy are reckoned through the oldest child irrespective of sex or paternity. The oldest child therefore acquires highest status, authority in the form of ability to exploit other members of the household, and prestige. He receives the tangible property such as the house, and has the ability to contract the most favorable marriage, and thus of becoming household-head and chief executive over secondary husbands. Since it is not always a man who gets this position, the conventions about primogeniture cannot be attributed to the desire to keep property in the male line; and since the oldest child can be adopted, the significance of actual paternity is lost. Whatever power the oldest child has is lost immediately upon the birth of his child. The practical effect of this situation is to give the highest rank and power to an individual when he is least likely to use it to the disadvantage of others. The institution undoubtedly has a mollifying effect on potential hostilities between men of the household.

The younger son is distinctly subordinate and cannot inherit anything but the tree which is his birthright. He usually takes the role of a secondary husband. There is little evidence, however, that this role is a painful one, or that it generates uncontrollable aggression. The reasons for this we have already mentioned. The men are banded together, and the most friendly relations exist between chief husband and those whom he outranks. The relations are coöperative and all have much to gain from mutual loyalty. The chief husband cannot really exploit the secondary ones, for the latter are not bound to the household; and besides prestige, he cannot enjoy any particular advantages in the form of personal wealth. The only individual in the society who exercises an arbitrary right to exploit anyone is the inspirational priest, who can tyrannize over an individual by threatening to curse him.

There is no opportunity in this culture to accumulate wealth, for it exists only in a form to be expended in ceremonies.[17] The social mobility of both household and the individual is considerable. There is, however, some envy of the rich by the poor. The only crimes known are stealing of food and killing for jealousy.

There is considerable struggle for rank and prestige; it must, however, be noted that there is no evidence that this conflict causes the necessity for severe repression of hostility within the group. The reason for this absence is to be sought in the freedom of impulse expression along sexual lines, the ability of the individual to share completely in the household prestige, and the fact that all the men are unconsciously banded together by hatred of the woman. In the long run it is the attractive woman who really controls the man power, by attracting desirable men. This tends to solidify the men and not to disrupt their solidarity.

In short, power and prestige among men in this culture cannot be abused; there are too many counterchecks, in the form of social mobility; the inability to use any advantage to another's disadvantage; too much mutual dependency among the men; and too much risk in abusing anyone.

The prestige conflicts are, however, much keener among the women. A singular proof of this is that they are the commonest targets for malevolent sorcery. This is really an astonishing fact. We are accustomed in other cultures to see the unconscious hostility directed toward individuals who have the power to use others for their own ends without due compensation, and toward those who can institute severe disciplines. In this culture the most feared and hated individual is not the bearer of prestige, authority, or power, but the woman, who has neither. She draws this hatred not because she has any actual authority or economic power. She does not even exert disciplinary functions.

[17] This is perhaps an additional reason why prestige is not the cause of much intrasocial hostility—at least not within household bounds. Power can be used only to give feasts, and the feasts are democratic; everyone, including enemies, eats his fill. So high is the regard for food that hostilities are suspended to permit enjoyment. The food provider is loved and not envied.

Her power is vested in her ability to frustrate an important need both in childhood, in the form of the child's need for support, trust, and security, and in the adult, in the form of the need for sexual satisfaction.

This gives us an important clue. It shows that aggressive and masochistic attitudes can be directed toward objects who do not have the power to exploit or discipline, but have merely the power to frustrate an important need, without the aid of the other two powers. The unconscious image formed of such an individual may be of the same character as that created by an exploiter or disciplinarian. If these constellations were evaluated in Marquesas as they are in our culture, then the father ought to be the object of hatred. In our culture, discipline, ability to frustrate important needs of dependency, and hence the ability to exploit—in other words all the attributes of authority, are often concentrated in the father. It would be difficult to classify the Marquesan as an authoritarian or non-authoritarian culture. Restrictive disciplines, in the sense in which we use this term, do not exist; the ability to exploit another is checked except in the case of the inspirational priest, and the only target for hatred is the frustrator of important needs. This explains the fact that the woman in folklore occupies a position very like that of the father in our culture, and is the most common target for malevolent sorcery.

THE BASIC PERSONALITY (EGO) STRUCTURE
OF THE INDIVIDUAL

We are now in a position to get some notion of the basic personality structure of the individual, resulting from the impact of these institutions on the individual. By basic personality structure we mean the effective adaptive tools of the individual which are common to every individual in the society. The term basic personality structure must be sharply differentiated from character. The latter is an individual arrangement of habitual ego attitudes, the formation of which depends on status and sex, and the particular selection of attributes resulting from individual reactions to the same institutions. Basic personality structure refers to the larger orbit of potentialities which the culture creates. The difference between these two concepts is not important when one studies the differentia among various individuals from the same culture. These are character differences. But when we study the differences between adaptive equipment furnished by different cultures, we study basic personality structure. One Eskimo may be obstinate and suspicious, another may be compliant and trusting; these are character traits. But the basic personality structure of an Eskimo is different from that of a Marquesan, because it is the product of different institutions. Since we know nothing about individuals in Marquesas, we can only study basic personality structure, the framework within which all character differences are contained.

In this general category we can include techniques of thinking, attitude toward objects, security systems, and "super-ego" formation.

Many of the thought processes we encountered in the Marquesans correspond to those we designate as scientific. We found them in the rational methods of dealing with food anxiety. These scientific methods of dealing with reality are developed to no small degree, but we are more interested in the methods of dealing with situations where the reality cannot be apprehended. In these instances we find a type of animistic thinking, a characterization which is not very precise.

The specific problem is to identify the forms in which the Marquesans represent their relation to human and inanimate objects in the outer world, and in the manner in which they manipulate their own feelings and those of others. Let us consider a ritual which is practiced to cure an illness. The Marquesans explain the etiology of the disease as due to the wandering of the soul from the body. The cure would therefore be to lure the soul back into the body. So far the thought processes are as logical as those involved in the scientific treatment of diphtheria with antitoxin. However, the derivation of the idea that the soul wanders from the body is not scientific.

Neither is the procedure of luring the soul back by placing food at its disposal. Both of these are ideas derived from specific sources and have, as far as the Marquesans are concerned, a high degree of plausibility. This conception of disease is very different from the one which conceives illness to be provoked by other people's magic or hostile wishes; and both these conceptions are different from the one which represents it as a punishment for disobedience or sin.

The Marquesan is utilizing in his conception of illness and its logical cure one of his own subjective experiences in connection with hunger anxiety. He is bound to the object who feeds him, and will desert the one who does not. The Marquesan is placated with food and can be moved to do something by this device. The principle used here is the same as the one used to deify an ancestor by feeding him ten humans. The miraculous powers of the inspirational priest are established by his ability to fast for long periods. It is not merely that there is a prominent food anxiety, but that the thought processes used in the representation of the anxiety become a technique for dealing with other situations in the outer world.[18]

This type of thinking we have designated as oral mastery. We could contrast this with that which prevails in scientific thinking by calling the latter manual mastery. Oral mastery is the type which prevails in the infant during the time when the mouth is the chief weapon of adaptation.[19] Children during the first year of life master objects by putting them into the mouth. As we see it in Marquesan institutions, oral mastery establishes a special type of relationship with an object, and prescribes the limits within which gratification from the object is obtainable.

[18] We need not review in detail all the clinical forms in which this type of thinking were used. We found it in the anxiety of children who died in birth, the interpretation of their rage as a hunger frustration; we found it in cannibalism; in the idea that the more one feeds a god, the better disposed will he be, etc.

[19] If all phenomena concerned with oral mastery were construed as evidence of the persistent pursuit of oral pleasure, then the whole series of phenomena here treated would be unintelligible. In terms of the libido theory it would means an arrest of development or a regression, in face of the fact that there are no sexual frustrations or obstacles to sexual development.

What problems of adaptation are appreciated in terms of, or solved by, oral mastery? We might learn something about this from psychopathology. This type of mastery can be revived in an individual in whom other types are inhibited, as in the traumatic neurosis. Not only are there these actual forms of oral mastery, biting and chewing objects instead of subjecting them to more advanced types of utility, but with these come extraordinarily exaggerated dependency attitudes. This technique is therefore indicative of a primitive type of relationship, not yet replaced by more highly developed forms of utility. It means that need tensions are greater than the means available to satisfy them. The persistence of this technique is therefore due to naïveté or to absence of other resources.

In the Marquesas this establishment of relations to others on the prototype of eating may be accentuated by the absence of severe disciplines in childhood (as we shall see later in studying Tanala culture). Discipline introduces a new element into these relationships with others.

The prominence of oral mastery in the Marquesas is the outstanding feature. The presence of projection and displacement of affect are not particularly distinctive.

A second feature pertaining to basic personality structures is the Marquesans' relation to the utility objects they create. These objects are regarded as extensions of the ego, and are endowed with attributes very like the possessor's own. The object increases in prestige with use. This is undoubtedly based on the pattern of the procreative act.

We now know that the Marquesans' thought processes are governed by scientific, oral, and sexual patterns. The security system of the individual must be evaluated in terms of the anxieties and frustrations he encounters, and the thought processes through which these are represented.

The basic anxiety situations in infancy, the demand for protection, are not satisfied by the mother, but by the father. Since the latter does not exercise severe disciplinary functions. the tie to men becomes very strong and a powerful weapon for insuring male solidarity. It also insures strong tender relations between daughter and father. This, as we have seen, is responsible for the unfriendly image of the mother, and later of woman as sexual object. Proof of this we found in the fact that rivalry situations between women are uncontrolled, and women are the commonest targets for malevolent magic.

The real situation of food anxiety creates both rational defensive measures and neurotic defenses based on unconscious hypochondriacal fears. The institutions resulting were identified as multiple naming, embalming, and cannibalism.

Unrestricted sexual development makes unnecessary the large number of defenses we saw in our culture. The most noteworthy consequences are the absence of parental inflation, the flexibility of dealings with the deity, and a general precocity shown in children's gangs.

The sexual situation with women leads to fear of the woman, but to absence of potency disturbances, and also to absence of inflated value of potency, and diminution in importance of paternity. The sexual dissatisfaction, as well as disappointment in tender relations with the woman, leads the man to strongly masochistic attitudes toward the woman—to sell one's postmortem powers in return for sexual favors (fanaua). No such attitude exists between man and man. Prestige conflicts are diminished, whereas these same conflicts among women lead to great hostility. The dead are not feared; but the woman and child who die in childbirth are.

Property is not a great source of anxiety; its chief function is to enhance the prestige of the donor by making him a great feeder.

There are two other ways in which basic personality structure can be verified—"super-ego" formation, and religion.

The neurotic super-ego[20] as we find it in our own culture has long served as a model for this hypothetical organ of morality. Extremely useful as a concept against which to standardize conditions under which phenomena of conscience, guilt, and

[20] See p. 71.

certain types of masochism arise, it is nevertheless a very inaccurate concept. The neurotic super-ego is the product of interaction between extreme dependency of the child and severe restrictive disciplines. The condition is established that love and protection can be guaranteed by renunciation of gratifications interdicted by society or its representatives. The "super-ego" is therefore a delicately poised indicator of the security system of the individual.

One may raise a purely theoretical question in this connection. The security of the child who is obedient to the conditions for parental protection is very strong. One may say that, in a relative sense, it is stronger than that of the child whose security depends on its own resources. Freedom to exercise resources cannot be identified with security gained through the protection of another individual. Free ego development does not necessarily confer greater security at all. It is, from the subjective point of view, a question of control. The condition of security in return for obedience is one which can be completely and absolutely fulfilled by the child—with the aid of neurosis, of course. From this a high degree of security can be derived, the security of dependency. The security from the exercise of one's resources does not have either the certainty or the quality of security through dependency. Judging from the tenacity with which the neurotic individual clings to this security system, the unconscious satisfaction derived from it must be very great.

In the case of the Marquesans, the kind of super-ego developed can have no relation to the repression of biological needs, at least as far as sexuality is concerned. Security is not based on this kind of obedience. This rules out the entire obedience system from super-ego formation. It does not mean that guilt and conscience are absent, but we must also see what occasions there are for the use of these functions. We encountered incest taboos, and as far as we can tell they are obeyed. Father-daughter incest is punished, but mildly; brother-sister incest, unless the taboo thereon is abrogated at cannibalistic feasts, is not committed. The absence of fraternal polyandry is probably evidence of the sister taboo and the suppression of fraternal rivalry. As far as other crime is concerned, the chief temptation is food, but not other articles. The "antisocial" impulses that can arise are very limited and are held in check by actual disadvantages that follow their exercise. But there is evidence of the high value of the esteem of others to the individual. The sense of shame, the need for "face," is very prominent.

We see, therefore, as much super-ego as the social situation makes necessary. The necessity to maintain face, status, affection, support, admiration, are all present; the omission is that system based on obedience to parental injunctions.

This discussion points up an observation made in a previous chapter,[21] that the derivation of the super-ego from the phenomenon of repression has led to misconceptions which conceal essential facts. At the basis of the whole phenomenon of super-ego lies the wish to enjoy the esteem and friendly feeling of others. When the conditions for winning this esteem and friendliness do not depend on renunciation of the satisfaction of biological needs, there is a residue to be found in every culture —the sense of shame.

The relation of super-ego formation to the effective external realities is well shown in the difference in the methods used by the men and the women in handling jealousy. The ability to trust an object makes it easier to suppress untoward feelings, hence the men handle their jealousy quite adequately. This suppression is undoubtedly aided to no small degree by the necessity for male coöperation. These conditions do not prevail among the women. No basis is laid in childhood for a friendly attitude of the girl toward her mother, and no need exists for the hostility toward her rivals to be repressed. It does not injure the economy, since women are a negligible economic force. To exercise their mutual hostility the women use no direct methods, but they use the men, through the *fanaua* or familiars, to execute their malicious designs.

In the case of Marquesan religion we have another oppor-

[21] See pp. 71–73.

PRIMARY INSTITUTION	BASIC PERSONALITY STRUCTURE	SECONDARY INSTITUTION
Male—Female Ratio 2½:1 └Maternal neglect ┌Jealousy of men ├─Expressed └─Suppressed	Anxiety—Fear of being eaten up Only when drunk Security in men Hatred of women	Hostile representation of woman, *vehini-hai* Suicide and love murder Male solidarity Taboos against women Homosexuality *vehini-hai*
Relation of Sexes ├─Male └─Female	Fear of exploitation by women Sexual dissatisfaction Interfeminine hostility Fear of having child stolen	*Fanaua* and familiars Sorcery against women, *fanaua* Pseudocyesis
Food Scarcity └Subsistence techniques	Rational methods Food anxiety Hypochondriacal fears Fear of disintegration Fear of being eaten up Food a means of enhancing ego	Multiple naming Food taboos Embalming Cannibalism Technique of deification

Basic Disciplines Absence of sexual restrictions or insistence on obedience	Unrestricted sexual development Super-ego: sense of shame	Absence of potency disturbances Absence of parental inflation Ease of relations to deity Precocity Children's gangs *Kaioi*
Social Mobility Primogeniture Rank	No anxiety of exploitation by men Prestige conflicts attenuated	Male solidarity: exchange of advantages Checks on prestige
Property Communal Personal	No anxiety—property not a means of enhancing ego	No theft except food Prestige—good feeder

Figure 1.

tunity to check on the correctness of our conclusions. The high-gods play no important role. The effective gods are the human spirits. They become gods by a cannibalistic procedure; but loyalty to the god is maintained only by his efficacy. The chief function of the god is to guarantee food and efficiency and skill. His aid is solicited by a simple feeding ritual and not by self-punishment.

The secondary spirits, *vehini-hai, fanaua,* and familiars are indicators of the sexual situation. Their functions and uses are eloquent testimony to the sexual tensions in the society.

Is there any indication in this society of an Oedipus complex? No, decidedly not, if by that is meant a wish for sexual union with the mother, and a desire to kill the father. By stretching the point a bit, one can say that the *vehini-hai* represent incestuous cravings for the mother presented in a negative form. If so, why should father-daughter incest be so explicitly presented? But there is evidence of strong tender relationships between father and daughter. Why no stories of killing father and possessing mother? The reasons are evident from Marquesan social organization and the disciplines to which "instinct" cravings are subjected. Previously, we posited that not the Oedipus complex creates social organization, but vice versa. This is an excellent case in point. In patriarchal Western society, we have both object and aim taboos, and the father is chief disciplinarian. We shall find that in Tanala folklore, where the conditions of the Oedipus complex exist, the story is made to conform to the social patterns. There the boy casts off his masculinity, returns the woman to his father, and makes a blood bond with the criminal, who is a brother of the boy's father.

In Marquesan society, the social picture is different. The boy has no opportunity to develop dependency attitudes toward the mother; she is cruel because she is frustrating. Dependency is more on the father and secondary husbands, and since they never discipline or frustrate him, there is no reason to hate them; in fact, this dependency becomes the greatest factor in cementing the bonds between men even to homosexuality, though in the latter case unconscious hatred and ingratiation are not necessary. We must not forget that the boy has, short of certain object taboos, equal opportunities with the father for sexual exercise. We would, therefore, expect no Oedipus stories, and not much of that homosexuality which depends essentially on fear of the father, ingratiation with him, and consequent abandonment of the heterosexual goal. But homosexuality on the basis of mutual support does exist, and in this case the perversion practiced is fellatio.

CONCLUSION

If we were to attempt to analyze this culture from the point of view of the evolutionary scheme, or the Freudian adaptation of it, we should soon find ourselves devoid of landmarks. The Oedipus complex is nowhere in evidence except in one tale, that of the hero Tohe-Tika. Here one could, with some stretch of imagination, say that it is a fantasy of killing the uncles, who can conveniently be made into father substitutes, and of then impregnating the mother so that she could give birth to successive children, whom the hero makes into parts of himself. To read the story thus would immediately raise the question why the other details of the story are of less significance. The fact is that the obvious pattern of the tale is one of successive rebirths to the end of making the hero more complete. The main demand on the mother and the cause of the hero's anger is a food frustration. To make this latter consistent with the Oedipus complex we would have to make the demand for food a sexual demand, disguised as an oral one because these people are arrested at the oral sadistic stage of development, the preeminent witness to which is cannibalism.

One could even make out a case for the female castration complex on the basis of the protruding eyes and tongue of the *vehini-hai* when she is not observed. This would give her a sufficient number of phallic attributes to make the case plausible. Moreover, Teemooniew has considerable resistance to intercourse in the story, which can be added to the first in evidence of this envy situation in female psychology.

If we grant these two points it would even then be no easy task to group all the remaining institutions as outgrowths from the very concealed Oedipus complex and female castration complex. If we had to operate on this scheme, the analysis would have to be abandoned at this point.

To begin with, any such preconception would in itself be a denial of the very processes which every individual experiences in any culture, and would be tantamount to saying that a Hindu is like an Eskimo because both of them may dream of an Oedipus complex. We made our point of departure the fact that the basic institutions which confronted the individual in the Marquesas were different from those in most patriarchal cultures. These institutions consisted of a male-female ratio of 2½:1; persistent maternal neglect; the absence of restrictive discipline; food scarcity; the absence of property as a means of enhancing the personality.

Secondly, we were obliged to note certain other institutions (see Figure 1) : the hostile representation of woman; the *vehini-hai;* the solidarity of males; the *fanaua;* the female neurosis of feigned pregnancy; multiple naming; embalming; cannibalism; a special technique of deification; and a highly original relation of individual to deity, etc.

This group of institutions would be very difficult to derive from the Oedipus complex. It would be more expedient to see what relation they have to the other group of institutions which we called primary. This relationship could not be established directly. But we did use another assumption: that the group of institutions called primary must have a certain effect on the basic personality structure of the individual exposed to them, an effect which was cumulative, and effective in the order in which he was obliged to adapt to them one way or another. Since these primary institutions are all data as far as the individual is concerned, and he has no hand in creating them, he must accommodate himself to them in some way. The particular constellations caused by the necessity of the individual to adapt to these institutions become a part of his effective functional tools of adaptation, and eventually a part of his sense of reality. We can illustrate this in the manner in which the conception of the woman is built up in this culture. As a result of his contacts with the inattentive mother, the child must get an impression, if only by contrast with the fathers, that she is not as kind as the latter, even if the child has no comparison with other types of mothers. It is not to be wondered at that the child therefore develops a feeling of confidence in the fathers. These two constellations formed by the several parental figures were the sources of our reconstruction of the emotional rationale of the secondary institutions. No matter how powerful the force of phylogeny (and it is a totally unwarranted assumption that behavior types are inherited), its influence would be dissipated if each successive generation were exposed to the influence of these primary institutions. The secondary institutions do not conform in pattern to those we are acquainted with in our culture, or in any culture like ours. Their origin cannot therefore be deduced from phylogeny, but from the actual conditions under which the basic personality structure is formed. The contact with these realities create a highly organized and interrelated series of "conditionings." These secondary institutions can therefore be understood only from the effects of the primary ones on the human mind.

We did note important differences in personality structure between males and females; but these were not reducible to the castration complex, unless one used the expedient of calling the feigned pregnancy a substitute for a penis. This interpretation could have no validity in a culture where the scarcity value of women and the absence of frustration caused by restrictive disciplines encourage the woman to use and enjoy the organs designated phylogenetically for pleasurable exercise.

A final point about method must be noted in contrast with the classical procedures of Th. Reik and G. Roheim. In these latter the unconscious constellation is noted, and its origin is attributed to a general arrest in development—presumably in the evolutionary march. Thus a constellation like cannibalism or the fear of being devoured has no direct connection with the actual realities encountered. Moreover, such attempts to identify the conscious systems from which the unconscious constellations are derived are not infrequently criticized as "superficial," in the sense of trite in contrast to profound. This contempt for the uses of the conscious systems is an old psychoanalytic prejudice. But it is easy to see that the omission of these conscious systems in the early days of psychoanalysis was in a large measure responsible for shifting the emphasis on phylogeny. This assumption made possible the belief in a universal personality structure.

In the procedure as illustrated by Marquesan culture, we can trace a continuous series between the conscious systems, and the ultimate unconscious constellations existing. Thus if we take a superficial trait like the absence of jealousy among men (except under special conditions) we find first an external reality, the scarcity of women, and from this point a long series of institutions and experiences, reaching back to infancy, which account for the ultimate attitude. It is. this series which traces the growth of the individual's sense of reality, and hence of his ego.

The truth or falsity of the procedure here used can be checked only experimentally. But it is at least a method subject to experimental testing. We shall have an opportunity in the chapters to follow to test this method on a culture where the basic conditions of life are very different from those prevailing in the Marquesas.

Chapter VII

THE TANALA OF MADAGASCAR

By Ralph Linton

OFF the southeast coast of Africa, extending from 13 degrees to 26 degrees south latitude, lies the Island of Madagascar. It is one thousand miles long and two hundred and fifty miles in average width. Although it has a considerable variety of environments, the island is largely mountainous, with a central basin. On the eastern side the climate is hot, with constant rainfall. There is a central plateau 2,000 to 3,000 feet in elevation, where the climate is temperate, with frost in the winter and seasonal rains.

The culture of Madagascar is sufficiently diverse to permit of delimitation of culture areas which do not correspond with ecological areas. The races are extremely diverse, great multiplicity of type being favored by endogamous group patterns. But certain main racial types are distinguishable with a fair degree of localization. In the plateau, the bulk of the population is mesocephalic, with light brown skin, long wavy hair, fairly heavy beard, and straight eyes. The language is of Malayo-Polynesian stock, closely related to Malayan.

All inhabitants must have come as migrants. The ancestors of the plateau population seem to have come originally from Indonesia, and appear to have been racially and culturally similar to the ancestors of the first Polynesian migrants. The earliest migrants must have come about 1000 B.C. In the twelfth century A.D. Arabs seem to have penetrated.

Of the current cultures in Madagascar the most archaic is that of the Tanala Menabe. These people live in a mountainous country, originally heavily forested. As the elevation is 3,000 to 4,000 feet, the climate is cool. The country is well watered, but without navigable streams. There is a very poor supply of game, all small animals, and fishing is incidental. Although there are some wild fruits and roots, these are of little economic importance.

The country is well adapted to agriculture by the cutting-and-burning method. Sufficient soil is available, although it is poor and requires ten to fifteen years of fallowing. The terrain has some swamp territories adapted to wet rice without irrigation. Timber is plentiful and there are localized supplies of high-grade iron ore, as well as some gold. The natives consider the region undesirable; it apparently served as a refuge for defeated groups driven from coast or plateau.

The tribe of the Tanala ("People of the forest") was never a political or even a cultural unit. At most there is among component groups a vague sense of remote kinship reflected in slightly different behavior in war and attitude toward captives. With slight exceptions, each group is economically and socially self-contained. Since not all groups had iron in their territory, they traded in iron and salt, and two or three groups smelted and manufactured implements for the rest. The goods were passed around from group to group by barter; there were no regular markets or traders. Small expeditions were made to get tools, and there were some trips to the coast for salt; some risks of capture and enslavement attended these trading trips.

The Village

Each village lays claim to certain land within the territory held by the gens; of this territory only a fraction is under cultivation at any given time. The land within the village is divided into wards, each of which is owned and occupied by a lineage. These wards are assigned by general consent at the time the village is set up. Each lineage has, furthermore, primary rights to a sector of land running from the village to the outer limits of the village territory. Each lineage works its sector independently. New land is cleared each year. The method of distributing land for cultivation among the families within the lineage is as follows: At the beginning of the season for agricultural work, the elders of the lineage arrange the heads of the various families along a frontage on the land to be cleared, and assign to each family a strip of certain width but of indeterminate depth. The men of the family then clear the jungle as far back as they consider necessary to meet their needs for rice. Care is taken to make the assignments of land to the families as equitable as possible; thus the family which got poor land one year will be given good land the next.

Agricultural implements are poor but adequate. The plow is entirely unknown. There is no incentive for any family to raise more than it needs, for crops can neither be sold nor hoarded. Each family has full rights over the land which it has cleared and planted as long as the land is in crops; thereafter it reverts to the general lineage property. A second, rather poor crop can be obtained from a field of this sort, but after this the land must be allowed to grow up in jungle and cannot be cultivated profitably before an interval of ten to fifteen years.

The rice crop is stored by the family and prorated to the various family members as needed. It is interesting to note that, although there is no famine, each portion of food is doled out, and every household includes in its equipment a series of measures of varying size used to apportion out the daily ration to men, women, and children of various ages. The old crop always carries over until the time of the new harvest. The Tanala have neither ceremonial attitudes nor magic connected with food. This fact is especially noteworthy since almost all the Malayan peoples have fairly elaborate fertility and other rituals connected with their rice culture. The only rice ceremony among the Tanala consists of a small family offering made to the ancestors at the time of the harvest. Other magics indirectly connected with rice are the charms kept in certain villages against hail or locust.

Eating habits are quite simple. One meal a day is served in the late afternoon. The father sits apart in an elevated position and is served separately. His food dish must be elevated above that of other members of the family; for this purpose elaborate stands of basketry are made. The oldest son, from the age of four onward, is also served separately. The mother and other children eat from a common dish.

The Tanala have cattle, but the utilitarian return from the herds is almost nil. They do not use the skins, and they eat meat so rarely that to dream of cutting meat is a bad omen indicating a funeral in the family. Milk is taken only when the cow has more than her calf can use. Even the manure is not employed in agriculture. At the same time, the possession of cattle gives a very high prestige return.

There is a constant division of labor, but aside from black-smiths there are no highly skilled or professional craftsmen. Men do all the wood and metal working; they also make bark cloth, heavy mats, and baskets of bamboo, the manufacture of which requires considerable strength. Women weave fine mats and baskets, caps, baby covers, and the mat clothing worn by both sexes. Women also do the cooking, keep house, and tend children; but a man may do any of these things without losing respect; in fact it is believed that men are somewhat better cooks than women.

PROPERTY

Unless they have been definitely disposed of, all manufactured objects belong to their makers. So rigid are the conventions about property that a husband cannot sell a mat woven by his wife or even a toy made by one of his children. Everything except land is individually owned; other persons have no claim over anything which the individual has made or gathered except that the head of the household may exercise his authority with regard to the disposition of choice food. At the present time a father also demands a share of his son's wages if the son is working as a contract laborer away from home. This is considered a legitimate reimbursement to the father for the loss of the son's services.

Within the family there is a general sharing of food, and general use of mats and utensils irrespective of exact ownership. Such things are considered their owner's contributions to the group. However, ownership reasserts itself as soon as there is any question of sale. There is some informal lending between households, but no exchange of gifts between persons of the same social level.

Apart from objects for wear or use, there were two types of property, the chief use of which was toward prestige goals. These were money and cattle. The money economy of the Tanala was at least two or three hundred years old. Spanish dubloons were probably introduced by pirates in the seventeenth century; but until very recently no gold or silver was used for coins or ornaments. All small trade was effected by barter; the use of money was a method of hoarding the surplus in an imperishable form until it was needed for large purchases such as cattle or a town lot, or as payment for an *ombiasy's* (medicine man) service, etc. Since theft was impossible for ordinary articles like cattle or manufactured utensils, both of which could be easily identified, money was the only object of value which was carefully hoarded and hidden. Although rarely used for ostentation, money was obviously the instrument of power. The chief use of money was to buy land, for this was the means through which an individual could set up a new lineage. The Tanala occasionally lent money, but even when this was done to a member of one's own family, it was done in the presence of witnesses, and often with an interest charge. A man who had money would guard it so closely that the closest member of his family would not know where he had concealed it. Nevertheless the theft of money was not uncommon, and when discovered was not as severely punished as thefts of other objects. Although possession of money was for the greater part the prerogative of the father, occasionally a woman would turn surplus into money, but would then bank it with her own relatives.

Cattle were the oldest form of surplus wealth, being through their reproduction the only interest-bearing investment. This is an extraordinary feature; for the value of cattle did not depend on their utility for consumption or fertilizer, or as draft animals. The latter two uses were unknown to the Tanala; cattle were killed only for sacrifices and funerals. The Tanala tried as much as possible to keep the cattle in the family, or at least in the village. A girl who married away from the village— a procedure that was generally discouraged—was usually given an equivalent inheritance in money and goods. All cattle were individually owned, and everyone tried to get as many as possible. The stealing of cattle was one of the main incentives for native raids, as distinct from wars.

We see then, that the prestige value of property was of tremendous importance in the native mind. It was intimately bound up with the whole pattern of family and lineage control. The main incentive for its accumulation was the desire for power and control over collaterals and descending generations. Such control did not extend upward, nor did it extend, except informally, to village control. The village headman required wealth to maintain his status, but he was by no means always the richest man, as we shall see later. Other factors also contributed to status and prestige.

With this tendency to accumulate wealth there was likewise a tendency to conceal the wealth from everyone in order to avoid the envy and consequent aggression of those in other families or lineages; but wealth nevertheless insured power within one's own group. Concealment was not always possible: when cattle were herded in common, it is clear that everybody knew what everybody else had.

In spite of the difference in possessions of wealth, there was little if any difference in living standards between rich and poor. Even at funerals and in the erection of memorial stones, there was no real display of wealth. Funerals usually consisted of adequate performances without ostentatious waste or overt effort to draw the envy of others. No overt power or office could be gained by competition to which one could only become incumbent through lineage. The only real way to power by the individual was the possession of an estate.

In the absence of trading and banking, the accretion of wealth to the gens was consequently very slow. Cattle raiding was practically the only sure method. The main wealth of the individual was that which he acquired by inheritance from the older generation, or by gifts. There was, however, an exception to this method: the case of the first wife, who received one-half of all the family profits, except that she did not participate in the inheritance of the husband after they were married. The only way in which a young man could acquire individual wealth from the outside was by cattle raiding or by becoming an *ombiasy*. However, the latter vocation usually required a long apprenticeship, to consummate which assistance from the parent was needed to meet the cost of instruction.

The rules of inheritance were highly conventionalized and rigidly enforced. A husband could not inherit from his wife, nor could a parent from a child. In the case of the death of a childless man or woman, the estate was divided equally among the brothers or sisters by the same mother; if these were deceased, it was divided among the brother's children. A woman's estate was divided equally among her children. Only the wife, or, in the event of polygamy, only the first wife, received one-third of her husband's estate, exclusive of inheritances he might have received after marriage. One-half of the residual estate would go to the oldest son, who also succeeded the father as head of the family, and the rest was divided equally among the other children; but the woman who had married outside the village received a smaller share. The oldest son of a family would also get the largest share of the mother's estate. Plural wives inherited nothing, but they had some rights in their children's share; for example they would retain the use of the house as long as they lived.

These rules were so rigid that a man could not make a will. However, he could make gifts at any time, in fact, on his death-bed. In this way, a favorite child, not the oldest, could actually become richer than the oldest son.

It is thus easy to see that the emphasis on wealth, together with the limited means of acquiring it by initiative, and the fixity of inheritance laws, made obedience and attempts to curry favor the dominant method of insuring status, and also promoted extreme jealousy among potential heirs. But however acute such feeling might be, its manifestation was curbed by the great fear of parental disfavor.

This practice of giving the oldest son the largest share in the inheritance was a means of insuring for him the real powers in the family line after the father's death. Such an oldest son could, by making loans to his younger brothers, keep them in debt and subjection. The aim of every man in this society was to accumulate wealth for himself in order to become the founder of a new lineage. This brought with it respect, authority, and power over others; and ultimately guaranteed for him worship in the ancestor cult, thus insuring his post-mortem use of the power he exercised in life.

SOCIAL ORGANIZATION

The Tanala were strongly conscious of being a group. They considered themselves people of the forest in contradistinction to the people of the plateau. There was, moreover, a very strong feeling of unity among villages within one gens if they lived in contiguous territory, with opportunities for contact. In a collection of villages of this kind, one was recognized as the parent, and its headman enjoyed a position of prominence; but he had no control over the other villages. The same was true of its priest. There was occasional intervillage marriage, but even this was rare, and was discouraged.

Each village laid claim to certain lands within those of the gens. The complete village establishment always included a series of features which were corporate property, used and kept

up by communal labor. These were the defenses, which consisted of a palisade eight to twelve feet high, a surrounding
ditch, and a common cattle pen. This was built near the gate
so that in case of attack the cattle could be driven into the village. In addition there were the public square and the assembly
house, which was built on any side of the square except the
west; this house could be used as a dwelling by the village
headman. There were also two charms belonging to the village
as a whole, one located at the gate to protect from attack, and
one buried in the public square to prevent pestilence and
lightning. These were made by an *ombiasy* at the time the
village was founded. Each village had, moreover, a sacred place
where memorial stones were set up for the dead, and where
sacrifices were held; this was sometimes as much as a mile from
the village. A settlement was not considered permanent until
deaths had occurred at the new site and memorial stones had
been set up. Finally, there was the village tomb, or tombs,
where all the village members were buried together. These
were often located many miles from the village, were more or
less secret, and were often moved when the village went to a
new site.

The occupants of a ward consisted of the descendants of an
original ancestor in the male line, plus wives and children, possibly a few husbands of lineage girls, and often a few hereditary
slave families. There was a cluster of houses, one for each
woman and her children, and also a children's house. As each
son married, a house was built for him, located to the east of
the house of the father's head wife.

The control of lineage passed from founder to eldest sons.
The founder had absolute control over all descendants as long
as he lived. He organized the work, divided the land for cultivation, took charge of funerals, and settled all disputes among
lineage members. He had a direct claim on the labor of all
males. At the death of the father, the oldest son took his post;
but this son had no claim on the labor of brothers or their descendants. His authority was less absolute, depending partly on

personality, and partly on the extent to which he was economically dependent. Rule then passed from the oldest son to his oldest son in turn. It is easy to see from this pattern that the lines from an original ancestor would have to split off.

Within the family the control over all descendants by the father was absolute. Elaborate rules governed attitudes of respect to him. The father also had authority over wives within limits set by the marriage contract; however, extreme violence to a wife was prohibited by the close residence of the wife's kin.

Socially, villages were almost completely isolated, although the men might coöperate with those of other villages if the territory of the gens was invaded. But ordinarily there was little contact among the village groups.

Marriage was almost always within the village, but outside the lineage. The couple always then resided in the ward of the husband's lineage. Marriage in the old days seems to have been about forty percent polygynous, but this rate has decreased with the cessation of war and an increase in the number of men; it is now about fifteen percent. The secondary wives in polygynous families are under the domination of the head wife; a man has to have his first wife's permission for plural marriage. There is a strong feeling against marriage across generation lines. This means that secondary wives are selected from among widows or from women who have been unable to make a first marriage. The regulation precludes the husband's bringing into the household a young and attractive plural wife, who might interfere with the prerogatives of the head wife. Succession as family head goes to the oldest son irrespective of his mother's status as head wife, or secondary wife.

Divorce is infrequent, although there are no supernatural sanctions attending marriage and the ancestors are not interested in divorce. In case one partner had divorced the other, this separation would never be taken as a cause of illness. The causes for divorce were always specified in the marriage contract. For the woman, they were usually adultery or incompetence as a housekeeper, or disrespect to the husband's relatives;

for the husband, adultery, marriage of a second wife without the first wife's permission, sleeping with one wife on another wife's day (the husband was expected to spend one day with each wife in succession in constant order), or extreme cruelty. Divorce is given to a wife by a village council, for cause, with an alimony award to boot.

A bride price given by the man or his father to the father of the woman was a necessary accompaniment of all legal marriages. However, the price was small—a spade, a shoulder cloth, etc. In case of divorce, there was no refund of the bride price. The real significance of this price lay in the fact that it reimbursed the woman's family for the loss of her potential children; it was in no sense a purchase of the woman herself. In case of remarriage of a divorced woman, the permission of the first husband had to be obtained, and he had to be reimbursed for the bride price; otherwise the children of the new union would belong to him, since he had already paid for them. Similarly, an illegitimate child born to a divorced woman would belong to the family of her previous husband. This arrangement was certainly related to the importance of children both in economic activities and as contributors to the well-being of the ancestral ghost, for the sacrifices which they would make.

LIFE CYCLE OF THE INDIVIDUAL AND BASIC DISCIPLINES

The Tanala nurse their children whenever they cry. A child is normally nursed only by its own mother; the plural wives may occasionally nurse a child not their own, but that is a matter of individual predilection. The age of weaning cannot be definitely decided, but the child is nursed until the next one needs the breast. If the mother becomes pregnant during the nursing period of the child, the latter is supposed to fall sick. The mother never nurses two children of different ages.

The child is constantly carried on the back of its mother. It sits on a belt pad and has a cover to protect it. These baby covers or "houses" are very difficult to obtain, for no mother will sell the house of her child. When the "baby house" is worn out it is thrown away, and it is buried with the child, should the child die.

Diapers are not used, with the result that the child is constantly soiling its mother; and since the clothes that the mother wears are difficult to replace, we have here an incentive for premature sphincter discipline. In fact, anal training is begun at the age of two or three months, and the child is expected to be continent at the age of six months. If after this time the child soils its mother, it is severely punished. In other words, the child is taught to be continent while on its mother's back. The child is however, permitted at intervals to leave the mother's back. It may be interesting to note that the woman is expected to be sexually abstinent for six months after the birth of her child. Thus the period of anal training of the child and the mother's sexual abstinence after the birth of the child coincide. Until the second year of life, the child sleeps with the father and mother. The removal from the bed of the parents imposes a severe discomfort on the part of the child, for it is then removed to a much colder place.

Thumb sucking has never been observed and masturbation in early childhood has likewise escaped observation. This may or may not be due to the existence of some taboo. The children run around nude, the boys until the age of five, the girls until four.

The personal cleanliness of the Tanala is noteworthy; they wash their hands and mouth before and after eating. Each individual has his own eating spoon.

Clothing is simple. The men wear tunics, and the women a tubular dress. There is a careful avoidance of exposure on the part of both men and women. Even the males show no tend-encies to exposure even among themselves.

Differential treatment by sex and primogeniture begins very early. So too do work requirements, which begin at the age of five and are stepped up with increasing age. There seems to be no serious discipline, punishment, or scolding, dependency on the parent for favors being the chief force in securing obedience. The relation to the parent is characterized by an insistence on respect and obedience from the child. The child is obliged to keep to the west of the house, and may not sit òn the same level as the father. Stools and mats are used to characterize comparative elevation of status. The distance between fathers and sons is rigidly maintained, but the relation between fathers and daughters is more cordial and less formal.

The boys form gangs, the girls do not. The play of the boys consists of war games, executed under the generalship and guidance of old men, who are very tough. The mother undertakes the systematic instruction of the girls; the boys are taught by the old men. It is the grandparents who are the best companions of the children, though the mother has a good deal of authority and willingness to help. Sexual play of children is strictly forbidden.

About premarital chastity one can form no definite opinion; affairs are at all events clandestine. Courting techniques officially allow no physical contact. While virginity is not greatly valued, promiscuous behavior is strongly disapproved and is believed to cause sterility. Whereas chastity is expected of the woman before marriage, it is not expected from the men. The boy is supposed to get his experience with older women and widows, and by adultery. The attitude of the husband whose wife commits adultery is unpredictable; there is no culture pattern for it. The lover may be fined, but this provision is not rigidly enforced. The age of puberty for boys is about fourteen, and for girls fifteen to seventeen. Despite their late puberty, the physical growth of the Tanala is rapid.

Fecundity and infant mortality are both high; the latter is fifty percent before the age of six months. Infanticide is not practiced, save as we shall note below.

The attitude of the Tanala toward sex is difficult to define. Ostensibly, it is puritanical and there is an effort to play sex down; but the emphasis on fecundity is high. The role of paternity is known, but some beliefs of the Tanala in this connection are obviously concessions to the strict formal morality. For example, they believe that the child is created by a mingling of the semen and menstrual blood. They believe, however, that the woman needs to have intercourse only once, and then goes on having children indefinitely. How they can maintain this belief, when they castrate bulls, it is difficult to see; it is obvious that the frank acknowledgment of the possibility of paternity in connection with each act of intercourse would create a good deal of difficulty; consequently they back up their practical morality with a series of convenient beliefs.

The parent needs children for the perpetuation of his family line and for the exercise of his personal power. But though the Tanala are very eager for children they will occasionally kill a child if, by divination, they find out that its destiny would be bad.

The incest taboos are the customary ones. They apply to siblings and parents, but in addition obtain for the father's plural wives and mother's sisters; and for the women, the father's brothers. Illegitimate children are not common, but notwithstanding formal taboos, are accepted. It is interesting to note the reasons assigned by the Tanala for their incest taboo. They say that breach of these taboos causes sterility and crop failure, and wrecks the whole reproductive system of the group. The immediate reason is that it offends one of the ancestors. However, those who break the taboo are not killed, but incur the obligation to propitiate an offended ancestor.

The age of marriage for the men is nineteen to twenty-two; for the women, not under eighteen. Marriage mates are as a rule about the same age level; there is, as we have already noted, strong feeling against cross-generation alliances, and plural wives are, for the greater part, left-overs. Marriages are generally arranged with the consent of all parties concerned, but as a rule the parent controls them. No great force is used; the couple merely court and notify the parents of their decision.

The preferred union, and one which is arranged by the parents, is that of cross cousins; that is, the boy marries the daughter of his father's sister. But the children of the father's brother are taboo. It is easy to see that this arrangement tends to perpetuate property within the male lines, and there is naturally a good deal of rivalry among the women for a desirable cross-cousin match.

The main rivalries in this society are between brothers. The Tanala have an institution whereby a man can enter into a blood-brotherhood bond, which obliterates rivalry conflicts. Such blood brothers, if they live in different villages, share their wives, but they do not if they live in the same village. Blood-brotherhood bond can be entered into by two men, two women, or a man and a woman. However, when a man and a woman enter such relationship, they may not have sexual intercourse; this is a very binding taboo. This relationship is chiefly entered by parallel cousins. This institution makes possible strong friendships and guarantees mutual assistance by different lineages.

HOMOSEXUALITY

Homosexuality is quite common, and so are male transvestites. There is, however, no information about female homosexuals or transvestites. Some of the male transvestites are actually homosexuals and can take the position of a plural wife. The social attitude toward this institution is completely neutral. The Tanala take it for granted. Many of these transvestites do not marry and are not homosexual; that is, they do not submit to sexual relations with another man. Being a transvestite is a common refuge of an impotent man, for it guarantees him a definite status in the community, as he can do everything that the woman can do and do it much better. Occasionally a young man will become a transvestite, but as a rule it is the choice of some old men who have become impotent. The recruits to this class come largely from the group of younger sons. The professional dancers are homosexual, but they oscillate a good deal between homo- and heterosexual practices. The fact that women do not assume the male role is quite evident from the social organization; the Tanala keep their women rigidly to the role of bearing children, and hence any deviation would interfere with the common objectives of the group.

DEATH

The Tanala do not fear death; they believe in a world hereafter, which, they are sure, is as good as the one they live in. Nor do they fear the dead; the dead are considered neither unclean nor polluted, and are handled with great ease and freedom. Pregnant women are, however, protected against the dead. The lack of fear, both of death and the dead, is in striking contrast to the fear of mutilation, the rationalization being that an individual after death maintains the physical status that he had when he died.

When an individual dies, he is kept in the house for as long as one month. Once a day the juices of decay are cleaned away. Then the corpse is taken to the village tomb, in which all the dead are placed, the most honorable preserving the place of dignity at the top of the heap. Each village has its sacred place. At the funeral there are an address, a feast, games, and then a formal introduction to the ancestors of the deceased. This is followed at some later time by the second funeral, at which a memorial stone is erected. The second funeral can take place anywhere from six months to four years after the original one. The memorial stone then erected depends on the status of the dead during life and how angry he would be if not placated.

The community of the dead is very much like that of the living. They have their own village, which is laid out much as the one they lived in, and their fate after death is a continuation of what they experience during life. They marry, get sick, are given food. The exact location of this village of the dead is rather vague; it may be on the site of an old village, or in another dimension. There is a continuous visiting back and forth between the living and the dead, and dreams are supposed to be caused by the visitations of the dead.

The Tanala believe that vital functions can carry on after life is gone. In severe illness, like tuberculosis, the soul leaves the body while the individual is still alive, and forms an association in an ancestor village. Insanity is said to be due to an absence of the soul.

Sacrifices to the dead constitute an extremely important ritual, which is performed on all occasions of importance among the living. They let the dead know everything that is going on, marriages, circumcisions, funerals, fulfillments of vows, undertaking in the case of illness, and especially if anything has been done that will offend the ancestor. The sacrifice consists of killing an ox, or oxen, cooking the meat and feeding it to the dead in order to keep them satisfied. There is some belief that the soul of the ox becomes part of the ancestor's herd in the next world.

The more important an individual was during life, the longer is his body exposed in the house, and the more sumptuous the funeral feast and the sacrifices to ancestors. There are, moreover, lengthy announcements of contributions to the funeral feast, showing the wealth of the relatives. Apparently there is no fear of the ancestors themselves, as they are believed to be controlled by sacrifices. But the Tanala are rather afraid of ghosts.

They refuse burial to lepers and those who have had smallpox. These are buried elsewhere for a period of three or four years. The same is true of the insane and sorcerers, and all those who would be disowned by their ancestors for having committed theft or incest.

Mourning is done by the spouse or spouses and their children. Mourning consists largely of keeping quiet, wearing old clothes, and not washing. The wife keeps this up for about six months, during which time there may be no remarriage. It is important to note the absence of contrition rituals. What is most feared of the dead is the ghost of a departed relative.

THE SUPERNATURAL

The prime cause and common denominator of all supernatural forces is Zanahary. He is the supreme being and life giver. He is represented, like the Christian God, as a defender of the poor and helpless. These attributes of Zanahary are, however, rarely used. The destiny of the individual is regulated or controlled through the household gods, who are ancestors. They are very irascible, and must be constantly pleased. Rituals indicate that the Tanala must have had at one time a whole pantheon of minor gods. But the attributes of these have now been forgotten, and the whole attention is focused on the ancestral spirits. These are the intermediaries between man and Zanahary, but Zanahary has been reduced to a sort of philosophical concept, to whom no native would ever think of praying directly. He is merely mentioned politely and incidentally in the prayers to the ancestors.

Even the dangerous or malevolent beings are all of human origin. The only nonhuman spirits recognized are a few minor spirits of streams and forests, to whom no worship or particular attention is paid.

All worship is directed to the management and placation of an ancestral ghost, of the family, lineage, village, or tribe: the hereditary head of the unit involved in the ceremony serves as ancestral priest. The ritual of sacrifice may be supervised by an *ombiasy*, since he is considered an expert in supernatural matters, but he cannot sacrifice anything himself. Sacrifices are held in connection with all important events, circumcisions, marriages, and especially funerals, and also in cases of sickness or of sins which it is thought may offend the ancestors. At all sacrifices all members of the group whose ancestors are being appealed to are expected to be present. There are also preventive sacrifices. When a marriage is on the border line of propriety—i.e., approaches an incestuous relationship—care is taken to make sacrifice and apology to the ancestors before the marriage is consummated. The ghosts of the ancestors are one of the most important instruments in social control; they are naturally always on the side of the proprieties and are consequently the executives of morality.

To the Tanala, ghosts are thoroughly individualized and entirely real. Every native will report seeing ghosts and talking with them. It is very often difficult for the people to distinguish between dream states and waking states. Hearing ghosts talk to one is so common an experience that natives often will not pay attention to you if you call them only once. If you call twice, they will know it is a man and pay attention, since ghosts call only once. The natives frequently encounter strange ghosts in lonely places, but are not injured by them. They dislike meeting the ghosts of immediate ancestors, parents or grandparents, since if you see a ghost of this sort, you must sacrifice to it personally. This system can be characterized as ghostly blackmail. The ghosts of women, however, are not much heeded.

There are several variations of the ghost cult. An individual may, while he is still alive, sell his potentialities as a spirit. An old man or woman may announce, "After my death, if you will make offerings to me of such and such a sort, I will answer prayers for such and such a thing." This device of seeking post-mortem power is rarely resorted to by anyone who is of importance at the time. A memorial stone will be erected for such a person, and nonrelatives as well as relatives may pray and sacrifice there. If the prayers are frequently answered, a regular cult of this individual may develop outside the true ancestor cult. But if the prayers are not answered, the individual will be neglected and his worship soon forgotten. Such liberties cannot, however, be taken with the gods of the ancestor cult. This relationship is binding, good or bad. Appeals to ghosts are always made on a direct personal basis, and usually in the form of a vow, payment not being made until the prayer has been answered.

There are also ghosts who become controls for medicine men. These are usually the ghosts of dead medicine men, who are thus able to keep their hands in the affairs of the living.

Lastly, there are other ghosts who possess those afflicted with *tromba,* a neurotic seizure indicated by an extreme desire to dance. Those who are seized with it often speak with the voice of the ghosts, make demands, give oracles, etc. During the time of the seizure such persons are treated with extreme respect. It is significant that most of those subject to *tromba* are persons of minor importance. A hereditary family head, an *ombiasy,* or a successful warrior rarely, if ever, has *tromba.* The possessing spirits in these cases are not family spirits.

Side by side with the belief in the ancestral spirits, there is a belief in impersonal fate or destiny. Destiny represents the will of Zanahary, but is regarded as completely mechanistic, a working out of cause and effect. The future is regarded as a result of causes and events which are already in train, and can be changed only by injecting new causal factors.

One aspect of destiny is connected with the calendar: there are days which are auspicious for various activities and days which are not. The day of birth indicates what the general destiny of the individual will be, whether high or low, good or bad. Being born on a propitious day imposes on the individual obligations to make good. The only occasion on which these people practice infanticide is when a combination of birth date and other indications shows that the destiny of the child is so bad that he is likely to bring ruin and disgrace upon the family.

This concept of destiny is of great social importance since it makes possible the transfer of blame for all sorts of misfortune, illness, etc., from individuals, even the ancestral ghosts, to this impersonal force. By means of this, hostilities may be drained away, and the fear of sorcery greatly mitigated.

OMBIASY

This is the name given to the native medicine men who are workers with destiny. Their activities are sharply differentiated from those of the family line cult. The same individual cannot be a priest and an *ombiasy* simultaneously. For this reason, an oldest son, who will normally become an ancestral priest at the death of his father, will never take *ombiasy* training; although the *ombiasy* cannot appeal to ghosts directly, he can make a charm which has the function of keeping ghosts away or counteracting their attacks. In other words, his control of ghosts is through a mechanistic device, not through appeal to them.

There are two types of *ombiasy*. The first is the *ombiasy nkazo*. This type is trained by other *ombiasies*. Such a man has no psychic peculiarities; his attitude toward his work is scientific and experimental. Such persons are usually very clever and worth appealing to in many difficulties. They take a keen interest in everything going on in the tribe and know where the best opportunities for cattle raids, for trade, etc., are to be found. Their advice is always couched in magical terms. In theory anyone can become an *ombiasy nkazo*, but because of the expense and time required for the training, women very rarely have the opportunity to acquire the profession. The second type is the *ombiasy ndolo*. *Ombiasies* of this type are controlled by the ghosts of dead *ombiasies*. Their function is to make the magical knowledge of the ghost available to the living. This type of *ombiasy* can be of either sex. He is selected for the office by the ghostly control. Although this vocation is open to women, it is most likely to occur with a primary wife who is childless or whose children have died. A secondary wife who tries to assume this role is viewed with a good deal of suspicion: Why should a good or powerful *ombiasy* ghost pick a person of such little consequence for his agent? The importance of the *ombiasy* does not depend on whether he is of the instructed or the inspired type, but on his efficiency and success.

The activities of the *ombiasy* consist primarily in determining the workings of destiny. In order to do this he must know an elaborate calendar of lucky and unlucky days. He must also know an elaborate form of divination called the *sikidy*, which is performed by means of seeds arranged in mathematical patterns. It is related to the Arab sand divination and also to the ancient Greek geomancy. The power of the apparatus is supposed to lie in the fact that seeds of a certain sort are used in combination with certain other objects. The divining set is in itself a charm, it is addressed as a conscious entity, but is not alive. You ask it what you want to know, but it is not a spirit and no offerings are made to it. The object of the divination is to determine the causes and current forces in a situation with a view to adjusting these to bring about a satisfactory outcome. Another use is to determine future events with a view to altering them if necessary. Thus an *ombiasy* can predict sickness or ill fortune, can give some general indications about who is the offending party, or definite indications about the offending ancestor who is responsible for bad fortune.

In all divination there is an indication of the *ombiasy's* probable chances for success. If the case is too difficult, he refers it to a more powerful *ombiasy*.

Future ill fortune is rarely indicated as due to the activities of ghosts; it is more commonly due to sorcery or fate. It is characteristic of the Tanala attitude that in this divination it is impossible to obtain direct information as to who is practicing sorcery against you. As a matter of fact, all phenomena pertaining to aggression or guilt in this culture are very oblique. There is a fear of direct action, or of direct assertion of hostility. Especially is this true of the relations of men to one another; the women are much more direct in their assertiveness.

Ghosts, next to destiny, are the most commonly ascribed causes of ill fortune. However, there is practically always an implication of sin on the part of the victim when a ghost persecutes him. Information as to what the sin has been is usually very vague in the divination. In such cases the *ombiasy* refers the patient to his ancestral priest, who placates the ghost by an appropriate sacrifice.

When sorcery is shown as the agent responsible, the identity of the sorcerer is left vague; the reason for his hostility can be readily filled in by the victim. In cases of sorcery, the *ombiasy* provides a protective charm and takes countermeasures against the sorcerer.

As a cause of sickness, ghosts are most common, sorcery

second, and fate least common. But with regard to ill fortune the order is reversed; fate is given the most prominent part, with sorcery next, and ghosts of least importance. In other words, ghosts find their primary role as causes of illness, which in turn is correlated with offense to the ghosts through the infraction of taboos or through antisocial behavior. Illness is almost always a result of sin, but it is a ghost who acts as the agent of punishment.

One of the chief functions of the *ombiasy* is to make and teach the use of charms. Every charm has two parts, an object, and a set of rules for behavior which are necessary to the object's successful functioning. The Tanala think of medication in the same way. If they are given a medicine, there must be associated with it a ritual of behavior, certain acts to be performed in conjunction with it. If such a ritual is lacking, they will have no faith in the efficacy of a medicine. The charm itself is usually worn, although parts of it may be taken internally. All charms consist of certain substances, for the most part various woods, roots, or herbs, which are gathered and compounded according to a definite formula. The making of such charms is purely mechanistic. They owe their power to the substances incorporated in them, and the way in which these have been combined. The completed charm has power and is addressed as if it were conscious, but it is not a spirit. The rules that go with the charm either aid its operation or prevent interference with its operation. For purposes of malevolent magic, it is desirable to bring the charm in contact with the victim by such a method as planting it in his house or rice field. If the *ombiasy's* divination shows that malevolent magic is the reason for ill fortune, it is part of the duty of the *ombiasy* to find the enemy's charm and remove it. No parts of the body are used for making charms, and there is therefore no fear of anyone else getting hold of such things as hair, nail parings, or excreta.

Each charm formula is either purchased or invented by the *ombiasy*. Its efficacy is not lost through sale. The effectiveness of a charm is judged entirely by pragmatic standards: if it does not produce results, it will be given up. On the other hand, if it is good, other *ombiasies* will attempt to obtain the formula by purchase or exchange of certain formulae of their own. The attitude toward these charms appears to be genuinely experimental, almost scientific.

Malevolent magic is always purposeful, i.e., directed against some particular victim. The *ombiasy* provides the equipment for injuring enemies with directions for its use, but only the user of the malevolent charm is held responsible for the effects. The *ombiasy* is regarded as a neutral in such cases. *Ombiasies* are rarely related to any of the lineages within the village where they live and practice. They are expected to afford their help equally to all. The use of malevolent magic within a lineage is practically unknown, since it would prove so offensive to the all-seeing ancestors that it would probably result in the death of the user. However, there is some use of magic as a weapon against members of other lineages in revenge of insults, for nonpayment of debts, refusal of a daughter requested in marriage. Apparently one of the focal points for malevolent magic is between plural wives who come from different lineages. Since these women are not related, they can employ magic against each other without incurring the revenge of the ancestral spirits.

There is also a favorable magic designed to insure success in all sorts of activities, and to keep away ill fortune in general. The charms used for this purpose are extremely numerous, corresponding to every imaginable native activity.

There are no post-mortem charms and no burial charms. From the point of view of the technique of magic, it is interesting to note an absence of the belief in the spoken word, a magical technique so common in most other cultures. A charm will be told to do such and such a thing, or to injure such and such a person, but the telling is not in a set formula and has no power in itself.

Mention must be made of the *mpamosavy*. These are individuals possessed by evil spirits who desecrate tombs, inflict general injury on the community, break down fences, ride cattle to death, and commit other malicious practices. It is believed that such persons may be entirely unconscious of what they are doing, and have no memory of it when the state of possession has passed. *Mpamosavy* who are suspected are tried by ordeal, and put to death if found guilty.

Legal Procedure

The Tanala had a well developed system of customary law, which was handed down by word of mouth. Such laws were invoked only in the case of disputes between members of different lineages. All disputes within the family were settled by the family head, whose power was reinforced by the ancestral spirits.

There was very little crime. Murder, aside from that by sorcery, was practically unknown, so much so that no formal statute in Tanala law covered it. Suicide was practically unknown, being attributed to insanity when it occurred. Theft was extremely rare, and easily detected within the community, since all objects were known. The only thing that could be successfully stolen here was money.

The feeling against theft, in spite of its rarity, was very strong, death being the penalty if the thief was caught in the act. Should the crime be proved some time after its commission, the thief was compelled to make restitution in addition to a severe beating. A repetition of the offense would be punished by disownment and the expulsion of the offender from the village. This punishment was considered more serious than death, since it excluded the individual from membership in the ancestral village in the next world. It condemned him to become a vagabond in this world, and in the next. The ceremony of disownment was a solemn and mournful one, accompanied by the giving of cattle or money to the heads of the various lineages within the village by the head of the disowning family. The idea was that the community was thus in part reimbursed for the loss of the services of the disowned person.

The Tanala regarded incest with equal seriousness, but its punishment was left to the family and the ancestral spirits. In extreme cases it might also result in disownment and expulsion. Accusations of sorcery were brought before the village tribunal. The individual found guilty would be punished by death if the sorcery had resulted in the death of the victim; otherwise by a heavy fine. It should be noted that the Tanala lacked the almost hysterical fear of sorcery present in many other Madagascan tribes. Actual deaths from this cause were believed to be rare. In connection with accusations of sorcery and also of theft, various forms of trials by ordeal were employed when evidence appeared inconclusive. The most drastic of these consisted in making the accused swim back and forth across a river where crocodiles were numerous. If the crocodiles did not take him he was considered innocent.

Civil cases involving property disputes and divorce cases were tried before the village council, with all able-bodied members of the village attending and expressing their opinions freely. In settling such cases legal precedents were important. Evidence on both sides was taken, and the final decision as handed down by the village headman represented the consensus of the community's opinion. The villages derived a great deal of amusement from these occasions, and from the long and witty speeches made by counsel on both sides; although there were no formal methods for enforcing the decisions of the courts, a person who failed to obey the rulings would incur ridicule and general disapproval.

FOLKLORE

The Tanala have neither creation myths, nor stories of gods. There are, however, rather prosaic historic stories of wandering gentes, with few episodes and slight personal reminiscences of family heads. In their hero tales there are no war-prestige stories. What is frequently stressed is conflict with the brothers or with the mother's family. A pattern very commonly found in their folk tales is that of fantastic boasting which is generally used to terrify the enemy and to compel him to submit. Trickery is another common device for gaining desirable ends; the most common form being to change one's shape. Thus one hears tales of monsters devouring relatives, who are then retrieved alive. Stories of animals in which the weaker gets the better of the stronger are a common type. The following is a typical legend:

There is a man, whose brothers steal his wives. The offended man confers with Zanahary, who tells him to marry another woman, which he does. The son of the second marriage avenges the theft of the father's two wives by stealing the wives from their new husbands; but in order to perform the theft he disguises himself as a woman. One of the original brothers pursues his nephew (the avenger of the original crime) ; they fight without hurting each other, and then end by admiring each other's prowess, and enter a blood bond, finally returning the wives to the father.

Status and Prestige Values

A survey of this culture shows us that social categories are very largely prescribed by birth and sex. Within these categories the training of the individual can begin at once. There are also achieved statuses, but these require special qualities in the individual. Status brings with it no differences in housing, clothing, or food. Its uses are largely to attract regard and to give opportunity for exploitation without any gain except in a feeling of importance. Though the Tanala love wealth, they look down upon ostentation or unnecessary spending.

In discussing the life cycle of the individual, we have already covered the beginning of differential treatment according to sex and birth. Further aspects may now be noted. As a young adult, the oldest son acquires wealth by an accumulation of paternal gifts. Marriage with a cross cousin is usually prearranged, so that for him there is relatively little sexual contact. There is a submission to the father, but with an increasing delegation of honorable activities. He does not need to participate in cattle raiding. He has few jealousies or rivalries with oldest sons of other lines, since competition for office and other honors does not come until later. The labor of the younger sons, as young adults, is preëmpted by the father. These younger sons stand a chance of gaining some gifts through absolute submission to the father, but there is very little chance of acquiring wealth through him. Such a young man must struggle with other males for the favors of women accessible to him. His marriage is not prearranged. He cannot very well engage in hostilities against his father or older brother because there is no technique for competition. However, several other alternatives are possible for him. He can surrender all his initiative and become a satellite of his father and later of his older brother; he can become a warrior, and accumulate wealth and prestige by cattle raiding. But notwithstanding all this, he is still subservient to his father during the latter's life. The father can, however, take only a small portion of his loot, and the older brother none at all. The younger son can thus enjóy a measure of independence from his older brother after his father's death, and, if he is sufficiently successful, he can secede when he himself has grown sons, and become the head of a new family line. Thirdly, he can become an *ombiasy*, although, as we have seen, this profession requires initial outlay for training. But having done this, he can leave the village, settle elsewhere, acquire wealth, and in his old age become the head of a family line. In the two latter alternatives, that is, as warrior or *ombiasy*, the rivalry is transferred outside the family, and tensions are worked off outside of his own group by raiding enemies or by working better magic. *Ombiasies* do not contend with one another directly.

As a middle-aged adult, the family head has an assured position and a constant increase of wealth from the labor of his descendants. By virtue of his capacity to give gifts he can command great respect. He may have rivalries with other family heads for prestige and possibly contend for the position of village headman; but this latter is determined largely on the strength of his family following. The middle-aged man who was a younger son can be head only of his own immediate family, remaining constantly dependent on the family head financially, and under the latter's authority. There is a great deal of jealousy of the family head and constant bickering, but for such rivalry there is no direct outlet. Such a man may develop *tromba* seizures.

In old age the head of the family acquires more respect and authority, as he is now reinforced by hopes of an estate and of acquiring importance among the ancestral spirits after death. In this latter position he exerts complete authority over all his own descendants and those of his brothers who have not broken away. He also has an automatic position in the village council.

There are, nothwithstanding, checks upon the absolutism of the father. He can even be deserted for cause. The younger son who becomes an old man has diminishing respect and authority, together with waning physical powers. As he has little to give he is often neglected by his sons. The only manner in which he can then exert any authority over his descendants is by the fear he may inspire as a potential ghost.

With regard to the women, the situation is somewhat different. There is no differentiation on primogeniture. A woman owes respect and obedience to all elders, but her relations to the father are easier than those of the sons. She has a close tie with all her brothers, but especially with her uterine brothers. She engages in housework and making articles. The development of skills is encouraged by the personal ownership of the product and the ability to solicit praise and small gifts. There is little jealousy between sisters until puberty, when they begin competing for the desirable man. The main requirements of a good match are amiability, ability to do hard work, skill, and good looks.

The status of women as wives differs. The woman becomes either head wife or a plural wife. There are no unmarried women. As a head wife, the woman enjoys an important position. She transfers her residence to her husband's house, but usually remains in the same village. She is then subject to the husband and the husband's parents, but with the constant support of her own family. As head wife she exercises control and disbursement of the new family fund. She has absolute right to all her own products, and to one-half of the increase in her husband's property, apart from inheritance.

There is some possible source of jealousy in relations with the women of the husband's line, and some possible jealousy of a plural wife on a sexual or on a gift basis. But as has been said, it is she whose permission must be sought for plural marriages. If such a head wife remains childless, her union with the husband's family is less strong. She is also likely to suffer contempt and jealousy of the wives who have children. But nothing can rob her of her executive position as head of the wives in finance.

The secondary wives play a distinctly secondary role. A secondary wife must obtain the first wife's consent to the marriage and must depend on gifts from her husband, which are usually made over the first wife's objection. There is generally intense jealousy of the first wife, and a struggle to displace her in the husband's favor. And there is a possibility of succeeding to the position of first wife through the latter's death—a fine situation, which calls for poisoning and magic. At the same time, there is a high degree of domestic coöperation between wives for mutual advantage. But a childless plural wife is in a very precarious position. She has no rights in inheritance and her husband can dismiss her at will. She is usually bitterly jealous of all the other wives, and is much disliked by the husband's family.

The middle-aged head wife is in a very strong position. Her own wealth is increased through inheritance and gifts, and she is constantly sharing in the increase. She also exercises control through gifts, and has a good deal of authority over sons and daughters.

The middle-aged secondary wife is in a fairly strong position. She has power over her own children, and is constantly attempting to get goods from her husband for them and herself, with consequent conflicts, jealousies, *tromba*, and occasionally claims for being an *ombiasy ndolo*.

As an old woman, the head wife has still greater power, amounting almost to matriarchy if she is widowed. She controls all her descendants with the hope of gifts, but has very little power if she remains barren.

The plural wife, as an old woman, has some power over her own children, but that is not very great. These are the women who constantly make deification claims and get *tromba*.

It is worth observing that although the hostilities between men cannot be very overt, those between women can. Women quarrel noisily and demonstratively. It is also noteworthy that there is very little antagonism between the sexes. Each sex is concerned with its prestige status; the prestige conflict is not between the sexes, but among members of each sex.

The focal point of social conflict is between the younger sons. There is no competition between brothers and sisters, or across generation lines. There is a great deal of jealousy of the oldest son, but it is impossible to dislodge him by anything short of death. Competition between sisters arises immediately prior to, but not after marriage. Some hostility to the women of the husband's family occurs, but no competition; the main competition is with the other wives.

The competition with individuals outside of the family is limited to family heads, warriors, and *ombiasies*. The goal for the family head is to become the village chief. This is generally gained by ability rather than by wealth, with the strength of the family helping. Warriors compete as individuals for prestige, but do not fight or work against each other. *Ombiasies* also compete as individuals; there are, however, rarely two in the same village. They do not use magic against each other. The office of village priest is strictly hereditary and is not subject to competition. The avoidance of direct conflict either in or out of the family is strictly according to conventionalized patterns.

Apart from what can be gained by seeking the favor of those who possess wealth or power other economic gains do not entail personal competition. Exploitation of natural resources is open to all. The fears and hostilities of the Tanala are highly individualized, being always directed toward a person, and hence provide excellent use for escape mechanisms.

If one can say anything about their character as a people, one would say that the Tanala are defensive but not warlike, and are obviously the descendants of defeated groups who moved back when defeated. Their aesthetic sense is poor, as are their craftsmanship in wood and metals and their mechanical sense.

The Change from Dry to Wet Rice Cultivation— Betsileo

The culture we have described is that of the Tanala of the dry rice cultivation. Wet rice cultivation, which introduced so many elements in social change that the whole culture was eventually altered, was borrowed from their Betsileo neighbors to the east. It was at first an adjunct to dry rice carried on by individual families. Before the new method was introduced on a large scale, there were already rice swamps of permanent tenure, which never reverted to the village for reassignment. But land favorable for this use was very limited, because of natural factors. Thus there gradually emerged a group of landowners, and with the process came a breakdown in the joint family organization. The cohesiveness of this older unit was maintained by economic interdependence and the need for coöperation. But an irrigated rice field could be tended by a single family, and its head need not recognize any claim to share it with anyone who had not contributed to its produce.

This group of permanent rice sites formed the nucleus of a permanent village, because the land could not be exhausted as was the land exploited by the dry method. As land suitable for wet rice near the village was presently all taken up, the landless households had to move farther and farther away into the jungle. So far away would they be that they could not return the same day. These distant fields also became household rather than joint family affairs.

The moving of the older unit from one land site to another had kept the joint family intact. But now single landless households were forced to move, while there were in the same unit landowners who had a capital investment and no incentive to move. The migrant groups were thus cross-sections of the original lineages. Each original village had a group of descendant villages, each one surrounded by irrigated fields and private ownership.

The mobile villages had been self-contained and endogamous. The settled villages were much less so. The joint family retained its religious importance, based on the worship of a common ancestor, even after its component households had been scattered. Family members would be called together on ceremonial occasions, and thus the old village isolation broke down. Intermarriages became common. In this way, the transformation from independent villages to a tribal organization took place.

The process brought further changes in the patterns of native warfare. The old village had to be defended; but not at so great a cost nor with the necessity for permanent upkeep. When the village became permanent the defenses had to be of a powerful kind, involving big investments and permanent upkeep.

Slaves, who were of no economic significance in the old system, now acquired economic importance. This gave rise to new techniques of ransom. Thus the tribal organization grew in solidity, and with the change the old tribal democracy disappeared. The next step was a king at the head who exercised control over the settled elements but not over the mobile ones. The kingdom came to an end before any adequate machinery of government could be established. This king built himself an individual tomb, thus breaking an ancient custom.

The changes were therefore, a king at the head, settled subjects, rudimentary social classes based on economic differences, and lineages of nothing but ceremonial importance. Most of these changes had already taken place among the Betsileo. The coöperative system made individual wealth impossible. Nor was the change devoid of serious stresses on the individual; a new class of interests, new life goals, and new conflicts came into being.

One of the Tanala clans, the Zafimaniry, was one of the first to take up the new wet rice cultivation. They continued it for a time, but finally abandoned it, and returned to the dry rice method. They offered as the reason for returning to the old method the fact that they had been attacked by an enemy, which scattered the men of the various households. The tribe tabooed the raising of wet rice, and still continues to refuse to take up wet rice despite depletion of the jungle.

Although we are not in possession of all the facts, and a great many unknown factors may have operated, we are justified in looking into the culture of the Betsileo for a contrast with the ultimate changes coincident with wet rice culture. The traditions of the Betsileo have it that there was a time when all people were equal and all land was held in common. Moreover, the cultural similarity to the Tanala leaves no doubt that in the main we are dealing with two cultures springing from a cognate source. Or to be more accurate, the changes we find in Betsileo culture were engrafted on a culture similar in all respects to the one we found in Tanala.

Whatever adventitious changes took place, basically we can regard Betsileo as the Tanala culture, after all the changes consequent upon wet rice had become consolidated, organized, and institutionalized. We are therefore observing an important experiment in the dynamics of social change.

In Betsileo society the gens is still the foundation of social life, descent being traced through the male line from a single ancestor. But the organization of the village as in Tanala culture is gone; it apparently disappeared according to the steps outlined above.

The local clan groups were administered by heads appointed by the king, one head for each gens. Members of several gentes live in the same village. Instead of free access to gens lands, as in Tanala culture, we have here a rigid system of ground rent levied on the land in the form of a proportion of rice produce.

Instead of the previous democracy as among the Tanala there is a rigid caste system with a king at the head, nobles, commoners, and slaves. The powers of the king are absolute over the life and property of everyone. The commoners are the bulk of the population, the nobles, to all intents, feudal lords whose chief control is over land by royal assignment; the slaves are war captives or their descendants.

The powers of the king far exceeded those of a lineage head in Tanala society and in some ways were greater than those of the ancestral ghosts. He could take the life, property, or wife of anyone; he could elevate and degrade the status of anyone at will, and no redress was possible. In accordance with these powers, a great many secondary mores, which accentuate the enhanced prestige of the king are present. There are taboos about his person and concerning his children; there are special clothes forbidden to anyone else; special words must be used to designate the condition or anatomy of the king. A king was not sick, he was "cold." He did not have eyes, he has "clearness." The souls of dead kings were called Zanahary-so-and-so. Succession was decided from among the king's sons, but not necessarily the oldest. Notwithstanding his great powers and prestige, he might work like a commoner in the rice fields. Though his powers were absolute and he could not be dethroned, he could be counseled to mend his ways.

Though the king owned all the land, he allotted it for use on a basis which was a charter of ownership, revokable at his will. The king dispensed this land in quantities proportional to the importance of, and the potential return from, the individual concerned. He would give the biggest allotments in return for the greatest support. The large landowner, a noble, could now rent any portion of his land to tenant farmers, who would pay rent in the form of a proportion of produce. Land thus owned could be sold or bequeathed as long as it did not become subject to another king. In short, here was a feudal system of a kind.

The staple crop was rice by the wet method; but other crops were cultivated as well—manioc, maize, millet, beans, and sweet potatoes. The chief adjunct to wet rice cultivation was the possibility of transporting water by irrigation, a factor which added to the permanency of the whole organization and took something of the premium away from the swamps and valleys. Irrigation methods made it possible to use the terraced hillsides for agriculture. But control of irrigation, and even perhaps its installation, made a strong central power essential.

The significance of cattle was the same as in Tanala culture; they had little economic but high prestige value. Cows were used chiefly for sacrifice and hence an instrument of power with the gods. The chief source of meat food were chickens, as with the Tanala.

Parallel to the powers of the king were the powers of the father in the individual household; in Betsileo he exercised an unchecked absolutism. All property belonged to the father during the latter's lifetime except his wives' clothes and the gifts he might make to his wives or children. The profits from exploitation of the land went to him. The inheritance laws resembled those of the Tanala except that land could now be inherited.

In the life cycle of the individual we begin to note important changes. The approaching birth of a child is not announced, for fear of sorcery. The afterbirth is buried and various superstitions are connected with it. As in Tanala culture, some days are propitious for birth, others are not. A child born on a certain day (the equivalent of Sunday) must be thrown on the village rubbish heap for a while, or washed in a jug of dirty dishwater. This is supposed to avert evil destiny. The belief is that a child born on one of these unlucky days will destroy its family. Children born in the month of *Alakaosy* are killed either by drowning, or by having cattle walk over them. Should they survive these exposures, they are kept, with the due precaution of changing their destiny through an *ombiasy*. Adoption is frequent; so also is the changing of names.

The basic disciplines are like those of the Tanala. But here in Betsileo society strong emphasis falls on the training in various shades of deference to elders and rank. Manners elevate the status of one individual as against another: the father is served separately, etc.

Incest taboos are the same as those of the Tanala, and observance is with the same general laxity. Premarital chastity is expected of women and punishment is sterility—as with the Tanala. The endogamy of marriage is now within caste lines, though elevation in status of a slave can take place. There is considerably more homosexuality than in Tanala.

The levirate is practiced in Tanala culture but not in Betsileo. A man who married his brother's widow would be strongly suspected of having killed his brother with sorcery or poison. Polygamy is the rule, as in Tanala.

The disciplinarian in Betsileo society is the father. He has the sole right to punish his children, a right which is, however, rarely exercised. Children may desert their parents in Betsileo, something which is almost inconceivable in Tanala. In one family eight children deserted their parents, whereupon the father changed his name to mean, "I have wiped away excrement for nothing."

The religion of Betsileo is much like that of Tanala; but significant changes can be noted. The rigid belief in fate is changed somewhat to mean that god arranges everything in advance. Sorcery (*mpamosavy*) is now the cause of illness, but the sorcerer is only an executive of god. We find new concepts in Betsileo culture which are unknown in Tanala. For example, god is angry if anyone oppresses the poor. There is a strong belief now in retaliation for aggression against anyone. A man is rich because his Zanahary is good.

The immediate supernatural executives are ghosts and spirits of various kinds. There are for example the *vazimba*, who once lived in the land of the Betsileo and were driven out. Their souls did not go to heaven but remained in the tombs and are, therefore, hostile. *Mpamosavy* bury bait in the tombs of the *vazimba* to kill the person from whom the bait was taken. They also believe in several other varieties of evil spirits in the form of birds or animals. The Betsileo make a clear distinction between life and soul. Life ceases with death, the soul continues. The soul may leave the body by breaking a taboo, through excessive chagrin or fright. The souls of the dead observe the same caste distinctions as obtained in life. The souls of the disowned are evil, and can seduce good souls to do mischief to their own families. A good funeral for a relative insures his good will after death. The soul of a king is transformed into a snake.

Possession by spirits is much more common than in Tanala. In the latter we noted occasional *tromba* (possession by a ghost), and very rarely *mpamosavy*. In Betsileo one is possessed by evil spirits. The incidence is very common and the manifestations much more severe. These spirit illnesses are due to either human or nonhuman spirits. In one type of possession (*aretondolo*) the victim sees these spirits which are invisible to everyone else. They persecute the victim in a large number of ways. They pursue him and he flees across the country; he may be dragged along and made to perform all varieties of stunts. But the remarkable thing is that the victim never shows marks of injury. These seizures come suddenly, and after the first attack, the victim is liable to others. His seizure ends in a spell of unconsciousness, from which he awakes normal. Another form of possession is called *salomanga,* which is possession by a once human spirit.

The chief method of worship is by means of sacrifice and thanks. The Betsileo make sacrifices for favors desired or received; they sacrifice for plenty and for scarcity. There is, however, a novelty in the form of taking a vow which in essence is a promise to make a sacrifice usually a cow or fowl pending the outcome of certain events in the individual's favor. The rituals are filled with all kinds of repetitious ceremonials; the same thing must be done a certain number of times to be effectual.

The *ombiasy* has the same functions as in Tanala. He cures

the sick, performs *sikidy,* designates good and bad days for undertakings, and makes charms. The *ombiasies* are as in Tanala, *nkazo* and *ndolo,* the latter being chiefly women. There are in addition to the legitimate *ombiasies* the malevolent sorcerers, *mpamosavy.* These are very scarce in Tanala, but very numerous—or at least suspected to be so—in Betsileo. The practice is secret, and hereditary. The *mpamosavy* is an agent of Zanahary and is possessed by the god. These sorcerers do evil deeds at night, and run out of their homes naked except for a turban. Everyone is suspected of being *mpamosavy.* They work chiefly by planting charms in places where they can do harm. The techniques by which the *mpamosavy* work are similar to those in Tanala. One such charm is a small wooden coffin containing medicines and a small dead animal. When this is destroyed the charm is broken. Nail parings, hair cuttings, leftover food, clothing, earth from a footprint, can be used to injure its owner; urine, feces, and spittle are not so used. In Tanala we noted that these could not be used for malevolent magic as "bait." As a result in Betsileo all nail parings, hair cuttings, etc., are kept in one common heap. The charms used by *mpamosavy,* powerful in themselves, are strengthened and reinforced by evil ghosts. Anyone apprehended in the practice of *mpamosavy* is ostracized or driven into exile.

There is perhaps one additional concept in Betsileo culture not found in Tanala: the breaking of a taboo can be atoned for by an act of purification.

Much more general apprehension exists in Betsileo than Tanala, as shown by the increase in belief in omens, dreams, and superstitions. The difference is quantitative. Some of the superstitutions are rather telling. When a person dies at the moment of a good harvest, he has been killed by his wealth. The superstitions all indicate some fear of retaliatory misfortune. The type of reasoning is largely by analogy. Thus, if anyone strikes a snake but does not kill it, the offender will suffer as the snake suffers; if it is sick he will be sick, if it dies, he will die.

There is also considerable increase in crime, stealing in particular, but also murder. For this latter crime there is indemnity and retaliation by vendetta. The Tanala do not engage in boxing; the Betsileo do. Suicide is very uncommon; but I have heard of a case of suicide in which the man vowed to use his soul to persecute the man who drove him to it. Blood brotherhood exists as in Tanala.

One additional custom should be noted, as of contrast to Tanala. There the village tomb contains all the dead. In Betsileo, burial was in individual family tombs, the women being laid on one side, the men on the other. The king's body was mummified, with special rituals insuring the liberation from the body of a small embryo which later turns into a snake. Tombs became one of the favorite ways of displaying wealth and ostentation. Technological development of weaving and pottery in Betsileo, was very much more highly developed than in Tanala. However, the Betsileo made contact with several neighboring peoples where these arts were highly developed, whereas the Tanala did not.

In conclusion we can say that Tanala and Betsileo cultures were identical in the main. The differences are traceable to the change in productive methods from dry to wet rice cultivation. This is proven by several circumstances: The traditions in Betsileo indicate an old culture very like Tanala; the institutions of both indicate a common source, and many of them are still identical; the changes in Tanala were gradual, and were well on the way to becoming identical with Betsileo when the French took over; and finally some of the Tanala tribes took over the wet rice method and abandoned it because of the serious incompatibilities it created in the social structure. The spread of wet rice cultivation cannot be attributed solely to diffusion; wet rice culture was endemic in Tanala and coincident with dry rice. Its spread was favored largely by the exhaustion of the dry method. Hence in examining the changes secondary to this main innovation, we need not depend exclusively on diffusion for an explanation.

Chapter VIII

THE ANALYSIS OF TANALA CULTURE

THIS account of the culture of the Tanala Menabe is complete enough to permit us to examine a society the primary institutions of which are very similar to our own. We have, therefore, an excellent opportunity to observe simpler types of secondary institutions which derive from the basic personality structure created by these primary institutions.

A second feature of this culture is the presence of checks on the drastic effects of some primary institutions by the substitution of convenient practical mores to offset the letter of the conventions, a condition which introduces into a rigid and oppressive system a good deal of plasticity and leeway for the individual. It is this which confers on the culture a high degree of stability and balance.

A third point worthy of note is the remarkable fact that though the oppression (according to our standards) of a large segment of the population is quite severe, this group, nevertheless, seems quite contented. According to Linton the Tanala culture attracts individuals from other cultures like the Arab, who become acclimated to it and like it. This is a high tribute to the satisfactions the individual can enjoy in it. The reasons for this must engage us.

A fourth important opportunity is created for us to observe the effects of changes in production systems—from dry to wet rice cultivation—on the social organization and the character of the intrasocial relationships. The culture of the Betsileo is the same as that of the Tanala except for a change in one of the primary institutions. We shall have the opportunity of seeing whether these changes create changes in basic personality structure and hence in secondary institutions.

Dr. Linton's account, as in the case of the Marquesan culture, contains much direct evidence, much that was reported by informants, a bit of folklore, and again a few invaluable personal impressions and reactions of the ethnographer. The one most worthy of note is the observation that the men are very shifty and indirect, whereas the women are quite straightforward in their conversation and dealings. This is the kind of observation which must be reconciled with the cultural picture as a whole.

The primary institutions which resemble our own are the general character of the family organization, the supreme position of the father, and the general character of the basic disciplines. These institutions differ from ours in that polygamy is common; in that the oldest son enjoys unusual privileges and immunities as well as opportunities for prestige; in that the younger sons have a completely immobile social status; in that the subsistence economy is very different from ours; and finally in the peculiar values in which prestige economy is expressed.

There is no numerical disparity between the sexes to create a special social problem. And there is no food anxiety of such intensity as to pervade the entire culture. The chief emphasis in this culture falls in places very like those of our own. The one feature which is pointed up in this culture is the character of relationship between the men, that between father and sons, and that between younger sons and the oldest son.

The contrapuntal character of the interrelationships in Tanala society creates difficulties in presentation. However, the most expedient plan is to discuss the main problem first, and then return to individual features for specific treatment. We shall therefore treat them in the following order: family organization and basic disciplines; subsistence economy; prestige economy; the basic personality structure of the individual; the psychology of ingratiation; the change from dry to wet rice cultivation (the Betsileo) ; the constellation of prestige.

FAMILY ORGANIZATION AND BASIC DISCIPLINES

The family is organized according to a patriarchal pattern save for the complication of multiple wives and the special treatment of the oldest son. The position of the father in the household is supreme. His powers consist of every known attribute of absolute authority, with a few checks on his behavior to wives and oldest son. On the younger sons his authority is most telling; for he has the ability to impose discipline, to exploit them for his own ends, and to frustrate important needs. He can command both within the prescribed customs and without, and from these conditions the younger son has no redress, if he wishes to retain the boons and protection that go with obedience. The father can compel the sons to labor for him on his own terms, and can frustrate the needs of protection and maintenance; and after death he can continue, as one of the lineage gods, to exert the same power, although by somewhat different techniques. The differentiation in status between oldest and youngest sons is demarcated by immunities from labor and tangible prestige values. The oldest son is not inducted into labor as early as the others, nor does his work ever take on more than a supervisory character.

The position of the woman and mother is distinctly secondary, though her prestige status is regulated by her relative standing as chief or secondary wife. The child's guardian in infancy and childhood is his mother, and the maternal care seems to be adequate and tender in many respects. The father's presence, in a family with multiple wives, must be intermittent, and hence his authority is consequently enhanced. However, the first and most significant discipline to which the child is subjected is effected through the agency of the mother. The basic disciplines are concerned with weaning, anal training, sexual mores in childhood, and induction into labor. There is no indication of mistreatment of the child by the mother except in connection with anal training. The infant is breast-fed until the next one needs the breast. The length of time varies, and there is no indication of anything traumatic about this phase of the child's life. Thumb-sucking was not observed by Linton.

Coincident with the bountiful treatment in connection with the mother as a feeder is a very early insistence on anal sphincter control. The reasons for this are purely practical and due to the absence of swaddling materials. Since the child must be continent at six months, and since this is established by punishment for failures, the entire process constitutes a very early conditioning. But for our purposes it is of considerable importance to see how this conditioning is constituted. At that age the child cannot have any appreciation of the end to which this discipline is directed; acquiescence must therefore be established on a pain-pleasure principle—the child must perceive that one condition is followed by pain, another by its absence. In the coincidence of the free access to the breast and rigid anal discipline, we have the constituents of a few basic constellations, which can be expressed as follows: "If I obey I will not be punished; if I obey I will be fed; if I do such-and-such, then there will follow such-and-such." No doubt some constellations are created which deal specifically with anal control, retention, suppression of feeling, and the rest. This we cannot tell without study of the individual. But the most important implication is the premature development of responsibility, sense of obligation, obedience, which later must manifest themselves as conscientiousness, fear of disobedience, and unswerving loyalty.

How much weight one can give a circumstance like this in the formation of personality in a culture is hard to determine. Such a situation cannot be of supreme significance unless the institutional arrangement later encountered continues the usefulness of these basic constellations. Nor can one say that this discipline is the result of patriarchal tyranny. It is inducted by the mother chiefly for purely practical purposes. It so happens that in Tanala culture there is, throughout the life cycle of the individual, and especially for the younger sons, a constant relationship between obedience and security, loyalty and protection. However, it would labor the point too far to state that these institutions are all patterned after the experience with anal training. Nor is it necessary to make any such assumption. The influence of these basic constellations, however, shows itself in some of the elementary thought processes.

The sexual mores are unfortunately not completely described; but the general outlines are clear. Sexual play between children is forbidden and masturbation was not observed. This can only mean that such sexual practices, if they exist at all, must be carried on in secret and receive no social approval. What laxity there is in dealing with these sexual situations is instituted after puberty. But it would not be extravagant to believe that there is probably a good deal of individual variation both as regards parental attitudes and those of the children to sexual behavior.

There seems to be a general laxity about enforcing sex mores, though premarital chastity is expected in women, but not in men. Although the young man is expected to have his adventures in any way he can, the girl is threatened with sterility if she violates the injunction. Notwithstanding, her illegitimate child is accepted without serious loss of face, and there is always a magic antidote to sterility.

The customary incest taboos against siblings, parents, and related groups prevail. There are, in other words, binding object taboos, and aim taboos as well, but with a not too rigid enforcement of the latter.

Here we begin to see some evidence of a common trait in this culture, to dull the edge of a serious prohibition, i.e., to deny its importance, and thus permit a circumvention of the formal mos. The sexual disciplines in Tanala ought to lead to jealousy among the men and ought to be associated with some failures in sexual development. What we actually find is a transposition of affect. Jealousy among men about sexual objects is played down, sexual activity being considered pleasant, but not very important. The emphasis falls on procreation, an emphasis aided by the actual fact that man power enhances the economic power and prestige of the paterfamilias. But the woman is considered permanently impregnated after the first intercourse with her husband and keeps on having children automatically, thus offering an opportunity for diminishing the significance of marital fidelity. This convenient belief evades the clumsy issue of paternity, which would otherwise unleash a good deal of hostility all around. This is quite different from the state of affairs in Marquesas, where potency has no outstanding value because of the absence of impediments to its free development. In Tanala the significance of paternity is not disturbed, but a convenient belief is superimposed to permit some sexual freedom. We cannot here use the check on potency disturbances as we did in Marquesas, because marriage was chiefly endogamous within the village and magic was too dangerous to use. Since this was a generally observed convention, no potency disturbance would ever be rationalized in this manner.

The necessity for sexual laxity becomes apparent when we examine the rigidity of the social organization and the almost complete immobilization of the individual. However, without the aid of biography we cannot tell the force of the sex mores; nor can we tell whether the sexual liberties behind the conventions have any relation to class lines, whether the most oppressed are the greatest libertines or the least.

Notwithstanding the sexual freedom behind the letter of the mores, we are safe in assuming that this freedom does not make itself felt in the individual until puberty; meanwhile, some interference with sexual development must have taken place in childhood. This shows itself quite patently in the incidence of and attitude toward homosexuality. Tolerance of the perversion is a strange trait to find in a patriarchal society where the emphasis on offspring is very great. The disapproval of this perversion has often been attributed to the fact that anything is perceived as a danger which tends to diminish population.[1]

---

[1] In this society homosexuality would have no influence on population. Children are of importance only to the head of the household, but not to the group as a whole. Hence the group cannot have any stake in the homosexuality of a few individuals.

The fact that homosexuals come from the ranks of younger sons or childless older men indicates that it has a relationship to the submissive role of the younger sons. But the fact that it is a socially accepted form of adjustment, even though it does not enjoy high standing, is a comment on the general laxity about sexual mores. The fact that the homosexual can take the position of secondary wife indicates the relative status of younger son and secondary wife. The former is evidently worse off. It is also a clear indication that sexual attitudes in childhood are much influenced by the dependency of the younger son on the father, especially since the boy's training in the paternal economic fold begins at about the age of five.

The disciplines for economic activity begin for the younger son at the age of five; from this activity the oldest son is exempted. The effect of this situation is to shorten the period of irresponsibility in childhood, and to establish work for the father as an essential condition for enjoying his protection and favors.

There is one important circumstance about their economic training. It requires chiefly diligence and application, but not skill. Skill is one of the qualities which permit enhancement of self-esteem, and in this society would permit some personal feeling of value to break the feeling of submission to the father. The individual loses an element of effective competition. For the younger son in this society, favors from the father must be won by another technique, the technique of ingratiation.

SUBSISTENCE ECONOMY

Tanala is not a scarcity culture. There is little evidence of food anxiety. The people have little difficulty and uncertainty in the exploitation of the environment for subsistence. This fact can be observed. It is certainly due to two factors: the availability of actual natural resources during the dry rice cultivation, and the fixity of the social organization for purposes of exploiting these resources. In other words, food anxiety may be due to actual food scarcity, or to the uncertainties of human organization in exploiting the resources. There is one striking fact which can be used to substantiate this absence of anxiety: there are no rituals to make the rice grow. This would indicate that there is no need for supernatural intervention to aid a sure and plentiful supply of rain and a sure fertility of the soil within certain limits. The Tanala have apparently complete confidence in their ability to control it themselves.

This does not mean that rice culture with the Tanala is devoid of hazards. While the cutting and burning method was being used, the fertility of the soil would periodically become exhausted, thereby necessitating a periodic removal of the entire village to a new site. A good deal of hard labor would thus be required to make the land fit to produce. Yet in spite of it the shift comes about without much anxiety.

This confidence in the ability to control the food supply does not come exclusively from these technological aspects—the knowledge of procedure and its consistent success—but from the certainty of the social and organizational aspects, which guarantee the labor necessary to exploit the opportunities. Each individual is so trained in his social role, as well as in techniques which require no great skill, that his fixity in his role is guaranteed by a rock-bound system of sanctions and punishments. Defections from the system of bonds to the father and to the economic role are possible for the exceptional individual, but are not the rule. The rigid social categories of status are aided to no small degree by the almost complete absence of differentiation of labor. The result is that emphasis falls on diligence rather than skill. The factor that contributes to the stability of this system is the equable rewards which diligence can bring.

The diligent son becomes a dependable factor in the machinery of production; and all factors which could be expected to bring about anxiety on the score of subsistence are circumvented because the opportunity for labor and diligence cannot be denied anyone. Land, the basic instrument of production, is communally owned and each individual has a subsistence claim on it. This holds for all the men in the household except the father and oldest son, who exact from the labor of the younger sons subsistence and prestige values as well. The diligence of the younger son is guaranteed by the threat of invoking the disfavor of the father. The level of prestige, standing, and status for the younger sons depends, therefore, not on successful competition in skills or superior values, but in vying with each other in winning paternal favors.

The warrior and *ombiasy* occupy a singular position in the social system. These individuals have daring and skill, and they fall outside the family economy.

PRESTIGE ECONOMY

The prestige economy of the Tanala is vested in certain privileges and immunities. The immunities are largely from labor. The privileges are the ability to command regard; to be treated with deference in contrast with those who do not possess these rights; to impose disciplines, tender rewards and favors; to inflict punishments and privations; and to discriminate against those who displease. The exercise of these rights cannot, however, interfere with the subsistence needs of any individual. These prestige rights are intimately connected with subsistence and also with birth.

The signal feature of the social organization is the concentration of these above-mentioned powers in the hands of the household head and on the oldest son, through whom this power is transmitted. It would appear that with the exception of the warrior and *ombiasy,* the life destiny of the individual is decided at birth.

The remarkable feature of Tanala prestige values is that these values are not translatable into any tangible advantages apart from immunity from labor. In the domain of subsistence needs there is no distinction between favored and unfavored.

Objects like cattle enjoy a high value in bestowing on their possessor claims for power, but have little, if any, utility value. The use of cattle is largely for purposes of sacrifice, and to establish the power of a deceased person. Money cannot be used much for trade in articles which give its owner greater comfort, convenience, or enjoyment, but again can only be used for purchase of land in order to establish a lineage. Nothing can be bought, for there is little trade, and most objects for personal utility are owned by those who make them, so even theft is practically impossible.

Notwithstanding the power of household head and oldest son, there are distinct checks on their power. The household head cannot inherit property from his wife or child. Instances are reported by Linton where a father can be deserted for cause, but this is uncommon.

In short, there is practically complete immobility of status for the younger son. This immobility, since there is no differentiation of labor, and since skills occupy relatively little importance, indicates pretty much the lines of intrasocial tension. Whether it is expressed or not, it must be between younger brothers against each other and against the oldest son, but not against the father, because the latter's position is so strong as to strangulate any hostility in that direction. This inability to show hostility to the father is guaranteed further by the post-mortem power that he retains to guard over the fixity of the social structure. One would, as a result of this social structure, expect two things: that hostilities would not be expressed directly or overtly, the family gods preventing any such display along lines where they would be most likely to assert themselves; and that adaptation by ingratiation would remain the chief way open to the younger son. The prerogatives of household head and older son are so completely safeguarded during life, and the power of household head is so completely retained after death, an effect which lasts at least as long as the life of a younger son, that for the latter, apart from ingratiation, only a few paths are left open within the limits of achievement. These are *ombiasy*, warrior, *tromba*, or homosexual. Of these four, only the first two require any real initiative; the latter two are masochistic accommodations. The striking characters in this society are most likely to be found in these two classes, *ombiasy* and warrior.

THE BASIC PERSONALITY STRUCTURE OF THE INDIVIDUAL

Under this rubric we can consider the following: techniques of thinking; sibling rivalry; the security system of the individual; checks by religion and folklore; the "super-ego" in Tanala.

In the accompanying figure (Figure 2, p. 326) we have a representation of the primary institutions, basic personality structure, secondary institutions, and counterchecks upon the latter. From the sketch of the primary institutions we can get some idea of the problems of adaptation which confront the individual and the basic constellations which are bound to be formed, and which are consonant with the social organization and subsistence economy.

We must note first of all that the basic disciplines predispose to an attitude of obedience to win rewards. Toward the father only two attitudes are possible, hatred or submission. The hatred is easy to suppress in view of the father's ability to confer favors and the son's ability to collect them. This renders ingratiation the dominant technique of adjustment. As long as the rewards of ingratiation are collectable, no serious problem of control of suppressed hostility can emerge. One may expect the aggression to emerge only when the rewards of submission are withdrawn. Moreover, the controls against any aggression within the lineage are well illustrated by the fact that among women, who do not have the same motives to repress mutual hostility, sorcery is commonly used across lineage lines, where the taboos do not hold.

How can we check on the correctness of this view? How do we know that there is any suppression of hostility to the father? This we can check by the secondary institutions. The Tanala do not fear the dead but do fear ghosts, and naturally the ghosts of the most important male individuals in the family cult. These ghosts can cause illness. To offend them, therefore, brings punishment. This is a replica of the actual social system. However, these ghosts can be propitiated by appropriate sacrifices, which in Tanala culture means depriving oneself.

We can also see the effects of the primary disciplines on the formation of basic rational constellations in the individual. The insistence on a compulsive ritual of obedience as part of a cure is an indication of the importance of obedience as part of the individual's security system.[2] With regard to sexual restraints we find evidence of the enigmatic Oedipus complex. But this is offset by convenient beliefs which render infidelity less damaging all around. Potency is valued, but we cannot check on the use of magic to create sexual impotence, because magic within the village is too dangerous to use.

The sibling rivalry situation presents some interesting phenomena. Hostility to the oldest brother must be suppressed because any breach of the injunctions against magic within the family line would immediately provoke the rage of the lineage gods. The suppression of it is again rendered acceptable by collecting rewards from the father and lineage gods. The sibling rivalry situation is permitted institutionalized compensation in blood brotherhood, where mutual fidelity is guaranteed. There are two more avenues of expression of defiance to submission to father and older brother without the aid of overt aggression or magic—the roles of *ombiasy* and warrior. The *ombiasy* is a worker with fate, who enjoys important immunities, social mo-

---

[2] In Tanala and Betsileo both we shall have ample opportunity to examine whether the compulsive and ritualistic character traits of both peoples are derived from anal erotism or from the reactions of obedience to discipline, of which the early anal training sets the prototype. The same is true of the hoarding and saving characteristics of the Tanala, and the high value of property in Betsileo. The crucial question is not whether retentive characteristics are present or not, but whether they are derived from the erotism or from the reaction to discipline. There is no doubt that once the basic *gestalt* is formed, security goes with retention and anxiety with irresponsible casting off, and that these constellations can later be elaborated in a great many ways. The irresponsible casting off (of feces) becomes by contrast with the social demand a piece of self-will, aggression, and defiance to discipline. Thus, one often sees in patients prolonged periods of constipation when the dominant emotion is an anxiety of losing support or protection. Anal training is essentially a training in retention and responsibility.

bility, and the capacity to accumulate wealth. The warrior is the enterprising individual who vents his antisocial trends outside of his village. He can thus acquire the means of becoming a lineage head. But it is important to note in the basic personality structure of the individual the complete shunting of direct hostilities, blaming one's destiny on fate, and then correcting the fate either by magic (ombiasy) or plunder (warrior). Direct aggression in the form of crime is severely punished. This explains the general shiftiness and indirectness in the men which Linton observed. It is absent in the women because they do not adjust by a technique of ingratiation and have no need to conceal their wants or displeasures. They have no status differentiation until after puberty, and do not come into open competition until the problems of mating arise. They do not therefore need the automatized cringing attitudes of the men.

Acquiescence in the submissive role to father and oldest brother does not, however, always result in a successful adaptation. The phenomenon of tromba, which is apparently some form of major hysteria, most frequently occurs in the younger sons, though occasionally in women.[3] Homosexuality also belongs to this category of unsuccessful combat with aggressive attitudes toward father and oldest brother. The fact that neither tromba nor homosexuality occurs in heads of households or oldest sons is witness to the close relation of both aberrations to the problems of adaptation confronting the younger sons.

From the point of view of the household head and oldest son, the constellation of prestige is dominant. Here the prominent constellation is the enlargement of the ego through possessions and property to the end of being able to control the activity of others. It is interesting to note that the mechanism of enlarging the ego is not on the pattern of eating, as we found in Marquesas. Deification is effected through sacrifices of animals; the meaning of the animal sacrifice is not the same as was noted in

[3] The phenomenon of "mpamosavy" is not accurately enough described to permit any definite conclusions. It seems a psychotic disturbance. For further details about it we shall use the material from Betsileo.

respect to cannibalism. The significance of the sacrifice of cattle is entirely a dispensation of property and hence not a form of depriving oneself of sensual pleasure, but a type of impoverishment of one's own condition and a corresponding enriching of that of the god. It may be based on the early constellation, "If I impoverish myself and suffer, the parent will come to my aid." How effective a check on overt aggression fear of ancestors can be, is well illustrated by Linton's account of how much of a nuisance it entailed to see an ancestral ghost (in this culture the equivalent of conscience), and be repeatedly obliged to make appropriate sacrifice.[4]

TECHNIQUES OF THINKING

Evidence of the nature of the thought processes of the Tanala can be found in their magic practices, in the manufacture and uses of charms, sorcery, and in the conception of illness. If we were to characterize all the beliefs and techniques connected with these as "animistic," we would overlook some important differences among them; for some of these techniques are based on a projection mechanism, and others on a scientific principle.

The differences between these two types of thought depend on two different criteria for evaluating phenomena perceived both in the outer world and in themselves. In the case of "projection," the reality is perceived in accordance with powerful subjective needs; in the case of scientific principle, it is perceived in accordance with observations made free of subjective emotional bias or necessity, and in accordance with the realities in the outer world.

Their conception of illness is an excellent illustration of projection phenomena. We here encounter the almost universal idea that illness and death are caused by magic or sorcery. This

[4] This explanation of the particular use of sacrifice has no relation to the ideas on the subject developed by Freud, where the sacrificial animal is a father-substitute. The sacrifice becomes therefore a form of killing the father and eating him up, and hence a descendant of a hypothetical totemic feast. However the case may be with this theory about origins, it has no bearing on the practical role of sacrifice in psychic economy of the Tanala.

magic or sorcery can be initiated through the agency of some individual. However, the wish or intention to inflict injury is not enough to set these forces in motion; the actual causative agent is the force released through the properties contained in charms, which do not derive their power from the ancestral cults, but from the properties of mechanical objects. It is therefore a purely mechanistic conception. However, behind this lies the intention of someone to inflict injury, and hence all defenses against magic would necessitate avoiding the hostile wishes, or counteracting the charm. However, the fact is that magic is not direct; it is really a form of modifying fate. Magic is an indirect method of injury without touching and without direct action of any kind. The modification of fate thus relieves some of the anxiety about direct application of injury to another individual.

It is interesting to note in Tanala culture the absence of magic by words. Instead, there is the idea that powerful forces in the world are mobilized through the agency of objects. The charm is thus made by placing certain objects with inherent properties in a certain definite relation with other objects, the combination of which will release a third force, which can then be directed toward a specific goal. The criteria by which the magic properties of these objects are established are apparently deductive, experimental, and are checked pragmatically; that is, they are considered effective only if they work. In the operation of the charm we have, therefore, the "scientifically" established efficacy of certain relationships between inanimate objects, which are joined to a wish to injure someone or protect oneself against injury. In the entire procedure of making a charm against illness, we see both the operation of a "scientific" principle and a projection.

The anxiety of being the victim of someone's hostile wishes is based upon a projection. This concept needs some elucidation. "Projection" is a form of ideational representation of a relationship between subject and object, whereby processes taking place in the subject are attributed to the object. "I wish to hurt you," when repressed, becomes a fear that "you will hurt me." This statement would create the impression that projection always represents a hostility unconsciously initiated by the subject but perceived as coming from the object, and that this transformation of perception is due entirely to repression. Such is not necessarily the case. This use of the term projection is very incomplete, for the perception of hostility may come from several other sources besides the one just described. Ferenczi has made some interesting conjectures about the origin of this type of perception.[5] One can supplement Ferenczi's brilliant ideas with a further pursuit of the unconscious ego activities that lie back of projection phenomena.

Illustrations of this type of unconscious activity of the ego can be observed in many of the phenomena that patients bring to our attention. Thus, for example, one patient described these ego activities very accurately. They first took the form of a conviction that the other person was doing something against him. On close examination it proved that this was not at all due to the repressed wish on the part of my patient to injure the other person, but by a rage caused by the fact that the other person was not doing what the patient expected him to do. This in turn was contingent upon another idea: that the other person was not a separate individual at all, but merely an appendage of the patient, like his arm or leg, and when the other person did not respond with the same readiness, and to the same degree with which his hand followed his will, the patient had a feeling of loss and desertion, which terminated in a rage. To this he reacted with great anxiety, feeling that the other person did not "love" him. This latter feeling was then perceived as hatred. His usual reaction was an aggression toward the frustrating object, but this aggression against the object was a defense against the aggression of which the patient felt himself to be the victim. Ferenczi gave this phenomenon the name of "loss of boundaries of the ego." However, through this formula it is

[5] S. Ferenczi, "Stages in the Development of the Sense of Reality," *Sex and Psychoanalysis* (Boston, 1916), pp. 213–238.

difficult to see the perceptive processes at work. We must stress these perceptive processes because they are indicators of what the ego or total personality is doing. This type of perception is ontogenetically very archaic, and, according to Ferenczi, stems from the earliest reactions to separation from the mother, and the recognition of the "separateness" of the ego from other objects. The symbiotic existence of the child in early life, the fact that its needs are gratified mainly through the agency of the mother, and partially through its own efforts, makes such a conclusion of the child (that the mother is an appendage of itself) warranted by the child's subjective experience. Freud had long since established the fact that the "persecutor" is the object by whom the persecuted individual expects to be loved. We can schematically represent the processes involved in projection:

The Perception is, "The other person wants to injure me."
The Premise is: "He does not do as I wish" (magic control of other person).

This frustrated expectation is interpreted as "not loved" but "hated," and hence the interpretation of the object as doing something against the subject.[6] In other words, it is not enough to recognize the fact that a bit of "aggression" has been repressed and is then perceived as coming from without, but to see that this aggression is due to the frustration of an expectation which is unconscious, and that the persistence of the expectation is a totally unconscious constellation of the ego.[7]

[6] At this point the subject may well initiate several types of defense, one of which is to submit sexually to the object. But this is a point we need not enter upon.

[7] In psychoanalytic usage such terms as "projection" were commonly used not only to describe dynamic transformations of impulse representatives, but also "explanations" of the entire behavior consequent upon the use of the mechanism concerned. Thus, once we had discovered that the individual "projects," no further explanation was deemed necessary. The explanation of "projection" here offered is an excellent illustration of the practical use of ego psychology. It describes at least one more facet of the locus of infantile fixations and describes the sources of the aggression and the motives for its repression.

What then is the meaning of the persistence of this type of perception in the grown adult, and in the institutionalized forms found in primitive societies? In adults in our culture, we find it a predominant type of perception in paranoid individuals, and we call it pathological. That does not mean that primitive people are "paranoid."

What factors make the use of "projection" so necessary in a wide range of perceptions which we find institutionalized in aboriginal cultures and in our own? An illustration from our own culture may aid in clarifying this point. Scientific thinking is widespread in many aspects of our culture, yet we find instances where certain emotional factors prevent the application of scientific methods. One of the most noteworthy instances of the persistence of nonscientific thinking was the belief that masturbation causes all varieties of disease. One of the diseases supposed to be caused by masturbation was general paresis. Until 1912, when the Spirochaeta pallida was discovered in the lesions of this disease, the older view was held and taught. The maintenance of this belief was not rational; but it had an emotional plausibility based on the experience of every individual in our culture in connection with our sex mores, viz., that masturbation is forbidden. There is a direct experimental connection between the idea of disobedience, the idea of punishment, and thence the concept of disease as punishment. It is interesting to note the difference in underlying concepts that characterize illness as due to someone's evil wishes, and illness as punishment. Behind these two different end results lie the cultural constellations built around the reactions to discipline. At all events, when there is an actual ignorance of the true cause of disease, the answer is supplied by an emotional evaluation. The belief about the consequences of masturbation is just as "animistic" as the Tanala belief about the etiology of disease.

The important things about projection are: the endopsychic perception of the power of hostile wishes; and the equally strong wishes to be able to make others do as you wish, that is, to treat them as appendages which follow your bidding, for example, as the hand follows the will. The significant thing about this phenomenon is that it explains illness on the basis of the hostile wishes of others. If hostile wishes are taken as manifestations *only* of hostile wishes attributed to the object, but perceived by the subject, we lose sight of a more important source of this perception of hostility as a frustrated expectation of being loved, protected, and therefore well. The prime mover is neither the wish to be loved and protected nor the hostility which is generated by the frustration of this expectation. The persistence of the wish is in itself an indicator of a permanent incapacity in the ego through inhibitions or underdeveloped functions, in lieu of which dependent attitudes appear. The entire constellation is an indicator of a localized ego failure.[8]

The human being's first perceptions of being "well" are those of the easing of wishes and tensions by the mother, usually by feeding, or by some other form of attention. It is reasonable to assume that in a helpless state the individual revives these expectations. Hence, illness has the subjective meaning of not being loved and protected, but hated. In psychoanalytic literature this idea has been expressed in a different form, especially in connection with hypochondria, where it was found that the diseased organ represents the person (father) from whom love is expected or desired, but not deserved, because of the hostilities of the individual toward him; hence the individual feels himself persecuted by the father (super-ego), and now by the diseased organ. This is really a roundabout way of saying that illness represents punishment for disobedience, and hence becomes a consequence of a repressed piece of assertiveness against authority. One would say, therefore, that the conception of illness in Tanala culture is similar to that of the hypochondriac. But in the former case, these conceptions are in part due to actual ignorance of cause, to the substitution, in place of a scientifically established eti-

---

[8] The relation between hostility and the wish to be protected is carefully studied out in many ramifications by Horney, *The Neurotic Personality of our Time* (New York, 1937).

ology, of one that seems the most plausible explanation—according to the patterns of infantile experience—of the tensions from which the individual suffers. The fear of illness through sorcery is, therefore, an expression of several ideas: a situation arises which creates a feeling of helplessness; the wish and need for aid are denied; the frustration is utilized as a perception of hostility coming from another individual. This anxiety, though almost universal in primitive culture, is most likely to be exaggerated in societies where mutual dependency is slight, and where actual hostilities between individuals are most likely to exist. For in these societies the expectation of help is countered by the hostility of the subject to object, and the consequent guilt. By contrast with this conception of the etiology of disease, we have demonstrated one in our culture in which the idea is based on the experience with punishment.

These considerations apply to the general ideas about, or reactions to, illness. The fact that actual ignorance of etiology of disease also aids in this formation must not be overlooked. But we have several other important features about the thinking techniques of the Tanala which seem to be derived from reactions to discipline. These are the universality of compulsive rituals as a cure, and the insistence on their use. Dr. Linton's illustration of their complete inability to understand the efficacy of a medicine without the aid of a compulsive ritual is a case in point. The medicine works, not because of its inherent properties, but because the users are obedient to some command; if they do so-and-so in conjunction with the medicine, then and then only will the medicine work. This view is at variance with the otherwise widespread belief of the Tanala in the mechanistic interaction of physical properties as shown in their manufacture of charms. Where does this insistence on an obedient ritual come from, and what experience, culturally determined, do all the Tanala have which leads to this conclusion? The answer is not hard to find. Anal training, the first discipline, is begun by this people at three months and completed at six months. There is a premature insistence on obedience, backed by punishment. If the child obeys, it suffers no harm. The insistence on some activity to be done or some gratification to be omitted, therefore, establishes the conditions for being loved, or not punished. Hence the ritual becomes a part of the cure, a guarantee of parental help, and, therefore, of recovery. Moreover, the pattern of love or security in return for obedience is the most prominent pattern of adaptation for the greatest number of people in the culture. In other words, this discipline does not make them "anal erotic" but creates a very basic constellation which becomes automatic from earliest infancy—obedience brings safety and security. The Tanala also have an insistence on cleanliness and orderliness, which is a perpetuation of the same type of obedience and derived from the same source. This is also present in the idea that angry ghosts cause illness.

The manufacture of their charms is another instance of this thinking technique; but only the *ombiasy* know just how the charms are made, and what principles or experiences are incorporated into their manufacture. There is obviously an experimental attitude about it. However, what kind of effects they expect from what causes is not accurately enough known to be examined. Even if this is not known, the procedure of making charms must be evaluated as scientific, and not based on infantile thought processes.

THE SECURITY SYSTEM OF THE INDIVIDUAL

The security system of the individual in this society is distinctly a function of his status, and is directly derived from the ego structure.

The younger son must suppress hatred toward father and oldest brother, be diligent, ingratiate himself with his superiors real and supernatural, anticipate offense with prophylactic sacrifice, or atone afterward. He has one additional, socially permissible adjunct to his security system: he may, through the aid of the *ombiasy*, tamper with fate in an attempt to alter it.

No wonder that the belief in fate is so rigid, for the mobility of the younger son is practically nil! We see some evidence of an attempt to express discontent by altering fate. Should this fail, *tromba* and homosexuality are still open. It is important to note the significance of the blood bond as a part of the security system of the individual. The role it plays in the folktale recorded by Linton suggests that it is a forceful way of binding oneself in mutual aid to another individual with whom there might otherwise arise a spontaneous need for great aggression.

The fathers and oldest sons do not have a security system guaranteed by obedience. They have obligations to the lineage heads or lineage gods. Their security depends on initiative to make important decisions. But for the greater part their security depends on keeping the younger sons in line. For this purpose they have the support of most of the institutions. The security of these individuals depends also on successful competition with other lineage heads for higher prestige. Their security system evolves around prestige and power but not around ingratiation.

The *ombiasy* and warrior are undoubtedly the strong characters in this society. They have social mobility and initiative, and their status is not created for them by birth. Their security depends exclusively on their cunning and resources. These roles require an unwillingness to take the humble position of the younger son, and an ability to make their services respected.

The adaptation of the woman is different from that of the man. Primogeniture is of no significance; her relations with the father are more friendly than those of her brothers. The jealousy problems between head and secondary wife present no unusual features. Here we have largely a struggle for security through children, and the security of both mothers and children by ingratiation with the father. There is no problem of suppressing jealousy, and failures in success as a woman often lead to *tromba*.

RELIGION

Let us check the conclusions we have reached about basic personality structure on the religion of the Tanala. The effective gods are the deceased ancestors, and hence are prototypes of the real parents. They operate as ghosts who are feared. They are pleased by obedience and sacrifices, and are constantly on the side of existing moralities. Conscience operates in this society by an unpleasant token of seeing an ancestral ghost. The power of the male parent is significantly emphasized in the fact that ghosts of women are not heeded. Loyalty to the gods of the ancestral cult is binding under any conditions (unlike the situation among the Marquesans). Illness is interpreted as the wage of sin, and hence appeasement must be undertaken.

There are also supplementary spirits who do not belong to the family cult. These are "elected" gods, loyalty to whom is not binding except on the basis of efficiency.

Ingratiation with the ancestral gods is achieved through suffering, impoverishment of oneself, renunciation of pleasure. The god is merely an inflated parental image, whose functions, like those of the father, are to see that no hostilities are directed against the individuals upon whom such hostilities would naturally fall. The religion merely guarantees the social status; guarantees the deflection of hostilities by promising rewards for "correct" behavior, and punishment for failure to do so.

This structure of their religion is consistent with our previous conclusions about the effects of severe disciplines on the individual. The parental image is exaggerated for purposes both good and evil, for rewards and punishments.

At this point we may raise the question whether Tanala society permits a good adjustment for its less favored members. The evidence is quite conclusive that it does. Notwithstanding what appears by our standards to be a severe form of oppression, the younger sons seem on the whole to be contented individuals. The institutionalized forms of expression cover the opportunities for those with initiative as well as those without. The ambitious may become either warrior or *ombiasy*; the failure a hysteric or a homosexual. The absence of stealing, murder, suicide, and competitive games testifies to the fact that the adjustments offered the individual are effective. The reasons for this are not hard to find: they lie in the checks on prestige powers, which we have elsewhere enumerated, and in the fact that the subsistence economy permits the realization of the rewards for submission.

The belief in fate—singularly effective in shunting direct envy and overt hostility—is a monument to the underlying absolutism which characterizes the culture. It shifts the responsibility from those who actually have power or advantages and places it upon a kind of mechanistic conception of human destiny. The chief function of this belief is to compel the individual to accept his role in life and not to bother those who exploit him, though he is given some right to attempt to alter his fate by magic means. If this fails, he has only fate to blame.

We can further check the validity of the basic personality structure on the Tanala folklore. The story recorded by Linton (p. 277) corresponds to the typical Oedipus story. It tells quite clearly where the social conflicts lie—between the brothers. The father is too powerful to draw any direct hatred, even in a folktale. The story, moreover, deals with sexual jealousy between brothers. It is the brothers who steal the wives away from the hero. It is the ingratiating son by another marriage who undertakes to avenge the crime of his father's brothers. To show his father complete renunciation of the claim as a sexual rival, the dutiful son disguises himself as a woman; (he kills an old woman and dons her skin) and recovers for his father the stolen wives. He enters into combat with his uncle, with whom the son has common cause for jealousy, but does not kill him. In fact, he enters into a blood bond with him, and returns the wives to his father.

This is a perfect hero story for this culture; it upholds the mores of the society; it exalts the role of renunciation of masculinity to ingratiate oneself with the father in order to enjoy the boons of his favor. The story does not punish incest as does the Greek tale of Oedipus; it forestalls the tragedy by the renunciation of the goal in advance. It encourages peace by submission and even perhaps homosexuality, and confers on the father alone the sole right to masculine prerogatives.

This tale is an illustration of the particular ego structure of the individual in Tanala society. It differs from other Oedipus stories in very particular respects, which are highly characteristic of the dominant modes of adaptation fostered by the social structure (or more particularly by the primary institutions there existing). The displacement of the seat of the conflict from father and son to brother and brother is not an arbitrary or chance maneuver; it springs from the fact that suppression of jealousy to the father is made acceptable by the possibility of collecting rewards of good behavior. No such possibility exists among brothers who are in open rivalry for the father's favor. This tale demonstrates that the folktale is a product of a special set of social conditions. Whereas the pattern of the tale is characteristic of all patriarchally organized societies which impose sexual restrictions in childhood, the particular way in which the characters behave is signal for this set of social conditions only.

THE "SUPER-EGO"

A final point in our discussion of ego structure is the character of the super-ego in this society. Another way of stating this issue is to ask what are the forces that hold the individual in place in this society.

Let us begin with the two principal ideas of Freud, that individuals identify themselves with one another, and that they develop a moral organ called the super-ego, which is capable of guilt, conscience, self-reproach, and the like.

We have already seen that the modalities of the ego designated by the term "identification" are not uniform, but express various types of relations between subject and object. One type of "identification" is based on a complete absence of resources of the subject and a parasitic existence through the activity of the object. This relationship may be represented as either swallowing the object, or being inside it. Another type of "identification" is based on complete independence of resources in the subject, but a recognition of a common claim with the other individual, on the basis of common interests.

We might ask which of these types of identification prevails in Tanala culture. The answer cannot be given in purely psychological terms. The younger son may make common cause with the father and brothers, i.e., identify himself with them under some conditions, and not under others. As long as the economy permits the gratification of subsistence needs, and as long as the rewards of obedience may be realized, the younger son can identify himself with his brothers and father. To a degree he is part of an ensemble in which, though he cannot actually live every part or function, he can to some extent vicariously participate in all. In view of the large number of checks on the prestige of father and oldest son, this is not a difficult task for the younger son, if subsistence and sexual needs are not frustrated. The father has a much inflated ego, and may identify himself with the younger sons in that he regards them as the limbs of his body, part of himself; he is therefore interested, not solely in their exploitation, but also in seeing their needs satisfied.

This whole situation could easily be changed—and we shall presently see that it was so changed—by the inability of the father to distribute the rewards for obedience, or by the inability of the younger son to collect them. Persistent and inflexible modalities of the ego are to be found only in the neurotic individual; otherwise they are plastic and contingent on realities. The reality which kept the Tanala society cohesive was the system of production by the cutting and burning method. Under this system the whole village could move to a new site when the fertility of the land was exhausted, and begin all over again. Under these conditions "mutual identification" is possible, the suppression of hostilities, with the complicated series of checks and counter-checks, is effectual, and the super-ego retains its tonicity.

In the case of the super-ego we find a similar situation. The structure of the super-ego, the internalized replica of the disciplines imposed on the individual, is very explicitly described in the institutions. Beginning with anal control at six months, throughout the entire life cycle of the individual, a series of constellations is built up by the actual contacts with reality, all of which confirm a single expedient, that if you obey you will be protected, not punished, you will be fed, healthy; you will not incur the wrath of the oldest brother, father, family gods, all of whom can institute serious reprisals. The internalization and automatization of this constellation is a great convenience to the individual. It enables him to anticipate and forestall false moves; for if he should fail, the external reality, in the form of institutions, will catch up with him. As long as the satisfactions guarded by the super-ego can be realized, the psychic tasks of living in consonance with the super-ego (and the institutions) are not too difficult. The individual is held in line by the anxiety of infraction, and the consequent loss of realizable gains.

Proof of the effectiveness of the institutions, or the internalization in the form of super-ego, is the absence of magic within the village, and the absence of crime such as stealing.

In connection with the ego structure of the individual, there are two constellations whose psychological fabric we must examine carefully in order to understand the secondary institutions that arise from them. Let us look at the psychology of ingratiation and of prestige.

THE PSYCHOLOGY OF INGRATIATION

What interests us most in Tanala culture is the psychology of the younger sons; for these must make up the bulk of the community. If one were to argue teleologically, one might say that the patriarchal organization in this society is thus circumspect in order to render the average member a very docile and obedient individual. First, anal training starts the pattern of "being fed in return for obedience"; the absolute power of the father and the fixed social lines continue this influence; and, finally, there is the inexorable belief in fate, which can be altered somewhat, though not in major details, through magic. The belief in the exact order of things is undoubtedly derived from the cramped feeling on the part of those in favored positions to maintain their advantage, as well as on the part of those in disadvantageous positions who cannot move within the rigid social lines. One may say that since they are born into this situation and trained to accept it, why look for evidence of some kind of unexpressed aggression? Jealousy and competition for favors must be very keen, but are held under rigid control by rigid sanctions. For those with some initiative, the vocations of warrior and *ombiasy* are predetermined and socially permissible avenues of expression. The *ombiasy* has the most powerful position of all; he operates with fate, and is himself relatively free from all group obligations, since he lives and practices in a "foreign" village. He enjoys prestige and wealth, depending on how successful he is. It is from the younger sons that we must expect the greatest imprint on this culture, and the manner in which they are kept in line becomes our first problem to solve.

It must be that there are definite rewards for the acquiescence of the younger sons in permitting themselves to be exploited to enhance the prestige value of the father and oldest son. They are guaranteed love and protection of the father and occasional gifts, and continued rewards after he dies. To breach the father's law or cross his will means certain punishment and a demand for an appropriate sacrifice, which can only be effected at the offender's own cost. If the sense of guilt asserts itself, the offender will see the ghost of an ancestor who must be placated with a sacrifice. It is therefore cheaper and easier to be acquiescent. There is one other consideration that may aid in explaining why this society holds together. The younger son suffers only in prestige. But those who enjoy prestige do not eat better, nor do they have more convenience or comfort than those who do not enjoy prestige, for there is a strong feeling against ostentation and display. The reason is obvious. If you display wealth, or flaunt enjoyments in the face of those who cannot have them, you must expect that they will make comparisons and consequently suffer a loss of self-esteem, and hence will be hostile to you, who enjoy these advantages. In short, the prestige is not translated into tangible forms, and those who do not have it are neither irritated nor exposed to suffering. There are no differences in subsistence values for rich and poor. We must put that down as one of the strange binding forces in this culture. Another is the relative absence of division of labor or high skills. In short, in Tanala culture, prestige means chiefly the ability to control others.

In other words, younger sons are kept in place by rewards for obedience; strong sanctions against aggression; absence of too much irritation on the score of their lower status; and rigid belief in fate, but with some culturally determined patterns for altering it. The last is almost a necessity, because it gives the individual, who thinks he is trapped by fate, some measure of control over it.

In this culture we see forces directed against the goals created by society—those of position, class, wealth, property, and prestige; and toward instinctual goals—those that appertain to sex and aggression. In order to understand the acquiescence of the younger sons, we must understand something about the psychology of ingratiation, which is the dominant mode of adaptation.

Ingratiation is the name of a technique, the object of which is to make onself loved or favored by another individual in such a way as to gain some end or advantage. It is a technique; which means it is an executive activity, which can be established on the basis of several ego attitudes. The most noteworthy attitude is that of dependency; but it may also proceed from the wish to be like the other person, or out of hatred of the other person (witness Uriah Heep). The technique employed in ingratiation must therefore vary with the objective sought or with the resources of the subject.

We have already discussed the psychological factors which are the basis of this attitude of dependency. The dominant method of procedure in dependency is to continue the attitudes and techniques of childhood established in the reaction types to discipline. The inhibition of resources consequent upon the repression of essential gratifications, as a means of establishing the conditions for being "loved," releases a large amount of aggression toward the disciplinarian; this is not vented toward the object, but, as Freud pointed out, increases the severity of the super-ego, increases the anxiety, and tends to inflate the powers of the disciplinarian to execute the subject's magic wishes. Such an individual must therefore constantly be on guard lest his defenses against the desired satisfactions and the aggression released by their frustration get beyond his control. This is notably the case in compulsion neuroses.

But repression on the basis of reactions to discipline is not the only means of ingratiation. It may be the technique of an individual whose resources are well developed, and whose expectations are not of a magical sort, but of a purely rational kind. An ingratiating attitude may serve merely the ends of expediency. In such a case we may expect that the suppression of hostility to the object will be more deliberate. In either case, be it through dependency or more consciously perceived objectives, ingratiation involves a considerable amount of ever-ready hostility to the object. In the case of the dependent or inhibited individual, this hostility does not show itself until the rewards of dependency are frustrated. In this culture safeguards are placed all along the line to prevent this aggression from becoming manifest.

It might be well to examine the technique of ingratiation through repression in order to win the objectives of dependency. This is most conspicuous in compulsion neuroses and in certain types of homosexuality.

A young man applies for treatment because of an inability

to work; this inability was predicated by several phobias against which he first protected himself by demanding that everyone in the world, including the analyst, make it his business to do everything for him except breathe and eat. After some time the patient realized that the specific phobias in back of the inhibition were concerned with his self-esteem. The only image he could conjure up when thinking of work was that he would be in a humiliating situation; his employer would order him around in an arbitrary way, and he would be helpless to rebel or defend himself. Then he spontaneously recognized that the danger was not from without, but from within himself; that he was defenseless, like a person in a hypnotic trance, and was impelled to do anything and everything that the other fellow wanted him to do. His inability to refuse the will of another was one of the dangers against which he was defending himself. This tendency, he recognized, would expose him to the dangers of being humiliated. As Rado[9] pointed out some years ago, the masochistic situation becomes a danger against which one must defend himself at all costs. For when the patient discovered this he picked up enough courage to get a job, and we both discovered to his chagrin that his fears were justified. He occupied the strange position in his place of business of being at once the chief consultant and errand boy. One day he would come with great elation and state that he had performed a remarkable exploit, and be convinced that he had great talent. The next day he would come with a story that someone had removed his desk from his office. The third day, that some minor official in the company had asked him to run an errand. On no occasion would he protest or do anything to defend himself. He could not protest. He behaved the same way toward his paramour, who was in the habit of calling him up on a cold winter night at 2 A.M. and asking him to come up and stay with her. But he would always appear next day with a vague feeling that he had been a fool, and ask, "Why did I do it? Why do I go like a little Pekinese when she calls me?"

[9] Unpublished lectures, N. Y. Psychoanalytic Institute, 1935.

The dynamics of this situation proved to be as follows. It began a long time ago in a rivalry situation with his siblings. He had murderous fantasies about them in order to preëmpt parental love. Now every impulse of self-assertion becomes, by virtue of the secondary effects of inhibition, exaggerated either into a grandiose fantasy of extraordinary achievement through which he expects to gain the love and admiration of everyone, and with which he will humiliate all rivals, or into a murderous fantasy. This is the value that self-assertion has to him unconsciously. He then had a sense of guilt for entertaining such an idea, and to consummate it, he must, therefore, mobilize tremendous energy. He then fears reprisals which the other person may institute, which is usually the withdrawal of esteem or love, and which he now overvalues in proportion to his aggressive (really normal) fantasies. The impulse must be denied, and the value of the love of the object correspondingly enhanced, and he then sets to work by his self-humiliating attitude to reinstate himself in the good graces of the object, who is not intrinsically valuable to him, but is overvalued because the object now has the one thing which can compensate him for the denied impulse. One can readily see that this follows the patterns of disciplines we employ with children. One may ask, are this man's capacities for love very great? They do not exist at all; he has no strong love for anyone. The preservation of love, or the tangible manifestation of it, becomes dynamically more valuable to him than his own self-assertion, or the fruits of it. He subsequently was able to work out the reasons for his submission to his girl. A very naïve idea it was. He believed she was the source of his power. "If she doesn't love me, and watch over me, I shall have to stand alone, and alone, I can't do anything." This is a magical idea of the influence of an object. When he is away from her, he is apprehensive. If she is the source of his power, naturally he will be afraid to offend her and risk losing her love.

Some further details about the psychology of ingratiation can be seen in homosexuality. Those who choose to center psychology around *instincts* would invoke the submissive instinct to describe the behavior of ingratiation, and by so doing, lose all the essential details of what is the psychology of this behavior. Once something is designated as an instinct, one does not have to think of it any more. In my experience there is no syndrome that so completely describes the psychology of ingratiation as do certain, not all, types of homosexuality.

A young man of thirty applies for treatment for homosexuality, generalized anxieties about everything, and severe discomforts in his work. His perverse sexual activities are rare, and when he engages in them, only seldom are they sexual. He usually picked as his subject a young sixteen- to nineteen-year-old boy with fair skin and feminine appearance. He would take these boys for a ride in a car, speak kindly to them, praise them for their beauty, give them presents, occasionally kiss them, and very rarely indulge in actual sex play; once or twice he unsuccessfully attempted actual anal intercourse, being both active and passive partner alternately. Sexual activity of this kind was not very enjoyable, and he often spoke of it as a nuisance. The most painful experience to him was to be rebuffed by one of his homosexual paramours.

It very soon became evident that the source of his discomfort in his business life was his father. He was his father's most abject slave. He could never oppose any wish of his father's, yet at the same time bore him a conscious, enraged, but helpless hatred. His only defensive weapon was an obstinacy and contrariness which was never overt, but which always found expression in some piece of behavior that did not immediately affect his father, e.g., before going to bed, it would occur to him to brush his teeth, something his father always told him to do when he was a child. Immediately he would respond mentally, "I won't, I won't." Occasionally he would think of spending the evening at home, but if by chance his father asked him to be home that very evening, staying home became a distressing obligation. For long periods he would be afraid to stay out after eleven, though his father had never said anything either to him or to his brothers, who would stay out until 4 a.m. It was apparent that these persecutions of his father were entirely self-imposed; but note that he had murderous fantasies about his father, the most unyielding obstinacy, together with an absolute abjectness of behavior.

The occasions of the homosexual activities were always wishes for a woman, and proved on close examination to be a ritual of ingratiation with his father. He was always doing to his homosexual mate what he wanted his father to do to him. His wishes for a woman remained unattainable, and his anxiety was always put to rest by a fresh gesture of ingratiation with his father.

The boy's early history was quite remarkable. At the age of five to six he was consciously in love with his mother; he described his infatuation for her in such vivid terms as the wish to smell her skin, to hug and kiss her all over. But she was not, according to his standards, responsive. She had two children after him, which he regards as evidence of her infidelity to him. His fallen self-esteem was bolstered in his fantasy by the claim that his mother must be stupid not to see his great superiority over his father and brothers. He used to sleep with her on every pretext, and remembers one occasion in which he went into a paralyzing anxiety when his father discovered him in bed with his mother, though his father did not utter a word of reproach.

About this time, aged five, his sexual curiosity was insatiable. He sought a little girl and got her to allow him to examine her genitals, which he did with great gusto. While thus engaged, he was detected by another little girl, who shouted to him, "I am going to tell your father." The terrors of these words still ring in his ears, twenty-seven years after it happened. From this time on he became more observant of his mother's indifference, and at about nine he sought a quarrel with her, after which his love for her completely vanished and was replaced by an indifference which he now has to every woman.

It would be interesting to observe, in connection with his sexual activities, this patient's behavior to me, which describes the dynamics of his anxiety about women. One day he told me that he had an engagement with a girl in whom he had shown a good deal of interest, but to whom he had made no sexual advances. The evening was set for an adventure. The following day he came and began his narrative with what had happened on the same day. Then there was a long pause, and he remarked, "I suppose you want me to tell you what happened last night?" Another pause. "I have the most obstinate reluctance to tell you anything about it. I don't know why. I feel compelled to tell you it was an unpleasant experience, and I dread a renewal of it. The strange thing about all this is that it was actually very pleasant. We kissed for a long time, and I had an erection which was very reassuring. I now feel a great hatred toward you." If we take this latter feeling of hatred toward me as our starting point, we can reconstruct the processes backward. His feeling is undoubtedly justified, if we note the basic anxiety and what events follow in its train. This is no function of his super-ego; but a response to a social situation with me, owing to certain now automatic methods of reacting to his own sexual desires. The attitude he once had to his father, now a part of his ego equipment, he takes to me, the analyst. He cannot avoid the feeling that I do not want him to have sexual gratification. He therefore hates me for compelling him to abandon woman and deny his desire. He fears telling me about it "because you will use the knowledge of that experience, that it was pleasant, against me. You will do something to me," meaning that I would punish him in one form or another, the most serious of which is to be abandoned. In telling me of the experience with the girl, he must therefore understate it, and in retrospect render himself anaesthetic. For the necessity to do this, he hates me.

What he fears is that his father will disown him (castration symbols as such rarely occurred even in his dreams or fantasies), throw him out of the business, and that he will consequently starve and not be able to find employment. All this was the wildest fantasy, in view of the fact that he was the most efficient

PRIMARY INSTITUTION	EGO STRUCTURE (son)	SECONDARY INSTITUTION	CHECKS
Patriarchal Family			
Absolute to power of father	Hatred—repressed	Fear of ghosts—cause illness	Propitiation by food sacrifice
Impose discipline	Submission	Immobility of lineage cult	Reward for repression of hatred
Exploit	Ingratiation	Loyalty to dead	
Frustrate needs (subsistence)		Concept of illness due to sin (displeasing a god)	
Basic Disciplines			
Oral—Nursed long		Cleanliness	
Anal—Continent at 6 months	Obedience to discipline rewarded	Insistence on compulsive act as part of cure	
Sexual—Object and aim taboos	Denial of importance of sex	Oedipus Tales—repressed female hatred	One intercourse keeps woman pregnant
Sibling Inequality			
	Sibling hatred	Fear of magic	Taboo against use in lineage
	Aggression repressed	Blood brotherhood—homosexuality	
	Aggression expressed	*Ombiasy*; warrior	Can control fate
			Can control property
	Crime	Law	Severity of punishment
	Acquiescence	Belief in fate	Fate can be controlled
		Tromba—mpamosavy	Neurosis-Psychosis

Subsistence Economy	Work for reward of love and subsistence	Smooth working of economy	Many checks on ostentation
Plenty	No food anxiety	Submission rewarded	Illness and absence of support
Communal land	No differentiation of labor	No rituals for rice	Punishment
		Emphasis on diligence	
Prestige Economy			
Social Immobility	Uselessness of strife	Deification and control over others	Malevolent magic
	Jealousy	*Tromba*—fate	
Property Laws	Property as means of enlarging ego	Rage of gods	
	Deification-Lineage cult	Law	

Figure 2.

man in the business, and his father a feeble old dotard of seventy or more. But we must note how the image of his father becomes inflated with a fictitious power, and how he overvalues what he gets from his father, and undervalues his own efficiency. As a matter of fact, his hatred of his father, notwithstanding his elaborate method of ingratiation, led to frequent acts of unconsciously perpetrated sabotage against the business and himself.

The night after his experience with the girl he had the following dream: "I find myself married to Jane, and we are driving in a car, but the road is stormy. It is slippery, the car skids and I lose control. It's very like the dreams I had when I was a child and had fever. I used to be afraid of dying, and wanted father and mother near me all the time." The meaning of the dream is self-evident. The stock interpretation of the dream might say it is a dream of fear of impotence. True enough, but why? His associations tell what he feels he has surrendered when he marries the girl, his main source of security. He now has only his own very limited resources, and not his father's strong and magic powers.

Now is that a biologically determined homosexuality? No, it is a replica of the behavior of monkeys in danger situations. The homosexuality is a method of ingratiation with his father, whom he hates; but in proportion to his hatred, he inflates his father's image and humbles his own. His initial powerful and precocious heterosexuality was no match for the resources he could command as a child, and hence he threw his most valuable attribute away to guarantee for himself other more basic values of survival, support, and hope of unlimited help from his father. These imaginary values he still finds today in his father, contrary to every bit of reality in the situation. To state that he "identified himself with mother as a result of the guilt from the Oedipus complex" may be an explanation, but it does not retrace the processes of nature.

The reason for citing this case is that it describes some important consequences of the dynamics of ingratiation, to wit, a great hatred of the object with whom he seeks to ingratiate himself, and a corresponding overenhancement of the value of the gain to be achieved by that means.

The essential points to be noted in the psychology of ingratiation are that it demands a sacrifice of gratification, exists at the cost of development, and ends in overvaluing the returns of dependency. The aggression which is held in check by the returns for submission can, however, be easily released should these rewards become incapable of realization. The two instances cited were neurotic manifestations, which simply means that the rewards of dependency are not realizable in actuality; but the system with which the individual operates is characteristic of childhood.

In the case of Tanala culture the aggression is ever present. This can be verified by the numerous sanctions and punishments against it. However, as long as the rewards can be collected, suppression is not very difficult.

The Change from Dry to Wet Rice Cultivation: The Betsileo

Dr. Linton has very fortunately preserved for us not only a check on the conclusions about the Tanala, but a remarkable text for the study of the dynamics of social change as well. This change was not merely an "economic" change; it went to the roots of the whole social organization, and hence created important changes in the basic adaptation of every individual.

In the attempt to survey what happened as a result of the change it must be remembered that only a few features of the culture changed; many remained intact. The changes were undoubtedly abrupt in some features and slower in others.

We can take as our guide-lines the actual changes recorded:

1. Techniques of labor—creating new problems of insuring water supply.
2. The social unit of locality (village) was changed to comprise cross-sections of many gentes. The individuals in the locale were therefore not bound by family ties, nor mutual coöpera-

tion, but by common interests and mutual antagonisms against which no religious sanctions could now operate.

3. Exogamous marriages, formerly rare, were now common.
4. Increasing significance of personal property; loss of significance of family ties.
5. Economic value of slaves.
6. Change from joint family to tribal organization to kingdom.
7. New life goals, and class interests; new types of conflict.

The basic disciplines—early anal training, sexual taboos, the formal character of intrafamilial relationships—could not possibly be changed by the new economy. But the significance and functions of the father must have changed. Under the new system he had a limited amount to dispense, and consequently there was a limit to what the sons could gain through ingratiation techniques. Under the old system, subsistence was guaranteed and prestige was graded, but there were a sufficient number of checks to relieve the smart. Under the new system, subsistence was not guaranteed and prestige could not be checked. Conflicts were not now limited to the brothers against each other; but were with brothers only during formative years, and with neighbors or competitors in adult years. A whole new series of loyalties and hostilities unknown in the old culture, had to be built up, to king, to noble, and to others. Undoubtedly there now came to be a high premium on enterprise, skill, cunning, treachery, aggression, plunder, and subjugation of others. After a period of consolidation there undoubtedly came to exist a highly developed check on these tendencies, at least within the group.

We can verify these conclusions concerning the Betsileo, and we need only stress those points at which the two cultures vary. We find first of all a graded hierarchy of rank so rigid that the differences continue after death. We find that these differences are associated with economic opportunities, as well as with difference in dress, demeanor, and other mores.

The significance of property (already quite pronounced in Tanala culture) is augmented until it becomes the sole means of enhancing the ego. The pursuit of property becomes the most important element in the security system of the individual. The powers and prestige of the king are an excellent indicator of the heights to which prestige may grow. His powers were far in excess of those of a deified ancestor in Tanala; he has unlimited powers to exploit, to frustrate important needs, to impose disciplines and punishments without redress. An ancestral god could be placated; a king could not.

Security of those beneath the king could not be established in any sure way. Ingratiation was a sure technique in Tanala, but a very uncertain one in Betsileo society. This same doubtful situation prevailed between father and son. The conflict between brothers increased in severity because the father's resources were limited. There was an influx of new needs for the individual. New needs as well as new anxieties were added to the individual's problem of adjustment. New needs were created in that the individual required different qualities to get along in this new society, and new anxieties in that he was susceptible to new dangers, dangers of poverty and degradation.

These are at least two sources from which there is an increase in mutual hostility and a corresponding increase in anxiety. That there were increasing suspicion and hostility between brothers is clearly shown by the fact that the levirate easily practiced among the Tanala is forbidden in Betsileo society on the grounds that a man marrying his brother's widow would be suspected of having killed his predecessor. This change cannot be attributed to any difference in basic disciplines, for they are the same in both societies. There is no reason why one Oedipus complex should be stronger in one community than in the other. We are here confronted by an unaccountable quantitative factor. It is remarkable that the "stronger" Oedipus complex should exist where the struggle for prestige, power, and property is keener. In this connection the increase in homosexuality is also significant.

Whereas the power of the father is increased in absolutism, we get an interesting sidelight on the character of the relations between father and children from the story of the father being deserted by his eight children. The father's remark that "he is one who has wiped away excrement for nothing" is eloquent testimony of his feeling that his expectations went awry. He performed all the most unpleasant tasks of parenthood without the rewards. There is little doubt that the parents' attitude is to exploit the child, without furnishing him adequate rewards. The story also proves the futility of ingratiating techniques where the father has nothing to give.

With regard to the basic disciplines we note an exaggeration of the training in denoting deference to authority and power, and an accentuation of homage and degradation. The constant reminder of gradations in status cannot enhance the security of the individual.

All these features would tend to a great increase in insecurity within Betsileo society, based upon a destruction of the frustration-satisfaction balance we found so effectual in preserving social equilibrium in Tanala. At the basis of the new system lies an anxiety which is basically a subsistence anxiety, a permanent claim on land. Upon this latter have been engrafted prestige values which reflect the anxieties of all concerned—those who have land and those who have not. The training in childhood predisposes to servility or exaggerated aggression. Servility by ingratiation cannot, however, bring rewards; the nature of the real economy no longer permits it. The only effect this can have is to release a great amount of anxiety and hostility. The increase in homosexuality also bears on this point.

This increase in general anxiety we find, and it takes a great many interesting forms. First of all, we notice two new concepts unknown in Tanala culture, *oppression* and *poverty*. These are sure indicators of the complete failure of the distribution of economic (subsistence and prestige) opportunities.

The underling's fear of the father, king or god is greatly increased. There is a formal change of belief which indicates the operation of new forces. The change is from the belief in fate, a somewhat mechanistic concept, to the idea that god arranges everything. This is quite consistent with experience in real life, where the king or father actually does arrange everything, and what one has is by virtue of his grace. But there is an interesting corollary to this, that the sorcerer is also an executive of god's will. This is a definite indicator of a fear of retaliation, different in character from the vision of an ancestral ghost in Tanala culture. In this latter case the anxiety was focused. In Betsileo culture it is diffused over the whole culture, "omnia contra omnes."

This retaliation fear in place of the fear of offending an ancestral ghost indicates the directness of the hostilities and the disappearance of the expectations from the father-king. The forms in which this retaliation fear is shown are the general injunctions against overt aggression. The type of reasoning is well described in the quotation that if you strike a snake, you will suffer as it suffers; if it dies, you will die.

The psychology of this retaliation anxiety was well illustrated by a patient who lived his early life in poverty, who had violent feelings of envy of his siblings. This child finally adjusted on a system of absolute parity for all concerned; that is, he would allow them no more than he had, and himself no more than they had. This compulsive justice did not work out practically, because he was always meeting people who had more than he had, and often met others who had less. These situations always made him uncomfortable. Totally unaware of his deeply repressed envy (for he always compensated on the side of generosity and concern over other people, and prided himself on having a noble character), he nevertheless showed great anxiety when anything "good" happened to him. This was associated with a great urgency to hurry and consummate the specific situation, lest it "slip out of his fingers," or someone else get it before he did. His attitude toward success was likewise filled with anxiety. Thus, on one occasion when he could little afford it he bought an automobile. He immediately began to have anxieties about being seen in it, for to him this would be an immediate indicator of his prosperity. The first thing that happened was that he began having an inordinate run of accidents, which marred the polish on the car. When his friends remarked about it he would stave them off by calling it "an old rattletrap" or "that cheap thing." In other words, though he had no conscious envy, he feared the hostile wishes and envy which he himself felt, but unconsciously covered up with a magnanimity and good will toward others. Each time he would encounter some such success in someone else, this patient would commit a little private crime in the form of petty stealing or of allowing himself some forbidden pleasure.

It is therefore not to be wondered at that in Betsileo society we also see evidence of a fear of success. A man dies because his harvest is too good. This is in no way to be construed to mean that the Betsileo fear, or are inhibited about, success. This tale is someone's fantasy and undoubtedly a culturally justifiable conclusion, in view of the great amount of mutual envy there existing, and is a testimony to the power attributed to hostile wishes.

The increase in crime is noteworthy as one of the overt forms of hostility. Though suicides are not frequent, the one reported by Linton, to the effect that the man killed himself to devote his soul to persecuting his oppressor, is quite consistent with the prevailing beliefs, and reveals a desperate means of acquiring a freedom to show aggression toward one he could not otherwise reach.

As contrasted with the Tanala, the general increase in anxiety among the Betsileo is clearly shown in the general increase in the superstitions and in the extraordinary development of compulsive rituals with their innumerable repetitions of this or the other act to insure its efficacy. It is in many ways according to the pattern we noted in Tanala; but it is much more intense.

Finally we have two important indices of anxiety and intrasocial decompensation: the great increase in various forms of spirit possession and in the use and fear of malevolent sorcery.

We noted in Tanala culture that nail parings, hair, etc., could not be used as bait for purposes of malevolent magic; in Betsileo, however, all these bodily parts or those appertaining to the individual can be used for the purpose, though interestingly enough, not urine, feces, and spittle. This is very baffling, both as regards the items susceptible to, and those immune from, use in malevolent magic. There is no way of deducing the significance without the aid of the individual. The ramifications cannot be traced according to some universal pattern; the immunity of feces, urine, and spittle cautions us to avoid any such universal deduction. But for our particular purposes this is not necessary. It suffices to indicate a hypochondriacal fear of injury through a systematic arrangement of ideas. It is designated "hypochondriacal" because these severed parts retain their connection with the body, and what happens to them will also happen to the body.

Another general indicator of anxiety is the secrecy which attends the birth of a child. It is manifestly a fear of sorcery. But there is another anxiety very remarkably described in the treatment of the child who is born on an unlucky day. This institution is very like what we found in Tanala. But there is in addition an extraordinary fear and brutality associated with it. The child is thrown on a dump heap, or bathed in swill water, or it is actually killed by having cattle trample over it. The implications appear to be that the cure for aggression is to degrade, to make into dirt, and to oppress the individual to death. This idea can arise only in the mind of the individual whose aggression has been crushed in this way; and this the individual in Betsileo has plenty of opportunity to feel.

The forms of spirit possession give us some further clues. In Tanala culture the *tromba* was designated specifically as possession by a ghost: in Betsileo, possession is by evil spirits. Not only is the incidence more common in Betsileo, but the manifestations are much more severe. The distinctions between the various forms of spirit possession do not give us very much help. One, however, seems to be descriptive of an acute hallucinatory psychosis of persecutory content. The victim hallucinates his persecutor, who makes him perform the most extraordinary feats of self-injury, against which the victim is helpless. The recognition and fear of evil spirits is the point of departure from Tanala.

The form of malignant sorcery, *mpamosavy*, known only rarely in Tanala, is extremely common in Betsileo. The techniques used are quite the same as in Tanala, but the agency of the evil spirit is much more in evidence than in Tanala. There the agency was largely inherent in the properties of certain objects. These objects are retained in Betsileo, but they seem to be merely catalysts for the evil spirits, who work in a more or less impersonal way. Another remarkable feature is the fact that everyone is suspected of being *mpamosavy*.

We can now attempt to locate the sources of these anxieties. To do this we may examine the basic personality structure found in Tanala culture. In comparison, we find a change in one of the primary institutions—the subsistence economy. This creates for the individual in Betsileo an ego problem not known in Tanala. The fusion of subsistence and prestige values is now permanent. No other variables are introduced, the family organization, basic disciplines, and sibling inequality remaining the same. Any changes in personality structure must therefore be due to new adaptations which must be made to the subsistence-prestige situation.

The ego-attitudes of this situation can be seen in the Tanala culture. Submission and ingratiation are ego-acceptable roles as long as basic needs are not frustrated and protection is guaranteed, and as long as the smart of being the underdog is soothed by the absence of ostentation. An ego organization built up by basic disciplines to expect reward for submission can do only a few things if this need for protection is frustrated; it becomes both anxious and aggressive. The prototype of the anxieties is to be found in the types of aggression observed. These take the form of envy, jealousy, wish to hurt, wish to rob, wish not to see others enjoy what you yourself do not have.

The anxieties—fear of being injured or robbed, fear of evil wishes of others, correspond to these hostile wishes.

The new needs for heightened self-esteem are strangulated by the rigid social system, which is now divided into immobile castes. However, the method of raising self-esteem is now exclusively through property, which has all the attributes of prestige because with it one can enhance one's ability to control others and win regard (and also hate).

The only forms of expression of those who decompensate under these conditions are the various forms of spirit possession (by evil spirits, not gods)—overt aggression in the form of malignant sorcery (mpamosavy), over which the family gods no longer exercise control, for the victims are outside the family line. For minor forms of decompensation there are still the services of the ombiasy, and for those who succeed, the hatred, unconscious or expressed, of everyone else.

The person of the king now has the highest prestige status and is distinguished from everyone else by personal taboos, special tokens of deference and submission. He is likely to be the most hated man, because he exercises the greatest control. Around him can now be built all the accoutrements of vested interests. These vested interests create great anxiety to their owners, and, to insure their integrity, the rights of property must be guaranteed with more and more force. This causes more anxiety all around and more hostility.

The disposition of the Tanala is assuredly "compulsive" in character; but it does not compare with that of the Betsileo in intensity. The source of this anxiety is not some racial idiosyncrasy, but the actual introduction of scarcity and anxiety into what is ultimately reducible to subsistence.

THE CONSTELLATION OF PRESTIGE

Prestige is a constellation in man which must be studied experimentally in various cultures before any reliable conclusions about it can be reached. The material from Tanala and Betsileo gives us some good opportunities to explore this constellation as it is constituted with some variations in primary institutions existing in each culture.

Let us begin by asking where does prestige belong as a quality appertaining to the individual? It may be examined from the point of view of him who possesses it and of him who bestows it, for prestige is a quality which no one confers upon himself. A man may have pride and vanity and conceit, but prestige is reflected only in what others think or feel about him. The quest for prestige, therefore, becomes a quest for assurance or the right to have a certain kind of ego feeling, positively toned, which enhances the size and the admirable qualities and powers of the ego. But it is a reflected quality, one seen or mirrored in others.

Where does the need for pursuing this goal come from? It is not an isolated phenomenon; it is one of many "narcissistic" human pursuits. There are many types of perception which the individual has, the function of which is to apprise him of his relative status with regard to others. When we see these types of ego feeling and ego attitude in the forms which mobilize hostile feelings toward others, we tend to regard them as pernicious qualities, and attribute to them only the capacity for creating disturbance of social equilibrium. This is decidedly not the case. These same emotional qualities are responsible for positive, cementing, and consolidating influences. Let us guess what kinds of social organization would be possible if humans were not capable of "identifying" themselves with others. What is true of "identification" is also true of the ability to perceive differences between oneself and others. The ramifications of this kind of perception are very elaborate, and often terminate in the basic feeling of hatred or anxiety when one encounters something unlike oneself, something "strange." Another tendency of humans, in connection with sameness and difference, is greatly to exaggerate or enhance the value of certain qualities in another person, the process of idealization, whereby the approval of those qualities is associated with a strong drive to emulate those qualities, or on the contrary, to have a feeling of hopelessness of so doing, and to preserve an ego feeling of smallness or unworthiness toward the thus inflated object.

One wonders in thinking of these various attitudes what their use is, and on what infantile patterns they are erected. The idealization of the parent by the child is a good place to look for the origin of these processes. Thus one patient, a girl of nineteen, had the tendency to idealize, to enhance the value of any female object who could perform any of the original maternal functions, i.e., to feed, discipline, or teach her. In her fantasies these objects are so remarkable as to defy description, and she always conceived of herself in relation to these objects as small and insignificant. She always thought herself lowly and unworthy, but did not appreciate that this was an effort to preserve an infantile status, to avoid effort and responsibility, which she did by a remarkable system of inhibitions. The objective of this attitude soon made itself manifest; it was the desire to be loved, cared for, and protected by these objects in much the same way as a child. The infantile prototype of idealization is to overvalue those qualities in the protector which offer the greatest security and pleasure. Such idealizations are often preserved even if the child has much reason to hate the parent.

In addition to idealization, one other quality associated with prestige, is its contagious quality. To be near, to associate with those who have prestige, is one of its most persistent qualities. This is a social cementing force of great power. Through it groups can become enlarged, and qualities in an individual which operate for the good of the group can thus be supported and emulated.

We mention these qualities associated with prestige only to emphasize that its appreciation and pursuit are useful and constructive. But what we most commonly see are the bad effects of the struggle for prestige. The boy who enhances the prestige of the leader because he profits by it, or feels he can emulate it, is not threatened by it. But the rival in prestige who has qualities that inspire awe, admiration, and fear, also inspires hostility, because he simultaneously lowers the ego feeling of the subject, who seeks the same objective. Submission is regarded by the subject as a dangerous attitude because he places himself in a helpless situation toward the object who has already robbed him of the love and regard to which he feels he is entitled, and he feels that the object will not use his high regard for the subject's benefit, but to his disadvantage.

Thus the struggle for prestige is an effort to preserve a kind of positive ego feeling which is threatened. On the side of the libidinous formulation, prestige belongs to those tendencies called "narcissistic," and pertaining to self-love. But to view it from this angle alone is to lose track of the function it plays in the social orientation of the individual.

We may venture a reconstruction of the factors at play in the struggle for prestige as follows: The chief components are: the wish to win love, to utilize the power that lies behind this being loved or esteemed; the wish to exploit others; and the fear of being exploited. In considering how these factors operate together, no theoretical fantasy can be a substitute for seeing them in action in the living subject. In most cases the pursuit of prestige is in part the unconscious reflection of the power the individual wishes to exercise over others. The manner in which the issue of prestige is handled by the individual indicates how the basic patterns of discipline and liberty of ego development settled in childhood.

In our own culture, from what we can observe, the quest for prestige is apt to be strongest in inhibited individuals; but this situation is too complicated to unravel. Prestige is a socially approved goal; but that does not tell us very much about its sources.

In Tanala culture we found a prestige system based on the idealization of parental qualities. But these must be specified; they were the parental qualities of feeding the subject and protecting him. Prestige was enjoyed by a special group of individuals, fathers, lineage heads, and oldest sons, who took over the paternal role and were in a position to fulfill the obligations to the subjects. The system of values on which the holder of prestige operated was partly of the same character; that is, he depended on deified ancestors and the continuation of their post-mortem powers. But prestige values operated also on another system, that of property, which was the means of maintaining the parental role of feeding and protecting. These parental functions were made possible by certain tangible resources. The chief of these was control over land, upon which no permanent vested interest could be based in the dry rice cultivation because its utility was exhaustible. Cattle and money had limited uses, were mere insignia of power rather than powerful economic tools. The moving of land site was merely a periodic inconvenience, as labor for exploiting it involved no special problems.

In Tanala culture, subsistence and prestige values each enjoyed a certain amount of autonomy. The presence or absence of prestige made little difference in subsistence. The democracy of the old Tanala was therefore vested in checks against the use of prestige to degrade, make small, or deprive anyone of inalienable rights. The fight did not necessarily concern prestige in itself, but was waged to reach the most favored position with the father. This failing, there remained, for those with initiative, the possibility of becoming *ombiasy,* warrior, *tromba,* or homosexual, all of which enjoyed acceptable status socially. Prestige could not be used to frustrate important needs; this is what rendered it innocuous, despite its seemingly despotic trappings. Any aggressions loosed by the sibling conflicts could be easily encapsulated. These encapsulated aggressions break their bounds in Betsileo. There the security system of the individual is tied up with property as a means of enhancing the integrity and size of the *ego.*

The wet rice system both in Tanala and Betsileo changed the whole character of prestige because it became inseparably tied to subsistence means, land, which was permanent in site and inexhaustible in productivity. At this point some very essential data are missing. How did the Tanala king get his power, by force, election, or in some other way? The lack of data about this step need not deter us from following its consequences. The union of prestige with command of subsistence means now created a new set of values for prestige holders, and a new set of values for the underdog. The rest is too complicated to see in every detail. Only a few points are visible.

Prestige values were set off and hypertrophied to the highest degree with the king, but remained equally significant in quality with all landholders. The increase in the inflation of the ego now is designated with all varieties of deference tokens which distinguish those who have control over food from those who have not. The possessors of power enjoy prestige, but not necessarily more security, because prestige and degradation are merely different polarities of the same anxiety based on a real scarcity situation.

If we take this anxiety situation as our starting point we can follow its progress into the constellation of prestige somewhat as follows:

The biological helplessness of man at birth predisposes him to need support and help from some superior person. The period of growth is, however, not associated with a feeling of helplessness, but with one of euphoria, of effortless control of the environment. The period of dependency ushers in an idealization of the parent. We have shown how this idealization is increased with restraints and frustrations. The constellation of prestige oscillates between the two polarities of euphoria and magic control of others and between the dependent attitudes and an idealization of the power of the prestige holder—who is to be either feared or worshiped, depending on whether the power is used for or against the subject. The subjective goal in prestige is essentially the ability to control another object, by an effortless domination, but at the same time to enjoy the attributes of the idealized object—originally the parent.

The situation which creates the anxiety in both Tanala and Betsileo cultures, and which is hence the basis for prestige, is the control of food. But it is not the only necessity about which anxiety can be created. Command of skill can and does create the same thing. Our clinical material up to the present shows that prestige conflicts are least violent where mutual dependency is guaranteed, and most violent where the rewards of dependency are frustrated. This latter can only lead to aggression and anxiety to possess, through one means or another, in order to satisfy the need to be in the securer position.[10]

A few technical points in connection with prestige must be noted. There is not much use in designating the presence or absence of prestige conflicts as culture patterns, or as some authors vaguely refer to them, as "culturally determined." Such generalities do not point to the real differentia which cause or provoke these conflicts. Affects are only indicators; they are not causes; and affects cannot explain each other.

In Betsileo we find certain modifications in ego structure as compared with Tanala. The entire security system of the individual is altered, and with it there is a consequent alteration in the so-called super-ego. The disappearance of ingratiation and the substitution of aggression takes place, and with this, an increase in anxiety. The aggression likewise gives rise to the necessity to control these impulses. Hence in the "super-ego" of Betsileo we cannot tell about the existence of guilt and conscience, but we can recognize retaliation, fear, and general anxiety of the aggression of others, against which new repressive measures must now be instituted. Some of these are direct, like the caste system; others indirect, as the enhancing of the magical properties of prestige and prestige holders. No society ever arbitrarily decides to have this or that emotion. These affects must

[10] We did not raise the issue about how vested rights came to be established. This is a historical question. But our guess would be that the constitutional differences between humans plays an important role. The one which probably counted most was the sheer strength of one individual to defend himself against another.

PSYCHIC POLARITIES OF
SUBSISTENCE-PRESTIGE ANXIETIES
IN BETSILEO

Basic Personality Structure

Submission
Ingratiation fails
leads to degradation and want
Aggression
  Expressed
    rational methods (acquisition of land)
    malevolent magic (controlled by policing)
  Repressed
    spirit possession
    increase in rituals ⎫
    omens   ⎬ Retaliation fears
    superstitions   ⎭
Increased regard for prestige
Increase in submissiveness because of inability to
participate in prestige and because it actually
degrades the subject.

Authority and Power
Hatred and fear of those oppressed

Increase in magic properties of prestige

Fears of success

Defenses*

more intrasocial oppression

caste system

slavery

Higher degree of individualization
Perpetuation of prestige after death

Figure 3.

*These institutions permit the economic arrangement to operate and are to some extent determined by it; but the entire complex also satisfies the internal anxiety situation.

all lead down to real frustrations due to inhibition, or obstacles in the outer world.[11]

CONCLUSION

The comparison of Tanala and Betsileo confirms the usefulness of the separation between primary and secondary institutions. The primary institutions are those which create the basic and inescapable problems of adaptation. The secondary institutions are creations of the result of the primary institutions on basic personality structure.

Tanala and Betsileo are kindred cultures in which most of the primary institutions are exactly alike. One of the primary institutions, technique of subsistence, changed sooner in Betsileo than it did in Tanala, probably due to a preponderance of swamps and valleys in Betsileo territory. There followed many important changes in secondary institutions, consequent upon the generation of great anxiety over a situation which in Tanala was quite free. The disposal of this anxiety created new classes based on the control of subsistence-prestige instruments.

This anxiety was not absent in Tanala, indicating that its sources were not exclusively in the subsistence aspects of adaptation. The controls of the aggression in Tanala were, however, so effective that the social balance could be easily maintained. This was done by a system of counterchecks and compensations for the less favored, which had the effect of blunting the irritating qualities of prestige differentiations and of guaranteeing for each individual an equable participation in all aspects of the culture.

When, however, anxiety was created about subsistence, this system of checks and counterchecks in Tanala could no longer operate. The opportunities for equal participation became limited, thus creating the necessity, because of anxiety, for fortifying the position of those who could control land. To some extent the institutions changed in regard to the policing meth-

[11] For a comparison of the views on prestige see Alfred Adler, *The Neurotic Constitution* (New York, 1917); and Karen Horney *The Neurotic Personality of our Time* (New York, 1937), Chap. X.

ods of control, and also by endowing the holders of these rights with insignia of prestige. These were to a large extent magical properties, designed to inspire awe, and create distance, both of which discourage aggressive attitudes.

However, the amount of anxiety and the aggression consequent upon real and threatened frustrations could not be automatically controlled. We would expect an inordinate increase in intrasocial hostility expressed in the only forms now available—magic, and severe forms of spirit possession. The only way to control this use of magic was by sanctions or force; the spirit possessions needed no external policing.

This is actually what all the new secondary institutions turn out to be in comparison with those of the Tanala. The new institutions can be derived from the anxiety defenses made necessary by the alteration in basic personality structure.

The resulting anxieties must be divided into two different categories, which merely represent different polarities of the same tension situation: the defenses of those who have subsistence-prestige and those who have not (see Figure 3, p. 344).

Those who have none of these values of subsistence-prestige or who suffer by comparison cannot profitably take dependent attitudes. The result is hostility in the form of actual hatred, together with increased use of magic and spirit possessions. But there is also fear of success and of retaliation. This leads to increasing expectation of failure and belief in omens and superstitions, with, however, the legitimate use of the *ombiasy* to change fate. On the part of those who have subsistence-prestige instruments, corresponding anxieties prevail which must lead to effective defenses. Instead of playing down ostentation, there is now an exaggeration of its magical properties and the introduction of fine gradations of deference in the basic disciplines of the child. The general use of "police" methods against magic are a second defense. Furthermore, there are the last external measures, the closing off of lines of social mobility by a caste-system including slavery. Both these systems are derived from the same anxiety. We do not intend to convey the idea that these measures are consciously and deliberately planned in order to keep others in subjection or to allay a consciously felt anxiety. They are no more consciously appreciated than are many of the defenses we observe in neuroses. Consciously these defenses merely appear as necessary or justifiable. The anxiety and the defenses are both unconsciously elaborated before they emerge as socially indicated measures.

Our analysis of this culture is open to the objection that whereas we have stressed the formation of the basic personality structure from the accommodations the individual must make to certain institutions in the order in which he is made to feel their influence, we have not demonstrated the relations of this basic personality structure to the adult personality. We have stressed the personality structure of the younger sons, but not that of the father or the oldest sons. To this objection we can only answer that, in the absence of biography, the opportunity was not sufficiently open to us. Secondly, to have written the analysis of this culture from the point of view of the father and oldest son would have created the impression commonly found in materialistic sociologies, that the fathers and oldest sons "run" the society in such a way as to produce in the younger sons a submissive attitude, thus assuring to themselves the power and prestige created by the abject attitudes of the younger sons. This voluntaristic attitude to culture is not valid, because the constellations in the father and the submissive son are merely different polarities of the same basic situation. The anxieties of the overdog in Betsileo are merely the opposite polarity of those which dominate the underdog.

From the point of view of the institutions, the fathers and oldest sons are subject to many of the same disciplines as the younger sons. They are, however, immune from others. Since these differential disciplines or immunities begin at about the age of five, their influence on personality must be considerable. However, we cannot pursue this investigation any further without biography. The impression is unavoidable that father and oldest son, although their psychological orientation is on the opposite pole of the ingratiation techniques of the younger sons, require no great initiative or independence. The *ombiasies* and warriors do need these qualities, and these are never oldest sons.

One point, however, stands out with great prominence in this culture. In old Tanala, the disciplines of childhood equip the individual adequately for his adult life without any change. The constellations there formed are effective without incompatibility with the world he meets as an adult. But severe discomforts are created when, with a change in economy, these early constellations are valueless. Then they divide sharply into the two polarities we noted in the subsistence-prestige constellation in Betsileo, both of which are equally pervaded by anxiety.

This is as far as our data permit us to go in the analysis of the relation of infantile attitudes to adult adaptations in this culture of Tanala. This analysis demonstrates that once the basic personality structure is established, any change in primary institutions will lead to personality changes, but that these changes will move only in the direction of the already established psychic constellations.

From the point of view of the libido theory a consistent account of Tanala culture can likewise be rendered. Treating their institutions as if they were characteristics of an individual, we could begin with the emphasis on early sphincter control as the predisposing factor for anal erotism. Many characteristics can be derived from that source, on the assumption that character traits are derived from anal erotism, by processes as yet unknown. The emphasis on retention and the organ pleasure coincident with it, could lead to displacements in the form of stinginess about money, property, and prestige. The relation between interest in feces and money is quite apparent. Other derivatives of anal erotism such as conscientiousness, thrift, and perhaps cleanliness would follow. With this conscientiousness we would expect a rigid and exacting super-ego to deal with the enormous quantities of aggression associated with anality. From this source we could derive the numerous compulsive traits, the rituals, repetitiousness, the constant struggle with cruel impulses and the masochistic sequelae. All this could be accounted for on the grounds of a regression due to the patent Oedipus complex and to the predisposition formed by early anal training. Passive homosexuality, both in folklore and practice, describes one outcome of this situation.

This analysis has the virtue of consistency with verifiable constants. One can, however, question several factors: the justification for treating a society as if it had the organic unity of the individual; the location of the sources of conflict in either the Oedipus complex or anal erotism without due regard for the fact that both are created by recognizable external conditions. The difficulty arises from the fact that the effect of the institutions must be derived from a repressed anal pleasure, and hence the whole character of the culture would have to depend on the continuation of this early sphincter control. The influence of dependency of the child, his fear of the powerful parent in enforcing this discipline would have to be passed over, or, if nominally recognized, would not be included in the final formulation of the processes which terminate in an accentuated anal erotism. The characteristics of interest in money, conscientiousness, obedience, compulsive traits, etc., are thus derivatives of a repressed erotism alone, and not of the effects of all these factors on the personality.

The comparison between Tanala and Betsileo would, moreover, introduce a quantitative factor, which is very difficult to account for on the basis of the libido theory. The Betsileo are more "anal sadistic" than Tanala, and every compulsive trait found in Tanala is exaggerated tenfold in Betsileo. In this comparison there is no escape from a consideration of the external factors associated with this change, namely the change in economy and the corresponding increase in anxiety tensions all around. One could argue around this point by stating that once the anal-sadistic character is established, any increase in external anxiety would naturally augment the internal discomfort, and hence the extent and intensity of the "instinctual" derivatives.

If our objective were merely to "explain" the cultural phenomena, we could make a strong and consistent case with the libido theory. Its use for comparative work would however be extremely limited, because many different types of culture will correspond to the formula "anal-sadistic," without supplying us with any standards for comparing the institutions of these various cultures.

The assumptions of the libido theory make it unnecessary to look to institutions as the sources of repressive influences and this is where "depth" psychology differs from an ego psychology. The assumption that repressions are phylogenetically determined, is one of the main supports of the libido theory; and this assumption is not substantiated by the comparative study of cultures. In our analysis of Tanala culture no such assumption was made, but it was demonstrated that the repressive mechanisms of man operate with a fair degree of regularity and produce similar results under similar provocation. The capacity for repression is a phylogenetically determined characteristic; but the circumstances under which these repressive forces are mobilized depend upon external realities, and on every influence that comes from education and discipline. If man's repressive powers were not mobilized in accordance with the external realities he encounters, but followed instead a phylogenetically predetermined pattern, then his adaptability would be no greater than those creatures whose adaptive weapons are all supposed to be completed at birth; and the advantages gained by man's long dependency and slow complicated development would be utterly vitiated.

The differences between cultures depend on the clash between the constancy of fundamental human needs and the variation in the forces that obstruct satisfaction of those needs: it is these obstructions which determine the arena of the repressive forces. One can agree with Freud that some of these obstructions are universal—as is the fate of the tendency of the child to become sexually attached to the mother. But how effective this situation is in creating difficulties in development depend not on this factor alone, but on two others: first, whether the child is institutionally permitted to express his sexuality in other ways, and second the failures in personal development due to constitutional and accidental factors. As regards the first factor, cultures vary, and the significance of such a parental fixation will correspondingly differ; as regards the second, personal failures can occur in any culture, irrespective of its institutions.

Part III

THEORETICAL

This part deals with the theoretical questions involved in the derivation and application of psycho-social concepts. It reviews the history of psychoanalytic social psychology, gives an exposition of the relevant principles of psychopathology, and describes the technique for applying them to problems in sociology.

Chapter IX

PSYCHOLOGY AND SOCIOLOGY—A
METHODOLOGICAL REVIEW

IN THE analysis of the Marquesan and Tanala cultures we used a technique for following transformations and changes in human affects and attitudes created by different types of social conditions. These analyses gave us information, a good deal of which was new, and not apparent on direct observation by the criteria of common sense. A good deal of this new information, although plausible, cannot be verified or checked except by comparison with other cultures where similar conditions exist.

The system of coördinates we employed comprised the immediate and inescapable problems of adaptation created for the individual by his natural and human environment. Whenever possible, and we did not always succeed, we attempted to describe the effects of institutions on the individual in terms of his direct experience, or at least to translate them into these terms.

This system of coördinates is not the only one used in current social psychologies. It would be useful for purposes of comparison to have a history of the types of psychological technique in use. The author is not, however, adequate to the task of recording such a history, nor is it entirely relevant to our theme. But what we can with some profit do is to examine some of the working concepts used by other psychologies and to study the principles of their use in sociology. In addition we can survey the history of the psychoanalytic concepts and the history of their application to sociology.

DIRECT EXPERIENCE, BEHAVIOR, CONSTRUCTS, AND EXPLANATIONS

There are certain difficulties common to all psychologies; and to these psychoanalysis is not immune. Roughly speaking, one can differentiate three types of psychological technique, which differ in the relative degrees to which they draw upon direct subjective experience, behavior, and the use of constructs[1] (or, to use Dewey's term, operational concepts) derived from both. They further vary in the kind of direct experience and the types of behavior they draw upon, and in the source and character of the constructs. Behaviorism and the reflexologies draw chiefly on behavioristic units; topology draws on analogical constructs, and psychoanalysis chiefly on constructs derived from direct experience. We need to examine each of these units briefly, because in our work we have employed all three.

In the living subject the experiences which we designate as "psychological" are continuous, even during sleep. The form in which these experiences occur in the subject, and are subsequently verbalized by him, can be called *direct experience*. The subject in describing this experience uses the first person. Thus "I think," "I felt angry," "I anticipate," "I am afraid that," "I dream". . . . The data collected in this way are one of our chief sources of information.

When, however, we wish to talk about the subject and his direct experiences, we talk of him in the third person, "he is afraid," etc. We can also make certain observations about his *behavior*, which he cannot do himself. If we want to study animals or children before the time they can talk, we have no choice except to study their behavior and to correlate it with certain identifiable provocatives or coincident circumstances which we can deliberately set into motion. These conditions we designate as *stimuli*, the behavior following a stimulus being the *response*.

[1] We are omitting the experimental psychologies.

In order to talk about both direct experience and behavior in such a way as to save time, we classify certain aggregates of experience, processes or reaction types, as entities. These are neither direct experiences nor behavior; they may be designated as *constructs*. Let us take a simple illustration of a construct. Little Bobbie sucks his thumb; his mother does not want him to do this and threatens to punish him. In direct experience Bobbie can say, "I want to suck my thumb but I'm afraid of mother." Behavioristically, Bobbie does not suck his thumb, but is irritable and naughty in other ways. If we want to describe the whole constellation we invent a word which is metamorphic, but suitable to convey the idea of the processes taking place, the word *conflict*. This word is a *construct*.

Without the aid of these constructs we could not economically describe anything. However, constructs differ in their accuracy and in the sources from which they are derived. Some of them are extremely complex, and extremely remote from direct experience. Behavioristic constructs are by their very nature bound to be less accurate, if direct experience is our ultimate check.

In addition to the difficulties created by the use of these three classes of concepts there is the problem of adequate verbal treatment. Practical illustrations alone can clarify the verbal difficulties we encounter and the risks involved in creating constructs from direct experience or from observed behavior. The statement "I am angry at Henry" is a statement of a direct experience. The statement "John is angry at Henry" describes a direct experience of John, but whether John is angry or not can only be decided by what John tells us. To conclude his anger from his behavior is not safe; for, instead of anger, the direct experience in the form of emotion may be anxiety, the source of which is not accessible to the direct experience of John. As to the anger, one has difficulty in establishing its cause by behavioristic standards. "I am angry" is easily intelligible; but "anger is a reaction of the ego" is very obscure. It seems to be a metaphor or a personification of a subdivision of the personality. The relation of "ego" to total personality is obscure, particularly in psychoanalytic usage.

The word "ego" is Latin for "I." It is a pronoun in Latin, but in English has been used as the substantive of "I." This usage permits us a very convenient word to express a specific idea; it permits the use of a substantive of "I" to describe direct subjective experience. For ordinary purposes this is not a great advantage, but in describing complicated types of direct experience, as in hysteria or compulsion neurosis, it becomes very helpful. A system of correlated ideas must be established between the pronoun and the substantive. In direct experience we may say "I can do so-and-so." With the substantive we can say "The ego has the capacity or resources to do so-and-so," without in any way distorting the meaning of the first. The word *ego* thus stands for the total personality subjectively perceived and not a personified function. The usefulness of this concept lies in the fact that we can establish from direct experience the structure or modalities of the personality, which cannot be expressed as direct experience.

In many instances the concept "the individual" or "personality" structure is adequate. The accurate use of these terms depends on the origin of the experience from which ideas about structure are derived. If their source is direct experience, "ego structure" is more accurate; "personality structure" is more accurate if they are derived from behavioristic data.

Once we establish this use of the word *ego,* we run into verbal difficulties when we attempt to denote modalities of this ego as *portions* of the total personality and attribute to these constructed functions anthropomorphic properties which can appertain only to the individual as a whole. This is notably the case with the concept "super-ego" and the concept "id," or the impersonal ego. Thus the extravagances committed with these constructs lead to unnecessary confusion. The idea "The ego feels that it is not loved by the super-ego" is a roundabout way of saying, "I do not approve of myself." The justification for this figure comes, however, from the fact that the deduction is not made from direct experience. The "super-ego does not love the ego" is an awkward attempt to describe a different type of direct experience from what is contained in the idea "I do not approve of myself."

A second difficulty confronting any psychology is the derivation and use of constructs. Constructs are abstract terms which are generalizations of types or classes of experience derived from direct experience or behavior. One difficulty created by constructs is that if they are not accurately derived from direct experience, they cannot be restated in terms of direct experience. One can see at a glance that a still greater risk is run in the derivation of constructs from behavior, because the meaning of behavior is always an inference, though in many instances a very safe one.

A third difficulty is presented by the final "explanation" which is usually derived from the constructs. An explanation may serve different purposes. It generally purports to make complicated entities comprehensible. This it may do in a pictorial, analogical, analytical, or dynamic manner.

From this discussion it would seem a miracle that one can ever draw any reliable psychological conclusions. This is not necessarily true if one is careful about the use of constructs and does not attempt to juggle them about as if they were mathematical formulae. The careless use of constructs often leads to explanations which do not add much new information and which are not accurate records of the processes of nature.

When a system of psychology built on poorly established constructs emerges in finished form, its usefulness for sociology is limited because these formulations in constructs are now offered as explanations which can satisfy only a few of the many conditions to which psychological knowledge can be put. Some explanations have as their aim merely to aid in thinking about matters psychological; and since psychology has a very limited number of concepts, analogizing with something more familiar, dramatizing, or rendering a concept pictorial, is a perfectly legitimate procedure. Such a rendering of psychological processes by analogies with the physical or mathematical sciences, by dramatization, or pictorial representation, is only an aid to thinking about psychological processes; but it is highly questionable whether this offers a more intimate approach to the essential processes themselves, and whether it offers any record of the psychic motions or transformations involved. A still further difficulty is created when the explanatory process creates difficulties in itself, as do mathematical analogies; much time and effort are thus lost in endeavors which do not approximate the essentials. That is, the investigator is compelled to explain the aid to thinking, rather than the original problem.

Although there is no quarrel with any explanation that aids in thinking about psychological processes, the limits of these procedures are reached when we attempt to use a criterion which psychoanalysis alone has introduced, namely, that explanations are to be used to confer control over the essential mental processes as a means of modifying subjective states or behavior. This objective creates new tasks which no analogical or pictorial explanation can help. An explanation which aims only to aid in thinking is not bound by the essential processes pursued by nature in reaching a certain psychological result; that is, it is not necessarily dynamic; but if the aim is to modify behavior, it becomes necessary to follow these psychological processes in a genetic order in terms of the actual conscious and unconscious experiences of the individual. An explanation which purports to be dynamic means that the actual psychic motion and transformations must be registered, if possible, in the units in which they occur, and not by means of an analogy or a pictorial representation, although these latter may also be considered "explanations." The understanding of obscure types of direct experience of the individual is an indispensable weapon to modify his feeling or behavior; the genetic and dynamic relationship of such experience becomes the object of study. The direct experience of the subject must be the starting point of every psychology, and the goal of every psychology is to reproduce all the steps in the creation of a given end result. But most psychologies differ in how much direct experience they need before calling in descriptive, analogical, dramatic, or pictorial adjuncts. Even psychoanalysis, which has gone further than any other psychology in attempting reconstructions of direct experience, has not been able to do without constructs and analogical, dramatic, and anthropomorphic methods, though in the past these were drawn mainly from biology, and not from mathematics or physics.

The distinction between psychologies based on direct experience and those which employ behavioristic formulas is a very sharp one. The situation is further complicated by the use of words of behavioristic connotation, which are often used to describe direct experience. For example the word *authority* is a behavioristic concept; it describes a result of certain interactions between individuals, yet it is often used to describe direct experience, notwithstanding the fact that the direct experience of each individual concerned is always one of several modalities in the total *authority* picture, the latter being the name of an interpersonal constellation.

In short, not all explanations are dynamic; they do not necessarily elucidate the processes of nature in creating behavior and types of feeling, and hence often fail on the pedagogic side as well as on that of emotional appeal, when the objective is to modify behavior or feeling.

Perhaps we are a bit extreme in overstating the aims of dynamic psychology and in underestimating the value of analogical explanations; we may, thereby, be letting ourselves in for an unredeemable promise. The word *conflict,* which we discussed, is a behavioristic construct based on an analogy. It would be difficult to find a word to convey the same idea as succinctly. A dynamic psychology which deals only with direct experience and uses only the purest constructs, which only tracks down processes of nature and does so without the aid of explanations, is today inconceivable. This is not alone the fault of psychology, but is due as much to the form in which direct

experience is registered on the individual, and the purpose
for which it is designed. These forms of direct experience are
not conceived to be of special use to the psychologist, any more
than the observations of practical sense about the physical
world are designed to give the physicist his insight into the laws
which govern physics, although they do supply him with his
primary data. When a man observes that the chair stands on
the floor, he is not taking into account the laws of gravity or
the counterpressure exerted by the floor. His observation only
records what it is necessary for him to know to the practical
end of utility and orientation, no more. The same is true of the
data of psychology. The processes of nature are not registered
in the direct experiences of the individual. Very often they take
forms which are unfamiliar and disturbing, and over which the
individual has no control or understanding. These processes
in back of the direct experience must in every instance be
deduced; whereas direct experience has a purely utilitarian
value of a very practical kind to the individual. These experiences apprise him of feelings, impulses, and wishes with respect
to the outer world or other individuals. They are the data of
human psychology.

The manner in which these data are used, the relation they
have to the total adaptation of the individual, the manner of
tracing their continuity through the entire life trajectory, the
particular sector of an experimential continuum which is
caught, the name attached to it, the verbal systems evolved,
and the special difficulties which all these verbal systems create
—in these, psychologies differ. There is a sharp difference between good theory and bad, and for purposes of selection, we
must have some standards. We are obliged to use a psychology
that is clinical, i.e., related to actual experience; a psychology
that deals with facts, and not with ideas detached from the
realities represented by them. The problems of sociology are
clinical. One of its important aims is to place social life under
human control.

BEHAVIORISTIC CONCEPTS

The reflexologies and behaviorism are types of psychology which either cannot or do not depend on direct experience. The techniques they employ are especially useful in animals and children before they can talk. Correlations between stimulus and response can, without question, be charted with great precision. Within the province in which these psychologies operate no question of their usefulness can be raised. This question arises only when concepts derived from the behavior of animals or children are used in relation to adults, for whom we have the additional check of direct experience.

The work of these schools has been helpful in establishing a psychological continuity between man and lower animals, and in checking experimentally the truth of principles used by other psychologies. The province within which the reactions of man and animals are alike has been established by the correlation of traumatic neuroses, organ neuroses, and "neuroses" in animals as the result of breaking established conditioned reflexes. In the domain of orientation, locomotion, basic reactions in procuring food, and some reactions to frustration, there is much similarity between man and lower animals.[2]

Regarding behaviorism, our chief concern is the necessity of using behavior as an adjunct to or substitute for direct experience. Conclusions about behavior in animals established on comparisons with man where some direct experience can be called on, are quite legitimate, and can hardly be a source of error. When we reverse the process, however, we are distinctly at a disadvantage.

When we observe the behavior of monkeys in combat, we can characterize the victorious monkey in a rivalry situation as *dominant*. This concept of *dominance* characterizes behavior of a certain type, as it is observed. We must now ask what this

[2] A. Kardiner, "Bioanalysis of the Epileptic Reaction," *Psychoanalytic Quarterly*, Vol. I, No. 3; H. S. Liddel, "The Experimental Neurosis and the Problem of Mental Disorder," *American Journal Psychiatry*, Vol. XCIV, No. 5, March, 1936; and Norman R. F. Maier, *Studies in Abnormal Behavior in the Rat* (New York, 1939).

dominant behavior looks like from the point of view of direct experience of the individual. When we apply this concept to man, we find that it can be appplied to a large variety of direct experiences in the form of motive, antecedent predisposition, command of resources, etc. For human psychology we must therefore be on guard about behavioristic concepts, which are to be avoided except where direct experience is unattainable.

A purist attitude toward behavioristic concepts cannot, however, be long maintained. They are often embodied in our concepts which describe direct experience. One can construct a dynamics on the basis of behavioristic concepts, one that can yield a good deal of new information even though direct experience is missing. In some instances it does not make much difference whether one uses the behavioristic terms or those of direct experience. The latter would often be entirely unwieldy, and one could hardly attempt to describe complicated phenomena without the aid of behavioristic concepts. For purposes of analysis, however, the direct experience becomes both a powerful analytic tool, and a conclusive check.

CONSTRUCTS

The *construct*, an abstract term describing general categories of experience, creates a new type of difficulty. It makes a great deal of difference whether the construct is derived from direct experience, from behavior, as is commonly the case with some psychologies, or from *analogies* with mathematical or physical phenomena.

Merely for the sake of illustration, we might pause to examine a type of construct that is used by the topologists K. Lewin and J. F. Brown. Brown[3] uses as his basic working tools, a good many of these constructs derived from analogies with mathematics and physics. It is important to understand how these are derived and the uses to which they are put.

[3] J. F. Brown, *Psychology and the Social Order* (New York, 1937). What is said in the ensuing paragraphs does not purport to be a review of this very stimulating work.

Brown follows Lewin in his distinction between the language of experience (phenotype) and the language of constructs (genotype). He believes that science consists of the transformation of one into the other (p. 33). The genotype describes the underlying dynamic situation. The prototype of this generalization comes from physics, where it is certainly true. But it is questionable that this is a justifiable procedure in psychology.

If we were to use the physical analogy and describe psychological experience in the manner of the law of gravity $\left(S = \dfrac{Gt.^2}{2}\right)$, we must restate the phenotype in terms of the genotype. Thus, the statement "The child wants candy" becomes "There is a vector toward a goal in the psychological field." Brown believes that by this type of formulation "many phenotypes can be understood as instances of one genotype" (p. 34). This would surely be an advantage if the information conveyed by the genotypic formulation were in any way new. It seems that the new version is very far removed from the direct experience of the child or of anyone observing it, and cannot be translated back into the original experience. The formulation of the law of gravity is the direct observation of the individual observer aided by more precise measurements than can be established by the eye; and the final formulation contains new information not directly available to the observer. This construct, contained in the formula, is a derivative of the direct experience, and is always convertible into the latter. The formulation of Brown is a translation of the direct experience into an arbitrary language of constructs, which not only adds no new information but actually obscures the experience it attempts to describe. It is very difficult to see what is gained by the transformation.

Calling the verb "want" a "vector" and calling "candy" a "goal" does not aid very materially except to form one clause of a law which must be stated in full before the analogy with the physical law is valid. Let us meanwhile make a few conjectures about what needs to be added to the proposition "a child wants candy" to make it material for a general law. First, "a" child is a nonexistent abstraction; but "Peter wants candy" is a reality. Peter has a history. Wanting candy is a factor, not in a vacuum, but in an actual life situation. What must Peter do to get candy? Is it the mere vocalization of the wish or the institution of a complicated series of maneuvers through Peter's nurse to Peter's mother, both of whom are distinct individuals with definite attitudes about Peter's wanting candy? The "want" in Peter either encounters no difficulty in being translated into action, or it does. The want is either gratified, or it is not. The frustration brings in its wake attitudes toward nurse and mother, and that night Peter may have a dream. Where are the limits of the total experience about which you want to make some generalization? The limits are very hard to define, and the psychological experience being a continuum, some arbitrary line must be drawn. We may investigate the form in which the perception of candy exists in Peter's mind; we may investigate the nature of the want, and track down its biological sources; or we may deal with a larger segment of the experience, ignoring the nature of the perceptions and the biological character of the want, and considering only how Peter deals with the satisfaction or frustration of the need, and what influences both have on the total experience of Peter for one day or one year, etc., etc. These three types of psychological endeavor are all different, and not at all incompatible with one another. But if we make a system of psychology only on the basis of what Peter does (behaviorist), we shall have to supply what goes on in Peter's mind from our general knowledge of norms under similar conditions. That would really be guessing, and we would, moreover, be missing out on those essential features which make Peter an individual. The situation can be obviated, for with a little trouble we can get a fairly complete picture of Peter's total experience, thanks to Peter's ability to dream and talk.

We can take two possible outcomes of the wish for candy.

(1) Peter expresses the wish, the nurse asks mother, who assents, Peter gets the candy, eats it, and goes to sleep contented. (2) Peter expresses the wish, the nurse refuses, Peter bawls, the mother intervenes and spanks Peter, not for wanting candy, but for being naughty; Peter frets himself to sleep, and dreams of a big box of candy on the table which suddenly disappears, though the feeling tone of the dream is pleasant. Each of these outcomes furnishes us with many opportunities to make psychological laws, by determining what psychological conditions are established when the wish is gratified, or by determining what happens when it is frustrated—to mention only two of the methods open to us.

Let us now consider the fate of Brown's procedure based on constructs derived from a mathematical prototype. He introduces a spatial concept called "the field"; then another spatial idea "goal"; and a third construct of "force behind behavior," which has magnitude, viz., vectors. These are followed by a group of constructs which seek to represent psychological facts in space (i.e., topological) and those which deal with motion; in addition there is the representation of barriers with varying degrees of permeability. So far, all we have in this method is a group of spatial and mathematical terms designed to characterize certain units of direct experience and behavior. We cannot tell how they work until they are put into action, but we can anticipate that nothing much can possibly happen. There is an inherent weakness in the whole system, which Brown recognizes. He states (p. 478) : "But a little careful thought convinces one that psychological vectors are just as valid as the concepts of vectors in the magnetic and gravitational fields, except that they are not subject to fundamental measurement." This does not state the case adequately. Even if the psychological vectors could be measured as to magnitude and intensity, we would not be getting the information that is most valuable to us for purposes of dynamics. Whereas measurement is the means of establishing laws of physics, the measurement of a "psychological vector" would yield relatively unimportant information.

If one were to measure vectors, one could measure only differences of intensity. But since we cannot measure them, the insistence on their use as in physics is misleading. This is the very point where the analogy between the phenomena observable in the physical world and those that take place in a living organism break down. The essential reason for the failure lies in the attempt to establish the coördinates in the outer world in spatial concepts, and not in direct psychological experience. The "vector," which in direct experience is *need,* wish, tension, is only a fleeting indicator of motion, change, or disturbance within the organism, whose origin, motion, and organization must be the object of study. The fact that the data of physics and psychology are epistemologically equal in their practical use by the individual does not justify us in treating the data of the two separate fields in the same way. Such a procedure would yield us little new knowledge about how and why humans act. The use of the data of physics must, by the nature of its premises, remain a manner of describing and ordering phenomena. From this new description one can draw many interesting and graphic representations of the activities of man behavioristically viewed, but very few that will tell much about the nature of the creature producing these phenomena.

The basic difficulties in the topology of Brown are those consequent on "explaining" psychological phenomena with the aid of constructs based on mathematical analogies. The procedure is justified by the hope that there is no essential difference between biological, psychological, and physical phenomena. These three types of phenomena arise from such widely different sources that it is hazardous to explain one in terms of the other. For example, the biological phenomenon of "growth" cannot be explained solely by what we know about "motion," nor can it be described only as "expansion." Neither of these descriptive analogies really touches on the essentials of growth, although motion and expansion are both observable phenomena in connection with it. Furthermore, the concepts used to describe the motion of inanimate bodies in space cannot be applied to feelings, even though we are employing concepts of force and direction when we speak of feelings being "directed at" someone. This would seem to make the concept "vector" as used by Brown applicable to "feeling." But feeling has another attribute not included either in the concept of force or in that of direction, and that is *subjective quality*. This is the essence of feeling; although intensity is also one of its attributes. Feeling cannot be described only in terms of intensity, for that would omit the consideration of the origin, purpose, modalities, change, and specific tone qualities associated with feeling. It is these latter considerations which occupy the greatest share of the psychologist's attention, in addition to intensity and direction. For these reasons one cannot be mathematically precise about the intensity of feeling, while ignoring the other aspects, and still continue to expect that our knowledge about intensity or direction explains all the other phenomena.

This long digression was necessary as a caution. Constructs are difficult enough to handle when they are derived from direct experience or from behavior. To make constructs based on analogies with processes in physics, on the assumption that such constructs are more accurate, removes us so much the further from our source material and greatly diminishes our chances of extracting any really new knowledge from it.

So far we have considered direct experience, behavior, and constructs as source material for deriving psychological knowledge. When we come to consider psychoanalysis as a method, we encounter a new type of direct experience, behavior, and constructs.

In psychoanalytic psychology direct experience includes a greater variety of factors than is the case in most psychologies. It takes in the wishes, impulses, drives which can be expressed in simple words; it includes fantasies and dreams, chance acts, emotions, and feeling tones which can be subjectively described, but of which the subject is not the master. The subject does not willfully direct them; many seem rather to control and drive him. Alterations of will and strange somatic sensations move the subject, and proceed from a personality in control of itself in some though not all respects.

This is the chief source of our data, though the behavior of the individual may not be markedly interfered with, and hence may be a very incomplete guide.

In short, psychoanalysis introduced the phenomena of neurosis into psychology; and with this material Freud attempted to work out a system of constructs to account for the continuity of the personality, despite the apparent breaks produced by the neurosis in the normal continuity.

The direct subjective experiences of a neurotic subject are of such a great variety that the array of material is bewildering. Out of this chaos Freud found a few threads which he could follow. He had then to invent constructs in order to follow what was going on in the subject. These constructs were based on certain assumptions. The first was a teleological assumption, meaning, concretely, that the neurosis was purposive. This teleological idea was attached to a behavioristic construct which Freud did not invent, but borrowed from biology—the concept of *instinct*. To this concept Freud added the direct experience of wish tension, need, drive. However awkward the concept was, Freud performed remarkable feats with it. By pursuing his assumption of the purposive character of neurosis, Freud developed the idea of dynamics and ontogenetic development. That is, he had the idea that "instinct," though phylogenetically determined, went through a course of ontogenetic development. This idea he worked into a more or less schematic plan in which ontogenesis was in some respects a phenomenon recapitulatory of phylogenetic experience.

However, with these phases of development as a base line, Freud needed some concepts with which to describe the continuity of the personality. These he found in a series of constructs which went under the general name of "mental mechanisms." They were designated by the terms: identification, projection, displacement, regression, fixation, reaction formation, isolation, and several others. These "mental mechanisms," which at first occupied an extraterritorial position with respect to the bulk of psychoanalytic theory, are really constructs which describe changing modalities in the organization of the total personality. The greatest share of attention first fell to the *content* on which these mechanisms operated, and the result was the instinct theory. These constructs are however useful only to describe the transformations in direct experience; they give information about modifications in organization of personality as well as the content involved in these processes; but they are useless in a behaviorist psychology.

This collection of constructs enabled Freud to describe the phenomena of neurosis and to ·reëstablish the apparently broken continuity of subjective experience and behavior which was found in the "normal." We found, thus, that "instinctual" objectives can be changed in accordance with the polarities activity-passivity, or in accordance with "instinctual" objectives arrested at certain stages of development. These alterations of objective were not always satisfactory to the individual, and in themselves created new conflicts in place of the old ones they purported to solve. It is these latter conflicts which create the façade of the neurosis.

By 1910 Freud had worked out a consistent system of constructs with the aid of which he could describe the phenomena of neurosis. This system he introduced into sociology. The chief innovation was the introduction of the concept of repression and its consequences, which took care of the important fact that in any social organization not every impulse can be satisfied, that some must be repressed, suppressed, or checked in some other way. The introduction of this idea into sociology was of the greatest importance. However, the particular manner in which Freud accounted for the repressions created considerable difficulty. The adoption of a psychology of direct experience to the phenomena of sociology was bound to create serious problems, chiefly because in sociology no direct experience is available, but only the shadows of this on the fixed precipitates of personal interactions, i.e., on institutions, which are behavioral phenomena. The crucial problem was how to bridge the gap between direct experience of the individual and the behavioral phenomena of culture. We shall first sketch the manner in which Freud solved this problem in his social psychology, and later contrast it with the procedure used in the present work.

FREUD'S SOCIOLOGY

In four essays, called *Totem and Taboo*[4] Freud presented the following theory of primitive society.

In the psychic life of the savage we have a well-preserved early stage of our own development. Therefore, we are able to compare the psychology of primitive races with the psychology of the neurotic. These primitive races have the most stringent taboos against incest. Individuals from the same totem may not have sexual relations, but must marry exogamically. Thus, primitive man does what we see the individual do in our society; the individual is attached to the parent of the opposite sex in childhood and then must renounce this goal. In primitive society we see that man in an early stage of development considered incest dangerous and hence instituted defenses against it.

Then Freud discovered the similarity between taboo systems in primitive society and the defensive measures of the compulsion neurosis. The basis of taboo is a forbidden action for which there is a strong inclination in the unconscious. Freud could not accept the idea that the taboo is merely imposed from without, but had to account for it on the basis on which it occurs in the compulsion neurosis. Both primitive man and neurotic believe in the omnipotence of their thought.

The facts about totemism which Freud stresses most are that the totem animal was considered an ancestor of the tribe; that the totem was hereditary through the female line; that it was forbidden to kill or eat the totem; and that members of the totem were forbidden to have sexual intercourse with each other.

[4] Translated by A. A. Brill (New York, 1912).

Freud's answer to this problem is derived from the consideration of the dread of incest. He follows Atkinson's theory about social origins: that the earliest organization of man was like that of higher apes, in which the strong male preëmpts the sexual prerogatives with the females. This would compel the exogamy of the young men.

In the animal phobias of children Freud saw a mental process similar to that which exists in primitive man. Since the phobic animal represents the father to the child, it may have the same significance in primitive man. In other words, animal phobias in children may be an "infantile recurrence of totemism." The psychology of the infantile animal phobia must therefore be the psychology of totemism. The love for the mother and the consequent ambivalence to the father necessitate the displacement of the fear and hatred of the father onto an animal.

Some of Robertson Smith's ideas on animal sacrifice complete Freud's material. According to Robertson Smith, sacrifice is a descendant of what was originally a totemic feast, in which the totem animal is killed and eaten by the whole group, an act for which no individual could take the responsibility. After this the murdered animal is bewailed and lamented because of a fear of retribution. The mourning is followed by festive gaiety. The individuals thereby strengthen their identification with the totem and with each other. The totem animal is a substitute for the father, and the ritual is a repetition of a once real drama, when the jealous sons banded together, slew the father, and ate him. This was followed by remorse.

All religions contain some features of this totemic complex. Christianity contains a record of this primal sin, for Christ redeems this sin with his own death; but he also satisfied the original wish to put himself in the father's place—he becomes a god.

Freud answers the question of how this complex is perpetuated through the ages by stating that "a part of the task seems to be performed by the inheritance of psychic dispositions which, however, need certain incentives in the individual life in order to become effective."

Freud was not unaware of the difficulties created by *Totem and Taboo*. He saw that this hypothesis and method did not at all explain why societies held together. For each human, subject to the same phylogenetic heritage, was something of a monad in the company of a host of other monads. To clarify this problem Freud wrote *Group Psychology and the Analysis of the Ego*,[5] which contains some of the most valuable ideas in his sociology, though they are incompatible with many of those expressed in the previous work.

In this book Freud rejected any method of dealing with the group as having a collective mind or group mind, and rejected the efforts to account for social phenomena on the basis of any special instinct like "herd instinct." He looked for the solution of this problem by investigating the character of the forces that bind one person to another. He also rejected imitativeness or suggestion or the "primitive induction of emotion" of McDougall as descriptive terms with which to describe interpersonal relations, because they do not deal with the underlying forces. Instead he derived these forces from the study of the individual in accordance with his theory of instincts.

Freud described the relations of person to person with the aid of the concept of *libido*, the grossest manifestation of which is in sexual love. He modified the connotation of libido to satisfy the manifestations of self-love, love of parents and by parents, friendship, love for humanity, devotion to concrete objects, and devotion to abstract ideas, and stated the problem as merely a question of whether the libido or Eros is satisfied in its aim, or whether it is deflected from it.

By way of illustration, he then applied this idea of the operation of libido to two artificial groups, the army and church. Freud maintains that the individuals composing the group are tied to one another and to the leader by special modalities of libido, one of which is that the love bond may become *desexu-*

[5] Translated by James Strachey (New York, 1922).

alized. Thus friendship between men is *aim-inhibited,* desexualized, or sublimated love. When these love ties are severed, as is the case in panic, the group disintegrates. In ordinary relationships this love relationship is not free of hatred; this hatred under ordinary conditions is easily repressed, but under other conditions, it becomes manifest. The two attitudes coexisting make for a psychological constellation called *ambivalence.* But this emotional attitude is the result of a conflict of interests in one and the same person. The readiness to hatred and aggressiveness is given an elementary character. In addition to the love bond, *identification* is still another mechanism expressing an emotional tie.

Under this term, identification, the following modalities are included by Freud: (1) The wish to take some other person's place, as does the little boy in conflict with his father for his mother's love. This identification is ambivalent. (2) A derivative of the oral libido phase, i.e., a wish to assimilate the object by ingestion and thus also reanimate the object. (3) Identification with an object may be a substitute for that same object as a love object. (4) Identification by a common claim, frequently noted in hysterical imitation. In this case, object love relationship is omitted. (5) Identification with an object that is lost as a substitute for it (melancholia). Only the first four play a role in groups.

According to Freud, additional factors in maintaining the relation between individuals in groups are: conscience; ego ideal; a later addition, the super-ego. Certain groups, especially those that do not have too fine an organization and have a leader, can be represented in terms of identification, ego ideal, and love object. "A primary group of this kind is a number of individuals who have substituted one and the same object for their ego ideal, and have consequently identified themselves with one another in their ego." In other groups the identification of members with one another is "forced" on the individual at the cost of repressing jealousy, and substituting for it the demand for justice and equality. "This demand for equality is the root of social conscience and the sense of duty." Thus social feeling is based on a reversal of what was first a hostile feeling into a positive tie having the nature of identification. In this work Freud still insists that the "primal horde" is the basic prototype of human society. It was the tyranny of the primal father that forced the sons into "group psychology," and his power over the sons was maintained by his being the group ideal. His power is maintained by an erotic hypnotic power.

Freud observes that discrepancies between ego and super-ego,[6] or ego and ego ideal, cannot be tolerated by the individual. He regards festivals as opportunities to abrogate the strictness of the super-ego, which is made up essentially of all the limitations to which the ego has had to acquiesce. Triumph is a manifestation of coincidence between ego and ego ideal; guilt and sense of inferiority are manifestations of tension between ego and ego ideal.

In *The Future of an Illusion*[7] Freud defines the aims of culture. They are to render nature subservient to human needs, and to govern the relations among the members of society and to divide the boons. However, culture is a protection for the individual. It demands certain renunciations on the part of the individual, which he finds hard to make. Society protects itself against the tendency of the individual to object to these sacrifices by instituting defenses for the institutions and compensating the individual for his sacrifice. Several factors make it possible to protect society against the hostility in the individual aroused by the demand for renunciation. They are: the fact that man has a tendency to incorporate external pressures, or super-ego formation; the desire of individuals to fulfill the group ideal and thus add to their feeling of worth; and the tendency of the individual to identify himself with those who oppress him. Among these cementing forces is religion, which is really a kind of illusion.

[6] In this work Freud does not yet draw the fine distinction between ego ideal and super-ego, but for purposes of clarity it is here used in the sense that it was his *The Ego and the Id*, translated by Joan Riviere (London, 1927).

[7] Translated by W. D. Robson-Scott (London, 1928).

Freud maintains that the value of religious ideas is that they help man to overcome his feeling of helplessness against the forces of nature. The personification of the forces of nature thus becomes an aid in that it gives the individual some technique for dealing with them, and puts them to some degree under human control. This technique has an infantile prototype; it reflects the relations of parent and child. Religion thus protects against dangers of the outer world and dangers arising from within society. We must note carefully that this orientation is very different from the one used in *Totem and Taboo,* for Freud now leaves room for differences of religion based on differences of vicissitudes of the group. But he fails to specify in this more recent work just where these difficulties, arising from within society, are to be located, studied, and examined in a comparative way. Furthermore, Freud recognizes that by introducing the idea of helplessness based on the infantile prototype, he introduces an ontogenetic factor in religion, whereas in *Totem and Taboo* the main source of these ideas was supposed to be a phylogenetic one, the reminiscence of a primal crime of parricide related entirely to the sexual rivalry of a primal father and his sons. About this point Freud says that the argument in his earlier work held for the origin of totemism, and not religion, though he sees some evidence of a transition from one to the other (p. 39). In other words, Freud now tries to reconcile the "father complex and helplessness and need for protection of man." And this he does in the following terms: It lies in the relation between the helpless child and the parent, and forms the basic prototype of the relation of man to God (p. 41).

In *Civilization and Its Discontents*[8] Freud attempts to answer the question "How does culture influence human instinctual dispositions?" Freud replies, "Some of these instincts become absorbed as it were, so that something appears in place of them in an individual we call a character trait." He chooses as illustration the anal character, thriftiness, orderliness, and cleanli-

[8] Translated by Joan Riviere (London, 1930).

ness. He observes, "How this happens we do not know," but notes that "order and cleanliness are essentially cultural demands."

Freud then postulates a second change that culture induces in instinct gratification—to change its path or direction by way of sublimation. It is from this source that scientific, artistic, and ideological activities become possible, as changes of sexual energy.

A third method, according to Freud, is the consequence of instinctual "suppression, repression, or something else," generally, non-gratification. The explanation that follows is firmly planted on an evolutionary basis: He states, ". . . if we wish to know what use it is to us to have recognized the evolution of culture as a special process, comparable to the normal growth of an individual to maturity, we must clearly attack another problem and put the question: What are the influences to which the evolution of culture owes its origin; how did it arise; and what determined its course?" (p. 64).

Again, as on many previous occasions, Freud prefers to answer this question about instinct repression by a phylogenetic reconstruction. But in addition to ground already covered in *Totem and Taboo* and *The Future of an Illusion*, Freud brings in some new material. He now notes that sexual love became to man the prototype of all happiness, and notes the far-reaching changes in erotic function that make this possible. The objective must be changed from the desire to be loved by turning from the sexual aim to an impulse whose aim is inhibited, a phenomenon which he calls desexualization. This makes possible the "all-embracing love of others"; it makes possible friendship. But "love opposes the interest of culture" and "culture menaces love with grievous restrictions." There are opposing forces to this love. The tendencies of culture are away from the family, though the ties of the latter are centrifugal. Women, "who are antithetical to cultural trends," cause another discord, and so "civilization has become more and more men's business."

Freud holds that culture sets restrictions on sexual life, first by incest taboos, "perhaps the most maiming wound ever inflicted throughout the ages on the erotic life of man." In addition there are more taboos, laws, customs (monogamy), and restrictions (perversions) which reach their greatest severity in Western Europe. These restrictions apply not only to adults but also to children.

Through these restrictions on sexual activity Freud believes that civilization levies a large amount of energy from the individual for the benefit of the group by way of identifications and friendships. But why is culture antagonistic to sexuality?[9]

Freud believes that "a powerful measure of desire for aggression has to be reckoned as a part of his [man's] instinctual endowment," which asserts itself in the wish to exploit, rob, humiliate, hurt, torture, and kill his fellows. This, he says, is one of the chief disintegrating forces in society, and culture "has to call up every possible reinforcement in order to erect barriers against this instinctual tendency by identifications, aim inhibited [desexualized] love relationships, restrictions on sex life, and the command to love one's neighbor, all of which is completely at variance with man's original nature. Society employs extreme measures against criminals, but not against the subtler manifestations of crime." Since Freud regards "aggression" as an instinct (presumably on a par with other instincts with identifiable somatic roots) he cannot regard inequalities in distribution of wealth and goods as a source of aggression, a tendency which already shows itself in the nursery. "Men clearly do not find it easy to do without satisfaction of this tendency to aggression in them; when deprived of satisfaction of it they are uncomfortable." Civilization, therefore, requires sacrifices of sexuality and the aggressive instincts. In exchange for these renunciations man has secured some measure of security.

Now, if aggression is an instinct, how do we trace its vicissitudes? At first Freud drew the distinction between sexual and

---

[9] It is worth comparing Freud's answer to the one given by Wilhelm Reich in *Der Einbruch der Sexualmoral* (Berlin, 1932), pp. 86–104.

ego instincts, object and narcissistic libido. But since the ego instincts are libidinal, he classes all of them, ego and sexual, under the name Eros; and its opposite, the death instinct, he classifies as seeking to disintegrate high states and to reinstate the inorganic state. Of this instinct one sees only those manifestations that become directed toward the outer world as aggression or destruction. Eros and the death instinct are in constant balance; too much death instinct exerted toward the outer world leads to destruction; too little intensifies the self-destruction. They never appear in isolation, but in admixtures. Sadism is destructive instinct plus love impulse; masochism is the same thing turned against the "ego."

Aggression is, therefore, according to Freud, the most powerful obstacle to culture. Eros binds men together, death instinct tears them apart. The meaning of the evolution of culture is therefore the endless struggle between Eros and death instinct.

Freud proceeds to state that society controls the aggressive instincts by "internalizing" them, i.e., directing them against the "ego." "It is there taken over by a part of the ego that distinguishes itself from the rest as a super-ego, and now, in the form of 'conscience' exercises the same propensity to harsh aggressiveness against the ego that the ego would have liked to enjoy against others." The tension between super-ego and "ego" is now the sense of guilt or need for punishment. Why does man obey this external agency? "It is easy to discover this motive in man's helplessness and dependence upon others," and "if he loses the love of those on whom he is dependent he will also forfeit their protection against many dangers"; and they may also punish him. "The more righteous a man is, the stricter and more suspicious will his conscience be." This explains the often observed clinical fact which Freud notes, that "external deprivation greatly intensifies the strength of conscience in the super-ego." Dread of authority and dread of super-ego are thus one and the same thing according to Freud. But as Freud notes, there is another clinical phenomenon of great importance. He says, "The first one (dread of authority) compels us to renounce instinctual gratification; the other (super-ego) presses . . . toward punishment. . . ." In other words, masochistic phenomena in man can be accounted for through the activity of the super-ego: . . . "every impulse of aggression which we omit to gratify is taken over by the super-ego and goes to heighten its aggressiveness (against the ego)." But what is the origin of this original aggressiveness? Is it a continuation of the rigor of parental authority? Or is it in some way a utilization of the aggression evoked in the child by the frustration which aggression the child cannot express? This is an excellent clue. But how does it work? By the child's identifying himself with the strict father, and thus treating himself as the latter would have treated him? In a roundabout way, the child therefore expresses the original aggression toward the father, and conscience originates from a suppression of an aggressive impulse. Freud says that both answers are right and are not incompatible with each other. The primal parricide is again evoked as proof.

As in individuals, says Freud, the sense of guilt is often unconscious, so in society; the sources are not perceived. "The anxiety [fear] of the super-ego and the need for punishment is an instinctual manifestation on the part of the ego, which has become masochistic under the influence of the sadistic super-ego, i.e., which has brought a part of the instinct of destruction at work within itself into the service of an erotic attachment to the super-ego." The basic clinical problem that Freud is trying to explain is why and under what circumstances aggression is turned inward.

"The aims of the individual and society do not coincide; there is in the individual a constant interplay between the egoistic and altruistic trends." "Society has a super-ego as well as the individual. This super-ego is based on the impression left behind of great personalities." "At various crises in history this cultural super-ego has made itself felt in the form of ethics, which is always a therapeutic effort directed against man's aggressiveness." Freud likewise admits possibilities of racial neurosis. The future of culture depends on how society "will succeed in mastering the derangement caused by the human instinct of aggression and self-destruction."

SURVEY OF FREUD'S SOCIAL PSYCHOLOGY

Freud brought to the study of neurosis several original principles which were altogether new to psychology. They were: a teleological principle, which meant in effect that there was something purposive in neuroses; a genetic, developmental or ontogenetic viewpoint; a concept of psychological motion, dynamics; and a principle of continuity in the personality, which could be detected only if one enlarged the range of data to be considered, which came to include the total experience of the individual. With the aid of these principles Freud introduced a new technique based upon the study of the individual. The mental processes found in neuroses, particularly those dealing with the disposition of impulses or needs whose satisfaction is frustrated, are to be recovered in the mental phenomena of primitive man.[10] However original these orientations all were, Freud handled them according to the prevailing scientific fashion of his day. Thus, the ontogenetic viewpoint was heavily tinctured with Haeckelian evolutionary biology; this was a part of the scientific atmosphere of the late nineteenth century and continued for a long time to influence psychoanalytic theory. The result was a distinct biological bias from the evolutionary standpoint to the disparagement of what we now call a sociological orientation. This viewpoint has continued to influence Freud throughout his work. Chief among Freud's achievements has been the establishment of definite units of experience, the continuity of which we could follow. This unit was "instinct," which was biologically oriented.

Thus the theory of instincts was largely the result of the biological orientation and was therefore handled in accordance

[10] In the ensuing discussion several criticisms of psychoanalytic sociology are included which were originally pointed out by Erich Fromm in "Die Entwicklung des Christusdogmas," *Imago* (1930), and by Wilhelm Reich in his *Der Einbruch der Sexualmoral* (Berlin, 1932).

with the prevailing biological theories. Moreover, the clinical material with which Freud was able to work lent itself easily to this end. There finally emerged an array of phenomena which made it seem highly probable that the "instinctual" development of man, notably the sexual "instincts," pursued a certain regularity, a fact which vindicated the use of evolutionary principles. This regularity in ontogenesis was interpreted as a repetition of phylogenetic patterns.

It was the success of this work on ontogenesis—in the sense of the verifiability of the constellations in question—which definitely committed Freud to the study of "instincts" and their vicissitudes as the best guide by which to study the continuity of the personality. The first dynamic principle was that of repression, which in its practical application simply meant that when a given "instinct" fails of gratification, the phenomena that take its place are in some way related to the repressed impulse, and hence no longer visible. When the ontogenetic theory and the theory of repression were put to work together, he then had an adequate explanation of a great variety of psychopathological phenomena. For example, if a woman with the hysterical symptom of frigidity dreams all the time of eating, these dreams are in essence sexual fantasies which derive their sexual character from the ontogenesis of the sexual "instinct." The truth or falsity of this statement cannot be gauged by its plausibility according to the conventions of common sense.

On the sociological side, Freud's orientation was very ambiguous, and the biological scheme was never thoroughly integrated with it. Freud partly recognized the importance of environmental pressure in producing repressions; but he allocated these environmental pressures to a very few social situations, tracing most repressions to organic or phylogenetic sources. The most notable of these was the group of interactions between individual and society which produced the constellation called the Oedipus complex. In essence, it merely meant that the child's sexual interests become focused on the parent of the opposite sex, a goal that was inevitably doomed to failure. The persistence of this goal in the unconscious generated a feeling of hostility to the parent of the same sex, and a concurrent sense of guilt. In the normal individual, this complex involuted, but it persisted in the neurotic, and could be identified in his dreams and fantasies. This Freud considered the nuclear complex of every neurosis.

The fact that this complex could be identified both in the individual and in folk tales of a large variety of cultures gave Freud his first clue; it made a bridge between individual and society. In the neurosis it played the role of the universal traumatic situation, gave the opportunity for arrest of development, and thus opened the way for regressive adaptation. In answering the question of how this traumatic factor becomes so important for the individual in our culture, Freud used certain methods, assumptions, and types of proof, which were subsequently taken over by Th. Reik and Roheim as well. This method and its conclusions were severely criticized by anthropologists like Kroeber and Goldenweiser, and by analysts, Fromm and Reich.

First of all Freud used, as Fromm has already pointed out,[11] an analogical reasoning. He sought to establish analogies between "primitive" and "neurotic." In essence we can concur entirely with Fromm's criticisms. The errors do not seem, however, to have arisen from the analogy between individual and group, but from the insistence that the individual inherits certain psychic dispositions and is dominated by phylogenetic repetitions. Freud was, moreover, encouraged in this procedure by the anthropologists of the day, who were working with a more or less evolutionary viewpoint, and whose data and methods he did not question. He expected to find that certain psychic processes that were "conscious" in primitive man were "unconscious" in the contemporary neurotic, and to use this as evidence of the phylogenetic origin of repression. He thus concluded that the struggle against incest in primitive culture

[11] Fromm, "Die Entwicklung des Christusdogmas," *Imago* (1930), pp. 366–367.

is conscious, and that a great many deliberate and easily recognizable defenses against it could be observed.

Had Freud stopped at this point of the phylogenetic-ontogenetic parallelism it would not seriously have influenced the procedure as a whole. But he felt compelled to draw another parallel, one premised again by the evolutionary viewpoint, that the Oedipus complex was not only the nuclear phenomenon in neurosis, but the nuclear complex about which all other factors in social organization and culture became concentrically arranged. This proposition made the character of the analogy final; processes in the individual and processes in society were similar, nay, identical. The individual has an Oedipus complex, society has an Oedipus complex, and the likelihood is that this is based on some occurrence in the remote past of the race, just as it is in the history of the individual. It is clear that Freud was trying to satisfy the condition of the recapitulation theory and was not deducing the conclusion from facts; and since such facts were not available, a "scientific myth"—so designated by Freud himself—was invented to satisfy the need.

The most probable source of the difficulty seems to lie in the lack of clarity about what the Oedipus complex is in the individual, the failure to distinguish the sociological and biological influences that go to make it up, and the attempt to preserve it as a "complex," a condition which facilitated its treatment as an irreducible constellation. Freud rejected the Jungian mystical concept of a "racial unconscious"; but viewing the practical use he made of the Oedipus complex in his sociology, it is hard to avoid the impression that it is not far removed from the Jungian idea. Freud[12] believes "that certain traits of totemism return as a negative expression in the animal phobias of children." This statement clearly affirms the recapitulation theory, and makes it unnecessary to deal directly with the problem of how the transmission through the ages was effected.

[12] Freud, *The Problem of Anxiety* (Tr. by H. A. Bunker; New York, 1935), p. 40; *Collected Papers*, Vol. III: *The History of an Infantile Neurosis* (London, 1924), pp. 577–578.

Perhaps the most serious consequence of this theory for sociology was the limited use it permitted of the data of anthropology. Since the nuclear Oedipus complex existed on the basis of an inherited disposition, all other features of culture not connected with the Oedipus complex were accidental, adventitious, and hence of no interest. The theory furnishes no way of dealing with the manifest differences between primitive cultures, and no room for considering the influence on their institutions of external realities and hardships under which a group lived. This type of reasoning was common among evolutionary anthropologists, who considered the tracing of the origin of an institution the only aspect worthy of attention.

The use of this recapitulation theory led to another serious handicap, in the form of an unwarranted assumption to which Fromm[13] called attention. The conclusions that Freud reached were derived from the study of individuals in our culture, and hence were not necessarily valid for human nature generally. In other words, Freud studied individuals who were products of a specific culture; he was not observing "human nature," but the influences upon it of a very specific set of institutions.

Although Freud used this assumption because it fell in conveniently with his other premises, he did not invent it. It was, in fact, one of the products of the evolutionary school of thought in anthropology, and was contained in many of the sources which Freud used, notably Frazer. Since human nature was the same everywhere, and society "evolves" from one stage to another, the data of anthropology could be used as evidence of survivals, and one could get a picture of the total by picking the parts from different cultures. Freud was following the best precedents of the day. Since he did not question these assumptions of the evolutionary school, it was quite natural for him to see the Oedipus complex as a survival, and not as the result on human nature of a special set of social conditions, a result

[13] E. Fromm, "Über Methode und Aufgabe einer Analytischen Sozialpsychologie," *Zeitschrift für Sozialforschung*, I (1932), Nos. 1-2, 33-38.

very wide-spread in basic pattern, to be sure.[14] The assumption of a primal Oedipus situation in the remote past, the myth of the primal horde, and "primal parricide" were, therefore, inescapable. The support of this thesis had to come from a carefully selected series of data to fit the theory. Thus, psychoanalytic sociology, proceeding in response to different needs and different theoretical orientations, found itself supporting the errors of the evolutionary school of thought in sociology with a psychological "proof." Though the Freudian effort drew fire on the score of introducing the concept of "fixation" into sociology, for elevating the defenses against incest as the prime mover in the culture, and for backing the argument with a synthetic myth about the Cyclopean horde which was treated as a historical fact, the original errors were made long before Freud. The biological and sociological adjuncts that Freud used were basically at fault.

If we recognize these errors based on the evolutionary hypothesis we can easily understand several others that crept in on the score of the theory of instincts. Two of these are outstanding; the use of the concept of repression and the use of "instinct" (*Trieb*) as the unit of experience, both of which failed in their application to sociological problems, though their usefulness in individual psychology has been amply demonstrated. The use of both these concepts is another instance of the miscarriage of the parallelism between phylogeny and ontogeny.

Freud, Th. Reik, and Roheim all assumed that repressions always fall in the same place in all cultures. The only evidence in support of this idea is the universality of incest taboos, considering the latter as a general injunction against sexual union with parents and siblings. First of all, what do we mean by repression, and what do we include under the concept "incest taboo?"

<hr>

[14] See also Fromm, *Autorität und Familie* (Paris, 1936), p. 89; and W. Reich, *Der Einbruch der Sexualmoral* (Berlin, 1932), pp. 105–112.

Repression is a function of the individual; groups cannot repress anything, though every individual in a given group can be subjected to the same pressures and sanctions that will compel each to abandon certain aspects of "instinctual" drives, which, nevertheless, cannot be altogether destroyed. In studying society, therefore, the emphasis must be shifted to those forces concealed in institutions which compel the individual to repress a given impulse, and to those tendencies or conditions in the individual which make him yield to these pressures contained in or derived from institutions. However, if this question is answered by postulating in advance that all repressions proceed from a phylogenetically determined constellation, then institutions do not create the forces of repression, but repressions cause institutions. In this case, institutions are purely adventitious, and all problems of culture can be solved by projecting the current psychological situation found in our culture into the remote past.

We can put this theory to test by an instance from Roheim.[15] In his Australasian essay, Roheim presents evidence to prove that a little native boy has an Oedipus complex. But the special conditions of the boy's life, the social organization in which he lives, its history, the institutions and economic practices of the group, have no bearing on the boy's Oedipus complex. Of course not, if it is phylogenetically determined. The influence of this assumption on technique is that it assumes what we are trying to prove, and takes away every possible motive for studying institutions. The motive for repression in the individual in our culture gives us no clue to the forces or motives that set the institution into motion. The institution is merely a part of the individual's environment, to which he must accommodate himself. These institutions are end results of instinctual or social conflicts established by necessity, force, or expediency; their origin is largely a matter of conjecture, for no reconstruction is possible without the aid of history. For this lost history, the theory of primal parricide is no substitute. The structure, tempo, and order of repression in the individual are entirely contingent upon cultural forces. These forces differ in different cultures. The individual is a finite being, and an organic unit with a fixed ontogenetic course; the group has no such organic unity, no such ontogenesis, and has no beginning and no end. Institution and repression are reciprocal influences and hence cannot be treated as identical even though they originate from the same source. The institution creates a force, repression is a symptom of its operation.

The concept "incest taboo" is altogether too vague and includes too many different meanings. Does "incest taboo" mean sexual union with an object, or marriage; is the one permissible and the other taboo? Does the taboo extend to those identified with parents or siblings? It does. This varies in different kinship systems.[16] Is the taboo of objects associated with prohibition or encouragement of the sexual aim in childhood? Are individuals allowed the normal sexual activities of childhood, or are these forbidden outside of the object taboos? All these variations, which we encounter in primitive society, have different effects on the individual and arise from different types of institutions. The only universal to be found is the mother-son object and aim taboo. The effect of this taboo on the individual depends on whether other sexual activity is permitted or not. This variability is disregarded by Freud, Reik, and Roheim. In Marquesan society we had an instance where sexual gratification for the child is plentiful, but where tenderness and maternal affection are lacking. The result on the folklore was striking.

The application of the instinct theory to sociology had consequences of a different order; it clearly demonstrated the difficulties created by transplanting the Haeckelian ideas into psychology and sociology. In this theory the basic concepts were founded on the character of the ontogenetic development of

[16] See B. W. Aginsky, *Kinship Systems and the Forms of Marriage*, American Anthropological Association, Memoirs, No. 45 (1935).

the sexual instincts, the partial impulses and the stages characteristic of them, oral, anal, phallic, genital. The sum total bearing on this development was included under the general heading of the "Libido Theory." In addition there was the important adjunct contained in the concept of "narcissism." These concepts were derived from the study of the ontogenesis of the individual. The observations on which the libido theory was based are easily verifiable and are as true today as they were when Freud originally noted them. The libido theory was a method of coördinating these observations into a purposeful and consistent whole under a biological scheme. The question, therefore, is whether or not this theory most effectively deals with all the associated facts, and not whether the observations on which the theory was based are constant and verifiable. However useful this theory was in accounting for certain consistent phenomena in the individual, its application to sociology created a great deal of confusion. It must be mentioned that Freud himself used these concepts of the libido theory very sparingly in his sociology; several of his followers exploited them more extensively.

In essence this application to sociology was predicated on an evolutionary viewpoint based on the parallelism with ontogenesis. The ontogenetic scheme, however, took in only a small segment of the individual, his sexual development, described in erogenous zone dominances. The development of the ego was hardly touched on, and this proved to be a serious omission. The early attempt of Ferenczi to study the ontogenesis of the ego, *The Ontogenesis of the Sense of Reality*, was overshadowed by the concept of narcissism, though Freud was keenly aware of this study of the ego as a necessary complement of the libido theory. He states,[17] "We know that a full understanding of any neurotic predisposition from the developmental point of view is never complete without taking into account not merely the stage of libido development at which fixation occurs,

---

[17] Freud, *Collected Papers*, Vol. II: *The Predisposition to Obsessional Neurosis* (London, 1913), p. 131.

but also the stage of ego development. Our concern has been confined to libido development and consequently does not afford all the information we are entitled to expect." He then refers to Ferenczi's work on the development of the sense of reality. Freud was well aware of the dangers of exploiting only the sexual phase of development. He moreover saw the indications for supplementing this knowledge as far back as 1913. He did not expect however that including ego development would necessitate a recasting of the entire libido theory. At all events, the net result of the use of the libido theory in sociology was that certain phases of primitive culture had to be ascribed to narcissism, others to oral, anal, phallic, and sadistic components. Animism was thus equated with narcissism.[18] Still greater difficulties were encountered in attempting to arrive at the libidinous formula which each culture was assumed to have. Egyptian culture was thus "phallic" (Roheim) ; modern bourgeois society was by common consent "anal sadistic"; religion became "a compulsion neurosis of the group" (Reik).

Let us consider for a moment, in the hope of getting some new knowledge concealed in this statement, a culture whose "libidinous formula" is based on anal erotism. What is anal erotism, and what characteristics of modern society are supposed to be derived from that source? With regard to the first question, we immediately strike confusion. Anal erotism is the pleasure associated with the anal zone. But this zone also has a utility function; it is the organ of evacuation. The expulsive and retentive functions of this zone (Abraham, Alexander) can be used to express attitudes of the ego. No one can deny that the anal zone can become a pleasure zone. Which of these features, the ego attitude or the pleasure element, is instrumental in forming the so-called anal character? In 1908 Freud noted what this character was: orderliness, stinginess, obstinacy; but the manner in which these character traits are derived from the erotism—the organ pleasure—has never been described. It

[18] G. Roheim, *Animism, Magic, and the Divine King* (New York, 1930), p. vi.

is quite remarkable that there seems to be no logical relationship among these various characteristics. Orderliness cannot be understood as a reaction formation against the pleasure associated with anal activity as organ-pleasure (*Organlust*). There is no discipline known to man that does or can interfere with this pleasure when it exists. The activity can never be stopped, and the pleasure, if any, is a factor in which society cannot have any stake. Why should the erotism be destroyed if conditions are established for place, time, or affect associated with its exercise? Then the reaction formation is not necessarily against the pleasure. But if we introduce a sociological factor, its meaning becomes clear. Sphincter control has a socially useful goal, cleanliness. We need not raise the issue of why this is so. It is taught to children by rigid discipline, and with it is associated the idea that the function is to be performed in a special place (and perhaps time and quantity), to the end of an objective not yet appreciated by the child. Orderliness, therefore, ceases to be a reaction formation against an erotism, but a complete compliance with a parental or social demand or discipline. Obstinacy is a refractory attitude to the same demand. Once such conditions become established, with or without the compliance of the child, then the pleasure element may become involved. There are types of anal discipline which do tend to enhance the erotic value of the anal zone; the frequent use of enemas, and observation of the quantity of feces as a general indicator of health make this the zone through which parental care and solicitude become known to the child. Stinginess, on the other hand, if related in any way to anal activity, is derived from the retentive functions. But there is a great variation in the number of things that can be thus "retained"; it may be aggression or it may be food; retention represents, therefore, an anxiety at a loss of something valuable. An endless series of ideas and feelings can be expressed by retention without reference to any erotism.

By introducing the concept of "reaction to discipline" to

describe the ego attitude, we have a concept that is usable equally for study of the individual and of society.[19] For sociology it gives us a comparative unit. By means of it we can answer the questions: What disciplines does a given society impose? How are they imposed? And what effects do they have on the individual? Discipline always interferes with previously existing adaptations and impairs the independence of the individual. To this imposition the individual can react in a variety of ways; for example, he can take a definite ego attitude, such as defiance or compliance. Discipline may also have various effects on organs of the individual if it is directed toward the activity of the organ. Discipline also channels out new types of gratification to the individual; but these are the result of secondary elaborations, e.g., spanking, as an erotic pattern. These considerations separate the two problems of the forces and pressures to which the individual is subjected through institutions, a sociological problem; and the effect of these disciplines on the individual in modifying his reaction types, an individual problem.

In other words, the libido theory as a tool for sociology failed because it attempted to characterize social forces by reference to a somatic pleasure source in the individual, and hence could not establish a base for the comparison of institutions. The problem, therefore, is not the truth or falsity of the libido theory, but whether the data it purports to treat can be verified in both the individual and society with the working ideas supplied by the libido theory. The answer is, decidedly, it cannot.

One final point in the sociological procedure of Freud, Reik, and Roheim is the explanation of certain crises in human affairs as attributable to the autochthonous recurrence of a sense of guilt. This is, of course, a part of the theory of primal parricide. It is a mystical hypothesis that is not convertible into a sociological technique.

---

[19] In clinical practice it would naturally make a great deal of difference whether one interprets anal phenomena from the point of view of an erogenous zone or of a reaction, compliant or refractory, to discipline.

The difficulties we have so far reviewed in Freud's social psychology all proceed from his evolutionary orientation and from the libido theory, which was the ontogenetic counterpart of phylogeny.

In his *Group Psychology* he made a more deliberate attempt to study, with the aid of the libido theory, the relations of individuals within groups.

First of all, the "groups" of which Freud speaks in this book are not prototypes of society as a whole. The army and the church are both non-familial hierarchies. They are organizations within a larger society and are made up exclusively of men. The women in the church are likewise removed from society as sexual objects. Such groups can exist only within the larger society, and conclusions drawn from them do not represent the forces operating in a society in which subsistence, sexual gratification, care of the young, etc., play such a prominent role. This does not deprive them of the right to be considered types of social order. The question is only whether their dynamics are typical of society as a whole.[20]

The army and church are not occupied with subsistence problems, and sexual rivalries are not part of the life of the soldier with his colleagues. The relationship of soldiers to leader can be taken as a prototype of only a few types of social relationship, even though one can agree with what Freud says about it. Here we must point out that the word "libido" cannot fully describe all the processes that operate between soldier and leader. "Libido" does not describe the attitude of dependency, nor does it describe the expectations that go with this "love" that binds them. These expectations are obviously not of a sexual character. If we say that it is "desexualized," it still does not describe the attitudes and expectations of this dependency, which may be protection, food, shelter, or even booty.

The reflections contained in Freud's book (*Group Psychology*) on the primal horde are of no more use than they were in *Totem and Taboo*, and it is difficult to see how the dynamics

[20] See also Fromm, *Autorität und Familie* (Paris, 1936), pp. 77–80.

of a hypothetical society can be used as a check against an actual one, since this society is by Freud's own words (p. 112) a "scientific myth."

But there is a second and more important source of confusion in this second sociological work proceeding from the use of certain words to describe clinical facts. It raises again the issue we found earlier in the relation between constructs and direct experience, and whether or not the construct really describes the direct experience. Let us note the following statement (p. 60) : "At the same time as this identification with the father, the boy began to develop a true object-cathexis toward the mother according to the anaclitic type" (*Anlehnungstypus*). This statement describes a complicated series of attitudes in the language of constructs. Let us dissect them, and try if possible to translate them into direct experience. The word *Besetzung* translated as "cathexis" is a term descriptive, from the point of view of the observer, of the experience "love" of the boy for his mother; but the word "cathexis" describes direction and energy charge both. It goes from subject to object. It is not the form of the direct experience; it is only a manner of speaking. Now an "object cathexis of an anaclitic type" does not describe accurately what it means to convey. By an "anaclitic" object, Freud means an object on whom the subject is dependent, i.e., an object of whom the subject expects that it will act as mediator for all difficulties in the outer world. Then what Freud really means to convey is that the subject has a sexual and a dependent attitude toward the same object. Toward the father, then, the attitude in terms of direct experience is dependency and hostility. We have not heard much about dependency in psychoanalytic literature as an ego attitude worthy of mention, yet we have discovered that it was concealed in the formula "anaclitic object choice." What then do we have in the Oedipus complex? We have a sexual love developing toward an object on which the child is dependent. Do these attitudes, love and dependency, have a biological common source, or, whether the source be biological or not, do sociological factors have something to do with shaping them? The answer to this must come from clinical evidence, and not from guessing. The only way to prove the point is to observe societies where dependency and sexual attitudes do not have the opportunity to be concentrated on the same object. There are such societies. In Trobriand and Marquesan societies we found such types of social organization. In Marquesan culture we found that dependent attitudes are divorced from erotic ones by social conditions, the child having in this society every opportunity for sexual attitudes toward other objects apart from the mother, who is inaccessible in this culture anyhow. But this contention could be definitely established only by studying the individual in these societies with the same criteria we use in our own culture.

We see, therefore, that the formula "object love according to anaclitic type" attempts to describe a complicated situation from the point of view of, and in the language of, what is happening to the "instinct," and an "instinct" has an aim and an object. It is not merely a question of language; this formulation does not describe the relationship of dependency.

Let us consider the basic idea of "libido" which Freud uses as the unit through which all social ties are to be understood. He uses three chief modalities: (1) the object may be oneself or another; (2) the libido can be "aim inhibited"; (3) it can be sublimated. The second of these, "aim inhibited" libido, raises the question, how is libido "desexualized" to emerge as friendship? What faculty of man performs this function? Is this again a manner of speaking, fulfilling a verbal requirement; or is it describing a dynamic process? Can we supply an illustration of the reverse process, an instance in which "desexualized libido" becomes sexualized? Indeed, there are innumerable instances in psychopathology that fulfill this condition. The most notable of these is "unconscious homosexuality" in the male. But that is not what the theory maintains; it takes the position that in unconscious homosexuality the high tension is of a homosexual nature; it is repressed and its manifestations hidden. In a dream of symptom it reasserts itself. This explanation does not reckon with the role of "defense" in creating these phenomena, nor does it reckon with dependency in creating the change in sexual objective. The concept "homosexuality" is treated as a substitute gratification and not as a type of defense.

What relevance has all this discussion to the basic problem in group psychology raised by Freud? It is important to understand what he means when he speaks of the relation of groups to leaders, and the relation of individuals to one another. It is important to decide whether these concepts satisfy the observations or whether they need to be supplemented by an understanding of ego attitudes, like dependency, and to see whether we can then utilize them to the better understanding of social phenomena. "Desexualized libido" is a concept we could use only if we knew of the mental functions that thus desexualize the libido, and could specifically identify the expectations that lie in back of this change. The expectations from the goal of dependency are very different from those which proceed from sexual love. The fact is that we do not know of any desexualizing agent. We have, therefore, only one alternative left; to investigate all possible factors that are thus condensed in the constructs of the libido theory. This we shall do in a later section.

There is one further issue in group psychology which Freud elaborated upon in *The Ego and the Id*. In this work Freud described the systematic arrangement within the personality.

This work is not intelligible unless we appreciate a few signal facts in the history of psychoanalytic theory. The theory was developed in response to clinical needs, and was relatively slow in growth. It is therefore natural to assume that many ideas used out of necessity in the beginning had later to be replaced by better ones. Such revisions were frequent and are still going on. But it often happens that retractions occur in Freud's later writings without his specifying those they replace. It is, however, true that the instinct theory remained the cornerstone of the entire system. Most of the mechanisms used by Freud to describe dynamics owe their origin to the vicissitudes of instinct that he was able to trace.

The division of the personality into ego, id, and super-ego was a product of the concept of repression. This fact is not only freely admitted by Freud, but he has repeatedly cautioned against the use of repression as a general yardstick for evaluating all of dynamics. In other words, the metapsychology is an attempt to formulate dynamics and structure of the total personality from what can be seen through the phenomena of repression. This was no arbitrary step on Freud's part, but was predicated by the nature of hysterical phenomena, in the creation of which repression plays such a prominent role.

We mentioned a few paragraphs above some of the advantages of describing psychic phenomena in terms of "instinct"; this procedure, however, brought with it many disadvantages. In his orientation on instinct, Freud left little room for the operation of societal influences. These we mentioned in connection with anal erotism as specific disciplines. The whole series of phenomena are considered by Freud manifestations of the anal erotism, and not a reaction to discipline.

In the metapsychology we find a similar difficulty. Freud has sufficiently indicated that the super-ego is a product of discipline; yet in the actual treatment of this concept the super-ego emerges as a compartment of the mind, a mental function which has severed its connection with the social environment. One can speak of super-ego as a construct; but in direct experience "super-ego" is merely the manipulation of habitual methods, established by discipline, of preserving certain infantile interests with respect to another individual or society as a whole. If we see the super-ego as a mental function, we tend to lose sight of the fact that it represents a habitual and automatic method of reacting to other individuals to the end of being loved or of escaping punishment. Here the distinction between normal and neurotic super-ego must be drawn. (See p. 73.)

The "id" is treated as the reservoir out of which the ego

develops from its contact with the outer world. However, clinically it is difficult to identify the impulse repressed, because this occurs in the form of, and mixed up with, a systematic defense. It is hard to tell which is which. A clinical illustration might clarify this point. On a given anxiety-provoking occasion, a patient dreams a "passive homosexual" dream. What, then, is the impulse in the "id"? Is the homosexuality the repressed impulse, or is it part of a complicated defense? It makes a great practical difference which interpretation one takes.

In the metapsychology, as one would expect, the "ego" is the least adequately developed. But this is a defect which ought to be remedied if the clinical need for it is demonstrated. This will be taken up in detail in a later section.

In *The Future of an Illusion* there is a distinct change in Freud's orientation. He there retracts some of the implications of *Totem and Taboo,* and states that these views hold only for totemism but not for religion. The latter Freud now derives from the dependent relations of child to parent. However, he stops short of pursuing this relationship to its logical conclusion. Fully recognizing the important role of the helplessness of the child, Freud does not follow its influence on the acceptance of disciplines, but continues to view the relationships of child and parent from the point of view of sexual object and aim. The child loves an object on whom he can be dependent, and this is evidently one of the chief factors in the creation of the Oedipus complex, ontogenetically considered. Much is to be gained in separating sexual needs for support from dependency, even though in our culture children concentrate these dependent and sexual attitudes on parents. At all events, in this work Freud definitely points to an abandonment of the evolutionary hypothesis on the one hand, although, formally, he retains it. "Religious ideas," says Freud in this work (p. 34) "have gone through a long process of evolution and in various cultures have become arrested at different phases." The recapitulation theory is reaffirmed (pp. 75-76).

In his later sociological work, Freud turns away from the pursuit of the relations of child and parent on the basis of dependency, and returns to the elaboration of his instinct theory of sociology. In this work he still insists that character is derived from the "absorption of instincts." Though he admits that no explanation of this process is possible, he recognizes that (in the case of anal character traits) cultural demands have something to do with their origin. Freud glosses over this fact that cultural demands have an influence in creating character, but stresses the "similarity between the processes of cultural development and that of the libidinal development in an individual" (p. 62). This is another way of saying that it is not of much importance that parents train, discipline, threaten, or reward children into acquiescing to sphincter control, and that the child may react to this discipline in a variety of ways; but that it is of great importance that phylogeny and ontogeny run parallel; that is, that the repression of anality in the individual runs parallel to the phylogenetic repression. This is an excellent illustration of how this dependency on the phylogenetic-ontogenetic parallelism interfered with Freud's perception of the social realities behind the phenomena he was observing from the point of view of "instinct." In the case of the sexual instincts, their suppression compels desexualization and hence sublimations, identifications, and friendships.

The chief interest in this work is in Freud's treatment of the "aggressive instincts." He states that mutual aggression is the most powerful obstacle to culture, but sees in aggression an autochthonous death instinct in opposition to the life instincts. This is another case in which Freud ignores the effects of institutions or reality situations in increasing or diminishing intrasocial hostilities, and in which he gives no criteria for diagnosing the causes of what appears phenomenologically to be an increase or a diminution of intrasocial aggression.

This treatment of aggression is one nodal point in Freud's sociology at which the instinct theory came to its logical conclusion. In applying a complicated construct like "instinct" to the phenomena of aggression one cannot avoid the inevitable impasse created by the clash between the logical demands of a theory and persistent clinical facts. Beginning with a high degree of specificity for the sexual instincts and their somatic executives, Freud predicated the "ego instincts" as a necessary hypothesis to account for self-preservation as their goal. The original dichotomy between the two was resolved when Freud called both sexual instincts and ego instincts (which were never described or clinically identified) manifestations of life instincts (Eros) in contrast to the death instinct.

In 1913 Freud credited Ferenczi with an attempt to identify these ego instincts; what Ferenczi was describing were certain attitudes and perceptions of oneself, the outer world and objects, but surely not "instincts."

It is important to review the data on which Freud based his theory of death instincts. These are first, repetitive phenomena in traumatic neuroses which he could not reconcile with the pleasure principles and hence put "beyond" this principle; secondly, the fact that when there were interferences with the satisfaction of established pleasure channels, he observed persistent sadistic or aggressive manifestations. He therefore concluded that in the normal pleasure function there was a *fusion* between erotic and aggressive (or destructive) components. Interference with the pleasure objective, by inhibition or force, leads thus to a *defusion* of erotic and destructive components. These clinical facts can be easily verified. But to attribute these aggressive or destructive phenomena to the activity of a "death instinct" satisfied only the biological assumptions on which the theory was based. It was equally effective in shunting attention away from the sociological forces which provoke or accentuate these destructive tendencies in man. The conflict between life and death instincts hermetically sealed the fate of the individual against social realities, as did the theory of primal parricide against the influence of man's subjection to social disciplines. The combination of instinct psychology and the derivations of the ego structure from the phenomena of repression ended in the necessity to designate the locus of conflict to the inner structural elements of the mental apparatus and thus to shut out the influence of an inhospitable outer world. The outer world and the difficulties created by social organization were thus exonerated of their share in human suffering, and the blame was placed squarely on the shoulders of the biologically determined need for pain.

The point of view embodied in the instinct theory is inconsistent with another tendency of Freud to include social forces in the formation of the super-ego, and to admit that man obeys discipline because of his helplessness and dependency on his protectors. These latter views, although couched in the language of metapsychology, opened up a new class of clinical data identifiable in the study of social phenomena. However, the relation between the death instincts and the social conditions which create an increase in destructiveness cannot be clinically established. One must believe either that the destructiveness must be identified in forces unleashed by external realities which confront man, or that it is unrelated to realities and determined by an autochthonous death instinct. The first view can be clinically verifiable, the second cannot. The first view can be established either by the study of comparative sociology, or by a historical study of the same society. The second must remain a matter of belief.

The remaining matters dealing with the aggression of the super-ego are reducible to the effects of social disciplines on the dependent individual.

To some degree we have, in the discussion of Marquesan and Tanala societies, attempted to answer the questions raised by Freud concerning both the source of intrasocial hostility or destructiveness and the increasing severity of the super-ego. We have found that the entire instinct orientation was unnecessary. In Marquesas we found hostile and masochistic attitudes directed against the woman, who frustrated tender feelings more than she did sensual ones. In Tanala-Betsileo culture it was clearly demonstrated that both aggressive and masochistic forms of destructiveness (spirit possession and the use of malevolent magic) increased when there was a scarcity created in subsistence opportunities; prior to this time the compensations for suppression of aggression were adequate to hold this mutual aggression in check. Once these compensations were removed in the form of tangible satisfactions, the aggression broke its encapsulated bounds. This precludes the necessity for any hypothesis about autochthonous death instincts. In this same Betsileo society we observed that these same forces created a more "severe" super-ego, in the sense that the necessity for curbing aggression was more frequent than in Tanala, and that the activity of the super-ego showed itself in the increase in belief in omens, superstitions, and retaliation fears, and also gave rise to fears of success.

We can say, therefore, of Freud's sociology that the only features which do not work out in actual practice are those based on the instinct theory and those derived from parallelism between phylogeny and ontogeny. He comes close to discarding the latter at several points in his sociology; but ends by including with the old, a new orientation, which he does not develop and which is inconsistent with the old. All these factors conspired to prevent Freud from examining current social realities, and from reconstructing the reactions of man to his effective social environment.

OTHER PSYCHOANALYTIC APPLICATIONS

The two main points of criticism of Freud's social psychology have been variously treated by different followers of Freud. Theodore Reik's work endorsed the entire Freudian standpoint without modification. For many years, that of Géza Roheim did the same thing. More recently, however, Roheim[21] has attempted a compromise between the pure Freudian position and one which diminishes the importance of phylogeny while increasing the importance of ontogeny, which means, essentially, taking into account the actual life situations of the individual.

[21] *The Riddle of the Sphinx* (London, 1937).

The phylogenetic orientation of Freud has long since been discarded by the other social sciences[22] as false and misleading. A new orientation based on the study of cultures as functioning units finds its best expression in Malinowski, Ruth Benedict,[23] and Ralph Linton.[24] From the psychoanalytic side such a revised orientation came from the introduction of the methods of historical materialism into psychoanalytic sociology. This was most effectively done by Erich Fromm[25] and Wilhelm Reich.[26] This orientation has been strongly endorsed by others, notably, K. Horney[27] and F. Alexander.[28]

Fromm's work was the first and most important of the series. It initiated a wholesome criticism of the analogical procedures in Reik's method (which was essentially Freud's) and pointed the way to a more realistic appreciation of the influence of environmental and sociological external realities on culture. This procedure was tantamount to the abandonment of the evolutionary hypothesis. The theory of instincts was retained by Fromm in several papers,[29] but later treated in a somewhat different manner. Fromm's specific illustration is the origin, growth, and change of Christian dogma during the early centuries. He denies the periodic recrudescence of autochthonous guilt feeling as responsible for religious crises in history, but seeks to derive these from specific difficulties in the environment. "Not ideologies make the man, but man, the ideolo-

---

[22] For criticism of this viewpoint see A. Goldenweiser, *History, Psychology and Culture* (New York, 1933), pp. 124–143. See also the works of Boas, Otto Klineberg, Benedict, Sapir, Kroeber, Radcliffe-Brown, F. H. Allport, L. Morgan, Gardner Murphy.

[23] Ruth Benedict, *Patterns of Culture* (Boston, 1934).

[24] Ralph Linton, *The Study of Man* (New York, 1936).

[25] Erich Fromm, "Die Entwicklung des Christusdogmas," *Imago* (1930) and *Autorität und Familie* (Paris, 1936).

[26] Wilhelm Reich, *Der Einbruch der Sexualmoral* (Berlin, 1932).

[27] K. Horney, *The Neurotic Personality of our Time* (New York, 1937).

[28] F. Alexander, "Psychoanalysis and Social Disorganization," *American Journal of Sociology* (May, 1937), Vol. XLII.

[29] Erich Fromm, "Über Methode und Aufgabe einer Analytischen Sozialpsychologie; Die Psychoanalytische Characterologie und ihre Bedeutung für die Sozialpsychologie," *Zeitschrift für Sozialforschung*, I (1932), 28–54, 253–277.

gies,"[30] and these are the product of specific conflicts on a particular group of people.

He demonstrates that when Christianity was the expression of an oppressed people its dogmas voiced the emotional needs of the oppressed; for example, the wish to be in the place of their persecutors. The dogma expressed the idea thus: Man becomes God. When Christianity became the religion of the ruling class, the dogma changed accordingly. It now reads: God was always God, and man can never become God. Moreover, the rewards of suffering are to be collected after death, thus facilitating the acceptance of suffering, and in fact, making of it a claim to eternal bliss after death. In later centuries God and his son Jesus give way to the Madonna cult, which is accounted for on the basis of corresponding social and economic changes.

Irrespective of the merits of Fromm's specific explanations, the orientation and methodology are more satisfying and workable than the evolutionary schematization. In an unpublished paper, the author traced the origin and development of the cult of Osiris in ancient Egypt, and can bring the demonstration to bear in support of Fromm's hypothesis. Moreover, recent workers in anthropology and sociology, whether unacquainted or acquainted with the methods of historical materialism or of psychoanalysis, confirm the point of view that one must work with cultures as units and derive their religion and ideologies from actual life situations,[31] irrespective of diffusion.

Thus, many orientations in psychoanalysis and anthropology are tending toward a similar goal; the question of technique and working concepts becomes, therefore, all the more urgent. The errors of the evolutionary hypothesis and the unclarities in the theory of instincts do not invalidate the psychoanalytic method. The data included and treated under the rubric of "instinct" can be restated and subdivided. After these diffi-

[30] Fromm, "Die Entwicklung des Christusdogmas," *Imago* (1930), p. 367.
[31] Benedict, Linton, Malinowski, et al.

culties are cleared the powerful tools of psychoanalysis must be reassembled for a fresh trial.

CONCLUSION

Freud brought to social psychology the most powerful analytic instruments yet devised. However, in the particular way in which he used them, the greatest emphasis fell in the direction of buttressing the weakest and least tenable aspects of the entire theoretical framework.

There are two aspects of Freud's defense of his recapitulation theory—for that is what it essentially is—that must be emphasized, the first a scientific one, the second a "moral" issue.

There is no clarity in Freud's clinical treatment of biological as against sociological factors. Having been one of the first psychologists to discover and describe with infinite care the reactions of the child to environmental influences, Freud insists in laboring the point that repressions and the material repressed are phylogenetically predetermined. Further research in social psychology along Freud's chosen direction became impossible, and it became the task of the investigator merely to confirm the established thesis. Freud's own research was decidedly along these lines, as witnessed by his latest sociological work.[32] In this work he still maintains that (p. 89) "religious phenomena are to be understood only on the model of neurotic symptoms." This statement can be used as a guide without the other weak assumption "that in the history of the human species something happened similar to the events in the life of the individual." (p. 126) And furthermore, he still insists that in the history of the race the processes are the same as those which take place in the individual according to the scheme "early trauma—defense—latency—outbreak of neurosis—partial return of the repressed material" (p. 126).

We cannot agree with Freud that this scheme is his most noteworthy contribution to sociology. No matter what defects the theoretical superstructure may have, Freud gave us a

[32] *Moses and Monotheism* (Tr. by Katharine Jones; New York, 1939).

method for identifying the reactions of man to the actualities of life, and for following their integration and continuity in the personality. This is his enduring achievement.

We must furthermore note that in 1926–27 Freud produced two works, one clinical (*The Problem of Anxiety*) and the other sociological (*The Future of an Illusion*), in which he introduced a new orientation applicable to both the theory of the neuroses and to sociology, an orientation which Freud himself did not develop because of the incompatibilities it created with the preëxisting theory. It is this new and undeveloped orientation of Freud which we have tried to exploit in this work.

The second issue which Freud's sociology raises is what may be called, by a stretch of meaning, a "moral" issue. Freud's sociology is fatalistic; it conveys a message of hopelessness and resignation to a fate predetermined in the past, which man cannot undo. This view is at complete variance with another message inherent in all of Freud's work, that through knowledge man can control his own fate, both as an individual and as a member of society.

We can attempt to resolve the theoretical dilemma in Freud's sociology in the following manner: to demarcate sharply the phylogenetic from the sociological. The capacity for repression is phylogenetic; it is a characteristic of man and of all animals capable of modifying their reactions in the face of failure or insuperable obstacles. The circumstances under which this dynamism of repression is brought into play depends on sociological factors, i.e., upon cultural institutions. The consequences of repression are of a different order. These are determined in part by the previous history of the individual. Regression, which is orderly and systematic, may be one of the consequences, and may in part have the function of substituting for the lost gratification. The consequences of repression or of frustrations in which no orderly retreat is possible, may be in the nature of phylogenetically determined reactions, as is the collapse of neurotic rats,[33] or complete disorganization of the ego in severe traumatic neuroses. But for the greater part regressions follow an ontogenetic path.

This plan gives us a clear range of vision on the effects of institutions on man, especially if they are studied in the order in which they occur to the individual, and note their compatibility with the normal processes of growth, and with the gradual increase in resources of the individual coincident with this process. This plan opens the danger of "sociologizing" in place of the previous "physiologizing;" but in the process we may learn enough to approximate the proportions that they have in nature.

[33] N. R. F. Maier, *Studies in Abnormal Behavior of the Rat* (New York, 1939).

Chapter X

PSYCHOLOGICAL PRINCIPLES AND
TECHNIQUE

THE social psychology of Freud was an application of his
theory of the neuroses: both took as their base-line the
instinctual endowment of man. Freud attributed many factors
in the ontogenesis of the sexual instinct of man to a parallelism
with phylogeny.[1] He did not, however, apply his conception
of the unitary character of the sexual instincts, generally
covered by the term *libido,* to his sociology until after he had
reduced the sexual and "ego" instincts into the single category
of *life instincts,* and had conceived of the *death instincts* as a
counterbalance. From this point of view he attemped to account
for the phenomena of aggression in social life as due to a
primary instinct, which in turn is only a manifestation of the
death instinct. As we have seen, this orientation militated
against the study of the actual environment and institutions as
agencies which created those phenomena regarded by Freud as
stages in the ontogenetic development of man.

In working with the individual in our culture Freud made
some assumptions about the universality of man's reaction types
which he attributed to "instincts" and not to the interaction of
institutions and human needs. He never expected that he might
be obliged to make comparisons between different types of
institutions, because the evolutionary hypothesis precluded the
necessity for any such comparison. He made some assumptions

---

[1] Thus the latency period in man is explained: "We believe that something
momentous to the destinies of the human species must have taken place which
has left behind as an historical precipitate this interruption of sexual development." *The Problem of Anxiety* (translated by H. A. Bunker, New York, 1935),
p. 131.

about the basic personality structure of man; but on the basis of the apparent universality of the Oedipus complex he assumed that special institutional conditions had no bearing on its formation. Hence he was able to make the Oedipus situation nuclear in social structure and to regard institutions as products of the central struggle against incest.

If we were to take this orientation as our starting point in Marquesan culture we would find ourselves at a serious loss. In some of the tales recorded, there is by implication something that can be interpreted as a very distorted Oedipus complex. The tale of the multiple births in which "the power of the god is so great" as to compel the mother to procreate may be interpreted as a mother-son incest fantasy. In the Teemooniew story the female's resistance to intercourse and her threats can be used as evidence of the female castration complex. However, it is difficult to see how one can proceed from this point to elaborate the interconnections between the institutions recorded. It is, moreover, a moot question why the Marquesans should make such a secret of the mother-son incest stories and talk with impunity about father-daughter incest. From the strict Freudian point of view in sociology one would either be obliged to disregard this culture, to consider the account hopelessly incomplete as recorded, or to be content with characterizing this culture as "oral sadistic."

In Tanala culture we are a bit more fortunate. In this culture one can make a phenomenological correlation between "anal erotism" (caused by the premature insistence on sphincter control) and the inordinately high value on property and especially on metallic gold, which, however, only chiefs can handle. There we also encountered an overt Oedipus complex in the folklore; but the specific form which it took left no doubt that the Oedipus complex was a derivative of a special set of conditions. It is, therefore, no accident that the Oedipus complex is absent in the Marquesas because the social organization which created it in Tanala was absent in the other culture.

In short, the attempt to apply Freud's conception of the individual in our culture to the study of primitive society met with failure because of the absence of an institutional picture of our culture. We have therefore attempted to standardize the findings of psychoanalysis against an institutional picture of our culture. This we did by identifying specific institutions in our culture, studying the range of reactions of the individual to them, and charting the psychic constellations created by them. This is another way of stating that we attempted to establish a direct connection between conscious (reality) systems and the unconscious.

However, when we came to the study of actual aboriginal cultures we had no individuals to deal with, but only a formal description of institutions and some products of fantasy embodied in folk tales. Moreover, with the exception of Tanala-Betsileo culture, we had no opportunity to picture these institutions in action. We had therefore to do most of the dynamic reconstructions from the relation of institutions to each other, with the aid of a few assumptions about the universality of the reactions of humans to frustrations of basic needs like hunger and sex.

This technique, as employed in the two cultures described, is liable to certain errors, which it might be well to examine.

Instead of using the general concept of "human nature"—which implies essentially, that the basic personality structure of man is universally the same everywhere, as witnessed by the assumed universality of the Oedipus complex—we used the concept of basic personality or ego structure as the precipitate of the reactions of the individual to specific institutions in the order in which they affect him. This concept is open to question, as is the method of deriving it from institutions.

In deriving the concept from reactions to institutions we begin to pay the penalty for the general term "institution." In any culture the institution only prescribes the general mold of behavior, which each individual uses in a highly specific manner. Hence the impression and effect created by any institution will vary according to the specific manner in which it is conveyed, according to the "character" of the parent, and according to the disposition of the individual upon whom it is imposed. However, we were obliged to assume that the institution, no matter how conveyed, must create a definite effect. How many ways is it possible to induct sphincter control in an infant from three to six months old? How many ways is it possible to place certain restrictions on sexual activity without creating a definite effect on the personality? There is really no escape. If by some chance direct threats or prohibitions are avoided in childhood, implied disciplines have the same effect. If the child is not apprised of sexual mores in his own home, he encounters them in the outside world. If he is forbidden sexual activity and exercises sexuality in secret, this factor of secrecy and social disapproval eventually catches up with him, sooner or later. The effects of these various devices on the individual will vary quantitatively; but the character of the reaction will be the same in all.

The concept *basic personality structure* is not a limited or exact one; it merely indicates that within the limitations prescribed by institutions, the individual is obliged to react in one way or another, and whatever the outcome in the form of *individual character,* the institutional background is the axis on which various individual polarities revolve. This is another way of saying that human beings are sufficiently alike so that if you put a hundred of them in a room and elevate the temperature to 105° F., they will all be hot; but that does not imply that they will all react in the same way to the heat, or that they all have a common heat regulating apparatus.

That basic personality structure varies in different societies is a matter of common agreement. In principle, Benedict[2] and Mead[3] have given much evidence in support of this idea. Mead's contrast between Arapesh and Mundugumore culture is eloquent testimony to the lasting influence of the various

[2] Ruth Benedict, *Patterns of Culture* (Boston, 1934).
[3] Margaret Mead, *Sex and Temperament* (New York, 1935).

forms of environment and discipline on basic personality (ego) structure.

Whereas the phenomenology of this basic personality or ego structure can be confirmed by common sense, the derivation of this concept from institutions, and the secondary effects attributed to its action on the individual and on the culture as a whole, is a part of the methodology which is most likely to be questioned.

The principles on which this method was based are of extreme importance both to psychology and sociology. The difficulties of presenting these principles are very great. The account given below is only a general indication of the direction to be followed; the precision and actual codification must wait for more experimentation and research.

Culture and Neurosis

Many of the constellations used in the reconstruction of Marquesan and Tanala cultures were based on the pathology of neuroses. This immediately raises the issue of the failure to distinguish between *normal* and *abnormal,* and the possible errors involved.

Normal and abnormal (or neurotic), are two types of adaptation to the same situation. There are certain "abnormal" types of adaptation which do depend not on cultural restrictions but on purely personal limitations. The development of the functions of orientation and mastery is never deliberately interfered with in any culture, although some customs, such as tying a child to a cradleboard, may accidentally have this effect. For the greater part, these disciplines are directional, not restrictive. Nevertheless, in our culture failures in successful mastery techniques may terminate in a pathological syndrome such as a persistent tendency to cruelty commonly observed in children.

The case is, however, a bit different in those instances where a cultural discipline is restrictive and actually interferes with a biological need, such as sexual satisfaction in childhood. The outcome of this situation in some individuals is a normal adaptation, which means in effect that no serious disturbances in the manifest comfort of the individual takes place. Another outcome is a disturbance of some kind with or without severe discomfort in connection with sexual or other activities.

It is commonly agreed (Reich, Fromm, Horney, Fenichel et al.) that when a culture persistently interferes with certain basic needs, neurosis results in a considerable number of individuals. This means that normal and neurotic both accommodate to the same situations by different techniques, one of which we arbitrarily call *neurosis*. But it is the neurosis which describes, much more accurately than the former, the institution which is creating the pressure. In producing this neurotic reaction, the offending institution is only one facet of the problem; the other is the equipment with which the individual encounters the institution.

From the study of our culture alone, psychopathology has acquired certain prejudices concerning the nature of the conditions that may create neurosis. The impression persists that sexual frustrations play a major role. This is an overstatement of the case, although there is no doubt about its general truth. The real difficulty arose from the fact that institutions were not supposed to play any role in creating the frustration. But Marquesan society and the neuroses there existing cast some doubt on how precise this formulation about sexual frustrations in our culture is. In the Marquesas no restrictions exist as regards the sensual aspects of sexual gratification; but there are considerable hardships on the score of feminine tenderness. The result is that there are no potency disturbances in either sex; but in the men there is a strong unconscious hatred of the woman, and in the women a strong unsatisfied craving shown in the form of feigned pregnancy. The latter is surely a neurotic manifestation; the former probably not—although it does represent a hostility, which, though safely encapsulated under most circumstances, can easily be mobilized, as we have seen, in the activities of the familiars and *fanaua*. The relation of the latter phenomenon to the scarcity of women is supported by the fact that this institution of *fanaua* is unknown in other Polynesian societies, and that this scarcity of women is likewise unique (Linton).

In short, the problem of culture and neurosis cannot definitely be solved now. Too few comparative studies have been made. A tentative solution is offered in the statement that no culture can exist without disciplines of some kind, and no culture can exist in which life goals and objectives are capable of realization by all the members with an equal degree of fullness. Since neurosis is the result of a personal reaction to a culturally determined situation, only the relative character of the reactions produced by one set of frustrations as against another can be established. It all depends on which particular impulses or needs a discipline operates, and at what time in the development of the individual he is made to feel the influence of these disciplines. One can speak with considerable assurance only about the systematic and complete interference with sexual and food frustrations, and those caused by the necessity to curb aggressive impulses. The more severe these restrictions, the more likely it is that the basic personality structure will be attuned to meet these exigencies. But neurotic or otherwise, all the reaction types must be built about the new problems of adaptation created by contact with these disciplines.

Hence we are not committing a methodological error in diagnosing the sources of these pressures from the reactions of the neurotic individual; because the only definite information we really get from the neurotic that is of use for general application is the location of the institutional factors to which he is reacting. It is at this point that the hypothesis that repressions follow phylogenetic prototypes is most damaging; for instead of examining the environmental factors responsible for repression, we must ignore these influences entirely or attribute to them a secondary or coincidental influence.

The reaction itself, which we call neurotic, can also give us valuable information. In Tanala culture we found a neurotic reaction, *tromba*, the characteristics of which we had no opportunity to examine. But we do know that it is present in the individuals who are in the least favored position socially. However, when this culture changed, we found a great increase in neuroses in the form of spirit possession. This presents a difficult problem. We cannot subscribe to the idea that this increase in aggression is due to some mysterious augmentation in the "death instinct." Nor can we subscribe to the idea that the increase in neurotic disturbance is due exclusively to the change in subsistence-prestige economy. This is only one of the factors. The other factor is that the individual is predisposed, by patriarchal organization and severe disciplines, to a compliant and submissive adaptation. As long as this compliance is successful in satisfying the wants of the individual, neurosis is rare. But when an individual accustomed to expectations of dependency is thrown into a position where he must be more aggressive, then spirit possession is more likely, as well as an increase in overt aggression in the form of malevolent magic. The overt aggression is *normal* under these circumstances; the spirit possession, *neurotic*. But both come from the same source.

The influence of culture on neurosis is therefore a cumulative one from childhood on, and depends on which basic attitudes are encouraged and which restricted in the child, and on the usefulness of these attitudes in the adaptations necessary for the individual later in life.

The important methodological issue as far as this essay is concerned is not in the relation between culture and neurosis, but in the derivation of the constellations common to neurotic and normal alike. This is where the method is open to question, for these constellations were derived from the neurotic individual in our culture.

The procedure is, however, much less of a leap than it seems. It is based on a few assumptions, accepted by most of the social sciences, that the biological needs of man must be the same in every human being irrespective of culture. In this assumption we included that a protector is needed in the early years of life, irrespective of the qualifications established for the effectiveness of the adult; that the process of growth is fairly uniform and that adaptations change with growth; that the methods of perceiving the outer world and of the individual's reactions to it change with growth, but that these changes are systematic and integrative; that reactions to frustration of sexual needs and other bodily needs, if not uniform, run within a certain narrow range; that needs, apart from bodily ones, can be created, stressed or underplayed by cultural forces.

If these assumptions are correct, then we have the license to identify the reactions of whole groups of individuals exposed to the same frustration, as we do those of a single individual to a specific frustration in our culture. On what other ground can we account for the consistently uniform representation of the woman in Marquesan folklore? These myths are the products of the fantasy of some individual, communicated and probably changed many times before we get them. The uniformity of the stories points to some common experience of all individuals in this culture, not remembered from the remote past, but currently experienced.

If this approach is not valid, then we must find some explanation for the fact that folklore is characteristic only of the group which creates it, and even if tales are appropriated by diffusion, they are rapidly changed to conform to the new conditions under which the adapters of the tale live.

In the case of the representation of woman in Marquesan culture, we have the right to see under what conditions such a representation takes origin in any individual in any culture. However, if this scarcity of women is a fixed social condition, then every individual in the group is exposed to some aspect of this scarcity, and it is more than likely that the representation of woman in folklore is a product of this condition.

To explain the reactions to this social situation we drew on our knowledge of psychopathology. We observed that the folklore dealt with the theme of the fear of being eaten up, and that the woman was the object from whom this anxiety proceeded, a fact which struck our attention because it was at such complete variance with actual experience. We were, however, able to identify a whole series of frustrations to which every individual was subjected by the scarcity of women from childhood on throughout the entire life cycle of the individual. Without a knowledge of psychopathology we could not localize the fact that the scarcity of women created any frustration, even though we might surmise it. Psychopathology gave us a bit of specific information; it informed us that certain discomforts were universally present, and that certain needs were not satisfied. The reaction which we used as an indicator of this dissatisfaction, the special representation of women in folklore, we recovered also from neurotic individuals in our culture; but the constellation is used by these neurotic individuals in a manner very different from what we found in Marquesan culture. In neurosis, representations of frustrated needs usually indicate coexisting inhibitions; in cultural constellations they depend on actual or institutional barriers. This trait in Marquesan culture of treating woman with disdain and representing her as a voracious cannibal is in no way a neurotic equivalent to each Marquesan, even though we drew our clue from the reaction of the neurotic. The elaborations of these basic frustrations in neurosis and in a cultural trait are very different. In the neurotic we found that this representation of the mother meant a need for her protecting influence because other resources were inhibited; in Marquesan culture we merely used it as an indicator that the woman actually did cause some frustrations, but these were not associated with inhibitions but with protests and derogation.

Our working tools were therefore assumptions of the universality of biologically determined needs, hunger, sex, and the need for protection. We took as our guides the existence of certain affects and attitudes; the existence of certain executive impulses such as aggression, some manifestations of which were disorganized, others more highly organized; and finally, evidence of the operation of certain attitudinized perceptions, an example of which was that the woman is regarded as an inimical object. This latter was an inference and not direct evidence. We watched for evidence indicating disturbances of potency and for hostility between men or women, and then tried to locate the sources of each.

These were the units we employed, and, moreover, we used them as being constantly interoperating and genetically integrated. We did not use "instinct" as a unit because by this means we could conclude only that the Marquesans were arrested at the oral phase of development, a statement which in this context gives us no information. In other words, instead of "instinct" as a unit we used a psychological constellation made up of needs, impulses, affects, attitudes, and perceptions, all of which coexist and interoperate in some form from the moment of birth on, and are constantly undergoing changes— subject of course to the integrative character of the mental apparatus—throughout the entire life cycle of the individual. These constellations change because the resources, the potentialities for activity, the perceptions, and the psychic preparation for activity, all change with the growth of the individual and in accordance with the external situations which confront him. The fixed forms of the individual's impact with these institutions we called his *character*. And this latter in turn is but a highly individual variant of the *basic personality structure*.

The derivation of these psychological constellations used in the formation of basic personality structure is therefore crucial for our endeavor, and their sources must be traced. For this purpose we might examine some of the reactions to simple frustrations.

REACTIONS TO FRUSTRATION

One of the ways to study the integrative processes of the human mind is to study the basic problems of adaptation with which the individual is confronted. In any culture the individual is bound to encounter: a need which cannot be satisfied; the blocking of an activity essential or intermediate to a gratification; a feeling whose manifestations may not be expressed; or an expectation which cannot be realized. It is desirable to follow out the fate of these vicissitudes, for which the general name of *frustration* is convenient. In following these vicissitudes one must bear in mind that mental processes change with the capacities of the individual to carry out certain objectives, and that these mental processes tend to become integrative. This means that only expedient patterns, or those which are so considered, are utilized for more complicated patterns.

In viewing these reaction types to frustrations, we wish to observe: the immediate reaction; the relation of this reaction to the total resources of the individual; the effects on the personality when it encounters a situation similar to the one in which it failed; the defensive measures mobilized and the degree of their permanence; the manner in which the frustration modifies the individual's perception of his own resources, of the world outside; and finally how all this modifies his total adaptation.

TOTAL DANGER SITUATION

Let us take first a total danger situation in which the resources of the individual are, in comparison with what the situation demands, zero. Such a situation we will find in the soldier on the battlefield in front of an exploding shell. The shell explodes, the soldier is blown to bits, the personality ceases to exist. Or the shell does not explode; nevertheless, the soldier dies. This was a common phenomenon during the war. There was much skepticism about these "fright deaths." A less contestable example is the death of captive birds which die, within a few days after capture, of causes without anatomical basis. Domesticated animals separated from their mates are known to die within a few days. These animals merely behave

PRINCIPLES AND TECHNIQUE 421

in an apathetic way, refuse food, and just die. Dr. Linton told
us of the case of the man who died within three days of violat-
ing a taboo. In our culture the death of aged people shortly
after enforced retirement may be of a similar character.
The mechanism of such a complete collapse of the total personality that death results is poorly understood, but we can
guess the probable path it follows. It is very likely the most
complete form of inhibition of the total resources of the total
personality all at once. The inhibitory forces concealed in the
personality have not been very thoroughly studied, but the
inhibitory reactions of infants show a similar mechanism. The
only reactions of the infant that coincide to these gross inhibitions of functions are those that deal with eating frustrations.
Difficulties in feeding at the breast may end in a refusal to take
the breast, and eventually to an inhibition of all gastro-intestinal functions, and a flight of circulation from periphery to
splanchnic area.[4] This reaction type involves inborn and automatic functions, but clearly describes that the automatic or
reflex reactions will not continue to function if not countered
by success. The mouth and gastro-intestinal tract are the most
completely developed portion of the ego in infancy. It is possible that marasmus is due to such a gross inhibition; but this
is only a hypothesis. We can hardly conclude anything else
when the pathologists report nothing but cessation of function
of pancreas, liver, and gastric and intestinal mucosa, associated
with internal congestion and flight of blood supply from periph-
eral to splanchnic areas. In the case which Dr. Linton reports,
death after breaking a taboo, the response of inhibition to what
the individual considers an insuperable force which he cannot
master must be regarded as an established fact. Nevertheless,
it is true that in most instances the inhibitions most commonly
observed follow more localized forms either in distribution or
in function, and do not jeopardize the entire personality.
This type of reaction is important for the study of sociology,

[4] Margarethe Ribble, "Instinctive Reactions in New-born Babies," *American
Journal of Psychiatry* (July, 1938), pp. 154–155.

for in many primitive societies the efficacy of a taboo is proved by such facts. It proves the great effectiveness of the taboo as a social force. How this happens, we do not yet know; how and why the individual meets the situation with such a complete collapse of the total personality is as yet an unanswerable problem. The reaction is probably in the nature of an inhibition in response to an overwhelming anxiety, and a reaction of avoidance of or withdrawal from a noxious stimulus, in its most extreme form. This is as close as one can get to its meaning.

FEEDING FRUSTRATION IN EARLY INFANCY

Regarding infantile reactions to feeding frustrations, we note that inhibitions are prominent. Theoretically such a reaction is possible only in the first few days of life, before gratifications have been established, and represents an overwhelming of the total personality. But once these gratifications are established, inhibitions are most likely to be preceded by fighting, kicking, crying reactions. In other words, inhibition is likely to be preceded by disorganized or organized aggression of some kind. Nor is this the only reaction type; thumb sucking may be instituted in reactions to certain feeding frustrations.[5] The inhibitory reactions in infancy are theoretically of greatest importance. It is questionable whether one really ought to call these reactions "inhibitions," for no psychic control of any kind is as yet established over these activities, and there is no repression. However, repression is a slow method of effecting something which is automatically effected with great rapidity in some types of reaction. The blindness that occurs after severe shocks is an illustration of this automatic contraction of function. It is most commonly found in traumatic neuroses. The deaths from taboo violations are in all likelihood the same reaction on a greatly extended scale.

[5] See David Levy, "Finger Sucking and Accessory Movements in Early Infancy," *American Journal fo Psychiatry*, VII (1933), 81, and "Experiments on the Sucking Reflex and Social Behavior of Dogs," *American Journal of Orthopsychiatry*, XVIII, 327.

FOOD FRUSTRATIONS IN THE DEVELOPED PERSONALITY

These reactions have been less carefully studied. In child-hood, food frustrations are dependency frustrations, because the technique of procuring food at that time is through the agency of the parent. When the individual is independent, food frustrations produce first a rage, and then apathy and depression, the rationalization differing according to the individual. At this time, since all ego resources fail, the individual is helpless, and early dependency cravings, the wish to have someone take care of him, are revived. We cannot understand this reaction unless we follow the reactions to frustrated dependency cravings. However, chronic forms of hunger anxiety may lead to particular forms of hypochondriasis, which we attempted to describe in connection with Marquesan society.[6]

REACTIONS TO FRUSTRATED CRAVINGS FOR PROTECTION

The need for protection is the most immediate need of the newborn, and it persists in some form for an indefinite time, depending on what the cultural norm for an effective personality happens to be. In childhood these cravings are directed toward the parent. To understand what happens, we must consider the representation of the craving, and the representation of the object from whom it is desired.

When the need is not satisfied the individual may represent himself in dreams or fantasies as helpless, or as failing in every activity he undertakes. The need for support and dependency is commonly represented in dreams by an eating symbol, or a shelter that is crumbling, and the object from whom support is expected as hostile. Even when food is no problem in the individual's life, a very common form of representing this idea is in the fear of having food taken away by some feared insect or animal, or more frankly expressed, a fear of being eaten up.[7]

[6] See p. 219.

[7] It is, however, important to note that in severe compulsion neuroses, where the protection is guaranteed by severe restrictions on the activities of the personality, or in homosexuality, where the dependency is guaranteed by a sexual attitude, these eating symbols are often lacking.

This representation corresponds to the usual transformation into a masochistic equivalent of the original gratification. From the fact that the earliest adaptation of the child is through the sucking reflex, and the mother subsequently becomes the chief support and feeder, it is natural that when the individual feels his resources curtailed, he should represent himself as in childhood, where the sucking was a successful adaptation. It was this fact which led Otto Rank to the conclusion that birth was a traumatic experience and the basic factor in all anxiety reactions, and to regard prenatal bliss as the basic prototype of all pleasure goals. But this does not explain why it should be expressed as a "fear of being eaten up." This is the negative of the original wish, its masochistic version. To understand this, we must go over some ground we have already covered in Chapter II, but add some important considerations.

In order to understand these reactions, we must summarize briefly what we have already said on the subject of dependency. The craving or need for support[8] (an apt phrase used by Rado) is biologically determined; it depends on the fact that the individual's executive tools are incomplete even as to their anatomical basis, and development is possible only with parental aid. The individual begins with a sucking reflex—the first zone at which gratification can be experienced—and an automatically regulated capacity for absorbing and digesting. This is what may metaphorically be called the ego-nucleus. From this point on we must consider personality development. Freud did this with the aid of the concept "instinct," and hence most of the ego development was described under the rubric of the pursuit of instinctual pleasure goals.

To limit ourselves to a study of instinctual pleasure goals leaves no room for consideration of all the steps at which adaptation may fail. The study of inhibition can teach us much about how the various factors in the personality inter-

---

[8] Freud used this conception of dependency first in *The Problem of Anxiety* (New York, 1935), and in *The Future of an Illusion* (London, 1928). They were never developed by him.

operate. Our knowledge today is very incomplete. But one may say in this regard that social life is possible only because there is a wide gap between impulse or drive and behavior, that is, the effector of its satisfaction, because it makes possible the element of social control which eventually becomes automatic. The concept "instinct" draws no distinction between drive and behavior. For the moment, we need not concern ourselves with somatic roots of those drives, though important conclusions eventually depend on the correct conception of the connection between soma and drive. In the case of some drives, this connection seems easy to establish, as in the case of the eating drive. But this directness of the connection is only apparent. The locus of hunger is certainly not in the stomach, although certain sensations in the stomach apprise the individual of the existence of a state of hunger. In short, somatic connections can be established only in the executive organs mobilized to satisfy the craving, although the latter does not necessarily originate in the organ or exclusively in it. But even as regards the organs through which a given drive asserts itself, there is a good deal of difference in the directness of the connection between soma and drive. Even in the case of the sexual drive, this connection is very difficult to establish; in the case of the drive toward mastery or aggression, such somatic connections are lost in vagueness. In the case of a function like vision it is impossible to identify any "instinct" which drives the function, although the executive organ, the eye, is easily identified.

This problem is of secondary importance. The problem of the relation between the drive and the activity which leads to its satisfaction is much more immediate. The word "aim" as used by Freud refers to the end result, for example, sexual union. The concepts that are used to describe the relation between the two, drive and behavior, have gradations of meaning. The conation of a drive is described by the epithet "desire" or "appetite"; whereas the word "impulse" conveys the meaning of desire plus an executive act in preparation. In the lower forms of life—and it is dangerous to draw inferences from forms of life whose drives we do not appreciate—one is led to believe that "instinct" covers both drive and activity necessary to satisfy it. In the case of man, it can be definitely said that only the drive is phylogenetically determined, and not the behavior necessary to satisfy it, as may be the case in lower forms of life. Otherwise the immature state of the human being at birth loses all significance in relation to his later adaptation possibilities. One cannot be altogether certain about this latter assumption, since it is impossible to reproduce anything like experimental conditions necessary to prove it one way or another. Neither can it be proved sociologically, for we have no knowledge of man except in some form of society. If our assumption were not at least in part true, how could we account for sexual perversion, or for the infinite refinements of the "instinct" of mastery?

The fact that in man there is this gap between an inborn drive and the technique for satisfying it constitutes his greatest advantage as far as survival and adaptation potentialities go in comparison with lower animals, but it is also, as the study of neuroses demonstrates, one of his severest handicaps. The fact that this gap is a psychological one renders the development and growth of the techniques for satisfying drives subject to environmental influences to a degree unknown to any lower form of life. This fact alone diminishes the chances of phylogenetic influences. The conspicuous difference between man and lower animals is the comparative poverty of man's adaptive mechanisms at birth, and the corresponding helplessness of the human infant. This biological fact has an anatomical correlate. The tracts which connect the spinal cord with the brain stem are undeveloped (functionally) at birth; they acquire their myelin sheaths, i.e., they become functionally active, gradually, and with varying degrees of rapidity. These are the tracts which form the anatomical link of "voluntary" motion. Connected with their development, there are psychic elements susceptible to modification and inhibition. The same process is true of some sensory organs. Indeed, it is the fifth cranial nerve, controlling oral activity, which is the first to be myelinated. Myelination is not completed until the third year of life. This simply means that growth, development, and functional activity all take place in association with purely *psychological components*, all of which modify the resulting *Gestalt*.

We can see at a glance two consequences of this. First, that the activities associated with drives have innumerable development and modification possibilities, and, in consequence, make the adaptation possibilities of man very numerous; and secondly, that such development possibilities depend on the particular direction, quality, and emphasis supplied by the particular social environment in which the individual happens to live. One can readily see that creatures in whom the behavior necessary to satisfy a drive is inborn can have but few adaptation possibilities. They can satisfy drives only under a very limited set of environmental conditions, because the individual cannot modify either drive, behavior, or environment. The same is true of animals which, like the guinea pig, complete the process of myelination very soon after birth; their adaptation possibilities are limited. One can safely predict the needs of such an animal. But one cannot predict the needs of man. In short, man is born helpless, the anatomical basis for voluntary action is slow in developing, leaving a large expanse in which modification and direction of behavior necessary to execute drives can take place. This condition also increases the variations in human needs.

The importance of all this for psychology is very great. If the gap between drive and behavior is conditioned by a psychological factor, we must investigate just what its character is. For the moment, we need only indicate its direction; it is pedagogic. And by this we do not mean "teaching" alone, but every conceivable influence, express or implicit, which molds the direction of feeling or activity in connection with drive and behavior. The most prominent among these influences are imitation, an extremely poor term and a poorly understood concept, and directional or restrictive disciplines, explicit or implied.

If these facts are borne in mind, then no observations about the development of any drive and its associated behavior can be made without reference to the social influences that have anything to do with it. We must be extremely careful what factors we attribute to "human nature," because there is no such thing; we know only specific types of "human nature" under specific environmental and social conditions. "Social influences" thus come to mean the specific idea and word pictures of a given drive, the manner in which it is executed, the mobility concepts, and the interconnections all of these have with each other and with the total personality.

In short, the helplessness of the human infant and the infinite number of adaptation possibilities are what makes sociological factors so important in the development of the ego. The dependency of the child renders him susceptible to all influences that are pedagogic or disciplinary, and culture is both.

Ferenczi has given us some valuable ideas about the subjective feelings of the child when its needs are satisfied through the agency of the parent. These we have already reviewed. But we must add an important corollary; the feeling of omnipotence and control is subjectively valid if the child is predominantly successful, i.e., if the aid from the parent is adequate to satisfy his limited wants. We have seen from our discussion on projection[9] that the feeling of well-being is also contingent on this experience; and that *illness*, or a feeling of being unwell, becomes the equivalent of being uncared for or hated. The parent who frustrates these longings is represented in dreams or fantasies as doing something actively aggressive against the child. This representation most often takes place in dreams, but often in conscious thinking. This is a second instance of a frustrated wish represented as the negative of the positive one. When the recognition comes later, as Rado has pointed

[9] See pp. 305–310.

out, the omnipotent feeling is projected on to the mother, and her powers are exaggerated and expected constantly to be at the child's disposal.[10]

I have in recent years been able to observe in paranoid characters that a result of marked interference with early omnipotence feelings is that the frustrating object, the one who does not satisfy dependency cravings, becomes an active harmful agent (persecutor) and that, in the subject, a premature and ill-founded independence and grandiosity is created. There is an absence of customary inflation of the parental image and a corresponding inflation of the subject's own. Among the influences in childhood which can disturb the normal feeling of protection, illness is perhaps the most important. Very often medical treatments, throat and nasal sprays, enemas, etc., give the child the impression that the parent is hurting him. In other words, in earliest infancy the disturbance of the normal feeling of well-being (for we cannot speak of dependency at this time) may lead to distrust and fear of the parent, to inflation of self, and to precocious development (intelligence). These

[10] This problem as stated has an important bearing on another moot point in the psychoanalytic psychopathology—the genesis of neurotic anxiety. The various theories about anxiety cannot be understood outside of their historical context. The relation between an unsatisfied biological craving and anxiety was solved by Freud on the basis of the libido theory as a "conversion" of libido into anxiety. The newer formulations of the Freudian ego psychology compelled him to retract this earlier conversion theory and to restate it as a reaction to danger which in turn sets into motion the whole dynamism of repression (1926). One idea, however, has remained the keystone of every theory of anxiety: that every anxiety is a reproduction of another anxiety previously experienced. The prototype of all anxiety thus became the act of being born. Rank exploited this idea and thought he had uncovered the universal formula for anxiety. The normal adaptation could thus be characterized as a "successful abreaction" of the birth trauma. The birth situation was thus treated from the point of view of instincts that were satisfied or frustrated, i.e., on the pattern of the sexual instincts. All of these theories operated on the basis that the actual occurrences during birth remained the prototype of anxiety, but did not take into account the resources of the ego or how they were established. Other authors pick out other associated phenomena, like aggression, and center the anxiety as related to aggression as the nuclear phenomenon. All of this proves merely that the problem of neurotic anxiety cannot be solved until the structure and functions of the ego are sufficiently understood to allow the proper place to all these phenomena that have been correctly observed.

are the ego activities on which the concept "narcissistic" is based.

The period of recognizable dependency coincides with the period of the greatest growth of the ego, the time when most culturally determined disciplines are imposed or absorbed. Some directional disciplines, like learning language, do not seriously interfere with preëxisting adaptations: if they create any disturbance at all, it is less serious than that created by disciplines which interfere with organically determined drives. By discipline, we mean the restriction or direction of impulses or activities which exist in some rudimentary form from the moment of birth. In other words, all disciplines aim to alter personality organization. We can easily see how difficult it is to meet this social demand for change, if we note that any type of adaptation must already have in its composition gratifications of one kind or another; and change, even on a guarantee of greater satisfactions to come, is always opposed, because it requires effort and sacrifice of established satisfactions. Such change is in addition a great injury to the child's independence and freedom from responsibility. If the previous infantile stage of development was one in which it controlled the world and mother, discipline establishes the reverse, a condition in which the parent controls and rules the child. If we add to this the fact that, for the greater part, disciplines are instituted without the child's appreciation of the purpose, need, or advantages to be gained therefrom, we have every possible reason why the child should oppose such restrictions. This situation confronts all discipline. Discipline is always coercion if it interferes with an existing adaptation. Since the dependency of the child is a biologically determined characteristic it naturally becomes the fulcrum on which the lever of discipline rests. Out of the inter-action between the two arise several basic constellations, which, expressed in the first person, read:

1. If I obey you, you will love and protect me.
2. If I am unloved (sick, miserable, unhappy, or unfortunate) it is because I have disobeyed.

3. If I repent, renounce, suffer, and promise in the future to obey, I can be reinstated in your good graces and enjoy once again your love and protection.

This set of constellations seems to represent a higher degree of organization than was found in the fear of being eaten up. To be able to use ingratiation techniques in a state of helplessness represents the existence of more effective types of adaptation, a finer appreciation of reality than is the case with the fantasy of fear of being eaten up. The group of constellations enumerated above can be formed only in a culture where restrictive disciplines are severe. We can contrast this group of constellations with those found in societies where disciplines either do not restrict the child, or establish an acceptable balance between satisfactions and frustrations.

To characterize disciplines as "severe" and "not severe" is rather loose terminology. One can speak of them as severe if the number of disciplines is great, and if collectively they greatly increase the responsibilities of the individual, or one can regard them as severe if they interfere with essential gratifications. There is, however, another factor which is perhaps the most important, and that is the conditions established around disciplines, the insistence and the punitive measures or threats of suffering. In societies like the Marquesan where anal disciplines are not severe in this sense and sexual objectives are not interfered with, the feeding by the parent remains the basic prototype of friendly relations with an object. It connotes, "If I feed you, you will feed me." This latter is not a love conditioned by obedience, but a simple exchange of similar pleasures highly valued by the individual. Tanala and Marquesan cultures describe in actual practice the difference between the constellations arising in the individual from these two types of basic attitude to parents. In many cultures the feeding pattern may persist in addition to the ingratiation-reinstatement procedure.

When dependency longings are guaranteed at the cost of heavy renunciation of gratification and when the suppressed tensions persist—as for example sexual cravings—the child must dispose of the impulses, and must develop some attitude to the forbidding parent. This he accomplishes by changing the representation of his impulses, and by changing the representation of the parent. The parental image becomes inflated, and with it the power for good or harm is equally exaggerated. The protecting object is represented as hating or injuring the subject. The child may represent himself as satisfying a permissible impulse by substitution; and the hatred and aggression toward the parent for the injury suffered is concealed. An example will clarify this. A frigid woman dreams of being in bed with her husband. They are about to have intercourse when a cross old woman enters the room with a tray of food. The patient resents the intrusion, which is repeated several times, but she cannot tell the old woman not to interfere. The meaning is obvious. She seeks compensation in food (oral gratification plus dependency) and hence cannot show her aggression against her mother. The hatred the patient feels as coming from the mother is concealed under the satisfaction of dependency cravings (food). In paranoid characters, the dependency longing is frustrated; then the "persecutor" pulls off his mask. Such characters then defend themselves against the persecutor by striking the first blow offensively, and inflate themselves instead of the parent.

A few clinical illustrations will show the various representations of the object from whom one expects satisfaction of dependency needs. We note that there is no uniformity in the following reactions; each depends on a different "ego" organization. Forms of these reactions are: (1) an anxiety appears in place of the gratification; (2) instead of satisfying the child, the object is represented as threatening to eat it up (Hansel and Gretel, Little Red Riding Hood); (3) the object is represented as injuring the subject (castration); (4) the subject takes an active defense against the object by active insistence of a criminal act such as stealing the desired gratification (kleptomania).

To illustrate the first variety, we may cite the boy of four whose mother had just given birth to a little sister. Moved out of his own room, he was angry, and vented his anger on his teddy bear, which he threw out of bed. It is not his mother who throws him out, but he actually disposes of her; or the act can be interpreted as dispossessing his little sister. Shortly afterward he began to have a recurrent dream in which he found himself in bed, while a large round object came closer and closer to him; just as it was about to strike him, he woke up frightened. The boy said the object looked like an orange, apple, or potato, and insisted that it had something to do with eating, because many times the object was "stuck all over with toothpicks." The boy was right. It did have something to do with eating. The round object is associated with a once pleasant experience now denied him, the breast. Now, instead of causing pleasant anticipations, it frightens him. The mother, at whom he is unconsciously angry, is represented as injuring him, though he represents her by her most valued attribute, the breast.[11] Was it oral gratification he sought, or had his sister interfered with his claims for dependency? It all depends on where the dominant interests of the child lie, in the organ-pleasure of sucking, or the more general claim for exclusive attention in a bewildering world in which he feels small and insignificant. His mother has ceased to be his magic agent as well as the source of sexual gratifications, both of which have ceased long ago anyhow. Subsequently, this boy took to stealing, and as one would expect, stole only food objects.

[11] This interpretation is open to some difference of opinion. Those whose chief interest in psychopathology is to study the transformations of affect will place the greatest emphasis on the "repressed anger" toward the mother and attribute the entire syndrome to this feeling. The threatening image is therefore a projection of his own hostility. This is a one-sided view. The syndrome is created by a constellation in which a need is frustrated, the impulses necessary to satisfy it are blocked, the affects of affection and hatred mingle—all these are active in making the total experience fail. Following this failure there is the creation of a perception of hostility coming from the object. This perception is created by the whole constellation, and not by any single element torn from its context.

Another illustration of a similar representation is to be found in the case of a man[12] who was subject to severe attacks of eczema all over the body whenever he encountered any unpleasant situation in his life. Infantile eczemas occur most frequently immediately after weaning, and often persist into adulthood. They are associated with itching and scratching, and the eczema is usually the result of scratching. This scratching, according to dreams, has the connotation of a violent aggression against the weaning mother, but is executed by the child on himself. The objective of the scratching, its meaning, changes. At first it is a primitive protest; it then becomes a process of boring his way back into the mother; and, finally, may become the equivalent of any of the gratifications which attempt to make good the loss, especially masturbation. This was the conclusion reached in several patients with eczema, whom I analyzed. The patient we are talking about had some interesting dreams. (1) A giant lifts him in his hands, but then the hand begins to close on him and to crush him. (2) He is in a large dark cave, but there is a wild animal there who may eat him up. He wakes with anxiety from both dreams. The first dream is the reproduction of an infantile experience of being lifted into the arms of the protecting parent; but instead of a fond embrace, he is threatened with being crushed. The second dream has the familiar intra-uterine character, with the added idea of being eaten up. The course of this man's illness has been quite remarkable. He often has gone into a hospital as a result of his eczema, where he has reproduced, under the stimulus of actual failures, the dependency state of childhood, lying in bed, being fed, and feeling irresponsible; and his eczema has then cleared up. Any new difficulty brings on a fresh attack. This man is a well-known figure in several New York hospitals.[13]

[12] This case was told me by Dr. Harold Kelman.

[13] The dynamics in this case are much more complicated than the explanation indicates. The points in his adaptation at which his control over his relations to the environment fails and the reasons for the failure cannot be taken up in detail.

The representation of the fear of being eaten up we have already discussed. The kleptomanic reaction is, of course, very different in character from the others. It represents a strong pugnacious attitude, an insistence on achieving the desired goal. What is the importance of all this psychopathology for our study of primitive sociology? It serves to indicate to us where the tensions in a society lie. The clue may come from a mos, a story, a ritual, but each of these clues must be verified in actual life practices. Thus, when we encounter the fear of being eaten up, we must attempt to identify the object from whom the gratification is expected, and what actual frustration this object is perpetrating. From most of the evidence we conclude that the frustration is a need for protection as a defense against anxiety[14] caused by inhibited or defective resources.

[14] It would be interesting to contrast this explanation with the one offered by the libido theory. Fears of being eaten up are generally dealt with as versions of castration fears, but expressed on the oral sadistic level. To the uninitiated this all sounds very mysterious. To understand the formula, we must first understand what information Freud was seeking; he was looking for evidence of what happened to the repressed impulse; this evidence was supplied by the phobia expressed in symptom or dream. At the time the libido theory was formulated Freud did not know what ego activities were represented in the phenomena; the libido theory only sought to account for the activities of the "instinct," which Freud knew could not be destroyed. He recognized the importance of ontogenesis, i.e., the developmental aspects, but interpreted all the facts, which are incontestable and verifiable, as evidence of regressions to earlier phases of the gratification of the same instinctive tendency. At the same time Freud urged that we should appreciate more of the ego activities (see above, p. 390). If we follow Freud's advice and Ferenczi's work, which Freud endorses, we can come to other conclusions with the use of the same data. But including ego activities is not merely adding to knowledge of what happens to the libido; it entails a recasting of the entire interpretation. The phenomenon designated as oral-sadistic represents a reorganization of the entire ego, to be sure, as it once was in childhood. But the frustrated wish is also represented in the wish to nurse and suck, to be protected, which the individual is eager to accept in lieu of the abandoned impulse. The ego activities are found in an unrealizable wish to return to a dependent state as in infancy; it is represented in the negative—being eaten up; the ego is represented as helpless. Thus the facts that Freud described, the dynamics, can be verified; the interpretation needs to be altered with reference to the ego. This we have here attempted. The libido theory was used only to give evidence of instinctual cravings, but not of ego attitudes. The incompleteness lies in the premises of the theory, not in the facts.

RELATIONS TO THE OUTER WORLD

Let us now consider another type of frustration, that caused by unsuccessful encounters with the outer world. The phenomena in connection with these reaction types will afford us some opportunity for clarifying the phenomena associated with masochism, and also something of their meaning.

When the personality is fully developed, one of its fixed functions is to orient the individual to the outer world. These functions include vision, hearing, and the other senses, together with complicated combinations of these. Thus vision alone does not impart "meaning"; in addition it requires knowledge of perspective, knowledge of utility of objects, and relations of the ego to them, such as use, pleasure, etc. When these functions are complete the individual is able to "adapt" to the outer world, and he never again questions their availability except when they fail. This they do in traumatic neurosis, in which the quantitative balance between resources and the demands made on them is impaired, with the result that no effectual adaptation can be made. Too little is known at the present time of the development of these adaptive functions, and too few of the vicissitudes of their failure have been observed. What we know about this phenomenon is largely the result of our study of traumatic neuroses,[15] the reaction to loss of special functions, as a limb, vision, or hearing. These functions which deal with orientation and use of the muscular apparatus for defense or work behave in a singular way when they are inhibited. The provoking circumstance is seen in those factors which cause traumatic neuroses. The net effect is that the world seems to withdraw its hospitality and those functions by which accommodation to it is effected become inhibited, blocked, so that they are no longer at the disposal of the individual. When this happens, the individual reacts like one in whom these functions

[15] See A. Kardiner, "Bioanalysis of the Epileptic Reaction," *Psychoanalytic Quarterly*, Vol. I. No. 3.

have been withdrawn, and exhibits abasia (loss of equilibrium, pre-walking stage), visual aberrations, tremors, inhibitions to work, and other disturbances. To characterize all these phenomena as regressions, a revival of infantile types of adaptation, would be too general. In many instances there seems to be no revival of infantile types, the original forms of which are not known. But in many cases the loss of meaning is quite apparent. Thus one patient heard people speak to him, but could not understand the language; he saw objects but could not appreciate his relation to them in the sense of meaning and use.

The dream life of these individuals furnishes us with some important clues. Their dreams are more or less stereotyped and consist of catastrophic endings to any action undertaken. For example, a man dreams of being in an elevator, but instead of going to its destination, the elevator plunges through the roof and falls down a great height. Patients with traumatic neuroses can repeat these anxiety dreams five or six times a night. During convalescence from this state they have dreams which suggest a reproduction of the phase of infancy in which the mouth is the sole organ of adaptation. One such patient who owned a chicken farm dreamed of the farm being covered with concrete, so that his chickens could not eat. In addition to having these catastrophic dreams and revivals of "oral mastery," such individuals are most extreme in their emotional reactions, which are either violently aggressive or absolutely abject. In the study of the traumatic neurosis we felt obliged to conclude that inhibitions and violently aggressive behavior in this disorganized form were related to each other; that inhibition of these basic functions causes the violent and disorganized aggression; that the latter was formerly channeled through useful methods of assertion or adaptation.

In the relation between the actual inhibitions and the dream life of the traumatic neurosis we encounter the simplest version of what we call "masochistic" phenomena. Before we begin theorizing about masochism, it is important to gather all the facts relevant to it. It is difficult to say how completely the recorded phenomena include all that happens. In the case of the traumatic neurosis we have the following steps. An "ego function" stands in a harmonious relation to the outer world; the individual employs it as a means to safety, orientation, pleasure. There is enjoyment of its use, no aggression is present in waking life or in dreams. Suddenly the picture changes, the ego function, let us say that of vision or of coördination, becomes inhibited, the individual cannot see, he dreams the world is falling on him, annihilating him. There is now no enjoyment, he is aggressive and irritable. His aggression is, moreover, disorganized. He is left with disordered types of adaptation. But his needs with regard to the outer world remain the same; they continue to push for satisfaction, and the result is an attempt at the same gratification although most of the adaptive tools to achieve it are blocked. The resulting picture we call "masochistic." This illustration is much more telling than an illustration dealing with sexual inhibition, for there we are accustomed to attribute to the masochism a punitive element due to the operation of the sense of guilt. Where is the guilt in the traumatic neurosis? We can draw some conclusions about the nature of these ego functions. Their job, apparently, is an aggressive pushing the world away in the first place, so that when their effectiveness is removed, the individual has the feeling of being unprotected, and hence the world now caves in on him. At least this is endopsychic perception of the world to the individual deprived of adaptive weapons. During the development of the individual, effective ego weapons of adaptation take the place of the supporting mother. These traumatic neurotics do not have anxiety in their waking states, but only irritability, a constant tension which prevents anxiety. The "masochism" is, therefore, created by the attempt to establish contact with the world, the executive agencies for which have become blocked. If with their aid the individual feels safe, and without them feels the world is falling in on him, then we must conclude that the function of these ego resources is to keep the world at bay. This is, of course, a very strange and mechanistic representation of organs with so passive a function as the sense organs. Diagrammatically one may represent it thus:[16]

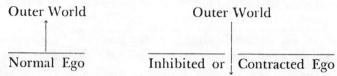

Outer World   Outer World

Normal Ego   Inhibited or Contracted Ego

There is no more crucial test for any psychology than in the explanation it offers of the phenomenon of masochism. This is a phenomenon which is comprehensible only through constructs or operational concepts, for neither direct experience nor behavior can explain it. The explanations tend to emphasize either a form of primary instinctual drive (Freud's primary masochism or death instinct) or the pursuit of certain affective states. No explanation of this phenomenon can be complete without an accounting both of the activity elements, otherwise designated as "instinctual," and the affective elements.

One of the difficulties with masochism is that the explanations are drawn from the phenomenon of the ordinary neuroses. This seems like starting with the most difficult and complicated phenomenon to attempt an explanation. The phenomena of the traumatic neurosis contain all the essentials of masochism in their most elementary form, and seem the logical place to start, and upon this the superstructure found in the neurosis is engrafted. A further qualification of the traumatic neurosis as the basic framework of masochistic phenomena is that in this neurosis we are concerned with the contraction of functions in the

---

[16] Freud's conception of this neurosis is explained in his *Reizschutz* theory (defense against stimuli). He maintains that normally this defense against stimuli is adequate, but in the traumatic neurosis this defense is broken through. This concept does adequate justice to the facts. But Freud does not tell us how this defense against stimuli is built up. The concept of defense against stimuli is correct, but not specific. According to the phenomena of the neurosis, the defense consists of the adequate functioning of the sensory-motor-equilibrium apparatus, with the aid of which orientation is secured, and the individual is able to employ the utility functions of the senses and limbs. Once this utility function is gone, the individual actually is unprotected. The individual who formerly mastered the world in a pleasant manner now sees this same activity as threatening and dangerous. This principle is true of other forms of masochism as well.

development of which no social influences of a prohibitory kind ever operate, and that the phenomena can be recovered in a traumatic neurosis whether it is of three days' or ten years' duration.

First of all, we note a change in the individual's adaptation, a limitation of general effectiveness. That this is a very deep-seated change can be seen from the dreams. The repetitive phenomenon noted in the dreams is not an indication of a repetition compulsion (which merely begs the question) but of permanent change in the ego structure, which means that the perceptions of the outer world, the capacities for action, and individual's attitude toward himself in relation to the outer world are now altered. He perceives the world as hostile, because his defensive or adaptive tools are inhibited and contracted. Of this the individual is not aware. This is the basic fact. The other associated phenomena, the retreat from the world and the outbursts of aggression, both follow from the inhibition, because the necessity for some accommodation to the outer world (despite his now contracted functions) persists.

The affective side of the picture cannot be treated by itself; it can be understood only as the result of the now completely altered adaptation. The individual's confidence is gone; he can now no longer freely exercise these functions which he formerly used with ease and which gave him certain gratifications. In their absence he seeks new types of affective gratification, compatible with his altered capacities. The outbursts of uncontrollable rage, when sudden demands for organized action are called for, his terror and sympathy when he sees someone in distress, are the consequences of the inhibitions.

This neurotic picture has no relation to the past; it may happen to any individual as, say, a result of an automobile accident. The reactions may be, but are not necessarily, reinstatements of earlier types of adaptation. And the cardinal feature of the masochism is the inhibition of functions of adaptation which formerly were effective. No masochism is possible without inhibition.

SEXUAL FRUSTRATIONS

If we try these principles described in the traumatic neurosis on a sexual inhibition, we find a very similar picture. It differs, however, in that its manifestations are much more complicated. The repressing force is not a sudden reflex contraction, but a gradual and persistent molding. Moreover, the sexual impulse is one which can be satisfied in many ways.

To illustrate these differences let us consider a severe compulsion neurotic whose inhibitions are of the most extreme kind. It is commonly assumed that an "inhibited" function is one whose development was complete, but whose exercise is blocked. In the case of many of the phenomena that look clinically like sexual inhibitions, the trouble is much deeper. The actual development of the function may have been arrested, so that the individual was never able to carry on the complete act because he never learned how. In the compulsion neurotic under consideration, sexual development was interfered with at the age of four under the influence of parental threats, and was never carried beyond what he knew of it at that age. The drive toward sexual gratification is inborn; but what to do in order to get sexual satisfaction is learned, not by perceptible means, but by a gradual series of successes. What is there to "know" about the sexual act? Each of the many intermediary steps between the formulation of the wish and the execution of the act has its distinct ideational representation and access to motility. Interference with any one of the steps may lead to inability to effect the completed action. It is natural to suppose that the earlier such an inhibitory influence is started, the more likely it is to interfere with all subsequent steps. We might take an illustration from the patient's current experience to observe what happens to the impulse that fails in its consummation, and to locate if possible where the obstacles are. The patient had been to a party one evening, and one of the guests who caught his fancy was a dancer. He flirted with her a bit. That night when he went to bed he began to have erotic fantasies about her. The fantasies at this time included a good deal more than they had earlier in the analysis. He was more assertive, had more feeling about his own genitals, and about the sexual act. He began to fall asleep and had the following succession of hypnagogic images. (1) Sexual fantasies about the dancer. (2) "I'm driving a hard instrument into a locomotive." (3) "I'm tied to a tree and some one is hitting me on the testicles with a baseball bat." (4) "I say this is all nonsense, I am master of the situation." (5) "I awaken with anxiety."

When the patient first came to the analysis, the only sexual activity of which he was capable was masturbation accompanied by intensely humiliating and cruel fantasies, as in the third hypnagogic image. Fantasies like these were already clearly established in his mind at the age of six. They took their present shape some time after his mother absolutely forbade masturbation, and threatened him with all kinds of dire consequences, insanity and the like, if he continued. He did continue, but with the aid of masochistic fantasies, of which having his penis beaten with a baseball bat was one. Coincident with the "masochistic" representation of sexual activity—from actively doing something pleasant, to having something unpleasant done to him—there was an interesting series of phobic images which would haunt him just before he fell asleep. These phobic images represent clearly the changes in the representation of the object who frustrates an important need. This child, from the age of three to five, was first haunted by fears of a witch coming into the room to strangle him. (His mother was in the habit of visiting him before he went to bed, first to hug and caress him, and later to warn him against masturbation.) Then followed fantasies of wild animals who would devour him, and finally burglars, who would not injure him if he remained perfectly quiet; but should he show any motion, they would bash his head in with a club. His immobility was his safety; by not masturbating he felt secure.

The current hypnagogic images represent quite clearly the inability to follow through his sexual fantasy in a normal way. In its place there are a series of images which represent it first as something extremely difficult, and then as a cruel act, in which there is some effort to salvage a bit of pleasure. His protest is clearly registered, as well as his fear of asserting this protest.

The situation is much more complicated than is the illustration from the traumatic neurosis, but the similarity is evident. The succession of images proved to the patient the fact that the "masochistic" fantasy was a transformation of the original pleasant one; that this transformation was effected under the persistent influence of a discipline which carried heavy penalties; that this discipline introduced a painful element into the activity not previously there; that he now had to meet the demands of discipline and of the sexual craving both; that the resultant masochistic fantasy satisfied both; that he not only had developed a tolerance for the pain in the fantasy, but that it had become the essential condition of the remaining fragments of pleasure; that the objective of masturbation had changed from a pleasurable goal to one whose purpose was to destroy the sexual wish tension; that the influence of the discipline was still active in his current life, though his resources were now generally much greater than they were when he was a child; and that he actually no longer needed to "obey in order to be loved," though he still acts as if he did. The fact that this idea was still very much alive was frequently demonstrated in his reactions to me, the analyst. It must not be overlooked that no small proportion of the patient's anxiety is due to his actual inability to consummate the activity, because so many steps in its development have been omitted. The link between the infantile conditions and his current adaptations lies not in memories which when recovered will automatically free the patient's resources, but in his present ego structure. This part of his adaptation must be thoroughly understood by the patient; the rationale of the adaptation can be recovered only from the infantile situation.[17]

[17] The author cannot agree with several current beliefs about technique which maintain that the past of the patient is insignificant, provided that one studies

The greatest difficulty in the understanding of masochistic phenomena pertaining to sexual activity (and this is true of other impulses as well) lies in the fact that we always find it mixed up with a complicated series of emotional accompaniments; at least, such is the case in the genesis of the masochistic activity. It seems as if the object of the activity has changed from active to passive, from pleasant to painful, from freedom of anxiety and guilt to the presence of both. The commonly accepted idea is that the objective changes because of the sense of guilt; but the operation of the same principle in the traumatic neurosis, where guilt cannot possibly play a part, gives us the clue that these emotional changes are secondary effects. But this is where our knowledge of the activities of the total personality is still defective. It would seem that the masochistic activity is an attempt to satisfy the original impulse by means of energy charges now blocked from their normal channels of expression, and by the utilization of the inhibited and thus "disorganized aggression"; but since the energy charges are not delivered to their original objective, the individual is deprived of an essential control or support, as when one performs a simple physical feat effectively. This explanation of masochism is incomplete; but for our purposes further pursuit is not essential. We know enough about it to know, when we encounter it in sociological phenomena, to look for two things: the presence of an inhibition; and a frustration of an essential need, be it through the agency of natural forces of the environment of the outer world, or from a source within the social organization.

We need not go into further details about sexual frustrations: the manifestations are too numerous because of the fact that,

---

only the current affective reactions and exhausts their possibilities in the reactions between analyst and patient. This procedure is indispensable, and is a most effective means of demonstrating the ego structure of the individual. However unimportant, therapeutically, the developmental aspects of these reactions in current life may be in mild character-disturbances where the individual's resources are very effectual nevertheless, in severe inhibitions, the infantile picture furnishes the analyst with a most important therapeutic tool, the emotional rationale of the behavior consistent with the then existing conception of the environment.

contrary in contrast to eating frustrations, the satisfaction of sexual impulse can be postponed, gratified vicariously, and expressed in innumerable different ways. From the sociological side, we need only stress two points: First, that when we speak of institutionalized frustrations, we must note carefully at what stage in the development of the individual they are made effective. If instituted in childhood, in the formative years, and involving both object and aim taboos, we can expect that they will modify the development of the entire individual for his lifetime. If the sexual impulse is allowed free expression in childhood, but severe restrictions are imposed after the development is completed (Trobriand), we must expect the social manifestations to be different from the first. The second point we must bear in mind is that when these frustrations are general, and apply to every member of the community, then we can expect some manifestation of this pressure in folklore, religion, and perhaps in other institutions. This is the point that Reik and G. Roheim were constantly trying to make, but which they accounted for on an evolutionary basis. Several constellations, notably the Oedipus complex, owe their origin to this source. This particular constellation describes the pressure created on man by certain forms of social restrictions on the sexual impulse, though the exact manner in which this constellation comes about is not yet fully understood.

In Marquesan culture we saw a type of sexual dissatisfaction which was not due to restrictive influences instituted in the formative years, but due entirely to the ratio of men to women. Instead of producing the usual Oedipus complex, we found that incest wishes toward the mother were not a feature of the folklore, though the incest between father and daughter was freely expressed. On the other hand, we found a very careful array of institutions which had the effect of diminishing the harmful effects of strife among the men for the women. The net result was that the woman occupied in Marquesan folklore a position very like that of the father in our society, not because she had any authority—in fact she had none—but because she naturally became a frustrating object since there were too few women to satisfy all the needs which the child and adult expected them to satisfy. But these needs we found not to be exclusively sexual. Not her authority, but her ability to cause sexual and other frustrations made the woman a hated, envied, and suspected object.

FRUSTRATION OF SOCIALLY "CREATED" NEEDS

We come now to frustration of goals created by society, i.e., needs created by the value placed on relative status or ability, wealth, prestige, class, and the like. It is questionable whether, strictly speaking, society "creates" these needs. Society does not create the need for these values, for as we have already indicated, they stem from a group of affective perceptions, which apprise the individual of his social orientation. Social life would be impossible if man did not have these perceptions. However, society can enhance the importance of relative status by various means. When these values exist, we must expect reactions to their satisfaction and frustration.

In the first place, the expression of the need is always conscious, though society can place barriers against ostentation or display, and can prevent abuse of others through the possession of prestige or wealth. These needs, especially when manifestly gratified for some individuals, are constantly stimulated by example in everyone, and hence are not easily subject to suppression. The deprived may exhibit a variety of feelings toward the fortunate:

1. Envy, hatred, aggression, the wish to take away from those who have and appropriate it for oneself, or even the wish to annihilate those who have. If there is a coincident dependency on the object of envy, the aggression against the object can be disposed of "masochistically," and may terminate in an increase in submission and efforts at ingratiation with the envied object, plus inhibition of one's own resources.

2. The envy or hatred may be suppressed and ingratiation procedures instituted, without inhibition, in the attempt to profit partially at least from the object's power.

3. Identification with the object. We have spoken of the contagiousness of prestige. Those who do not have it take up the cause of those who have. This is one of the reasons why those who enjoy prestige can enlist and attach vast numbers of others to themselves without reward. There is some vicarious gratification in this; to associate with those who have prestige gives one a shadow of the original quality. This attitude involves no hostility to the object; on the contrary, great loyalty, because the cause of the object becomes the subject's cause.

4. One may seek compensatory gratification on the principle, "I haven't this, but I have that." This follows on the principle of overemphasizing an advantage to compensate for qualities which one lacks. This is a mechanism which Dollard found very prominent in the American negro.[18]

5. Complete destruction of the prestige values of the object, and the elevation of masochistic goals in their place. This was prominent in early Christianity, where the objective of frustration, suffering, abstinence, and degradation became elevated to a new scale of prestige values. The more you suffered, the higher your prestige. Asceticism can thus become a high social goal.

Concerning ingratiation, it must be noted that all ingratiating procedures are maintained by the promise and potential realization of real or fancied rewards. This means, socially, that hostility always lurks behind ingratiation if the reward is not forthcoming. In Tanala culture we saw how this was maintained by the threat of punishment by a powerful god (a dead ancestor) who made good his promise with ample rewards.

When we speak of social mobility through class and prestige lines, we speak of a hope or objective which the individual can maintain as a life goal. The absence of such mobility, as exists in caste systems, ought theoretically to augment anxiety about achievement of prestige; but practically this anxiety eventually disappears and is replaced by attitudes of resignation and submission. Where class lines are free and the individual can acquire prestige, the anxiety about achievement is likely to be greater because the objective never disappears, and as long as the individual feels belittled by his lack of achievement, he is

[18] John Dollard, *Caste and Class in a Southern Town* (New Haven, 1937).

constantly prodded by his anxiety. This failure to achieve is then rationalized on the basis of guilt, inadequacy, fate, and the like.

CONTROL OF AGGRESSION

The last factor in frustration types to be considered is the interference with aggression itself. We have not yet encountered a society which does not control this impulse in some form, which does not channel permissible outlets, and even encourage others.[19] It would take us too far afield to discuss all the sources and causes of aggression. What concerns us chiefly is the control of intrasocial aggression. We have seen that aggression is a reaction type to every frustration; whether it is an instinct or not, is of secondary importance. Therefore, our problem, from the sociological side, shifts somewhat to a new locus. It shifts to the ground of looking for the frustration behind the aggression. These frustrations, however, do not all arise from the social organization; they may arise from the actual inadequacy of the individual.

This brings up the problem of social control of aggression. Freud has already discussed this point at great length.[20] It consists of two basic means: intrapsychic control, which Freud calls super-ego formation, and all its complicated relations to guilt and conscience; external control, government, police. This problem has already been discussed in connection with the Marquesan and Tanala cultures.

In the reactions to frustration we have encountered a large variety of types of aggression proceeding from this source. This is not the only source of aggression, but it is the one we are most concerned with. The chief interest lies in the forms in which the aggression is expressed. The two chief types we encountered were overt and suppressed forms. The overt forms were malevolent magic; the suppressed forms, some type of hysteria (*tromba* and spirit possession).

[19] See p. 116.
[20] See pp. 379–382.

The suppression of aggression can succeed only when the frustration-gratification balance can be adequately maintained. Tanala-Betsileo culture showed us that this balance can be upset by imposing barriers to basic satisfactions for a large number of individuals.

When the aggressions are walled off by corresponding rewards, evidences of the fact appear in the products of fantasy. This is one of the reasons why folklore is so useful in locating the sources of intrasocial hostilities.

SUMMARY OF REACTION TYPES TO FRUSTRATION

The reaction types to frustration which we have encountered serve as practical guides in the study of the effects of various types of social organization. This account of reactions to frustration does not pretend to exhaust all the possibilities, but rather to describe the method of studying a fair sampling of them. Notwithstanding the somewhat schematic representation, we must hasten to add that there is no uniformity in the reactions which the same external frustration will cause in the individual. Not all dependency cravings are expressed in oral symbolism. We do not as yet fully appreciate all the factors which lead to expressing this need in oral symbolism. We have a striking illustration of this in the difference between Marquesan and Tanala culture. In the latter, the entire dependency constellation is expressed in the form of obedience and ingratiation. In Marquesan, this constellation is not formed in the individual and it is no wonder that we find no evidence of it in the folklore. On the other hand, Marquesan fears of being eaten up and of starving, undoubtedly have something to do with the oral symbolism. We cannot, therefore, diagnose frustrations from any single feature in the adaptation of the individual, but from the total ensemble of the actual life practices.

Psychologically, these reaction types to frustration are one of our most useful sources of information as to how the total personality is organized. By studying the results of these frustrations we learn about the defenses and accommodations which are initiated. We learn one important fact, that the individual can use only freely accessible resources. A man may actually be very poor, although he has millions concealed in a vault in a foreign country to enter which he cannot secure a passport.

THE TOTAL PERSONALITY FROM THE POINT OF VIEW OF "INSTINCT"

It was no less true of psychoanalysis than of other psychologies that the structure and functioning of the total personality were derived from those particular concepts used to describe an arbitrarily selected segment of adaptation. Freud's notations were all derivations of the concept "instinct," with its assumptions about phylogenetic parallelism. In contrast to those of Freud we might mention those of Adler, who chose out of the total process of adaptation to follow the destinies of certain affects and attitudes. The structure of the total personality will accordingly vary depending on the line of sight established by following the destinies of instinct, or by tracing the modalities of ego organization. Our interest is not to prove one right and the other wrong, but merely to see how they complement each other, and how relative each is to the data included.

The earliest structural concepts in psychoanalysis were confined to topical (or topological) differentiations of which "unconscious" and "conscious" were the first. These notions came to take on a spatial meaning. The dynamic viewpoint reëstablished the continuity of the personality with the aid of the so-called mental mechanisms (identification, projection, etc.), and the economic viewpoint indicated the purposive character of the modification; both of these viewpoints contributed to form working concepts of the structure and functions of the total personality.

Unlike its history in other psychologies, the concept "instinct" in psychoanalysis was tied to the tether of certain medical preconceptions, the most significant of which was the guiding notion of a specific etiology for neuroses. Freud decided upon its use after a series of preliminary maneuvers with the idea of trauma or injury as a principle with which to trace specific etiology. Then followed the concept of trauma as a specific, shocking, psychic experience in the sexual domain. The idea of specificity then attached itself to the idea of the time when the sexual injury or trauma was experienced. Finally, since it turned out that not all individuals who had shocking sexual experiences in childhood succumbed to neurosis later, Freud had to abandon this in search of another more specific factor. He then looked for the special factor which affected one individual and not another. The result was that sexual trauma came to mean an arrest of development, probably the most valuable find of this period of Freud's work. This idea has outlived all attempts to overlook or to replace it. There are, however, many ways of interpreting the meaning of this arrest of development, each of which has different clinical implications; one may refer exclusively to pleasure goals, another to perceptual, coördinative and executive functions.

This idea of arrest of development or fixation led to the discovery of infantile sexuality, which was deduced from the correlation between sexual perversions, infantile memories of neurotics, and certain persistent and regularly recurring phenomena in neuroses and dreams.

The term "sexual instinct" was in common usage, and it seemed possible that the ontogenetic scheme evolved in connection with the sexual instinct could be used on other instincts. This proved not to be the case. Some of these other instincts, as the "ego instincts," were merely identified by name; but no progress could be made in studying them. The criteria established for the sexual instincts were made to embrace the entire adaptation of the individual; under the term "erotic pleasure" a great many things were included which deserved separate treatment, or which might have been treated differently if divorced from the assumption that all activities must be derived from that source.

The difficulties with the theory of instincts began at this

point, because the phenomena, correctly observed, were interpreted exclusively as manifestations of the "instinct" in its course of ontogenesis, in back of which was the phylogenetic push, and were not interpreted as manifestations of the total process of adaptation of the individual to a special set of environmental situations. The arrests of development were designated as *fixations,* which emerged as persistent infantile sexual goals to which the individual could regress. The vicissitudes of life were supposed to have an influence on this development, but only in accordance with the ease with which the individual progressed from one stage to another. A failure would always result in a regression (a return to an earlier phase). Thus the entire process of adaptation was seen from the point of view of development, growth, change. This point of view was of inestimable value; without it many phenomena of psychopathology are incomprehensible. The trouble was that this development was watched from a biased viewpoint, and made adaptation a pursuit of sexual pleasure goals. This seems to have been an oversimplification, even though Freud originally claimed that he was only looking for the meaning of neurotic symptoms and was not attempting to elucidate character.

There seem to be two sources of error in this point of view. First, the "instinct" was viewed too exclusively as phylogenetic and physiological; and second, the base was too narrow to hold the entire process of adaptation. The phylogenetic point of view obscured the actual vicissitudes in the life of the child, its dependency, its reactions to discipline; and the pursuit of sexual pleasure goals was too limited to include all the factors which enter into the complicated process we call adaptation. The result was that the phenomena Freud observed did not include the record of all the factors taking place in the adaptation. All divergences from Freud among his pupils took place on the interpretation of what was the essential thing to observe in the total adaptation of the individual. Any psychology which ignores biological needs must (in accordance with past experience) go astray; but it is likewise highly questionable whether the concept of "instinct" is the most accurate method of dealing with these needs.

The phenomenon of repression became, as a result of the instinct theory, the chief guide to the structure of the personality. Nor was there even sufficient differentiation between the "normal" and "neurotic" in this regard. The personality thus became divided into an "ego," "id," and "super-ego." Though Freud recognized that this was merely a tentative scheme and that repression played too great a role in the final formulations, the use of the scheme persisted.

The only change made in recent years is one suggested by Anna Freud. She took this scheme of personality as a base line, and enlarged on the protective functions of the "ego." She now includes in the defensive measures of the "ego" all the mental mechanisms which previously were merely isolated characteristics of the human mind and are so important in following dynamic changes in neurotic processes.

However useful may be Anna Freud's conception of the mental mechanisms as defensive processes, considerable ambiguity persists in that these defenses are considered activities, not of the total personality, but of that portion of the total personality which is called the "ego," as apart from super-ego and id. A further ambiguity derives from the fact that the conception of the total personality as ego-id-super-ego is the representation we get when the total personality is acting under the influence of repression and defense. A still further unclarity arises from the definition of the "ego" as a differentiated portion of the id.

This structuralization of the total personality is one of the sequelae of the influence of psychopathology and more particularly of the phenomenon of repression as a guide for the structure of the total personality. And this in turn is traceable to the instinct-hypothesis.

The instinct-hypothesis with its definition of goals in terms of pleasure principle (or more specifically organ-pleasure-principle) gave rise to another important series of concepts, which although phenomenologically correct (i.e., verifiable) nevertheless were distorted in meaning. These concepts were *fixation, displacement, transference,* and *repetition compulsion.* All of these have been of great use in following the continuity of the human personality, but their meaning changes when they are divorced from the interpretation of behavior as a pursuit of instinctual goals. The question is only as to how fixation is to be located—as the pursuit of a special infantile organ-pleasure goal, or as the organization of the total personality? When seen from the latter point of view all these four "mechanisms" describe the continuity of the personality in its perceptual, coordinative, and executive capacities.

The instinct-psychology which defines adaptation in terms of the pursuit of instinctual goals, did so with the aid of a group of constructs which, like the mental mechanisms, enjoyed for a long time a position extraneous to the main body of the theory. This situation was changed when Freud reintroduced the concept of defense (1926). In this new point of view the extraneous concepts are now drawn into the whole ego structure and in fact describe its changing modalities.

The personality scheme evolved from the instinct-psychology left open gaps between repression and repressing forces, between symptoms and character, pleasure principle and reality principle, and, most important of all, the relations between the conscious and unconscious idea systems. The first attempt to bridge these gaps was made by Ferenczi; but in order to do this he had to step outside of the frame of reference of instinct psychology, and to regard attitudes and idea sequences compatible with the comprehension and resources of the child as basic units with which to deal, units which could not be construed as derivatives of the so-called "ego instincts." Further work along this line has more recently been done by Anna Freud in her book *The Ego and the Mechanisms of Defence,* and by Horney, Rado, and Reich. If we continue the line of reasoning by both Ferenczi and Anna Freud, we come to a conception of the total personality as follows in the ensuing pages.

The Total Personality from the Point of View Of the Ego

This essay is an attempt to show that different institutions create different personality structures. For this reason it is of the highest importance that our technique be attuned to the capacity for comparative work. One of the failures of the instinct theory is that it established no basis for the comparison of institutions and their effects.

In our study of the reaction types to frustration we have attempted to show that a large series of obstacles can be placed in the way of the smooth functioning of the total personality. And furthermore that the structure of the personality, since it is integrative and cumulative in character, will be persistently molded in accordance with the social forces with which it makes contact from birth onward.

The simplest illustration of how an obstacle to the functioning of the total personality will modify its entire structure is to be found in the traumatic neurosis. The particular functions involved in this neurosis, those which pertain to orientation and mastery of the external environment, are of a kind to which no culture ever creates obstacles; but the effects on the total personality are much easier to envisage.

Let us consider the case of a man who fell with a crashing airplane some 1,500 feet and was only slightly injured in the fall. When I saw him seven years after this accident, he had the following symptoms: convulsive seizures or losses of consciousness occurring three or four times daily; inability to sleep because of nightmares in which he is being annihilated in one form or another; vertigo; lack of coördination of limbs, so that he could not walk confidently or use tools with any accuracy; a very marked irritability, especially toward noise or toward any persistent effort; a headache localized on the left side of the forehead; a hemianaesthesia involving the whole left side of the body; a partial amnesia about the accident itself; a disinclination to work and a complete inability to perform any work; outbursts of rage at mild provocation.

It may be noted that these symptoms, though extreme, are similar in character to those which any individual exposed to an accident may have. The difference lies in the severity and persistence of the symptoms.

In this type of neurosis the concept "instinct" gives us no orientation because the executive functions of orientation and muscle coördination do not have any identifiable "instinct" which drives them. These functions have, primarily, not a pleasure function, but a "utility function"; they are means to an end which may eventually be pleasure or mastery. No somatic source can be identified as the source of these activities, but only the executives—eye, ear, muscle, etc.—can be identified. What we do know about these functions is that the potentiality for using them existed at birth, but that their development was slow and became more and more complicated. We know that as long as these functions were intact this man was able to lead a normal life, all of which was restored to him after treatment. What has happened in the neurosis is that these functions became protectively contracted, and were no longer at the disposal of the total personality.

This is the basic psychopathology. The symptoms are the secondary effects of the effort to continue the former adaptation without the use of these important instruments. It means that the entire personality structure became altered, and that a new type of adaptation, based on his now altered capacities, became imperative. The great disadvantage to the patient was that the functions involved cannot be replaced by any other functions. The ear cannot see and the eye cannot touch. In many of these neuroses all the sense organs cease, for a time, to function.

How do we know that this is essentially the pathology? Because these functions of orientation and activity formerly were in order, and now they are not. What has happened to them? We can only assume—on the principle that a child who touches the flame and gets burnt will avoid the flame thereafter—that they are protectively inhibited. That these functions were not permanently lost[21] was demonstrated by this patient's complete restoration to effective life.

Now we are in a position to understand his symptoms. This man, after his illness, seeks to derive the same gratification from the outer world as he did before, but cannot do so. His "self-confidence" is gone; his picture of himself as effectively consummating a given act no longer exists. Every time he makes an attempt to tax his contracted resources he meets with a repetition of the accident (his convulsive seizures). His dreams, in which he is continually failing, are another witness to the fact that this man can no longer command the resources he formerly did. With all his effectiveness gone, he has the right to picture himself as helpless and insignificant, and to picture the outer world, which has lost its meaning to him, as hostile and ready to annihilate him. In place of the previously organized mastery of the outer world, he now gives vent to disorganized outbursts of aggression and destructiveness.

As a result of his now diminished resources, this man's perceptions of the outer world and of himself have become altered. He is in a constant state of apprehension and irritability lest his enfeebled personality be overthrown by any stimulus too great for him. His anxiety is organized around the memory of his failure, the contraction of his resources, and the feeling of helplessness. The outbursts of aggression, so prominent in this neurosis, are due neither to a death instinct nor to a regression to a sadistic organization; they are merely an effort to express mastery, the normal channels of which have become blocked. There are other details in this illness which we can safely delete as not bearing on our theme.

This case gives us some important clues about the total personality. Under cultural forces—except in the case of violation of taboo—we never observe such a complete contraction of

[21] This case was demonstrated to the N. Y. Society for Clinical Psychiatry, March, 1924.

the total resources. But we find, instead, persistent pressures which also modify the personality in circumscribed segments of organization. When such a personality change has taken place in the individual as a whole, his perceptive, coördinative, and executive capacities operate in accordance with this altered organization. This new organization is present in his character or in symptoms.

This is demonstrated in the case of the man whose dream we previously recorded (p. 208). There we saw, as antecedent to the dream, a culturally determined interference in childhood with the impulse to masturbate, and in adult life with the patient's free use of his sexual impulses. This interference was conveyed to him in a particularly forceful, if not brutal, manner. At the present time this individual is unable to perform normally not only his sexual functions, but also a great many other activities, as he is under the constant obligation to keep watch over this impulse, lest it escape its defenses. This possibility causes him much anxiety. In his dream the total personality is seen operating under the necessity to keep a powerful impulse under control. Since he has omitted one of his most essential defenses, to narcotize the sexual urge and his defensive capacities out of existence by alcohol, the original desire promptly asserts itself in a dream, whereas in the waking state he has no sexual desire. The dream now tries to dispose of the wish by crushing the protest against the prohibition.

Why does this individual still have to crush both his desire and his protest against the interference with it, when the external conditions in the world no longer demand of him to renounce it as he did in childhood? Is it because he has become "fixated" on some other substitute gratification? This has not shown itself to be the case, though some of his symptoms have the character of oral substitutes, when one would theoretically expect to find those of anal origin. Strictly speaking, there is no more a substitute for the sexual impulse than there is one for hearing; when an individual is compelled by circumstances to press another organ into use for the purpose, the results are highly unsatisfactory to the personality as a whole. When a blind man educates his sense of touch, we cannot make the assumption that this is done on the principle that seeing and touching are of cognate origin, although they are both forms of sensation. Does our subject continue to repress because his super-ego is very strict? This explanation is not an implausible one under the circumstances, except that we cannot accept or operate with the concept super-ego as a fixed compartment or function of the mind, any more than we can apply this concept to the child who burns his fingers.[22] Likewise we can identify the "id" impulse in the wish to make love to a girl, an activity which is abruptly interrupted. The "ego" can also be identified as the castrated man who protests against the outrage, and the "super-ego" as the man who crushes the protesting figure with alcohol.

This scheme of the total personality makes some very damaging omissions. We cannot make clear to ourselves the meaning of the "super-ego," even when we add the fact that it was acquired by a process of "identification" with the mother, who was the original prohibitor of the activity; this is especially true since "identification" includes so many different attitudes.

We might get a clearer picture of the personality structure, as operating in this dream, by translating the entire fantasy into terms of direct experience. Thus it says in effect: "I have sexual desire which I want very much to exercise; but I fear to do so, because if I do, some very important interest which I really cannot identify will be jeopardized. I cannot control this desire of mine, although in fact it no longer appears as a desire but as a murderous impulse of some kind. I must therefore crush this desire which exposes me to unknown danger. I have trouble on another score because I am afraid that unless I crush this desire I will commit some horrible deed—at least it appears to me that way. Moreover, I feel a terrific protest against not

<hr>

[22] This dilemma Freud encounters frequently, as we see when the sense of reality is sometimes described as a function of the "ego" and sometimes as a function of the "super-ego."

being able to exercise my sexuality; but I dare not offer any protest because if I do all kinds of terrible things will happen to me."

This is as far as we can go in reconstructing the patient's direct experience. But there are still some things the subject does not know, and of which there is no record in the dream; they are truly unconscious. He does not know that his entire perceptual system (i.e., the stimuli in the outer world he is reacting to) has undergone important changes; his coördinative systems, as can be seen from the dream, are very distorted; and, finally, his executive capacities are seriously curtailed. He cannot do anything that will yield him sexual satisfaction. But his coördinative and executive capacities are contingent on his perceptions, which are now attitudinized and habitual, and therefore a fixed part of his ego structure. These perceptions involve the outer world and himself. If we ask him what interests he is safeguarding by this entire procedure, he does not know. And for a very good reason. He cannot make them plausible in the world in which he lives, for his practical relations with people are conventionalized. From his reactions to the analyst, however, one can see something of the interests he is trying to defend. This interest, in a man of thirty-seven, can get no recognition nor enjoy any plausibility. He wishes to be approved and protected by me and everyone else, and attributes to me remarkable powers to do him both good and harm. But these conditions of gaining approval are sought after by those very techniques he used as a child of four, though these no longer have any currency in his present world. This is the picture of approval, safety, security which our subject built up from the disciplines to which he was subjected. These are the terms in which he perceives his relations to others.

In short, the continuity of the personality can be traced in the specific conditioned perceptions, the coördinative, and the executive capacities of our subject, and not in the pursuit of specific infantile sexual goals or objects. These latter, when they do exist, are effects and not causes. If this is true, then *repetition compulsion, transference, displacement,* and *fixation* are all evidences of fixed modifications in the personality structure of the subject. The structure of the personality into an id ego, and super-ego is a schematic method of representing the direct experience of the subject; but it represents only one specific arrangement: the individual perceives himself and his capacities in accordance with the conditions for being loved in return for obedience. Another type of arrangement of perceptive, coördinative, and executive tools of the individual can be found in the phenomenon descriptively called "projection" (see p. 305).

Thus, when we attempt to describe the structure of the personality according to the fixed scheme deduced from the phenomenon of repression, we put ourselves in an awkward position if we use this as a base for describing all its other modalities such as projection, identification, etc., and conceive of them as activities of the "ego"—which is itself now a neurotic residue in Freud's personality scheme. In actual practice the scheme does not work, for it is not even true of all forms of repression. We have already examined one neurosis in which the super-ego plays no role, yet the total personality has undergone very far-reaching changes in its executive and perceptual functions.

As a substitute for this rigid personality scheme we are obliged to use one which lacks the concentration and patness of the ego-id-super-ego scheme, but which gains in plasticity. We are obliged to remember the phylogenetic endowment of man at birth with an ego or total personality of a very rudimentary kind, which in the process of growth and integration is constantly undergoing continuous change. However, at any time after birth we find that this organization has the following elements:

1. Needs: either of a bodily nature (food and sex, etc.), or created or accentuated by the society—prestige, etc.
2. Perceptions: of the outer world, of oneself, and of oneself in relation to the outer world.

3. Impulses: in a disorganized state, or in an organized state to the end of mastery or control.

4. Affects: which are indicators of the tensions of the personality as a whole, e.g., anxiety, jealousy.

5. Attitudes: which are really preparations for action, whether it is consummated or not, e.g., obstinacy, crossness, etc.

6. Goals: pleasure, rest, freedom from tension, satisfaction (hunger) mastery, utility, etc.

It is to be noted that all of these units are forms of direct experience.

The final formulations about the personality as a whole will depend largely on which of these elements are singled out for pursuit, and on whether the human being is conceived of as an *acting* or a *feeling* creature. Some authors, notably Adler, prefer the latter conception. All these elements are equally important and the dependency of feeling on the capacity for action is so intimate that one cannot emphasize one over the other without distorting the entire picture. If such an arbitrary selection is made, the trouble really begins to arise when the total personality must be reconstructed from the selective information gathered from affects or instincts. The result is bound to be incomplete. It is the interaction of all these elements mentioned which tells eventually on the individual's capacity for free and uninhibited action.

NEEDS

Hunger and sexual needs are probably the most basic needs of man. These are apparently somatically rooted. Other needs, like the need for protection, are not somatically rooted, but are not therefore less urgent. It is the characteristic of man that his needs are not stereotyped and change under different conditions. Needs can be created or accentuated by a given milieu.

PERCEPTIONS

To the physical world perceptions are "educated." Perspective is such a type of educated or trained perception. The utility of objects is another result of trained perceptions. The complicated forms of attitudinized perceptions both of other individuals and of oneself are the most important for our consideration.

IMPULSES

These have been given various names, such as *elementary drives* (Rado). When organized, impulses have a goal—mastery or satisfaction. The most complicated types of integration take place in the organization of activity to consummate these drives or impulses.

AFFECTS

These must engage us at some length. Affects differ from attitudes; affects are perceptive, whereas attitudes are executive. An affect describes the quality of a feeling; an attitude, a preparation for action. Love is an affect; diffidence or submission an attitude. Affects and attitudes are considered together because the relation between the two, especially the chronological one, is not equally understood in all cases.

Complicated forms of affects and attitudes are most likely to come into play when the individual is not acting or feeling as a unit, i.e., if he has several interests to meet simultaneously. Let us consider a very complicated attitude like "crossness." A young woman in analysis becomes cross, contrary, uncoöperative, sulky, and abusive whenever the concept "sexual" crosses her mind. This is the attitude. The affective state underneath it proves to be very complicated. She has an unconscious attitude of obedience to certain injunctions against sex once imposed by her mother. Of this she is not aware. This prohibition is organically sealed in a sexual anesthesia; she can perceive no sexual pleasure. Whenever the sexual impulse, now conceived as an impulse to disobey, arises, she is anxious. On the other hand, she resents being compelled to obey this injunction because it interferes not only with sexual pleasure, but secondarily with a great many other pleasures. Her crossness is a helpless rage; but it is now directed at anyone who stimulates sexual desire, not at the one who originally prevented its gratification. Behind this crossness there is the necessity for obedience, resentment against it, and anxiety.

Attitudes and affects become important for the diagnosis of the effectiveness of the total personality. Affects indicate something pleasant or something dangerous, or may point to the existence of conflicting interests. Attitudes advise us of the executive position of the entire personality toward the situation provoking the affect.

The study of psychopathology has demonstrated that this problem of affects and attitudes is very complex. Affects are not always direct indicators because the perceptions from which they arise cannot always be located. This is, of course, notably the case with anxiety. Anxiety, for example, may be the expression of a direct conflict with an object or situation in the outer world, a wild beast, the apprehension of famine, etc. On the other hand, in neurotic phobias, affects are not the result of any direct perceptions. However, neurotic or otherwise, anxiety is always an indicator of a deficiency of resources to combat what the individual regards as a threat to his existence or safety.

The *fear* of a specific object is an affect. The attitude with respect to this affect may be humility, submissiveness, awe, ingratiation, combat, or flight. Anxiety is usually accompanied by helplessness or a tendency to flight. Others would interpret anxiety as an indicator of the helplessness of the individual. With love, on the other hand, a great many attitudes are associated, as, for example, tenderness, sympathy, trust, kindness, protectiveness, pity. Hate has a long series of attitudes associated with it, such as mistrust, spite, obstinacy, cruelty, scorn, contempt. Other affects are more difficult to differentiate from ego attitudes, as for example, envy, jealousy, and rivalry.

Affects and attitudes bear a relationship to another series which can be called ego feelings, for example, satisfaction, contentment, elation, depression; pride and disdain record ego attitudes in relation to comparison with others. The phenomenon of guilt is particularly difficult to classify in this regard. In a general way we can state that the affect is a signal, the attitude, executive in character. In addition there are the ego-feelings, which are affects about oneself. These attitudes are basic in the formation of a final category of personality, namely, character. The formation of character is thus a piece of psychic economy enabling the individual to mobilize attitudes based upon past experience which will act as automatic guides to future behavior.

Let us consider a specific affect and attitude, namely jealousy. How does this fit into our personality scheme? We have indicated that jealousy describes a state of tension among various interests of the personality, and we made an analogy with sensation. The emotion and the attitude accompanying jealousy imply a complicated series of events simultaneously: (1) A specific kind of ego feeling which indicates that the individual is not at one with himself. (2) A comparison with another person who is either enjoying more or suffering less. (3) A wish to have what he has or to be what he is. (4) Hostile feeling toward him. (5) Self-abasing feeling toward oneself. (6) An anxiety that one has lost what the other fellow has, based on the assumption that the desired state stands in the same relation to the object of jealousy as it would to the subject.

To say that there are humans who have no feeling of jealousy may be correct, but to say that there are humans who have no potentiality for jealousy is, in other words, to say that their personality is defective in the very important and socially useful function of apprising the individual of his relative status. In many ways, such an individual is exposed to dangers similar to those of the person who has lost the power of feeling the sensation of pain, as for example, when touching a hot stove. But to state that certain social conditions preclude the necessity for jealousy because they supply deferred or vicarious satisfaction or relief thereof, must not be taken to mean that the potentiality for jealousy does not exist. Its absence in an individual may be testimony to his adequacy and resourcefulness. No society can impose upon the individual that he should either feel or not feel jealousy; society can only curb its manifestations, render its usefulness for adaptation minimal, or devise methods for restoring the state of equilibrium in the individual. A society may, however, render the manifestations of jealousy overt and even encourage its manifestations. It may be pointed out that the Todas are a people among whom there is no jealousy. The Todas have a polyandrous system of marriage. This observation may be phenomenologically correct. Rivers[23] notes, however, that there is a special place in the netherworld for those who feel jealousy, thereby clearly indicating that there are sanctions against the manifestations of jealousy. Moreover, it is very probable that such feelings among the Todas are easily repressed, for various reasons contained in their social organization. It would take too long to describe the conditions under which jealousy can be repressed. In a personal communication Linton reports that sanctions against jealousy are so effective among the Todas that after monogamous marriage was legally enforced they reverted to group marriage, in which the man has several wives, and each wife has several husbands.

Now why is all this discussion pertinent to our theme? It is because culture molds the specific direction and activities of the personality. Culture can do this because the total personality is slow in formation. Not all of it is done by force; most of it is done by a kind of osmosis. This influence of culture is, of course, necessary for the preservation of the solidarity of the group. Though the immediate executive of a culture is the parent, or the protectors during the formative years, the disciplines to which the individual is subject are culturally determined. This leaves plenty of leeway for the individual. Society cannot prescribe the specific reaction to a given discipline; this is determined by the individual alone. In our society for ex-

[23] W. H. R. Rivers, *The Todas* (London and New York, 1906), p. 530.

ample, we prescribe sexual aims, but the reactions to these by the individual are legion.[24]

In the clinical study of the neurosis, the analysis of character has in recent years taken the prime position. This point of view was first taken by W. Reich.[25] It is also the working basis of Horney, Rado, and myself. W. Reich, however, derives *character* from infantile experiences as evaluated by the criteria of the libido theory. In this book we sacrificed no important facts included in the libido theory. The facts were, however, evaluated in accordance with express indications of Freud, and by a technique initiated by Ferenczi. The essential difference is that phenomena which can be described as "anal sadastic" from the point of view of substitutive pleasure goals take on a different meaning from the point of view of the ego. The substitutive pleasure function of such phenomena becomes one of many secondary alterations in the total ego structure.

BASIC PERSONALITY STRUCTURE

From this point on, our chief interest is in the role that institutions play in the formation of the basic conceptions of the individual concerning his relations with the objects in the outer world. This must depend on what special influences the child is subjected to, and must be integrated in the order in which the influences occur, or rather in the order in which the child can appreciate them. If shortly after birth the child is deprived of free mobility by being placed on a cradleboard, it is reasonable to expect that this will have an immediate

---

[24] We have not had any occasion to discuss the third unit of Freudian metapsychology, the "id." This concept has the same obscurities connected with it which we found in "super-ego." As long as psychoanalysis proceeds from the viewpoint that all data of mental life are to be focused on the issue of what instinctual goal the individual is pursuing, the concept "id" has a definite meaning. If, however, a more complete analysis of the ego shows us that the data of mental life must include factors other than pursuit of instinctual goals, such as defense, dependency, etc., then this concept loses its sharp outlines. If, for example, we encounter in a dream an indication of unconscious homosexuality, it is very difficult to describe this merely as an expression of the "id," without taking into account the factor of defense.

[25] Reich, *Characteranalyse* (published by the author, 1933).

retarding influence. How permanent this retarding influence is will not depend on this circumstance alone. There is reason to believe that when this restricting influence is removed, there may be an initial retardation, which can, however, soon be overcome.[26] There is little reason to suppose that such an influence in early childhood will have a permanent effect unless the influence is continuous and is associated with other elements that convey the impression of pain, obstruction, or mistreatment. Let us suppose two kinds of treatment associated with the cradleboard. In one case, let us suppose the treatment to be unkind: the infant is neglected, it is fed carelessly—these or other factors create painful impressions. In this case we could expect some association of restriction with the cradleboard and an unpleasant affect associated with the mother. If, however, we suppose the mother's treatment to be kind and tender, then the cradleboard would not necessarily create a painful impression.

Likewise in considering obstructions to certain impulses or satisfactions it is questionable whether any fixed constellations can be formed around episodic or unrelated phenomena. The case of early sphincter control in Tanala society is a case in point. It is doubtful that this isolated fact can create a lasting constellation, unless followed by others of a similar type. Both in Tanala and Marquesan culture we found that the most important constellations were those which were continuous. As a result, a group of constellations are formed which become for the individual a part of his sense of reality.

This can be easily proved by examining some of the thought processes used by different cultures to represent relations between the individual and other objects. The structure of the constellations in the basic personality structure may be represented from the particular instance of sphincter control as follows:

1. The child begins with an automatic functioning of the bowels. This may be accompanied by feelings of release of tension.

[26] René Spitz, in a personal communication.

2. The automatic functioning is replaced by a necessity for control of the bowel, and this, in turn, necessitates a recognition of certain sensations, and the initiation of a new series of behavior patterns in connection with them.

3. If control is learned, the child is approved; if he fails, he is either punished or disapproved.

4. A basic constellation is now created, "If I do as is expected of me I will be approved." Orderliness and cleanliness are thus cultural demands, the significance of which the child does not appreciate; but when he is clean, the child is led to expect approval. This is at first a constellation of obedience; but it may later become one of responsibility and conscientiousness. If the conditions are fulfilled by the child, and the rewards are collected, a working balance may be struck. If however the child is obedient and then is not rewarded, increased anxiety and inhibition is one result; another is pugnacity and defiance.

The situation which creates this series of constellations in the individual is the primary institution. From this point on it may become a part of the individual's sense of reality that obedience brings protection—or any plausible variation of the same idea. The power of the parent becomes inflated in accordance with the deflation of that of the child. When this same individual is an adult, and is confronted with a situation in which he is helpless and demands aid from a deity, he has a ready-made technique for securing the aid of this superior being, the truth and expediency of which is self-evident to him. He can insure it by obedience, or by a system of reinstatement techniques, such as punishment, fine, sacrifice in the sense of depriving oneself, all of which are derived from his actual experience. Thus the secondary institution, the religious practice or ritual, is a product not of the primary institution directly, but of the constellation produced by it in the individual. This constellation, now a part of his sense of reality, the individual automatically uses when any situation like the original one arises. The religious practices in fact have no direct resemblance to anal discipline, but the actual practices in the religion are comprehensible only in terms of the constellation in the basic personality structure created by these early disciplines.

We were fortunately able to check the operational efficacy of this conception of basic personality structure in two cultures in which the basic disciplines, and hence the constellations in the basic personality structure, were radically different. In both cultures the need for a superior being to aid the individual when in a helpless state was present. In both instances the superior being was actually the departed parent or a close substitute for him. But the methods of soliciting aid and the binding character of the relationship to the deity were different in each culture.

Some of these constellations in the basic personality structure were derived from the causal relations established by discipline. Others were derived from persistent frustrations in objects (in the Marquesas, the woman) and the outer world (attitude toward food supply). In each instance the institution was shown to be derived from the constellation created in the individual by the frustrating experience in real life. The summation of all these constellations constitutes the basic personality structure.

In deriving these constellations from frustrating experiences we used our knowledge of psychopathology, and found in each instance that the constellations could be reduced to simple types of experience, many of which could be verified by common observation. The manner in which these images of frustrating objects became altered can be traced in any child subjected to severe restrictions. The series of phobic images recorded above (p. 442) are the general lines along which they develop. The change from witches to burglars represents the change in the plausibility of the image to which the anxiety is attached. This "displacement" already indicates the fixity of his perceptions and the interests which his fantasies were intended to serve. These were the transformations of the representation of his mother, who was his persecutrix as regards masturbation, and his protectress in every other way.

The exact manner in which institutions like *fanaua* originated cannot be answered without history. But such an institution can arise only from the constellations produced by frustrating contacts with the mother in childhood and with other women later. The correctness of these derivations can be checked only by comparative studies of various cultures, but from the study of the individual in our own culture, they seem quite correct.

Primary and Secondary Institutions

We stated at the beginning that we have to divide institutions into primary and secondary; that psychology can cast no light whatsoever without the aid of history on how these primary institutions took their final forms. So far as we know, no satisfactory explanations have ever been made of primary institutions. All we know about them is that there are a limited number of possibilities in the attempt to satisfy certain biological needs of man. However, we can explain secondary institutions and their relation to primary ones. Among the primary institutions are family organization, in-group formation, basic disciplines, feeding, weaning, institutionalized care or neglect of children, anal training, and sexual taboos including aim, object, or both, subsistence techniques, etc. Among the secondary institutions are taboo systems, religion, rituals, folktales, and techniques of thinking.

A primary institution is one which is older, more stable, and less likely to be interfered with by vicissitudes of climate or economy. To this the one exception is subsistence technique, which must be considered primary, although abrupt changes in it can take place in any culture. However, the presence of these primary institutions is never noted by the individual; they always seem as self-evident as breathing. We cannot think of any more basic institution than the family. This is the kind of institution about which explanations are scanty. The fact that father, mother, and child must at least temporarily constitute a social unit needs no explanation. But the various types of family organization and the various factors which produced the particular arrangement found in each culture constitute an historical problem.

But the formal organization is the least important aspect of the family as a social unit. Of far greater importance are the particular relations of father, mother, and child, and the disciplines to which the child is subjected together with the division of his loyalties and obligations; for it is in these relations that the differentiations in family organization, insofar as they affect the individual, begin to occur. Certain types of family organization are predicted by systematic numerical disparity between the sexes induced by female infanticide (Todas).

The origin of the disciplines to which the child is subjected is largely a field for speculation in which we have little interest. Occasionally we find a culture, such as Tanala, in which very early anal training is founded on a practical convenience for the mother, due to the absence of suitable swaddling material. In general, one could account for the origin of anal training on the basis of mutual convenience, while living in fixed abodes. At all events, the origin of the family, the special types of organization, and the reasons for these basic disciplines, are fields for speculation, for without the aid of history, it is futile to attempt to reconstruct them.

It may be possible at some future date to trace the history of anal training and sexual disciplines; but for our present objectives the origins of these are too remote in every culture, and therefore history alone can supply the clues. There is, however, one phase of this primary institution in which we can allow ourselves some plausible hypothesis; that is the sex behavior permitted to children. This, more than any other of the basic institutions, seems to be a function of the entire culture. By that we mean that in the type of sex behavior permitted the child, we have a general indication of the tensions already existing in a given society. The relation between primary and secondary institutions can only be checked in an experimental way, by demonstrating that when one changes, the other will also change. We had an opportunity to observe this in the change from dry to wet rice cultivation among the Tanala. This change in economy brought about a whole series of apparently unrelated changes in secondary institutions, ranging from the establishment of a king to an increase in homosexuality.

The anxieties coming from the external environment can only be evaluated in terms of the effectiveness with which man deals with them. The ability to store and save food can lessen the anxiety of famine. It is a source of security to learn to control what is originally beyond control, but in this latter case, where there is no control, there is a way of soliciting aid from a divinity. The relationship of the group to this deity is based on the prototype of the relation of parent to child, where the resourcelessness of the latter is supplemented by the omnipotence delegated to him by the child. In Zuni, the chief function of the *catchinas* is to give rain. This is the simplest illustration of relieving anxiety by direct appeal to a deity. What you cannot do yourself, the all-powerful parent will.

However, the character of the demands made on the deity and the conditions under which such help can be solicited from him, are derived from the disciplines to which the child is subjected. He is thus taught the primary techniques by which aid can be secured from a more powerful individual. If the disciplines established by the parent are severe, the means of placating the god must likewise be associated with privations and punishments to establish the conditions for reinstatement of the conditions for being loved. The easiest way to verify this is to study the rituals for placating a god, or for reinstating oneself in his good graces in order to be able to call upon his omnipotence once more. Several of these have been noted by Freud and Reik. But they did not see in this phenomenon a reflection of the disciplines to which the individual was subjected, but a reminiscence of the original parricide, i.e., historical survivals, etc. This latter hypothesis raises the question whether institutions without functional significance can survive in their original form. They can; but their meaning is altered.

In those societies where restrictive disciplines[27] are slight, as in the Marquesan, we note the relations to the major gods described through the simple relationship of parent and child with respect to food. What is fed to the god is determined by various factors; here in the Marquesan culture we find expression of the primitive idea that the power of the god depends on how many men he eats. The idea is derived from only one possible source, that of nursing or being fed, which remains the basic pattern of solicitation from the parent.

The anxieties created by the primary institutions we have already described elsewhere. They depend essentially on which particular impulses are subjected to discipline. We have already surveyed in a previous chapter the forces at play in the establishment of a discipline. It is the interplay between authority and dependency which establishes the basic patterns in which human relations are formulated. If the idea in back of conditioned love, "If you obey me, I will protect you," is established early in life, we can follow its numerous ramifications in many of the practices of primitive people. In Tanala, cure of disease depends on the performance of a compulsive ritual in which obedience to some arbitrary command is essential. In Marquesan and Trobriand culture we found no such insistence, but in the case of the Marquesan we have a pure feeding ritual. The reason is self-evident; in Tanala, discipline is enforced early; in Marquesan, it not enforced at all.

Now, if a culture creates a necessity for repressing certain tendencies or impulses, what are likely to be the effects of this on other institutions? What institutions does this repression in itself create? In order to understand this we must first see what influence repressions have on the perception systems of the individual. This is extremely difficult and complicated and may not be convincing. We can only describe it clinically.

[27] Anal training is, strictly speaking, a directional discipline. It takes on the character of a restrictive discipline because of the marked interference it creates with the previously existing adaptation.

There we must make use of a distinction between those disciplines which end in inhibitions and those which end in suppression.

Let us consider this problem from the point of view of an individual who has a character disturbance which can be called paranoid. This man is the same individual from whom we derived the phenomena of projection in terms of direct experience (see p. 305). His relations with others were disturbed by the unconscious operation of two conflicting attitudes: a deeply repressed insistence that others should submit to his will, and a conviction that this wish is bound to be frustrated. His manifest attitude was one of distrust of others and of grandiosity, the latter being in effect a denial of his strong unconscious dependency.

One of this man's dominant interests was the wish to change the institutions of our society in such a way as to make it suitable for his particular needs, to make them satisfy a long repressed craving for dependency. Though he always looks everywhere for the satisfaction of his craving, a part of his personality structure, an attitude of mistrust, makes it impossible for him to satisfy it in his actual life contacts. On the one hand every rival or superior is assumed to be his enemy, and he then proceeds to antagonize them by showing them how little need he has for their love and admiration. This relationship was formerly covered by the concept narcissistic; this word, however, does not describe the dynamics of the actual relationship. The basic reservoir in the human cannot be considered narcissism; but dependency is one of the basic ego attitudes, and the techniques derived from it are among the basic means of consummating the ends of so-called "narcissistic" needs. The frustrated dependency creates the situation which looks like self-love. On the other hand, this same patient had a blind worship of certain characters whose teachings promised him the wished-for realization of his dependency craving. The institution which he wishes to create is a projection in the outer world of the discomforts created by his own manner of perceiving reality. Though his perceptions have been conditioned by a series of frustrations, their effect has been indelibly imprinted upon his personality organization.

If our assumption is correct that primary institutions create certain constellations, then secondary institutions in society must satisfy the needs and tensions created by the primary or fixed ones. The technique of such institutions must of course, vary with the consciousness of the need and particular terms in which the need is represented. Among the techniques encountered in primitive society, taboo is one of the most remarkable. This is undoubtedly an instrument of social balance capable of a great many different uses. The interest which a taboo safeguards may not be consciously appreciated, though the emotion giving rise to the taboo must be extremely powerful. If we note for example, that women are excluded by taboo from the communal activity with men in Marquesan society, this taboo may have been established as the result of actual disturbances in the past; or it may be unconsciously appreciated as a source of danger. It does not matter which, for both are true. In other instances, it seems very unlikely that the objectives which a taboo purports to safeguard should not be consciously appreciated. For example, in a gerontocracy where all the young women and the choice bits of food are taboo to any except the older men of the community, it seems difficult to believe that this is not appreciated as a conscious objective. However, in this instance one must explain why the young men obey the taboo. The old men may have something which would disrupt the society if they were killed. In the case of the Marquesans, we offered the suggestion that these taboos point to an anxiety about disrupting the solidarity among the men. The implication is that there is a great deal of latent jealousy among the men, but at the same time there is an appreciation of the danger to the entire community and to each individual in it, if this jealousy becomes manifest. The institution of taboo is, therefore, a weapon of social equilibrium, a legitimate and necessary protection against the disrupting influences latent within the social organization itself. I do not believe it is possible for a member of the Marquesan society to appreciate the sources from which this feeling of danger comes; he need not even be aware of the fact that there is such a thing as male solidarity. We do not appreciate such factors in our own society. We did not (until Freud pointed them out) appreciate the effects of sexual aim taboos.

Let us examine some of the other secondary institutions in Marquesan culture, the minor deities, the familiars, and the *fanaua*. One group of these are male ghosts, who sleep with incestuous objects, and are obviously the fantasies of women. This institution is a record of a definite social taboo against incest between father and daughter. The familiar may, however, be some other illustrious figure of the past. The woman can thus use the illustrious figure or incestuous object to execute her own wishes against another woman. In the case of the *fanaua* we see other evidence of the sexual dissatisfaction of the male, who as a *fanaua* enjoys the opportunity to have sexual intercourse with a woman after he is dead. But why cannot a *fanaua* injure the husband of the woman possessed? The reasons are obviously the same as those that obtain in actual life, the preservation of male solidarity. This latter illustration shows us how close to the actual social patterns the religious concepts are, and the actual experiences from which they proceed.

The most difficult part of the scheme that we have outlined is the one which deals with the alteration of perceptions as the result of repressions, and the structure of the new institutions on the basis of the perceptions now altered to coincide with the repression. Let us consider a compulsive neurotic who lives in a complicated system of taboos. As a result of severe and rigidly enforced external prohibitions against masturbation, every bit of self-assertion on his part is represented in his dreams or in his fantasies as a piece of wanton destructiveness. Now according to the libido theory our patient is arrested at a certain phase of ontogenetic development, the "anal sadistic."

The man is simply describing to us, according to the principles laid down in a previous chapter, what happens to an inhibited impulse. The important thing to note is that our patient is no longer defending himself against the consciously perceived sexual impulse, but against the form in which it is now represented in his unconscious. The latter in turn is a replica of how the patient actually regards the prohibition, and how much force he would have to use to overthrow it. On this principle, namely that a repressed impulse has a new ideational representation in the unconscious, we may describe cannibalism as an active defense created by the unconscious images in which frustrated dependency is represented, namely the fear of being eaten up. It is not likely that any current or ancient practice of infanticide could make the anxiety of being eaten up active among Marquesans without drawing on the actual frustrations that they experience in real life.

This brings up a point which we had occasion to discuss in connection with Marquesan culture, namely, why do certain beliefs persist against all reason? Let us take one of the myths of our society, the myth that masturbation is harmful. This myth is traceable to the predynastic Egyptians and has gone through a long series of rationalizations in Western culture. This belief was even embodied in our notions about anatomical pathology as late as 1910. The medical profession backed up this myth with a series of imposing "scientific" checks. This story could not be perpetuated if it did not have some emotional plausibility. One does not have to look very far for the answer; it is to be found in the whole line of forces that lie back of sexual aim taboos in our society. If these taboos are violated, parental love and protection may be withdrawn from the child. It is, therefore, a belief which only a very dependent or uninformed character can maintain. Those for whom the myth does not serve the end of corroborating an unconscious conviction, do not tell it to their children.

We are now in a position to appreciate the significance of certain social syndromes as checks upon our diagnosis of the forces operating in institutions. We are naturally most interested in the one on which psychoanalysis has devoted so much attention, namely the Oedipus complex. This constellation derives its name from an ancient Greek myth. Freud discovered it in the dreams of contemporary individuals, and occasionally as an actual episode consciously remembered by the child. He ascribed to this syndrome the significance of the universal trauma in man's phylogenetic history, and assumed that the drive for sexual union with the mother was a biologically determined and transmitted constellation.

The significance of this syndrome in the individual neurotic is far from established. Freud's original assumption was that the longings of the child toward the parent of the opposite sex were sexual. A vast array of facts gathered in the past forty years have failed to disprove this assumption of Freud's. However, the interpretation of "sexual" gives us a good deal of leeway in our thinking. There is no question but that sexual cravings begin in the child during the period of greatest dependency. Any one who doubts this might examine the sexual activity in societies where there are no aim taboos, Trobriand and Marquesan. Infantile sexuality had to be "discovered" in our society by mining down through a long series of blind spots and defenses. The confusion in psychoanalytic literature about the significance of the Oedipus complex has resulted from the failure to recognize that these sexual longings were mixed up with and were expressions of dependency cravings. The greater the dependency, the more prominent the Oedipus complex. The individual seeks to make the object of dependency his sexual object as well. In the face of social barriers to satisfying sexual curiosity on other objects, and even to masturbation (one of the functions of which is to aid the child in weaning itself from the mother), the Oedipus complex would seem the expression both of the extreme dependency of the individual, and of social barriers. The natural dissolution of this complex in the normal individual has been described in terms which are unquestionably true as far as the phenomena are concerned.

Yet it is extremely difficult to vizualize, in terms of this complex alone, why one child is able to seek another object in place of the mother, and another child remains "fixated." This formulation does not describe where the actual failures of adaptation take place. The failures can be located only in the lack of autonomy and persistent dependency. This is a fact which can be verified when one analyzes the falling in love of patients with their analyst. What they demand is the satisfaction of dependency longings expressed in sexual language. The testimony of what one of my patients said about the woman with whom he was supposed to be "in love" describes these dependent attitudes in sexual guise. To this patient the loved one had the function of enhancing his self-esteem. Having very little of it himself, he always wanted to be seen with her because she was attractive, and people would say, "what a man to be loved by a woman like that!" Secondly, she was the source of his power—a purely magical idea—and only by virtue of her love could he be effective. Therefore he feared to do anything that would displease her, because if she ceased to love him his whole ego would collapse. If she went out with another man he was seized with most violent jealousy, by which he meant that she was giving this power to someone else, and not to him. He was in a constant dread to be without her; in short, it was the love of the child for a parent. Nevertheless, this love showed itself in the usual sexual way. These same demands showed themselves to the analyst, not in a sexual guise, as often happens, but in the form of the most extraordinary expectations of what the analyst would do for him. They included taking over every responsibility in life for the patient. It was an interesting corroboration to find that when this patient recovered a good deal of his independence, he fell "out of love."

We must therefore conclude that the Oedipus complex represents a fusion of dependency and sexual cravings on the same object. Its persistence is thus an indicator of failures in ego development in which sexual aim taboos have indeed played a significant role. From the point of view of culture its existence

can only be diagnostic of societies in which dependency longings and their sequelae are exaggerated by sexual aim taboos.
Where a society does not prescribe aim taboos, the sexual phase
of ego development is permitted free growth. This prevents
the fusion of dependency goals and sexual goals. To explain
this Oedipus complex on the basis of survival is to rob institutions of any dynamic significance. It is a survival not of a
phylogenetic complex, but of the institutions which created it
in the first place. This can be verified by the study of societies
different in organization or disciplines from our own. It is
much more likely that this complex is an indicator of the forces
operating within the society itself. It cannot be an accident
that only the neurotic, in whom it is decidedly an indicator of
retarded development, preserves this constellation in an active
form. From the diagnostic point of view, we can therefore check
up by comparative sociology. Thus far we noted the complex
only in societies where the sexual goal is interfered with in
childhood. Why, for example, is the Oedipus complex absent in
Marquesan and Trobriand culture, where no restrictions to
the sexual aim exist? It is this fact which makes it highly
probable that sexual activity compatible with childhood aids
and does not retard the development of the individual. This
interference with sexual development creates exaggerated dependency, the inflation of parental image, an overvaluation of
the boons of dependency, and the encouragement of secondary
outlets for the repressed hostility to the interfering disciplinarian. This is what Reik correctly observed in rituals of several
primitive and archaic cultures.

However, even in those societies which interfere with the
aim of sexuality, we find that this constellation is also an indicator of the frictions created by the social organization. In the
Tanala Oedipus story the greatest rivalry is represented as between brothers; moreover, the son is represented as ingratiating
himself with the father by abandoning his sexual role, returning the father's wives, and entering into a blood bond with the
criminal brothers. The Osirian myth represents the jealousy

not between father and son, but between brothers for their sisters, with whom marriage was socially approved. If these myths are based on the principle of survival, why do they at the same time indicate the sources of the greatest rivalry latent in the actual social organization?

Let us now proceed to examine the compatibility of institutions with one another in such a way as to result in some social stability. In Tanala we saw a society capable of functioning well as long as labor was undifferentiated. When the inevitable claims of skill in labor, opportunity, plunder, and privilege were introduced, the entire system had to be readjusted. The results were a great increase in spirit possession and magic, and against the latter new institutional defenses had to be created.

What influence does the problem of status have on social balance? Many of the institutions we encountered in Betsileo culture had the express purpose of maintaining the new status gradations (e. g., the system of personal taboos) as well as those which maintained and emphasized the privileges of rank. These we found to be institutions created by the anxiety derived from the new subsistence technique, to which those of prestige soon became attached. In old Tanala culture, it is the younger sons who have the greatest need for the idealization and deification of the father; if there is resentment or hatred, it is held in check fairly well by the threat that if they do not behave they lose the call on the help of the deified father. However, the society permits the career of *ombiasy,* homosexual, warrior, or *tromba.* All these careers may be pursued without destroying the entire system of institutions.

Some of the primary institutions, family organization and basic disciplines affect every individual in the society, but leave plenty of room for varying individual reactions. In our society, sexual aim taboos strike everyone, irrespective of status, and again, individual reactions are very varied. The basic constellations formed from this source are the same in everyone, except that these constellations differ with male and female. They are elaborated into the personality in different ways according to a large variety of factors, of which some are constitutional and some accidental, while others pertain to the status of the individual. In other words, secondary institutions do not serve the same need for everyone. Because of the varying needs which institutions must minister to, we must expect to find that co-existing institutions in the same society cross each other's purposes. The more complex a society, and the wider the range of variation of individual characteristics and class differentiation, the more incompatibilities we may expect to find. In primitive society the individual variations of personal fate cannot be as numerous as they are in ours, and the incompatibilities in institutions are therefore likely to be less striking.

The relation between primary and secondary institutions can best be studied when we observe a culture in motion. An excellent illustration can be found in the transition of institutions from the Plateau tribes who eventually became the predatory Comanche. In this transition some of their primary institutions pertaining to subsistence technique changed, and, with this change, some of the secondary institutions of the old Plateau tribes disappeared; some were altered, others remained unchanged. Those that disappeared had a direct conscious representation; those which persisted arose from intrasocial tensions which had little conscious representation.

Summary and Conclusion

The technique used in studying the relations between personality and culture is an elaboration of the common-sense observation that a Hindu is "different" from an Eskimo. Each is the product of a different culture.

The necessity of rendering this common-sense observation useful in an accurate and comparative way obliged us to establish a group of suitable criteria. This work is not by any means finished, but its general direction can be indicated.

We studied the effects of institutions on the individual by means of certain accidents called neurotic reactions, which were created by personal failures to adapt to conditions created by institutions. Comparisons between successful and unsuccessful accommodation to the same institution gave us our first insight into what an institution does to the individual. From this point on the effects of institutions had to be studied in accordance with two standards: the order in which the individual encounters them in his progress from infancy to effective adulthood; and the biologically determined dependency of the individual.

It would seem from our account that the greatest emphasis falls on the influences of institutions on the child, hence that basic disciplines are crucial in the formation of basic personality structure. This emphasis is more apparent than real. If the character of the human mind is integrative, then it follows that the earliest constellations are basic, and if they prove expedient they will form the groundwork of all subsequent integrations, because they become a part of the individual's appreciation of reality. From the rituals alone one cannot fully appreciate their meaning in Tanala in placating a deity; the emotional rationale can be recovered only from the constellation "if I suffer you will love me," a constellation which is created by an endless series of restrictive disciplines. And this constellation is the result of continuous impressions of the practical effectiveness of this formula from childhood on. Freud did not regard this concept of basic personality as necessary because it was assumed to be the same in all human beings irrespective of culture. The differentia among aboriginal peoples had therefore to be evaluated in terms of the degree to which they had evolved, in the evolutionary scheme. This hypothesis had to be changed because it allowed no opportunity to compare cultures in regard to the specificity of their institutions and because it ignored the effects of these institutions in creating basic personality (ego) structure. It was assumed in this book that the character and meaning of institutions were in every instance conveyed to the individual by the behavior of others and always became known to him by some form of direct experience.

The basic personality structure stands midway between

primary and secondary institutions. The practical way in which this interrelationship was followed out could be demonstrated either in Tanala or Marquesan culture. By virtue of severe disciplines and restrictions in early childhood in Tanala, with consequential premature assumption of obligations, the constellation formed in the basic personality structure is: "If I am obedient I will be protected." This constellation governs not only interpersonal relations, but also relations with the deity. The religion, a secondary institution, embodies this constellation in various ways. When the reality situation permits the use of this adaptation without discomfort no serious problems arise. But when it no longer is effective two outcomes are possible: outbursts of overt aggression, or spirit possession. As the primary institution changes, the secondary changes with it.

The structure of the basic personality was derived from the observed reaction types of man to frustration; and the various conceptions of secondary institutions are derived from the representations in the unconscious of these frustrating experiences. The *fanaua* in Marquesan culture was demonstrated as derived from this source.

From this point of view the Oedipus complex, which Freud regarded as evidence of a universal personality structure, turns out to be the expression of a definite series of primary institutions.

This essay purports to answer only a few fundamental questions; it leaves a great many others unanswered. It remains to be seen whether the method can be used effectively on a variety of cultures with different types of institutions. However, this preliminary essay in part fulfills the expectation that a psychological approach to sociology should yield new knowledge. Meanwhile it is well to note what this essay does not purport to answer:

1. It does not purport to describe the institutions solely from the "meaning" of the psychological origins. The uses which institutions serve may change. Embalming in Egypt may well have

originated in certain anxieties about food. That does not mean that this is the use which the institutions served in dynastic Egypt when the problem of food anxiety had been adequately dispelled. The history of Egypt shows conclusively that this institution came to have the meaning of a special prestige value, and eventually this prestige problem became the central focus of anxieties coming from other sources. This in turn became the cause of a social conflict which ended with democratization of burial rites previously accorded only to the elite. The establishment of the cult of Osiris, the popular religion, as the state religion of Egypt signalled one of the many changes of the meaning of the original institution of embalming.

2. This essay does not take into account a vast array of institutions of purely rational origin.

3. It takes little note of artistic pursuits because no reliable psychological criteria exist for studying them, since "sublimation" is a questionable guide.

4. No very consistent attempt was made to study the role of status in the total social ensemble because the biographical material for pursuing this was not at hand. Neither was any attempt made to define from the material differences in the social structure caused by the fact that the same individual may have different roles, as an individual, or as a special executive of the culture such as a chief or warrior. This is a part of the problem of status.

5. No attempt was made to study the origin of primary institutions, because history was not available. Theories about the possible origins were considered irrelevant.

6. We did not take up in any detail the significant fact that similar types of neurosis make their appearance in cultures of widely different institutional patterns. This is a problem on which we had no data.

Notwithstanding the present limitations of this work, it distinctly encourages the view that a science of society is possible. And for this purpose the study of primitive society is indispensable, for in it is concealed the most valuable record of the relation of man to the external vicissitudes he encounters and the institutions he contrives as a result of this impact. None of the other social sciences give us the same opportunity to study in a macroscopic way the outcome of the various combinations of institutions on the comfort and effectiveness of man. In addition, this work gives us a new vantage point for the critical study of our own culture.

The future of this work is clearly indicated. Twenty or thirty cultures studied in the manner here delineated will offer safe ground for generalizations based on reliable comparisons. The laws which govern the psychodynamics of social change can then be approximated, if not precisely stated.

INDEX

INDEX

Freud, Sigmund (*Continued*)
Psychology and the Analysis of the Ego, 374, 394–97; *Moses and Monotheism*, 406n; *The Problem of Anxiety*, 385n, 407, 409n, 424n; *Three Contributions to the Theory of Sex*, 134n; *Totem and Taboo*, 372, 374, 377, 378, 394, 399
Freudian psychology, basis of psychological technique, xxi, 12, 90
Freudian sociology, dilemma of, 407
Friendship, 375, 378, 396, 400
Fromm, Erich, xxi, 414; concept of super-ego, 64–67; "Die Entwicklung des Christusdogmas," 382n, 384n, 404n; in *Autorität und Familie*, 387n, 394n; "Über Methode und Aufgabe einer Analytischen Sozialpsychologie," 386n, 404n; "Sozialpsychologischer Teil," 64n, 77n
Frustration, aggression a reaction to, 448; effect on child ego, 24–28, 34–44; feeding, in infancy, 205, 422; importance in neurosis, 414; in relation to outer world, 436–46; institutionalized, 445; Marquesas, 414, 445; of socially c. ted needs, 446–48; protection, 423–35; reactions as basis of study, 419–50; reaction types to, 449; relation of hostility to, 130; relation of projection to, 307; sexual, 414, 441–46; woman's status a basis of, 213–16
Functionalists, viii
Future of an Illusion, The (Freud), 76, 376, 378, 399, 407, 424n

Genotype, 365
Ghosts, Betsileo, 287; Tanala, 268–70, 271–73, 301, 304
Goals, 462
God, relation of concept to disciplines, 75, 76; relation of dependence to concept of, 38
——attitude toward, Marquesas, 187, 211, 221, 246, 248, 474; Tanala, 313, 484; Zuni, 473
Goldenweiser, A., 381; *History, Psychology and Culture*, 404n
Group psychology, 374–76
"Group Psychology" (Freud), 67

Group Psychology and the Analysis of the Ego (Freud, S.), 373, 394
Grundzüge einer Genetische Psychologie (Rank), 26n
Guilt, sense of, 380, 384, 438, 465

Haeckelian evolutionary biology, 381, 389
Handy, E. S. Craighill, xv, 230; *Marquesan Legends*, 191n, 197, 221n; *The Native Culture of the Marquesas*, xvi
Hansel and Gretel story, 224, 432
Herd instinct, 374
History, Psychology and Culture (Goldenweiser), 404n
Homosexuality, Betsileo, 287, 331, 332; Marquesas, 218; relation to ingratiation, 322–25, 328; Tanala, 265, 296, 303, 312; unconscious, 396
Horde, primal, 376, 387, 394
Horney, K., xxi, 414, 454; *The Neurotic Personality of Our Time*, 20n, 28n, 51n, 309n, 404n
Huxley, H. M., *The Jewish Encyclopedia*, 200n

Id, 358, 453, 461; as subdivision of personality, 398–99
Identification, 36n, 64, 67, 338, 370, 400; analysis of, 375; Tanala, 315–17
Immortality, concept as social tool, 76; ideology of, 90–92; Marquesas, 182–85; Trobriand, 81, 91
Impulse, sexual: relation to dependency, 395–96
Impulse control, factors of, 129
Impulses, 461, 463; defined, 425; somatic roots of, 425
Incest, *see* Taboos, incest
Individual, as unit of study, 3–12; Freud's technique based on, 382; interaction with institutions, vii; relation to culture pattern, xiii
Individuals, centripetal and centrifugal forces between, 63 ff.
Infant, *see* Child
Inferiority, feeling of, 51n
Ingratiation, Betsileo, 332; linked to hostility, 447; psychology of, 317–29;

INDEX

Will, basis of concept of, 27
Woman, antithetical to cultural trends, 378; hostile representation of, Marquesas, 203, 213–16, 229, 248, 417, 445; in folklore, 213–15, 216, 237
——status of, xiii–xv; Chuckchee, 122; Marquesas, 69, 154, 158, 162, 184, 200–204; Tanala, 279–81; Western culture, 22
Work, emotional characteristics of, 50

Zuni culture, xxiii, 111–16; aggression, 112, 114–16, 127, 129; authority, 113; coöperation, 113; dependency, 114; environment, 111; jealousy, 88, 112; life goals, 115, 119; magic, 111; marriage, 111; mastery technique, 112; organization, family, 111; organization, social, 111; property, 111; religion, 111, 113, 473; secret societies, men's, 114; sex mores, 112; shame, 69, 74, 112, 114; taboos, 112